Muses and Measures

Muses and Measures:

Empirical Research Methods for the Humanities

By

Willie van Peer, Frank Hakemulder
and Sonia Zyngier

**Cambridge
Scholars**
Publishing

Muses and Measures: Empirical Research Methods for the Humanities

By Willie van Peer, Frank Hakemulder and Sonia Zyngier

This book first published 2007. The present binding first published 2007.

Cambridge Scholars Publishing

Lady Stephenson Library, Newcastle upon Tyne, NE6 2PA, UK

British Library Cataloguing in Publication Data
A catalogue record for this book is available from the British Library

Copyright © 2007 by Willie van Peer, Frank Hakemulder and Sonia Zyngier

All rights for this book reserved. No part of this book may be reproduced, stored in a retrieval system, or transmitted, in any form or by any means, electronic, mechanical, photocopying, recording or otherwise, without the prior permission of the copyright owner.

ISBN: 978-1-84718-421-4
ISBN (Ebook): 1-84718-421-9

You cannot hope to build a better world without improving the individuals. To that end each of us must work for his own improvement, and at the same time share a general responsibility for all humanity, our particular duty being to aid those to whom we think we can be most useful.
—Marie Curie (1867–1934)

The main things which seem to me important on their own account, and not merely as means to other things, are knowledge, art, instinctive happiness, and relations of friendship or affection.
—Bertrand Russell (1872–1970)

This book is dedicated to our partners-in-life

TABLE OF CONTENTS

List of Figures, Tables and Graphs ix
Acknowledgments xiv
Foreword xvi
Notes on Contributors xix

Chapter One 1
Empirical Studies

Interlude: 25
Some Misconceptions about Empirical Research

Chapter Two 33
Basic Insights from the Philosophy of Science

Chapter Three 57
Types of Research Methodology and Research Design

Chapter Four 75
Methods of Data Collection

Chapter Five 108
How to Construct a Questionnaire

Chapter Six 138
Experiment

Chapter Seven 166
How to Enter and Manipulate Data in SPSS

Chapter Eight 190
Descriptive Statistics

Chapter Nine 227
Inference statistics: Preliminaries

Chapter Ten 252
Inference Statistics: Test Selection, *t*-test and Non-Parametric Equivalents

Chapter Eleven 278
Inference Statistics: ANOVA

Chapter Twelve 312
Communicating Results

Epilogue 350
Bibliography 358
Index of Names 365
Index of Subjects 367

CD-ROM with assignments, feedback and materials

LIST OF FIGURES, TABLES AND GRAPHS

Figures

Figure 1.1:   The Wundt curve
Figure 1.2:   Figure 1.2: The Wundt curve for aesthetic experience
Figure 1.3:   Novelty and the perception of beauty
Figure 1.4:   Distance between metaphor concepts
Figure 1.5:   The Wundt curve for several persons
Figure 1.6:   How 'just' is each person?
Figure 1.7:   How 'considerate' is each person?

Figure 2.1:   The development of the three synoptic gospels

Figure 3.1:   Possible relations between variables
Figure 3.2:   Example of a PsycINFO search result
Figure 3.3:   Example of a PsycINFO file

Figure 4.1:   Candid camera observation of two age groups' responses to different degrees of retaliation for amoral character behavior. Adopted from Zillmann and Bryant (1975)
Figure 4.2:   Two measures and two moments

Figure 5.1:   Closed question: a semantic differential (Limbert & Polzella, 1998)
Figure 5.2:   A nominal measure
Figure 5.3:   An ordinal measure: the rank-order rating scale
Figure 5.4:   An interval measure: the Likert scale
Figure 5.5:   A ratio measure: the constant-sum rating scale
Figure 5.6:   Checklist (taken from West et al. 1993)
Figure 5.7:   A non-ordinal multiple choice question (Andringa, 1986)
Figure 5.8:   14- to 15-year-olds
Figure 5.9:   16- to 17-year-olds
Figure 5.10: Graphic rating scale (non-comparative)
Figure 5.11: Graphic rating scale (comparative)
Figure 5.12: Itemized rating scale
Figure 5.13: Itemized rating scale (numbered) (from Gibson et al., 2000)

x   List of Figures, Tables and Graphs

Figure 5.14:   Itemized rating scale: unbalanced
Figure 5.15:   Fractionation rating scale
Figure 5.16:   Profiles of two dance performances (A and B)

Figure 6.1:   Pre-test post-test control group design
Figure 6.2:   Pre-test post-test control group design with two experimental conditions
Figure 6.3:   Alcohol at the Comedy Club
Figure 6.4:   Case study
Figure 6.5:   One-group pre-test post-test design
Figure 6.6:   Afterwards comparisons of existing groups
Figure 6.7:   Non-equivalent control group design
Figure 6.8:   Solomon design
Figure 6.9a: No pre-test effect
Figure 6.9b: Effect of pre-test

Figure 7.1:   Opening dialog box of SPSS
Figure 7.2:   SPSS Data Editor
Figure 7.3:   SPSS Variable View
Figure 7.4:   Example of a filled-out questionnaire
Figure 7.5:   Variable View with one variable entered
Figure 7.6:   Value Labels dialog box
Figure 7.7:   Compute Variable dialog box
Figure 7.8:   Compute Variable: example
Figure 7.9:   Recode into Same Variable dialog Box
Figure 7.10:   Old and New Values dialog box
Figure 7.11:   Recode into Different Variables dialog box
Figure 7.12:   Recode into Different Variables: example
Figure 7.13:   Select Cases dialog box
Figure 7.14:   Select Cases If dialog box: example

Figure 8.1:   Scatterplot of differences between individual observations and the mean
Figure 8.2:   Example of a normal distribution
Figure 8.3:   Standard deviations within the normal distribution
Figure 8.4:   Two overlapping distributions
Figure 8.5:   Enter frequencies to obtain descriptive statistics
Figure 8.6:   Dialog box to obtain frequencies
Figure 8.7:   Dialog box to request statistics
Figure 8.8:   Output of FREQUENCIES
Figure 8.9:   Enter several variables for descriptive statistics

Figure 8.10: Output of FREQUENCIES of several variables
Figure 8.11: Output of descriptive statistics of several variables
Figure 8.12: Defining different groups in VALUE LABELS
Figure 8.13: Entering data as defined by group
Figure 8.16: Output of BASIC TABLES
Figure 8.17: Dialog box for Reliability Analysis
Figure 8.18: Dialog box for Reliability Analysis: STATISTICS
Figure 8.19: Output of reliability analysis (Cronbach's alpha)
Figure 8.20: Interpreting Cronbach's alpha
Figure 8.21: Dialog box for Bar Charts
Figure 8.22: Dialog box for Define Simple Bar: Summaries for Groups of Cases
Figure 8.23: Example: Bar chart for respondents' gender
Figure 8.24: Dialog Box. Define Clustered Bar: Summary of Separate Variables
Figure 8.25: SPSS output: Bar charts for separate variables
Figure 8.26: Dialog Box for Scale Axis in Editing Graph
Figure 8.27: Dialog Box for Scale in Graph Adaptation
Figure 8.28: Bar chart on original scale
Figure 8.29: Dialog Box for Boxplot
Figure 8.30: Dialog Box. Define Simple Boxplot: Summaries for Groups of Cases
Figure 8.31: Output of Boxplot

Figure 9.1: Distribution of preferences for story outcome with two participants
Figure 9.2: Distribution of preferences for story outcome with four participants
Figure 9.3: Region of rejection
Figure 9.4: Region of rejection at both ends of the curve
Figure 9.5: Example of a positive correlation
Figure 9.6: Example of a negative correlation
Figure 9.7: Scatterplot showing a positive correlation
Figure 9.8: Scatterplot showing no correlation
Figure 9.9: Scatterplot with regression fit line and R-square
Figure 9.10: Dialog box to obtain Pearson's bivariate correlations
Figure 9.11: Dialog box to obtain Spearman's rho
Figure 10.1: Dialog box to obtain histograms
Figure 10.2: Dialog box to obtain normal curves with histograms
Figure 10.3: Histogram for Line 1
Figure 10.4: Histogram with normal curve for line 9

Figure 10.5: Dialog box to explore data
Figure 10.6: Dialog box to show normality plots
Figure 10.7: SPSS output of Kolmogorov–Smirnov test
Figure 10.8: SPSS output of Q-Q plots
Figure 10.9: Decision flowchart for test selection
Figure 10.10: Dialog box to obtain an Independent-Samples t-test
Figure 10.11: Dialog box to Define Groups in t-test
Figure 10.12: Descriptive statistics in Independent-Samples t-test
Figure 10.13: SPSS output of t-test for independent samples
Figure 10.14: Dialog box to obtain a Paired-Samples t-test
Figure 10.15: Output of descriptive statistics in paired-samples t-test
Figure 10.16: SPSS output of paired-samples t-test
Figure 10.17: Dialogue box to obtain a Two-Related-Samples Wilcoxon test
Figure 10.18: Options for descriptive statistics with the Wicoxon test
Figure 10.19: Output of descriptive statistics in the Wilcoxon test
Figure 10.20: Output of Wilcoxon test.
Figure 10.21: Output of Mann–Whitney U Test
Figure 10.22: Descriptives output of Kruskal–Wallis Test
Figure 10.23: Output of Kruskal–Wallis test
Figure 10.24: Dialog box of Friedman's test
Figure 10.25: Output of Friedman test
Figure 10.26: Requesting chi-square with Crosstabs
Figure 10.27: Output of chi-square with Crosstabs
Figure 10.28: Chi-square statistics in Crosstabs
Figure 10.29: Further output of chi-square test
Figure 11.1a: Distribution within and between groups (ANOVA)
Figure 11.1b: Distribution within and between groups (ANOVA)
Figure 11.2: Dialog Box for one-way ANOVA
Figure 11.3: Dialog Box for one-way ANOVA: Options
Figure 11.4: SPSS output of descriptive statistics with ANOVA
Figure 11.5: Dialog box one-way ANOVA: Post Hoc Multiple Comparison
Figure 11.6: SPSS Output for Bonferroni test in a one-way ANOVA procedure
Figure 11.7: Dialog Box Multivariate GLM
Figure 11.8a: SPSS output of GLM: Multivariate
Figure 11.8b: SPSS output of GLM: Multivariate
Figure 11.8c: SPSS Output. Multivariate tests
Figure 11.8d: SPSS Output. Multivariate test results
Figure 11.9: Repeated Measures ANOVA
Figure 11.10: Dialog box for Repeated Measures
Figure 11.11: Dialog box for Repeated Measures: Profile Plots

Figure 11.12:   Dialog box for Repeated Measures: Contrasts
Figure 11.12a: SPSS Output: Mauchly's test of Sphericity
Figure 11.12b: SPSS Output: Test of Within-Subjects Effects
Figure 11.12 c: SPSS Output: Test of Within-Subjects Contrasts
Figure 12.1:   Level of appreciation (from Mendes & Menezes, 2003)
Figure 12.2:   Example of a poster layout

Tables

Table 2.1:   Matrix of quasi-identical text locations
Table 2.2:   Extended matrix of quasi-identical text locations
Table 3.1:   Relevant journals
Table 6.1:   Scariness scores
Table 6.2:   Paired matching for preference for scary movies
Table 6.2a: Calculate the scores for scary movies
Table 6.2b: Arrange in ascending order
Table 8.14:   BASIC TABLES dialog box
Table 8.15:   Statistics selection in BASIC TABLES
Table 9.1:   Table of outcomes of preferences for story outcome with four participants
Table 9.2:   Table of outcomes of preferences for story outcome with eight participants
Table 9.3:   Decision Matrix for Error Types
Table 9.4:   Output of Spearman rank correlations
Table 9.5:   Output of Spearman's rho
Table 10.1:   Overview of inference tests

Acknowledgments

This book has had a long history of experimentation and reading. Many people have helped shape it. We are grateful to all those involved in some way or other in helping us sharpen the concepts and who have read the many different versions of the manuscripts. Our special thanks go to Els Andringa, Mick Short, Don Kuiken, Max Louwerse, Paul Sopcak, Peter Dixon, Marisa Bortolussi, Marcelo Oliveira, Alexey Tyurikov, Jan Auracher and the students who participated in all the REDES Seminars in Munich. The book would never have reached its completion were it not for those students of the Institute for Media and Representation at Utrecht University who helped collect data, namely Willemijn van der Bent, Jery Hsu, Femke Penning de Vries, Paul van Beckum, Ilonka Kupecz. David Miall has also been so generous as to offer a one-semester course testing the materials with his students at the University of Alberta. Our special thanks also go to all our REDES junior researchers in Brazil who have contributed to all stages of the volume, especially Alessandra Mitie Spallanzani, Alexandre José Cadilhe, Carla Xavier, Danielle Menezes, Érika Coachman, Fabiana Fausto, Gabriela Marques, Gabriela Oliveira, Juliana Jandre, Kelly Carvalho, Leandra Luciano, Milena Mendes, Natalia Braguez, Natália Giordani, Olívia Fialho, Raquel Haua, Roberta Boechat, Suzana de Deus, Vander Viana. Anna Chesnokova and the REDES members at Kyiv National Linguistic University have also put all the concepts and experiments here to test and returned to us with precious comments.

To all we thank and offer, in return, the volume, which we hope will be useful to many more people.

FOREWORD

Before you start reading and — hopefully — enjoying this book, we would like you to consider the picture on page xv above[1]. What do you see? What do you feel when you look at this clock? On top, you can see a child, a dog, a basket with fruits ... and a book. It is a reading lesson, in fact, combining the picture of the child reading with a dog in her lap. Intuitively, many ideas may spring to your mind: the innocence attached to it, the open-minded attitude, the uncompromised involvement of the little child holding the dog's paw, trying to teach it how to read, and below, the clock, measuring time.

Indeed, our question really centers on what art is. More specifically: how artists provoke emotions in us through their work and how we respond to them. Can we account for these responses, some of which may play an important role in our lives? As students of media, culture and the arts you may have pondered on these and other issues concerning aesthetic and affective reactions. Your questions are not new. Since the 1970s, there has been a growing awareness of the importance of the specific person to whom novels, theater plays, movies, or paintings are directed.

You may still not know, but much has been said and thought about the processes and effects of comprehension, interpretation, and evaluation of literature, the arts, and the media. Especially in the world of the media, where advertising and marketing strategies are so relevant today, these issues play a central role. By and large, the concrete body of research on such processes and their outcomes has grown over the years and there is now a considerable (and expanding) field of empirical studies of cultural artifacts and their processing. But you may by now be asking yourself: "How can I start learning about it? How do I enter this field?"

Humanities departments do not have a tradition of empirical research methods and usually lack the methods required for carrying out this kind of research. This book deals with fundamental aspects of empirical methodology to study cultural and artistic phenomena in their diversity, richness, and depth. Its main goal is to introduce you to this methodology, offering systematic guidance through various methods of enquiry, and including a wide variety of examples,

---

[1] We would like to thank IRPA-KIK for allowing us to use the picture on the cover (Copyright IRPA-KIK); we are grateful to Mimi Debruyn for having suggested we used it and to Ione Galeti for the cover design.

exercises and illustrative studies, as well as help for self-instruction and simulation exercises. To make you feel comfortable, we would like to tell you that all materials have been tested and used in course work with students like you in as diverse contexts as Brazil, Germany, the Netherlands and the Ukraine.

So, back to the illustration on page xv: the work of art here is very symmetrical, with the three female figures arranged in one single triangle, making us consider them as related. The relaxed posture of the child, mindless of anything but her reading, makes us think of the two levels of activity involved in the appreciation of art — the rational and the affective. Notice that, although she is at ease, she is sitting up to her reading, revealing concentration and intensity. Her little feet are raised and the dog is looking up at her, attentively. Her chair seems to be very sturdy and fixed, but if you look at it carefully, you will notice that the legs end in beaks of swans, which immediately destabilize any rigidity and introduce the idea of floating. There is definitely a sense of pleasure and happiness in this activity. The child's dress is falling off her right shoulder, baring it. We cannot avoid noticing sensual implications, also suggested by the promises of spring and the smells and tastes contained in that basket of ripe fruits. Below, the winged victories (the mythological female figures) holding a wreath on the clock contrast with the everyday life depiction of the little child. The figures have their backs to the pointers, and seem to be flying away from Time. Their dresses are also floating. Would they be offering laurels to those who know how to enjoy art? They also seem to be illustrating how Art defeats Time and Mortality, so typical in poets, like Shakespeare, who try to hold back the destructive force of Time by immortalizing their loved ones in their writing. Besides a means for telling time, the clock here can also be seen as a symbol for measurement.

These brief comments illustrate in a way how we would like you to see empirical studies: by combining the pleasures of aesthetic experience and the mechanisms of science. We would like you to indulge in the intuitive and naïve posture of this child, open to new ways of seeing but also bearing in mind that we need measures and methods to understand our experience. Moreover, in a quite curious way, this work of art reflects the purpose of our book: it reminds us of one of the instruments available to researchers in this field, for instance, to measure the pace of reading: the clock.

In this volume you will find initially some general introduction to the field, followed by an Interlude, where we review a couple of prejudices against empirical work that prevail in the Humanities. We have to win many battles first. The Interlude has been written in dialogue form, so that you can engage in the challenges we pose. You can then proceed into Chapter 2, which explains underlying concepts from the philosophy of science. Ten subsequent chapters progressively acquaint you with the practical application of research methods. These chapters guide you through the entire process of carrying out an empirical study. They help you formulate your initial idea for a study and provide valuable hints on conducting a proper literature search. We will discuss how a critical reading of the literature available or of the theories of your field can lead to a concrete plan for research. We will look not only at the most prevalent methods, but also how you can pick the one that fits your purposes best. You will learn how to collect and analyze your data. Finally, you will find practical guidelines on how to communicate your results in a way that matches professional standards.

You will find that a number of chapters are dedicated to statistical techniques, which you may need in your research. It is important to note, however, that our aim is not to provide a complete course in statistics; this would require an entirely different book, or rather several volumes. Here we will explain how to choose the appropriate technique and how to interpret the results. The word "statistics" does not always have a positive ring to it, to put it mildly, especially not in Humanities. Therefore we place great emphasis on clarity and simplicity so that you can gradually build a thorough understanding of the fundamental concepts of its methodology. We will run you through easy-to-understand, hands-on examples, using original data sets, some of which were collected by students. Exercise materials in the form of databases are provided on CD-ROM to help you consolidate your knowledge. And when the time comes to conduct your own study, the text will be a cookbook to you: you may follow the instructions step by step. Our experience using the method of this book is that this can lead to high-quality research. The research abilities you will acquire through reading and doing the exercises are essential to academic training and will prove to be extremely useful inside as well as outside the University.

We hope that you become as enthusiastic in empirical studies as the three of us have been in developing these materials, many of which are also based on our own research in the field. We hope you will join the community of researchers soon.

NOTES ON CONTRIBUTORS

Willie van Peer holds a Ph.D. from Lancaster University, and is Professor of Literary Studies and Intercultural Hermeneutics at the University of Munich, former President of IGEL (International Association for the Empirical Study of Literature) and of PALA (Poetics and Linguistics Association). He has been Visiting Scholar in the Departments of Comparative Literature at Stanford and at Princeton University, and in the Department of (Cognitive) Psychology at the University of Memphis. He is also a Fellow of Clare Hall of Cambridge University. He is the author of several books and many articles on poetics and the epistemological foundations of literary studies, including *Stylistics and Psychology: Investigations of Foregrounding* (London, 1986). He edited *The Taming of the Text: Explorations in Language, Literature and Culture* (Routledge, 1988), together with Seymour Chatman, *New Perspectives on Narrative Perspective* (SUNY Press, 2001), and together with Max Louwerse, *Thematics. Interdisciplinary Studies* (Benjamins, 2002).

Jèmeljan Hakemulder has a background in literary theory and comparative literature. He conducted his Ph.D. research (1998) in the Department of Literary Studies at Utrecht University and the Department of Psychology at the University of Illinois (Urbana-Champaign). He specialized in the psychology of literature, focusing on the effects of reading literary texts on attitudes. On this subject he published a book and several articles, among them *The moral laboratory. Experiments examining the effects of reading literature on social perception and moral self-concept* (Amsterdam: Benjamins, 2000), and "Foregrounding and its effects on readers' perception" (*Discourse Processes*, 38, 2000, 193–218). From 1998 to 2001 he conducted (post-doctoral) research at the Free University of Amsterdam, looking at aspects of literary communication that may be responsible for the effects of reading on inter-group attitudes. Since 2001 he has been Assistant Professor at the Institute for Media and Representation (Utrecht University), where he conducts studies on the reception of film. He trains students in the humanities in methodological aspects of research, especially experimentation.

Sonia Zyngier is Associate Professor of English Language and Literature at the Postgraduate Program of Applied Linguistics at the Federal University of Rio de Janeiro, Brazil, where she has acted as Director of Cultural Affairs and Continuing Education for five years. She was Secretary of PALA (Poetics and Linguistics Association) and is co-editor of the IGEL Newsletter. She has an M.A. in English Literature from the University of Liverpool and a Ph.D. in Applied Linguistics from the University of Birmingham. Much of her work has been on stylistics and the teaching of literatures in English. Specific research interests include discourse analysis and pedagogical stylistics. She has published widely on literary awareness, stylistics, and corpus analysis of literary discourse. She has developed a program of research in the area of the Empirical Science of Literature and its implications for literary education. Her latest publication is *Literature and Stylistics for Language Learners*, co-edited with Greg Watson and published by Palgrave-Macmillan.

The three researchers have set up the REDES Project, an international and multicultural program aimed at training young researchers (www.redes.de/portal and www.letras.ufrj.br/redes).

CHAPTER ONE

EMPIRICAL STUDIES

In this chapter we do several things. To begin with, we contrast two world views: that of the Humanities and that of the Sciences (Sections 1.1 and 1.2) to argue later that these views are not mutually exclusive. We hold that the way in which science looks at things can be profitably used to study cultural phenomena (Sections 1.3 to 1.5). We then look at a range of examples demonstrating the way this can be done (Sections 1.6 to 1.9), and conclude with two studies that show the relevance of empirical methods (Section 1.10). As we understand it, the chapter should provide you with an introduction to the methodology of performing empirical research.

1.1. Understanding versus Explaining

Most people experience at some point in life the effect of drinking too much. What may have started off as a benign feeling while conversing with an interesting partner gradually evolved into a small catastrophe. How could it happen that something so agreeable turned into something so unpleasant a couple of hours later?

Here you have a clear example of how human behavior can be explained. The phenomenon is called the 'Wundt curve' – after Wilhelm Wundt (1832–1920), the German psychologist and founder of experimental psychology who, together with his co-workers in the first ever laboratory to study human psychology, in Leipzig, discovered the law around 1874. Since then the Wundt curve has been confirmed in scores of experimental studies for a wide range of phenomena, so that we can now say that we understand the mechanism involved rather well. Most importantly for us in this book, the law is also at work in the perception and appreciation of art works. But before we discuss the example of getting drunk, which we will do in Section 1.6, we should think about two verbs: **understand** and **explain**. These two words already open up a vista of discussions that have kept several generations of scholars busy. Usually, these terms set off alarms with people in the Humanities. Why? What is at stake? The pair is usually seen in its German original as 'verstehen' (understand) and 'erklären' (explain), as they originate in the work of the philosopher Wilhelm Dilthey (1833–1911). Dilthey saw in the mental operations of understanding and explaining two opposing modes of coming to terms with the world around us. Explaining ('erklären') was the typical mode of the Natural Sciences, he argued, where *causality* is a central concept and where researchers try to explain how X causes Y, for instance, how a meteorite *caused* the extinction of the dinosaurs, or how UV rays from the sun *cause* skin cancer in humans. Understanding ('verstehen'), by contrast, was seen by Dilthey as the typical way in which the Humanities try to understand the world through an operation that centers not on causality, as in the Natural Sciences, but on trying to unravel the personal meaning of the phenomena involved. 'Explaining' the drunkenness would be done by describing the chemical characteristics of alcohol and their effect on physiological processes in the body, how they affect the nervous system and numb the senses, how they affect the liver and the other digestive organs, and so forth. 'Understanding' the drunkenness would be done in terms of the situation in which you found yourself. Such situations can be highly different. Perhaps it was your first experience with alcohol and you did not know its properties and the danger of drinking too much. Or you drank too much because you did not feel too happy at that party. Perhaps a love was unanswered, or something went wrong at work that day, or you had had a quarrel with your father. All these situations are different and will imply different personal meanings to the person involved, which the Humanistic tradition – in contrast to the explanatory approach of the Natural Sciences – will try to 'understand'.

Here is another example. Consider AIDS. To the medical scientist, the disease is caused by the human immunodeficiency virus. Someone infected with this virus may develop the disease. Although not all people infected eventually become ill, all people who do must have been exposed to the virus before. Without such exposure there will be no disease; in this sense, the virus 'causes' the disease. Natural scientists are satisfied with such an explanation once they have isolated the cause(s) of an event. Typical for the natural scientist is the attempt to eliminate explanations that are false, ideally leading to the isolation of single causes or of the exact composition of single factors in a multicausal chain or complex.

This example can now be contrasted with the act of 'understanding', which according to Dilthey (and his followers, who are by far the majority in the Humanities) is the method dealing with the 'human' (some would say 'cultural') side of the world. Often the term hermeneutics is used for it, deriving from the Greek word 'hermeneuein', already used by Plato in his Dialogue *Kratylos*, where it means things like 'to understand', 'to enunciate', 'to proclaim', 'to translate'. From this point of view, what matters is less the cause of the disease than its meaning. A person who contracts a serious illness will soon ask "why?"

or "why me?" These are questions that involve the person's own subjectivity, and are thus not amenable (or so it would seem) to the methods of the Natural Sciences, which do not deal in subjectivity. For instance, the person may think that he or she became sick as a punishment for his or her behavior in the past. In this sense, the condition is now 'understood' through its acquisition of a 'meaning': it is no longer limited to a natural cause but involves an understanding that can be embedded in the person's biography and value system. This 'understanding' may call forward a range of emotions, which may influence the person's further norms and behavior. This concentration on meaning is at the core of Dilthey's understanding ('verstehen').

Note that there may be competing modes of constructing such a meaning: religion offers certain possibilities but does not exclude the non-believer from the processes of meaning-making. One may understand AIDS in terms of a blind fate by which one has been struck, or one may reproach oneself for not having taken the necessary precautions. Typical for 'verstehen', however, is that there is no (or very little) attempt to eliminate different ways of understanding, and one may even encounter many of them side by side in a person's reaction to an event. Multiple meanings are therefore possible – and often also live side by side.

1.2. Some problems

Dilthey's view, however, raises some problems. It cuts the world in two, a view called *dualism* in philosophy. This idea was not of Dilthey's own making. Although the roots of dualism go back to Plato, the French philosopher René Descartes, who in his *Discourse on Method* (1637) introduced the difference between two sorts of things, extended substances (Latin *res extensa*, i.e. nature) and thinking substances (Latin *res cogitans*, i.e. humans), is credited with having introduced it.

But what about the existence of only one world? This is called *monism*[1]. Monism holds that in the real world you find all sorts of interactions between the natural and the cultural worlds – and in both directions. The meaning we ascribe to things is influenced by our scientific knowledge of them and our scientific work is linked to our cultural views, norms and values. How else to explain, for instance, that the research budgets spent on depression (a typical Western disease) are many times higher than the budgets spent on malaria research, although this disease kills one million people every year (most of them children under five years of age) and affects one in ten people on Earth,

---

[1] In philosophy the terms Monism and Dualism are also called Naturalism and Anti-Naturalism, respectively.

stifling economic growth and prosperity and drawing whole countries into a spiral of bitter poverty. If science was only 'explaining', without any meaning attached to it, as the Diltheyan world view propagates, then it becomes difficult to explain why research is guided in such a skewed way toward diseases that, although being cruel and disabling in themselves, are not the most prevalent among human beings all over the world.

However, the interaction also runs in the opposite direction. Thus persons who believe themselves to be at risk of being infected with a life-threatening disease will not only immerse themselves in questions of meaning, but will also use the best methods to find out whether they carry the virus, something that only the Natural Sciences can provide. In cases where the persons find that they have been infected, the actual cause of the infection (a 'scientific' matter) will again call forward questions of how to deal with this fact (a matter of 'meaning'), which will raise the problem of whether there is a cure (a 'scientific' question), the answer to which will further generate matters of 'meaning', and so forth. Dilthey's defenders need to look closely at the ways in which the natural and the cultural worlds are connected. To us, the authors of this book, the 'division' of the world into 'understanding' and 'explaining' is less rewarding than seeing (and studying) the *interaction* between these two forms of knowledge.

In spite of this problem generated by a dualistic world view, Dilthey's opinion is widespread in the Humanities, and is reiterated in various forms and disguises all the time. One finds a similar expression of the division between the scientific and the humanistic view in the philosophy of Jürgen Habermas (1929) or of the hermeneutics of Hans-Georg Gadamer (1900–2002). Look, for instance, at what he has to say about the notion:

> The experience of the socio-historical world cannot be raised to a science by the inductive procedure of the natural sciences (...) historical research does not endeavour to group the concrete phenomenon as an instance of a universal rule. The individual case does not serve only to confirm a law from which practical predictions can be made. Its ideal is rather to understand the phenomenon itself in its unique and historical concreteness. However much experiential universals are involved, the aim is not to confirm and extend these universalized experiences in order to attain knowledge of a law – e.g., how men, peoples, and states evolve – but to understand how this man, this people, or this state is what it has become or, more generally, how it happened that it is so. (...) the human sciences arrive at their conclusions by an unconscious process. (1975: 4–5)

Later, he adds: "This gives the word 'understanding' an almost religious tone" (1975:211). And there are related views. The German philosopher Wilhelm Windelband (1848–1915) distinguished between *idiographic* and *nomothetic* (sometimes also called *nomological*) world views.

Idiographic approaches are appropriate in cases where no law-like patterns apply, because the events observed and studied are unique and occur only once. The battle of Waterloo, for instance, in which Napoleon was finally defeated, is not something that can be studied from the scientific point of view (so this argument goes), because you *cannot repeat it*. Nomothetic approaches, however, do just that: they attempt to discover underlying regularities in the events studied, sometimes leading to the formulation of 'laws'. At first sight, the idiographic methods seem to side with Dilthey's 'understanding', and the nomothetic ones with his 'explaining'. So one could say that idiographic methods are typical for the Humanities while nomothetic ones are typical for the Sciences. There are some difficulties, however: geology studies the history of the Earth, a unique event, not to be repeated – yet geology belongs to the Natural Sciences. That means that it is possible to study unique events with the help of scientific methods. The question is: if this is possible in geology, why would it not be possible in the Humanities? The answer that this book will give is simple: it *is* possible.

The view held by Dilthey, Gadamer and their followers also suggests that there is no 'understanding' involved in a scientific explanation, something which may sound strange, because much work in the Natural Sciences demands an understanding at a very deep level. Alternatively, to suggest that understanding is fully isolated from explanatory modes of thinking is also counterintuitive: surely I must ask myself whether and how I can have contracted AIDS before I can even entertain questions of understanding it. There is also no need to carve up the world into two halves: one is not under the obligation to choose between those two methods as exclusive alternatives, because a third alternative is available. This is what C.P. Snow was looking for when he defined the Third Culture.

1.3. Two cultures?

Charles Percy Snow (1905–1980), an influential novelist and former scientist at Cambridge University, highlighted the contrast between the Sciences and the Humanities in *The Two Cultures* (1959), not in a normative way as Dilthey had done but in a descriptive way. He showed how the working cultures of these two groups of disciplines gradually grew apart over the past hundred years. ('Culture' here is to be understood as the ways, habits, customs, etc. of people.) Since Snow was both a scientist and a well-known novelist, his description must be taken seriously – he was speaking on the basis of first-hand knowledge and experience in both domains. At first sight, his description seems to underpin the view propounded by Dilthey and his followers in the Humanities. Snow seems to concur with them that there are two fundamentally different ways of looking at the world. There is a paradox in this, however. A Diltheyan view implies that the methods of 'understanding' and 'explaining' are incompatible with each other, that one has to choose between the two, and that adherents of either view cannot meaningfully communicate with each other. While Snow gave many examples of such a deep gap between the cultures of the scientist and the humanist, he himself was a living example of the contrary: he was at home in both worlds and had made significant contributions to both. He maintained that one does not have to choose: the two methods can be combined and communication between them is a real possibility.

Maybe Snow may have felt this paradox himself. In a kind of postscript to the second edition of his book he added that there may be a way out of this double-tracked view, in that an alternative way may exist. He calls that the 'Third Culture':

> It is probably too early to speak of a third culture already in existence. But I am now convinced that this is coming. When it comes, some of the difficulties of communication will at last be softened: for such a culture has, just to do its job, to be on speaking terms with the scientific one (…) [(1959) 1993:71]

In 1959, when Snow proposed this way out of the problem of a dualistic world view, it was not altogether clear what he meant by it, nor what the implications could be. Our book firmly takes its position in the possibility of this Third Culture. Let us consider in more detail what this means.

1.4. The scientific study of meaning

Our own view is that the relation between the Humanities and the Natural Sciences is complementary rather than one of opposition. In the Epilogue after Chapter 12, we will inspect critically several ideas that we believe misrepresent and confuse this relation. For the time being, let us specify our position further.

Many people in the Humanities think that scientific methods cannot deal with issues of meaning, and that by using them one misses the 'essence' of what the Humanities are all about. We reject this position: questions of meaning can and have been studied in a scientific manner for about one hundred years now, beginning with the work of the British psychologist Francis Galton (1822–1911).

Human cultures are centrally concerned with questions of meaning, of justice, of order, of normality, of value. Such questions play a predominant role in the lives of individuals and of social groups: how to live in the right way, how to ascribe meaning to one's life, how to be knowledgeable about values? To abolish such questions would be, in our mind, to disregard cultural phenomena.

It is through questions like these that we manifest ourselves as human beings. They express that we are human and humane, that we maintain a relationship with our surroundings, that we mean something to ourselves and to others. Any study of human culture that refuses to deal with these issues is not worth its name. Hence the point of view taken in this book is that such questions must be confronted head on and need to be investigated by the very best methods we have at our disposal.

Hence we need more, not less, study of the role such meaning processes play in the lives of individuals and cultures. But the way we carry out this study matters. The methods traditionally used by Humanists are often merely speculative, in the sense that there are very few checks on the assertions made. Often they are also of a rather subjective nature and tend to rely on methods such as introspection (subjectively tracking one's own thoughts). These approaches may have their benefits in some respects, but they do not yield particularly reliable forms of information. They generate more concepts, more theoretical constructions, but do not propose to test their points. It is our contention that questions of meaning in human life (or in societies at large) are too important to be studied only through the means of investigation that Humanists offer. What we propagate is the empirical investigation of culture, a form of study that approaches matters of meaning in a more accountable way – as Dilthey rightly insisted – by relying on methods from a scientific repertoire. *Empirical* can be defined here as a kind of reasoning and a kind of research that is based on real evidence, that is, on evidence from the real world, which can be inspected by anyone. That does not mean that such investigations provide all the answers: scientific methods do not reveal what the meaning of life is, of course but they do illuminate how such questions come into being or how they function in the lives of individuals and societies. What we are proposing, therefore, is a piecemeal contribution to the study of culture, one that bridges the gap between the Humanities and the Natural Sciences, in the realization that both need each other for a better understanding of the world.

Some may be of the opinion that the search for patterns, regularities, or laws has no place in the Humanities. As we hope to show you, the contrary is the case: there are many cultural issues where we can observe clear patterns of behavior and we will instruct you how to discover such regularities yourself through the various methods we will describe. What are these methods and why do we think that they are more appropriate for the study of some problems in the Humanities? That is the central topic of this book, and we will introduce you to it as we go along. For the time being, however, let us just say that by scientific methods we mean two things. First, we mean methods that are coherent, logically clear and transparent, that avoid all tautologies or contradictions. Second, and more importantly, we mean methods that employ independent forms of observation. Observations are here understood as forms of systematic data collection and analysis. These methods are used to check whether our intuitions (upon which we depend to begin any investigation) are reliable – whether they provide us with correct information about the world. Sections 1.8 and 1.9 of this chapter will give clear illustrations of this. But first, let us pay a visit to Wundt's laboratory, to see how some of the above-mentioned issues work out in practice.

1.5. A visit to Wundt's laboratory

In Section 1.1 we wondered how a state of drunkenness came to be the result of actions that initially were so pleasant in themselves. In order to understand how it came about, we have to invoke the spirit of Wilhelm Wundt (1832–1920), the generally acknowledged father of modern psychology. One could say, as Hunt does (1993: 127), that psychology in our present-day sense of the word was born on a December day in 1879, when Wilhelm Wundt first established his research institute in Leipzig, Germany. In order to get a clearer picture of the kind of work Wundt was doing, let us pay a visit to his laboratory in our imagination: we can see small groups of three or four men standing around (women were virtually excluded from higher education at the time), with various instruments, observing the people involved in using them, and making notes all the time. Here a man is requested to close his eyes while someone whispers something into his ear. He opens his eyes again; the others look at a small machine and write things down. In a corner, someone utters words after being prompted by someone else, while over there a group of men looks at a metronome, setting it at different paces and reporting their sensations.

If this description does not tell you precisely what is happening, that is because the research that is being carried out is highly detailed and needs technical knowledge to be understood. At first sight, then, this does not really make an impression of greatness. Rather, it presents a picture, on the one hand, of boring work that seems not to hold great promises of understanding the world and, on the other hand, that has a ring of treating humans as machines, studying their reactions as if they were some kind of robots.

None of these impressions, however, is justified. To begin with the last view, Wundt's experiments do take human life in its fullness and richness seriously. It is because he took the matter so seriously that he concentrated with all his energy on the precise processes involved in human thinking, feeling and acting. How else could we become better informed about the processes that run in our mental (hence invisible) apparatus than through concentrated efforts at elucidating their structure? That some of these procedures may look a bit abstruse today is an effect of historical distance. Just imagine how people will judge our work in a hundred years' time. It is not certain that they will be impressed by our contemporary 'primitive' forms of investigation from their perspective, when so many more powerful devices to study human culture may be at their disposal and the history of thinking will have also changed its course. We are in the middle of an ongoing process in the development of research and you will soon be part of it.

As to the first objection, whether such work is boring or exciting, it depends to a considerable degree on what one mean by such words. Is it not exciting to explore how the human mind works, how perception is guided by preformed categories, how feelings guide our actions? There is no better way, however, to experience the thrill of discovery involved in such empirical work than by doing it yourself. Let us do a typical experiment that could have been carried out by Wilhelm Wundt's co-workers. At first, you may wonder what it has to do with research in the cultural sphere, but just bear with us, and momentarily take our word for it that its relevance for things cultural is not in doubt. All you need to carry out the experiment is a cup large enough to put your hand in, a thermometer (*not* a clinical thermometer – it may burst), a piece of paper and a pencil, and a person willing to cooperate with you.

1.6. The Wundt curve

Start off by filling the cup with water and put it in the fridge. After a couple of hours, take the cup out and request the person participating in your experiment to put his/her hand in the cup, then ask him or her how (un)pleasant it feels. Measure the temperature of the water with the thermometer. You now draw up a coordination system, where you enter the temperature on the horizontal axis and the 'feelings' of your partner on the vertical axis. The zero point, where the two axes cross, will be the point of departure. Do this in the following way: mark 10 points on the vertical axis at equal distances; for the first experience, take the zero-point on both the horizontal and vertical axis. Everything above the horizontal axis means that the feelings of 'pleasantness' are positive relative to the first experience, everything below it will be negative experiences relative to the first time your partner put his/her hand in the cup. Suppose the temperature of the water was 5 degrees Celsius (15 degrees Fahrenheit). Now heat up the water to 10 degrees C (25 degrees F) and again request your partner to put the same hand in the water. Again ask how it feels *compared to the previous experience*. If the answer is 'more pleasant', go up one point on the y-axis and enter the coordinate for both axes; if the answer is 'less pleasant' go down one point on the y-axis and enter the coordinates. Now repeat the procedure with temperature intervals of 5 degrees C (10 degrees F) each. Request your partner to indicate whether s/he experiences a more or a less pleasant sensation and enter the answer each time in the coordinate system. Stop when you come to a point where your partner no longer wishes to cooperate simply because the water becomes too hot. Now link all the points in the coordinate system with a line. What does the result look like?

What you are looking at now is what psychologists call the 'Wundt curve', first of all because it *is* a curvilinear shape and second because it was probably discovered by Wilhelm Wundt in his laboratory. It reveals that, relative to the initial position, a gradual increase in temperature of the water also gradually increases the feeling of 'pleasantness,' but only up to a certain point, after which the pleasant feeling gradually diminishes, until it reaches a point where it actually crosses the *x*-axis, indicating that from there onwards, the feelings become quite *un*pleasant. Compare your findings to the 'ideal' Wundt curve, which looks like this:

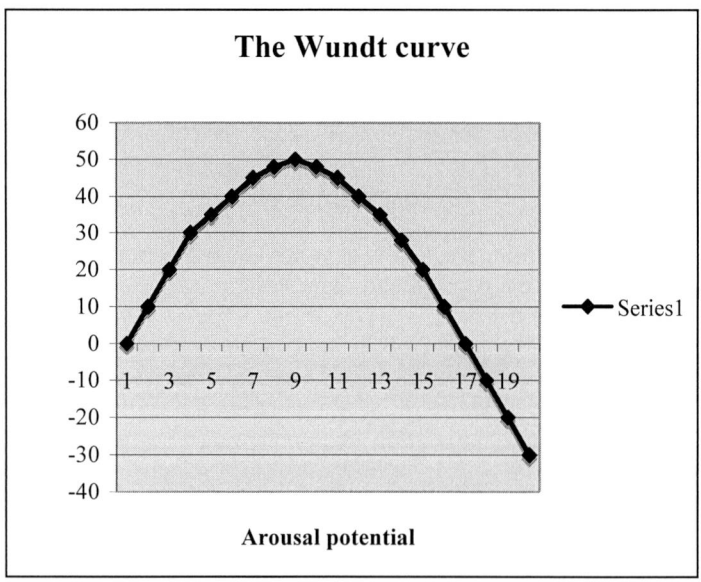

Figure 1.1: The Wundt curve

If your graph deviates somewhat from what you see here, do not worry: in all likelihood, this is caused by the limited number of measurements you carried out as well as by the rather primitive 'measurement' of 'points' when asking your partner about the sensations experienced. When, however, your graph differs *fundamentally* from the Wundt curve, something is amiss and you have, in all probability, made a mistake somewhere. But supposing your results match the Wundt curve more or less, the question arises in what way these findings bear on cultural matters. The answer to that question is relatively simple: the Wundt curve has been observed in many areas of life, including the cultural domain.

Let us get back now to our example of getting drunk in Section 1 above. The Wundt curve explains how a moderate intake of alcohol initially increased the benign feeling in the drinker; further intake increased it even more, but only up to a certain point (which is partly different for different people, depending on body weight, the extent to which the body is used to alcohol, etc.), after which the benign feelings start to decrease, in some cases even rapidly. Because alcohol numbs the mind, making an adequate perception of the decrease more difficult, one may not have felt having crossed the zero-point, where now any further dose is going to increase displeasure, ultimately leading to the unpleasant experiences of dizziness, vomiting, and the general feeling like being a wet rag. The Wundt curve explains all this in a simple and elegant way.

Wundt apparently did not base his curve on empirical data, but formulated it on the basis of his everyday expectations. However, Alfred Georg Ludwig Lehmann, a Danish student of Wilhelm Wundt, carried out the experiment you just went through already in 1892. You could also run experiments in which you have people taste solutions in which the amount of salt (or sour or bitter ingredients) is gradually increased, and you will find the Wundt curve in each case.

1.7. Empirical aesthetics

Interesting as it may be to discover the relation between temperature and corporal feeling, or between the intake of alcohol and getting drunk, what use is that to students of culture? The question is a legitimate, even an important one, because its answer shows even more the brilliant idea behind the Wundt curve, and this is that the same kinds of relation as expressed by the Wundt curve are found in the cultural realm as well. One of the researchers who has done most to exemplify this was the Canadian psychologist Daniel E. Berlyne (1924–1976). First, let us look at the way in which he reinterpreted Wundt's curve.

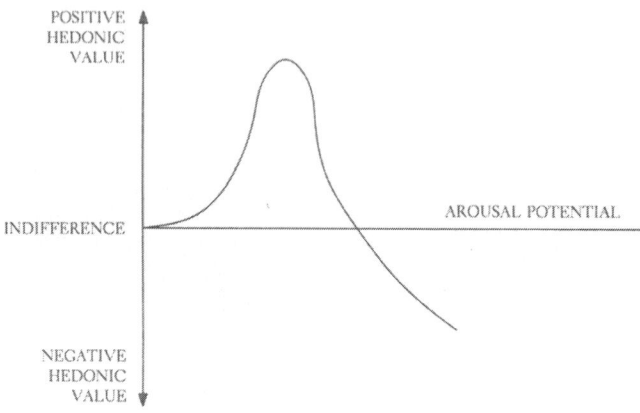

Figure 1.2: The Wundt curve for aesthetic experience (from Berlyne)
(from *Aesthetics and Psychobiology*, p. 89)

For feelings of pleasantness, Berlyne uses the term positive *hedonic value*. Unpleasant feelings are categorized by him as negative hedonic value. The intensity of the stimulus itself is represented on the horizontal axis; the axis itself represents neither positive nor negative hedonic value, hence indifference. Berlyne reinterprets the Wundt curve in such a way that the horizontal axis represents not merely stimulus intensity, but "also other stimulus properties that tend to raise arousal, including biological significance and the collative properties like novelty and complexity." (Berlyne 1971: 90)

Arousal is defined by him as a psycho-physiological concept, indicating the degree of activation: how conscious one is, how excited, how alert, and so forth. The lowest levels of arousal are experienced during sleep, while during waking hours, arousal levels may fluctuate. At some times one is more relaxed, while at others one may be more emotional; arousal levels will be higher in the latter case. (It will be evident that sometimes alertness may be highly required – for instance in emergency situations – hence Berlyne's reference to its 'biological significance'.) However, it is not the actual level of arousal in a person that is set out on the horizontal axis, but the arousal *potential*, the properties of the environment which that person is experiencing, i.e. the temperature of the water, the proportion of salt in the solution, etc. The revolutionary leap made by Berlyne is that he included the properties of cultural artifacts within the concept of arousal potential. Novelty and complexity are two such properties.

Novelty refers to the subjective experience of surprisingness, in other words, how 'new' you experience something that you perceive. Berlyne's assumption was that subjective novelty raises hedonic value, while diminishing (or absent) novelty decreases it. If you want to test that assumption empirically, make a pile of seven or eight cards and write a sentence on each of them, for instance "I love you not." Now write on card number 9 "I love you notwithstanding". Present the cards one by one to a group of friends and after each one ask whether the person thinks this is an interesting/pleasant sentence. You are looking for 'hedonic value', i.e. pleasantness after each card. What do you notice? Here are the results of such an experiment we carried out (Van Peer, Zyngier & Hakemulder, 2007): 27 undergraduate students of Humanities at the Federal University of Rio de Janeiro were presented with a 'poem' line by line on an overhead projector. The first eight lines were identical and ran *'não te amo'* (I love you not) in Portuguese; the ninth, final, line ran *'te amo não obstante"* (I love you notwithstanding). Participants were requested to mark their appreciation of the *beauty* of the poem as it unfolds on a 10-point scale. Here is what came out of the experiment:

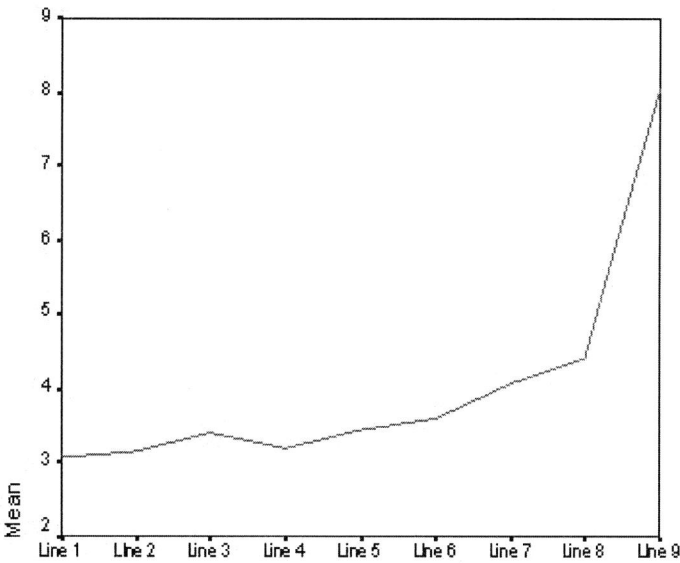

Figure 1.3: Novelty and the perception of beauty

The horizontal axis contains the nine lines of the poem as it unfolds. The vertical axis represents the average ratings of their perceived beauty. As can be seen, ratings of beauty remain relatively low and stable as long as there is little novelty – due to the mere repetition of the same phrase. But there is a sharp rise in the beauty ratings for line 9, which contains something totally new – and hence unexpected. The results clearly illustrate Berlyne's view that novelty has a positive impact on hedonic value.

An interesting aspect about such experiments is that they can be *repeated*. You can test the theory by carrying out a similar study to see whether in your case, too, the values will remain low except for line 9, which shows a marked jump upwards, because its sudden novelty is experienced, after the repetitions of the previous eight lines, as beautiful. But you can also check whether similar results would be obtained if you had asked participants to indicate the degree of pleasantness, interest, motivation, or the like. Familiarity breeds monotony, while some degree of deviation from the expected raises hedonic value. The Wundt curve captures this relationship in an abstract and detailed manner: rising novelty (as subjectively perceived, of course) results in higher hedonic values, but only up to a certain point, after which the thing perceived becomes 'too novel' for the observer to be readily interpretable. Values will diminish as novelty is further increased, until they become unpleasant and negative hedonic value sets in.

Such preference for novelty starts very early in life, and may therefore be part of our cognitive wiring. Slater et al. (2000), for instance, found evidence for this with newly born infants (3 days old), who were presented with a complex visual stimulus. Researchers monitored how long the babies looked at it and noticed that with repeated presentations the babies spent less and less time looking at the stimulus. When they spent less than half the initial time looking, a new stimulus was presented; the babies looked for significantly longer at this new stimulus than at the original one. This study shows how even at the very beginning of our lives we are already prone to automatization and the emergence of habituation, while at the same time being sensitive to the rewarding experience of novelty. What we have been dealing with in this section are people's experiences of beauty, of pleasant feelings, of captivating experiences caused by simple stimuli. Works of art, theater plays, sculptures, TV productions, or novels are also stimuli. Here we enter the field of *empirical aesthetics*: the study of what people find beautiful, captivating and pleasurable when they explore such aesthetic objects. D.E. Berlyne was not the first to base such study on empirical observations. That was Theodor Fechner (1801–1887), a German philosopher, but Berlyne was perhaps the most important one in the 20th century. He showed how several properties of art works, novelty being one of them, influence the spectator's aesthetic experience. Going beyond Berlyne's studies, the psychologist Colin Martindale, in his 1990 book, explored the notion of novelty in an even more systematic way. This work is so fundamental that we devote a special section to it.

1.8. The Clockwork Muse

The title of this book expresses Martindale's thesis that the history of cultural products and processes is highly predictable; its subtitle indeed is: 'The predictability of artistic change'. Martindale starts from the insights proposed in 1917 by the Russian Formalists, most notably by Viktor Shklovsky, about the nature and the function of art:

> And art exists that one may recover the sensation of life; it exists to make one feel things, to make the stone *stony*. The purpose of art is to impart the sensation of things as they are perceived and not as they are known. The technique of art is to make objects "unfamiliar", to make forms difficult, to increase the difficulty and length of perception because the process of perception is an aesthetic end in itself and must be prolonged. (Shklovsky [1917] 1965: 12)

Basing his work on this insight, Martindale sees novelty as the major drive in the history of art and literature. Our daily world is built on habits and routines – we would not be able to survive otherwise. Art, however, builds an antidote against the debilitating effects that our everyday automatisms create by allowing us to experience things again in a new and fresh way. In order to make this possible, however, artists are under constant pressure to produce novelty in their works. Contrary to more traditional scholars, Martindale is not content to assert a theory. He also carried out a considerable body of research that actually *tests* his idea. The critical attitude of testing your intuitions against independent data – independent not in the sense that researchers themselves are not involved, but that they try not to influence the outcome – is typical for the empirical method of research, and will crop up in this book time and again.

As an example, let us look at the way in which people use metaphors. In daily life we may say a thing like "The president is a fox". Everyone will know that we do not mean that the president is a quadruped that catches chickens and rabbits. We understand the utterance because metaphor belongs to the language repertoire. In some way that linguists still do not fully understand, we transfer some quality, for instance cunningness, from the one concept (fox) to the other (president), so that we will interpret the sentence as meaning that the president is cunning, not that he is covered in brownish fur and has a tail. Many such metaphors become standardized, 'dead' metaphors, as when we speak of the 'foot' of the mountain, the 'leg' of a table, or a 'cut' in wages. In literature, however, what we see is that poets constantly strive for new metaphors, as when Romeo says of Juliet that she "is the sun". Here we have to transfer some qualities we associate with the sun (light, warmth) with Juliet – something already less predictable than in the case of the fox. We could say that the psychological distance between the concepts of 'sun' and 'Juliet' is greater than that between 'fox' and 'president'. This distance may become so large that the metaphor becomes really hard to understand.

Martindale suspected that, because of the drive for novelty in cultural history, the distance between the two concepts involved in metaphors would increase over time. To this end, he composed a sample of poems written by French poets born between 1790 and 1909, divided into consecutive 20-year periods. For each period, the three poets with the most pages in the *Oxford Book of French Verse* (ed. St John Lucas and P. Mansell Jones, 1957) were selected. From the works of each of these poets, 50 pages were drawn randomly from the most recent and most complete edition of their works, and in each case the first eight lines were used. This produced samples of some 3,000 words per poet. Martindale then carried out a content analysis of the *corpus* that he had thus obtained. A computer program was developed to measure the distance between concepts in metaphors. This measure is plotted on the vertical axis, while the horizontal axis represents the 20-year time slots. The result of this study can be seen in the following graph.

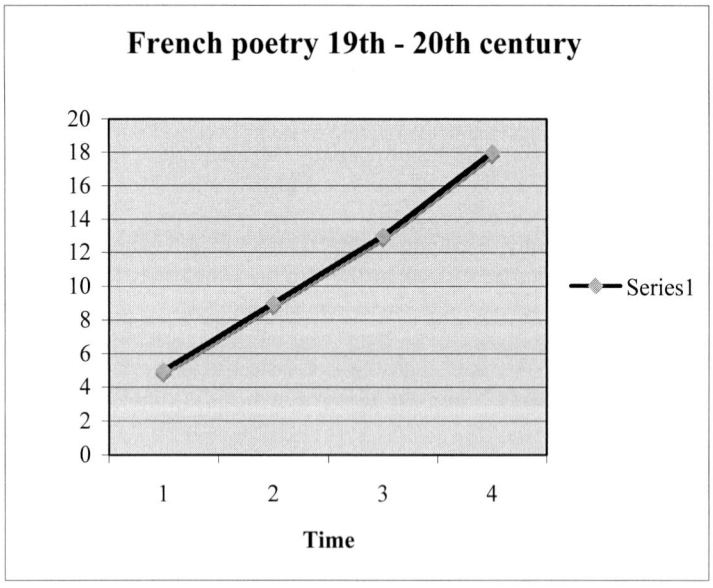

Figure 1.4: Distance between metaphor concepts

As can be seen, and in accordance with the theoretical prediction of the theory of novelty, the distance between the metaphoric poles indeed goes up as time goes by. The line represents the 'fit' of the individual poets into a general trend. Martindale has performed scores of studies like these, testing his theory again and again, not just for French poetry, but also for music, painting, short stories, popular music lyrics, Gothic architecture, and other cultural artifacts. Thus we can now safely say that Martindale's theory about the importance of novelty in the history of culture is supported by a considerable body of *independent* evidence.

1.9. Complexity

Returning once more to our previous discussion of the Wundt curve, we must now discuss an observation that you will soon make when you observe ratings provided by participants in research: it is that often Wundt curves obtained through ratings look very different. How can this be explained? Two factors are at work here. The first has already been mentioned: complexity. In general, we can distinguish different levels of complexity on the basis of the number of units and sub-units of which a work is composed and on the basis of the number of relations that obtain between those various (sub-)units. Now cultural artifacts differ greatly in this respect: a Roman watch tower is so much less complex than a Romanesque church, which is in itself less complex than a late Gothic cathedral. This is not the place to elaborate on the notion of complexity, but it will be clear that variable measures of complexity can be employed. Thus, for instance – other things being equal – a longer piece of text is more complex than a shorter one. The notion of 'other things being equal' is crucial here. It is also referred to as the *ceteris paribus* notion. It means that you compare only comparable things: a novel with 10 chapters is more complex than *that same novel* with only nine chapters. Note, however, that the chapters must be roughly of equal content. If you are dealing with a mystery novel and Chapter 10 is the final one, in which all the mysteries are resolved, then a version of the novel with only nine chapters may be more complex to the reader, in the sense that the reader is unable to link the various pieces of information in a meaningful way. Always in research we will have to keep the *ceteris paribus* principle in mind. Thus, other things being equal, a novel's complexity increases with the number of characters, the number of relations established between the characters, the number of different traits the characters and their relations possess, the number of themes and issues brought forth, etc.

Suppose you ask people to listen to a simple song. Chances are high that most people will find it of medium to high hedonic value. Now have them listen to a Mahler symphony. In all likelihood, the ratings for hedonic value will be lower. The explanation for these different ratings lies in the different complexities of the two pieces of music. For various reasons, we must call the Mahler symphony more complex than the song: it is much longer, is executed by a much larger orchestra, containing more different instruments that build, moreover, ever-changing combinations, and its melodic patterns are more intricate and unusual (hence it is also more 'novel'). The way we describe the differences here hopefully makes clear that the notion of complexity is not a normative one; in itself complexity is not 'good' or 'bad' or 'beautiful' or 'ugly', though it is linked to such normative notions in an indirect way.

Now suppose we expose listeners to the song repetitively, and we do the same with the symphony. What one will observe is that after several trials, the hedonic value ratings for the song will start falling, while those of the symphony may start rising. The complexity of the sound texture of the symphony makes it nearly impossible for most untrained listeners to be appreciative on a first or second hearing: its richness is simply not taken in. With repeated exposures, listeners may begin to grasp its variations of melodic and orchestral patterns, its structure of repetitions and contrasts, and its multi-layered levels of tone and rhythm. A similar process is at work in processing the song, of course, but there the musical 'material' is many times less rich, so that after several exposures, it seems to have yielded all the hedonic value it can provide. Thus, different levels of complexity of cultural artifacts produce differences in hedonic value; this has indeed been found in research (see Skaife, 1967).

But there is also a second factor explaining different ratings of hedonic value. Consider three persons listening to the song and to the Mahler symphony: one of them has no musical background, the other is a lover of classical music, a third is a conductor of a professional orchestra. Chances are high that the hedonic value experienced by those three people will differ considerably. The conductor, used to thinking and feeling in complex musical structures, will see through the complexity of the Mahler symphony much faster than the layman, and will thus start appreciation of it at a much higher value. Typically, people's background – in terms of their past experiences, their attitudes, their motivations, or their skills – explains why the same phenomenon may provide highly different ratings of hedonic value. Thus the Wundt curves for different people, though showing the same underlying pattern, will simultaneously reveal a somewhat different course, as in the following figure:

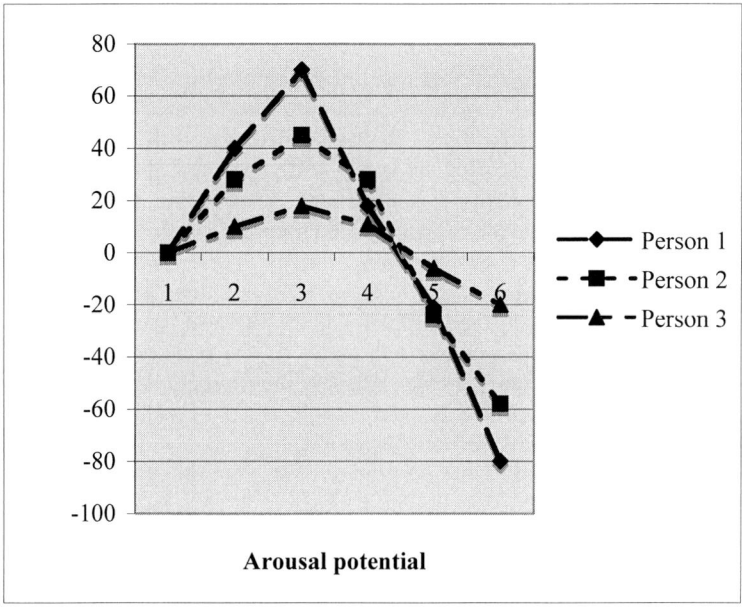

Figure 1.5: The Wundt curve for several persons

The picture has become more complicated now: next to novelty there are also complexity and a person's background influencing aesthetic appreciation. We will later study in more detail how the *interaction* between several such variables can be investigated in a rigorous way. Each of the factors plays its own role in determining the outcome of an aesthetic experience, and certainly there are other factors still that exert influence, for instance the degree to which something is expected (surprise), the information value (uncertainty), interest, etc. It is likely that the particular emotional state you are in or the amount of attention you pay also shape your reaction to music. How many such factors are there? We do not know. But presumably other factors are irrelevant: whether I am wearing black or white socks, or whether the date is an odd or even number, or whether I wear a digital or an analogue wrist watch, these will in all probability not influence my reactions directly. Hence cultural preferences and experiences are highly complex in themselves, because many factors are involved in them, and you have to estimate the relative weight of each of these factors in the overall result. On the other hand, we know the effects of some of the factors and their relationship. The Wundt curve expresses some of these relationships in a clear and meaningful way.

1.10. Why methodology?

Empirical research is not the only way through which you can inform yourself and explore the world, but it is one of the most powerful, perhaps even the very best of the methods we have as humans to learn to know ourselves and the world in which we live. Natural scientists discovered this some 400 years ago; psychologists and sociologists some 100 years ago. In the Humanities, things are different. Many Humanists, perhaps the majority, do not work in an empirical way and few devote themselves to empirical investigations. The result is that Humanists are still largely ignorant of many aspects of their own field. To name only a few areas: if you wish to know what emotions a particular kind of painting produces, art studies must remain silent. Suppose you want to know the effect of literary reading, whether it changes in the course of time (or not), literary scholars will shrug their shoulders – they simply do not know. You could make a long list of highly interesting aspects of cultural life that one would like to know, so that we would have a better understanding of the cultural world we live in, but you will find precious little empirical research on most items on your list. Of course scholars in literary studies also acknowledge the complexity of the world, but most of them do not engage in empirical studies to unravel that complexity. Or if they do, they make use of methods that are many times less reliable and are often extremely speculative, so that they develop a history of thinking about the subject, rather than discover anything new about it. This is sad, because it means that we remain ignorant about crucial aspects of our cultural life. It is also sad because it need not be so: the methods of finding out are here. It only requires reading a book about empirical research methodology, and you can start. It is really that simple.

Let us give two examples of empirical research that shows the kinds of things that you can discover. The first one is simple and is concerned with psychoanalytic approaches to literature. Psychoanalysis holds that the semantic content of literary texts allows readers to come to terms with feelings of repressed sexuality in early childhood and puberty. More specifically, Freud has argued that reading fairy tales produces feelings of hate against one's mother and also incestuous feelings for one's brothers and/or sisters. To some, this may sound like a wild speculation, but many psychoanalysts take this as truth. The claim itself, however, is not speculative at all, because you can put it to a test: you can actually have people read fairy tales and question them whether they indeed have these feelings – and then compare their answers with people who read something from a newspaper, or a text totally different from a fairy tale.

That is precisely what Ingrid Stöger, a former student of ours, did. Of course the researcher has to be somewhat careful here, since you can hardly ask readers whether they hate their mother or whether they would like to go to bed with their brother or sister. Van Peer & Stöger (2001) therefore approached these feelings in a somewhat roundabout way, by asking questions like whether they felt the atmosphere in the family pleasant, whether they had wished to have had more presents from their parents, and so forth, and also asking them whether they wished to have spent more time with their brothers/sisters, whether they would have preferred to sleep in his/her bed, and the like. The results of the investigation were interesting, in that they showed that in virtually no cases did readers react in the way Freud said. It did turn out, however, that several readers reported feelings in the direction of Freud's predictions ... in the control text. In other words, a text that according to psychoanalysis was not meant to produce such feelings did, while a text that was meant to do so did not. What this empirical investigation shows is that Freudian theory about reading is wrong when it comes to this aspect dealing with the reading of fairy tales. It shows that the theory makes claims about reality that are obviously false when one observes how real readers go about reading. Perhaps other claims by literary psychoanalysis are also false and you may now wish to be on your guard when psychoanalysts claim something about readers or reading.

This piece of research has a rather clear outcome: at least part of psychoanalytic theory about reading literature is untrustworthy. But sometimes empirical research may also create a more puzzling picture. One such study in which we have been involved concerns the point of view from which a story is told. Many scholars in literary studies assume that if a story is presented from an 'inside' perspective, so that you not only know what that person does in the story world, but also what he or she thinks and feels, then readers will more easily identify with that person. And they may have more sympathy for that character. Investigating such theoretical claims Van Peer (2001) presented readers randomly with one of three versions of the same story in which a conflict between a husband and wife erupts. In one version, the events were told in a more neutral way; one other version presented the events from the 'inside' of the male character and yet another one similarly from the perspective of the female character. This was done by adding bits of text like "'Can he never think of that himself,' she thought" or "'Can't she ever leave me in peace,' he thought." Since the conflict formed the central point around which the story develops, it is interesting to see whether the internal point of view influences the amount to which either of the protagonists is viewed as 'just'. The results of the investigation showed that indeed, internal point of view did have an effect, as can be seen in the following figure:

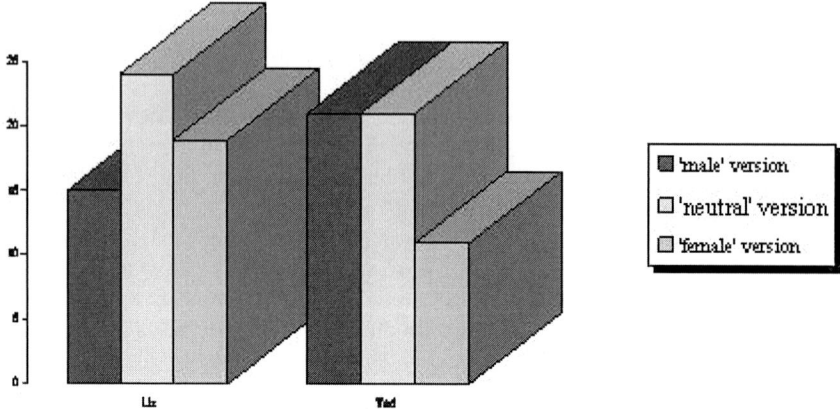

Figure 1.6: How 'just' is each person?

The dark bar, indicating the degree to which the male character ('Ted') was perceived as just, is indeed higher than the gray bar representing the ratings for Ted by the group of readers who had been given the version with the internal female perspective, and vice versa: for the female character ('Liz') the dark bar (readers who read the 'male' version of the story) is lower than the gray one, representing those readers who had read the version with the built-in female perspective. Hence the investigation seems to support the claims made by narratologists about internal point of view. The observed differences are also statistically significant (something about which we will say more in later chapters).

However, a closer look reveals that things are not quite that simple. First of all, one would expect readers' rating of the version with the 'neutral' perspective to be somewhere halfway between the other two versions. For the male character, however, the 'neutral' version elicited exactly the same ratings as the male version, and for the female character, the ratings produced by the 'neutral' version are higher than those of the other two versions, which clearly does not make much sense in narratological terms.

Readers were also asked who of the two characters they considered more 'considerate'. In line with narratological theory, we expected similar results as for the question how 'just' they thought each character was.

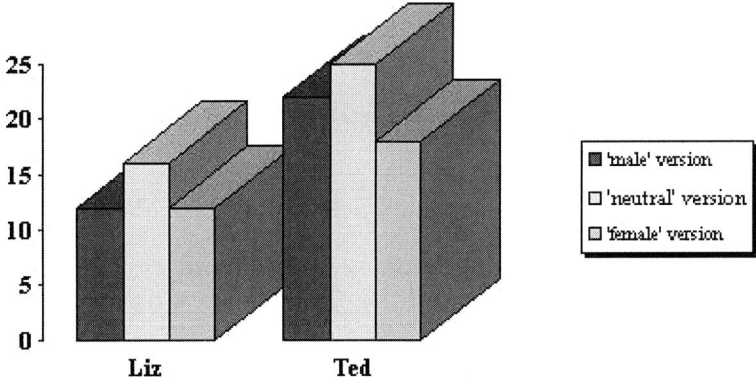

Figure 1.7: How 'considerate' is each person?

As can be seen in Fig. 1.7, however, narratological theory is in a bit of trouble here. This time the 'neutral' version elicited higher ratings for both characters. Moreover, there is indeed a difference in rating for the male character, and it is in the predicted direction, but the difference is marginal (and not significant in statistical terms.) Finally, there is no difference in rating the female character between the versions with the male and the female perspective. Obviously it did not matter to the readers from which point of view the story was told when they rated the degree to which they judged the protagonists 'considerate'.

Some people find it irritating that research muddles up the clear picture that narratologists have developed over the past decades. Indeed it makes life more difficult, for we can no longer be so sure that our theory makes correct claims about the world. But would that be a reason to renounce such investigations? We ourselves think that what this piece of research shows is, again, how much more complex the world, especially the cultural world, is than we initially surmised. We would argue, however, that it is precisely because this cultural world is so complex, that we cannot do without empirical research. If our understanding of culture is to advance with any degree of success in heightening the reliability of understanding, then empirical investigations are unavoidable.

Appendix

Assignment

To be carried out before turning to Chapter Two

Read in the New Testament the following passages in the Gospel by Luke and try to find the comparable passages in Mark and Matthew. Then chart your results (think out a method yourself) and see whether you can generate any remarkable insights from them. Can you explain what you have found? The passages are indicated in the usual way: the first number indicates the chapter, subsequent numbers after the colon indicate the verse lines in that chapter. Hence 'Mt 1: 1—3' means 'Gospel by Matthew, chapter 1, verses 1 through 3'.

The passages from Luke to be investigated are:
3: 3–6	3: 7–9	3: 21–22
4: 1–13	4: 14	6: 12–19

[Please note that in this task we consider the Gospels as literary texts. This is by no means an exceptional view, since New Testament scholars have amply demonstrated their literary character. That view should not hinder any person to consider these texts as a source of religious belief. Personal conviction is a valuable thing in itself, but not one that we shall deal with in this book. Science is about general things, not about particulars].

INTERLUDE

SOME MISCONCEPTIONS ABOUT EMPIRICAL RESEARCH

One thing you will notice when you become interested in empirical studies is that many Humanists remain skeptical of their methods. Often it is because they hold specific preconceptions about empirical studies that are at least debatable. We believe it is instructive to review some of these traditional and current attitudes toward the empirical approach, and see how they relate to what empirical methods are really about. We will discuss them very briefly, hoping in this way to contribute to a better understanding of the power and the limits of empirical work.

1. You cannot do empirical research without having a theoretical framework.
That is correct but a lot depends on what you mean by 'theory'. If it means that you need an elaborate construction of concepts (and relations between them) before you can start out doing research in the field, it is quite mistaken. If it means that one needs ideas on where to look for interesting hypotheses, or an intuition of what aspect of culture to study in more detail, then the idea is correct. Often, reading the theoretical literature may bring about such ideas or may activate intuitions. But that does not mean that one has to buy such theoretical writings wholesale. Nor does it mean that you have to bury yourself in the library for an extended time to come up with a 'theoretical framework' before you can start doing research.

2. Empirical studies reduce culture to some superficial object, without doing justice to its richness and depth.
If that is the case, then it is a poor piece of empirical work! Empirical studies can – and should – take into account the depth of feelings generated by cultural processes, and they are certainly not blind to the richness of symbolic meaning or the importance of detail for understanding and experiencing them. There is one sense, however, in which the reproach contains some truth: empirical studies of culture will – indeed must – reduce the object being investigated. The reason for this is simple: without some concentration on one or on some aspects,

valid investigation is not possible. This is not to deny depth or richness, but because this is the only way in which you can study anything at all: isolate some feature and study it in detail. All approaches that proclaim not to narrow the focus of their object of study in some way, and instead promise some 'holistic' method should be viewed with distrust, because it is not really possible for human beings to pay attention simultaneously to all aspects of a complex issue.

3. There is no way in which aspects of the cultural world can be measured.
One would like to know why this would be impossible. We gave some clear examples in Chapter 1 of how certain cultural aspects were measured. If you say that you cannot measure aspects of the cultural world, you are basically saying that you cannot observe any differences between cultural artifacts, which is, of course, rather absurd. But if you can observe differences, then there is no reason why you cannot measure particular aspects of the difference. It is true, however, that in the Humanities we have relatively little experience with this. That can be changed if we creatively search for ways to improve our work in this respect.

4. Empirical studies are concerned with present-day people and are thus a-historical.
This is patently untrue. Although much empirical work is carried out with present-day participants, there is no principled reason why one cannot study the cultural issues of the past, as the research by Martindale (discussed in Section 1.8 above) eloquently demonstrated. In the course of this book, we will provide further examples of the empirical study of cultures in the past.

5. Empirical studies are involved in hair-splitting issues and are thus a-theoretical.
It is true that quantitative analyses play an important role in empirical work. But why would that mean that this makes empirical work a-theoretical? Is physics an a-theoretical discipline because a lot of it is based on numbers? Our view is that the most productive kind of research is one in which theoretical views are combined with quantifiable observations. This usually enriches the theory, while the theory will make the observations more meaningful. To quote Kurt Lewin, a famous psychologist (1890–1947):

> A science without a theory is blind because it lacks that element which alone is able to organize facts and give direction to research. It is necessary to have a theory (…) that is empirical and not speculative. This means that theory and facts must be closely related to each other (in Rogers & Shoemaker, 1971, p. 44).

6. Empirical studies generate just numbers and numbers do not tell you anything.

On the contrary, numbers often give much more (and much more precise) information than everyday language can. Why would numbers about the kind of people who visit museums not be able to tell us something interesting about the world, something we would not know at all without such numbers? Usually it is descriptions in everyday language, or even in the technical language of the literary critic that are vague or uninformative.

7. Empirical methods are artificial instruments that do not have a status in real life and therefore cannot be used to study real-life situations and processes.
A thermometer is also an artificial instrument. It does not grow in gardens or on trees, yet it is highly useful to study real-life situations. Why would it be different in the cultural world? What we need to keep in mind is that instruments do not replace real-life situations. If we know that the cultural world is more complex than a research setting, there is no problem. Research situations can be used as terms of comparison to other, more everyday situations.

8. By doing empirical research, one actively changes the situation one is investigating, thereby destroying the very basis upon which one wants to base one's theories.
The first part of the sentence is correct. That is often (though not always) the very essence of empirical research: one manipulates a variable in order to see its effect on its surroundings. But precisely in doing so, it creates a transparent basis on which to base conclusions as to the influence of this particular variable. If you want to know what a new medicine against AIDS does, you have to introduce it in a concrete situation and subsequently observe what it does. In doing so, an empirical approach does not destroy, but rather creates a thorough basis from which you can derive clear conclusions.

9. Empirical methods pretend to be 'objective' but in fact are as much involved in imposing an interpretation on the world as other methods.
It is true that empirical methods do require interpretation. Empirical studies without interpretation of analyzed data are poor, if not worthless. This kind of interpretation, however, is different from the kind of unrestrained or wild interpretations you often see in cultural studies. It basically means trying to eliminate all alternative explanations for the pattern observed or, where this cannot be done, give them their due, and design new studies that will adequately reveal the power of these alternative explanations.

10. Empirical studies claim to be neutral, but this is an illusion. In practice all observation is interpretive.
This is true only up to a certain degree. Whether one sees a yellow or a blue circle in front of one's eyes is in most cases not a matter of interpretation. Whether the thing lying on the ground in front of me is a stick or a snake may be partly a matter of interpretation, but not with an arbitrary outcome! What empirical studies try to avoid is interpreting without being conscious that one is being interpretive. In empirical studies, a clear distinction is made between the data that are collected, and the scholar's own interpretation of such data. In this way, a serious attempt is made to be as neutral as one can be. If this is not total neutrality, at least it is a neutrality that is many degrees higher than in many non-empirical approaches.

11. Empirical studies are not adequate to describe the object of the humanistic disciplines, which are subjective in nature.
This argument seems to presuppose that the language of science must 'echo' the nature of the object it studies. Does that mean then, perhaps, that military history should be belligerent and the study of deafness should be mute? Is the language of psychiatry confused, that of musicology supposed to be melodious? Subjectivity is indeed an integral part of cultural processes and experiences, but there is no a priori reason why such subjective processes are not amenable to a rigorous description and analysis, as the discipline of psychology amply demonstrates.

12. It is of no value whatsoever to try to be impartial or objective – since these are unattainable ideals. It is much better to admit this limitation from the start and hence accept the fundamentally subjective nature of looking at the cultural world.
'Objectivity' and 'impartiality' are two different things. Let us look at each separately. If people say that impartiality is of no value, then they are basically saying that nothing matters at all, that everything is of equal value, that there is no difference in expertise, that everyone has exactly the same skills, that there are no differences in the world that deserve to be noticed. Clearly this is at odds with the facts. Some people are better at some things than others, some facts are less problematic than others and some theories are better supported by evidence than others.
'Objectivity' can mean many things. If you take it to mean 'controllable' or 'repeatable' by other scholars, it loses much of its ambiguity. It is mainly in this sense that we use the word in the present book. 'Objectivity' can also mean: having characteristics of its own, independent of the researcher's opinion. It is also in this sense that we use the term 'objectivity' here: that much of the world

'out there' has characteristics and a structure of its own, which research can try to bring to light. Prime numbers form a good case in point: once prime numbers are defined as natural numbers that are divisible only by themselves and one, it is now an objective question whether 13, 27 or 1 438 777 009 are prime numbers or not – and the answers are certainly not 'partial' or 'subjective'.

13. Empirical studies pretend to know how the world is ultimately structured.
If someone pretends anything of the kind, then you may rest assured that that person is not working in the empirical frame of mind at all. Moreover, it is not methods or approaches that are pretentious, but people. If empirical scholars turn out to be pretentious, then they behave at odds with the basic tenets of empirical research, which tell you to be modest and humble rather than arrogant and pretentious. Empirical studies do not provide answers to all questions, nor do they explain all phenomena. They do offer a valuable perspective from which one can analyze people's dealings with cultural issues, draw solid generalizations and replicate them, and thus augment our understanding of and insights into the way in which culture operates.

14. It is not possible to 'measure' the attitudes of readers or spectators.
Interestingly enough, psychologists have been doing this for almost a century now, and in the process have developed highly valid and reliable methods for doing so. Someone asserting the above concept displays an embarrassing ignorance of psychological research methods.

15. Empirical methods are (neo-)positivistic: they pretend to offer absolute certainties.
This is debatable. In fact, quite to the contrary: empirical methods are fundamentally anti-positivistic. They do not presuppose anything, but instead subject all views to independent tests. The empirical method as it is applied in this book goes also against one of the basic tenets of Positivism, i.e. that there is no place for investigations of things that one cannot observe. As is clear, most empirical research of culture is directed toward cognitive and emotional processes that are themselves invisible. To say that empirical studies are positivistic thus shows a profound misunderstanding of what Positivism is (apart from also misunderstanding what such empirical studies try to do).

16. Empirical studies employ methods borrowed from the Natural Sciences, but these methods were never developed to study human culture.
The first part of this sentence is a half-truth: some methods in empirical studies, for instance statistics, are also used in the Natural Sciences. But many of the methods used in the Natural Sciences (for instance microscope observations,

litmus tests, or particle accelerators) are completely alien to empirical studies of culture. Most of the empirical methods to study culture were not derived from the Natural Sciences, but were developed precisely for their own aims in the course of the last half century.

17. The 'experiments' carried out by empirical scholars in the Humanities are not 'real' experiments in the sense that Natural Scientists do experiments, because one cannot repeat them and come up with exactly the same results.
Well, many experiments in Natural Science do not come up with exactly the same results either. At the spearhead of scientific research, there is constant bickering over research results. But more importantly, many experiments in the social and human sciences have been repeated time and again, like the ones leading to the Wundt curve (see Section 1.6. above), with (*ceteris paribus!*) exactly the same results. Where the replication studies yield different results, they inform us of shortcomings still inherent in our theories and methods, so that we can use these discrepancies to further deepen our theoretical and methodological grasp of the issues at hand.

18. Empirical studies can never lead to generalization, because all one has done is to study a small group of people and one never knows whether other people will behave in the same way.
Exactly! But that is the case for all sciences. Geologists can only study fractions of the Earth's crust and must generalize beyond the samples they have studied. Physicists do their experiments in their laboratories, but they can never be sure that next time results will not turn out differently. A biopsy takes only a small portion of the organ to check whether it is cancerous. Rather than a criticism of the empirical method in cultural studies, this is an appreciation of its scientific merit: all science must be content to study samples of reality and then to conjecture beyond that sample. Here statistics play a vital role: statistical analyses allow you to estimate how probable your conjectures are in the world at large, beyond the observations of your sample. This is an enormous asset of empirical studies over traditional approaches, which necessarily remain in the dark regarding the probabilities of the assertions they make.

19. Empirical studies of culture cannot work, because such studies are unable to define what culture is in the first place.
The second part of the sentence is certainly true. But no other approach is able to do so either. As far as can be seen, there is no consensus on the notion of culture anywhere to be found. Thus the empirical approach is in exactly the same boat as all other approaches.

20. Empirical studies cannot really show the effects of being exposed to art, film, or literature, because there are always tens (if not hundreds) of other things that may play a role at the same time.
But that is exactly why one needs a good grasp of empirical methodology! That, for instance, is why in empirical studies the use of a control group is so vital: the control group is comparable to the participants who take part in the experiment (hence they share all other characteristics with those participants), only: they have not been exposed to the specific cultural process one is studying. Differences in outcome between these two groups allow you, yes, precisely, to control all these other variables!

21. One of the major shortcomings of empirical studies is that so far they have only produced trivial results.
Is this not an overgeneralization? Certainly the results of research presented in Chapter 1 can hardly be called trivial, we think: to call the Wundt curve a trivial result of research is certainly at odds with what most experts in the field believe it is: a profound discovery. Whether something is trivial will in the last resort be judged by the future, however, not by us. Was the relation between aesthetic appreciation and novelty or complexity known before Berlyne? Was it known that psychoanalysis makes wrong predictions about readers' reactions to fairy tales? Did we know that some assumptions about the effects of narrative perspective are deficient? If this was known long before empirical studies demonstrated them, then why are there so many people in the Humanities who still do not know about them?

22. Empirical studies do not belong in the Humanities. They are part of the Social Sciences. This is where they belong.
Why is that such an important matter in the first place? But if one insists, there are good reasons for carrying out empirical studies in the Humanities as well. If the aim of the Humanities is to learn to understand ourselves better, as cultural beings, then why condemn certain methods a priori? Why not use all methods to try to attain a deeper understanding of cultural issues? There are many questions that traditionally belong to the Humanities and in which most social scientists are not really versed (or interested). Matters of aesthetics, of beauty, of responses to art works, or their emotional impact, these are all topics that are at the core of the Humanities.

23. Empirical studies negate the uniqueness of each individual and thereby cannot account for the endless variation between people, but must deal with averages only. They also entail a view of human life as something inherently deterministic.

In various chapters of this book, we will emphasize individual differences and will actually instruct you what methods you may use to explore such issues. But next to individual differences, general trends and patterns are also important. If there is one thing that the empirical study of culture reveals again and again, it is the richness and variety of the world, not only the variation between individuals and groups, but also – often – the patterns and regularities that are there under a surface of variation. People are unique, but they are also highly similar in many ways. One of the best ways we can describe the relationship between constancy and variety is with reference to medicine: a physician who does not treat you as an individual and unique patient is a poor doctor. But at the same time, s/he has to treat you according to what is known generally about human biology. Each arm is different, unique, and a good doctor will take that uniqueness into account when treating a fracture. But simultaneously, arms are very similar – and that similarity allows medicine to develop treatments that are nearly the same for most, if not all, of us such as immobilizing a fractured arm so that it can heal.

24. To conclude
The empirical study of culture can heal too only if it takes these two sides of culture – its enormous variability on the one hand, and its structured nature on the other – as the basis of its own research program. This book attempts to acquaint you with methods to research this complex, intricate, double-sided nature of the cultural world.

CHAPTER TWO

BASIC INSIGHTS FROM THE PHILOSOPHY OF SCIENCE

In the previous chapter, we introduced you to a number of notions concerning empirical forms of research. Here we will continue to do this by offering some theoretical support for the methodological chapters in this book. This is necessary to help you understand the philosophical and historical foundations upon which such research is based, since methodology itself also exists in a social context. Some disciplines, like the philosophy of science, study that context and are therefore relevant to our concerns here. We will begin with some everyday notions and then gradually develop more rigorous concepts and insights.

2.1. The word 'science'

As you might know, in English the word 'science' has traditionally been reserved for the natural sciences. This is unfortunate, and contrasts with some other European languages. Whether in French, German, Dutch, or Portuguese, it is not awkward to talk about a 'science' of culture, literature, theater, or media. Indeed, why should it be? It is certainly possible to investigate cultural objects in a scientific spirit – in the sense of the Third Culture outlined in Chapter 1. If that sounds strange to native speakers of English, we invite them to reflect on the reasons (mostly accidental, we believe) why English has built in this restriction in the word 'science'. In any case, here we depart from the premise that things cultural can and are studied from a scientific point of view. Indeed, the book is an effort to guide you through the various methods that such a study requires.

Perhaps a productive way to understand what is meant by science is to look at its history. How did it come into being? Although the search for knowledge is perhaps as old as Humanity itself, what we nowadays call science has its origins in various cultures (China, India, the Western world) at different points in history. Let us look at the way in which a daily phenomenon such as movement has been questioned in a scientific way in the Western tradition.

2.2. Motion

Small children already know that inanimate objects can be moved by the force of our muscles and that such movements are limited. They quickly learn that objects thrown into the air will fall down and that going up a mountain costs more energy than walking on a flat plane. During Antiquity, the most refined theory about such movements was developed by Aristotle (384–322 BCE). According to this theory, everything in the universe has a 'natural' place where it belongs. The Earth is the center of this universe and is therefore the natural resting place of all objects. Therefore, things 'fall' down to the Earth: and each object 'strives' toward its 'natural' rest. But various obstacles can thwart that movement. When I hold a pebble in my hand, the force exerted by my muscles prevents the pebble from falling. When I let it loose, we notice how the natural movement sets in immediately and the pebble falls down, only to be hindered by the crust of the Earth's surface from falling further to the center of the Earth.

Aristotle's views look plausible. Indeed, we *see* that objects fall toward the Earth's surface. Such a view that is seemingly in accordance with perceptual observations can be called a *theory*. A theory is accepted as long as it does not confront anomalies that contrast with its content and because science must start somewhere, theories are an important starting point. From such theories, we can (through the force of reason) deduce conclusions that allow us to develop further insights. For instance, we observe that one particular stone is heavier than another. In the framework of Aristotle's theory, that must mean that the heavier stone has a stronger 'tendency' to fall toward the Earth's center than a lighter one, since it is believed that the heavier stone will fall with greater speed than the lighter one and this is indeed what we can observe: snowflakes and feathers are very light and so they fall down with much lower speed than bricks or rocks.

We can now formulate a preliminary conclusion: science attempts to fill in the holes in our incomplete knowledge. Whenever our knowledge is deficient or incomplete, science develops a theory to deal with such a hiatus. That we *wish* to know what we presently do not know seems to be a fundamental trait of human beings. We are curious by nature. Thus science is born out of questions and sees them as problems. In that sense, science is *problem solving*.

2.3. Foundations

Usually, however, more than just a theory is needed to speak of science. We have all sorts of 'theories' in everyday life, but we do not call them 'scientific'. What is required of science is the inspection of our theories: we want to know whether the assertions it makes are correct. This can be done in two different ways. A first method is to investigate whether it contains internal contradictions. A theory that states that the Earth is flat and at the same time denies that it is flat is an example of such a contradiction. Presumably everyone agrees. We call such a view a *foundation*. Foundations provide science with the bedrock of certainty we need to be able to proceed with our work. There is a paradox involved in here, however: how to provide a solid base for such 'foundations'? If we keep questioning our basis, will we ever reach stable grounds? The answer to this question is simple: there are no ultimate foundations. One way out of this difficulty is to argue that to refute certain rules (e.g. to avoid contradictions), one has to have recourse to … those very same rules! In this way we presume the importance of logical 'foundations' even when we know that we cannot 'prove' them.

There is also a more pragmatic way to support such foundations, namely that their value has been demonstrated during centuries of human thinking and experimentation. There is indeed no adequate way to prove that theories without contradictions are better than theories that contain them. But we can critically reflect on the issue and still come to the conclusion that even though we may not be in a position to say why, contradiction-free theories are better adapted to the aims of science than theories that do not fulfill this criterion. Since this book is a practical handbook for 'doing' research, we shall occupy ourselves no further with such considerations and shall move on to the assumptions underlying them.

2.4. Contradictions

Let us confront the question whether Aristotle's theory of motion is free from contradictions. Suppose we do the following: we take a big, heavy rock and a small, light pebble and put them both in one bag. We now drop the bag. What will happen according to Aristotle's theory? Well, that is not clear. In fact, the theory allows two possible outcomes:

(1) The heavier stone will 'want' to fall at a great speed (because of its naturally greater tendency to fall toward the middle of the Earth), but the lighter stone will slow it down (because of its much weaker tendency), so the bag will fall with a speed that averages the separate speeds of the two stones.

(2) Because there are two stones in the bag, its total weight is larger, so it will fall with a speed exceeding that of the heavier stone alone.

Both (1) and (2) look interesting as speculations, but the point is that they cannot both be true. Since both statements derive from Aristotle's theory but exclude each other, we must conclude that there is something wrong with the theory. Note that we are not interested here in carrying out such an experiment. Indeed, it is one of the great advantages of logical exercise that such investigations can be considered without further equipment or tools besides human imagination and the powers of reasoning. Our thought experiment revealed that the theory of motion as advanced by Aristotle allows contradictory conclusions, and that suffices, because such theories are not true. Logic tells us that a contradiction is never true. That is, if a theory is found wanting in this respect, it is further inspected and if efforts to remedy the contradiction turn out to be fruitless, it is usually discarded. In short, a first way to inspect the correctness of a theory is a *logical* one: the theory is subjected to an analysis of its claims. Whenever logical problems (such as contradictions) are spotted, the theory must be either changed to do away with those problems, or it will be rejected. Another way of saying this is that scientific theories are required to be *coherent*, that the assertions they contain *cohere*, that is, that they form a conglomerate of claims that do not contradict one another.

2.5. Predictions

There is also a second way to critically inspect a theory, which can be illustrated as follows. We can derive from Aristotle's theory of motion the *hypothesis* that an object should always fall with the same speed – because its 'natural resting place' is always the same. A hypothesis is a concrete claim derived from a theory. Or put the other way: a conglomerate of related hypotheses together forms a theory. From this hypothesis, we can further derive a still more concrete assertion, namely a *prediction*: if the hypothesis is correct, then an object will always fall with the same speed. Let us examine this prediction. Take a sheet of paper, drop it and observe what happens. You see that it will make swirling movements as it gradually and slowly falls to the ground. Now take the same sheet of paper, squeeze it into a ball and drop it again. You observe that now the sheet of paper falls much faster to the ground. But how can this be? Its 'natural tendency' mass has not been changed by squeezing the sheet into a ball! The prediction derived from the hypothesis is not borne out by your observation. Therefore, there must be something wrong with this hypothesis. This spells trouble for the theory as well.

The inescapable conclusion is that through a simple experiment in reality you can observe that one central hypothesis of Aristotle's theory is flawed: it generates incorrect predictions. With 'incorrect' here we do not mean that it is logically contradictory, as in the previous section, but rather that the theory is not in accordance with the facts of reality. In this instance it is not logic that refutes the theory, but the *facts* of reality, facts that have nothing to do with our liking of the theory or not. Such a refutation rests not on logical, but on *empirical* grounds.

The word 'empirical' derives from the Greek 'empeireia' meaning experience, especially experience through the senses (seeing, hearing, feeling, smelling, tasting). This meaning complements the definition of 'empirical' that you read in Chapter 1: there we referred to the objective nature of the investigation, that it should be based on facts that anyone can inspect independently. You may well have wondered *how* such inspection would be possible. The results of empirical research can be inspected independently because they are based on observations: whether they are taped interviews, think-aloud protocols, or filled-out questionnaires, anyone can inspect and re-analyze these data by looking into them.

2.6. An experiment

According to legend, the first independent inspection (and subsequent refutation) of Aristotle's theory of motion took a dramatic form in the famous 'experiment' carried out by Galileo Galilei (1564–1642). In his native town of Pisa, he is said to have mounted the famous leaning tower and to have simultaneously dropped, before a group of spectators, a large heavy ball and a tiny one. Aristotle's theory *predicts* that the heavier ball would hit the ground first. Also today, this is what many people think. However, the two balls hit the ground at exactly the same moment. Galileo measured the distance the balls traversed on a slope and the time they needed for this, and found that the relation between time and distance of falling objects can be expressed as follows (you may remember this from physics classes in school):

$d = g\, t^2 / 2$

The distance (d) travelled equals half the square of the time (t^2) multiplied by an acceleration constant (g), this constant being (on Earth!) 9.8 m/s^2. In other words, the distance is proportional to the square of the time elapsed during the fall.

The significant point is that Galileo's equation does not contain what was central in Aristotle's theory, namely the **mass** of the falling body. According to his theory, a body with greater mass will fall down with greater speed than bodies with lower mass. This is a *folk theory* – something that is widely believed, but scientifically speaking wrong, in spite of the fact that it is still adhered to by large portions of the population, especially by those uninitiated in the natural sciences. Galileo's measurements showed that mass does not figure in this equation and that it therefore plays no role at all in the motion of bodies. That is, all things fall with equal speed – but beware!

This equation is but an *approximation*: it is indeed the case that feathers (or, for that matter, the sheet of paper we used) fall slower than bricks, but this is due to the resistance of air, which such lighter bodies encounter. In a perfect vacuum, the feather and the stone will fall with equal speeds – and this can be demonstrated (as can the correctness of Galileo's equation) time and again by anybody who takes the trouble to investigate it. Maybe you have seen this demonstrated in a laboratory or in a space shuttle: a feather falling in a vacuum with the same speed as we are accustomed to see for heavier objects is indeed a spectacular thing the first time you see it!

Hence we must conclude that Aristotle's theory is incorrect, not only on the grounds that it contains hidden contradictions, but also on the grounds that it does not accurately describe what happens to falling bodies in the world at large. The predictions derived from it are not borne out by observation. Such empirical refutation of theories plays a predominant part in many disciplines, including several Social Sciences.

Of course we are not dealing with calculations of velocities, accelerations or distances when we study cultural phenomena but also here it happens that theories are refuted because empirical facts do not correspond to the claims of a particular theory. For instance, a theory asserting that literary texts do not exert any moral influence on readers, as Stolnitz (1991) does, seems to be unaware of several studies, summarized in Hakemulder (2000) that have demonstrated the opposite unequivocally. Hence the theoretical equation of literature and functionless entertainment is rejected on empirical grounds.

2.7. Comparison of theories

Galileo's experiments ultimately led to a theory that was, on the one hand, free from contradictions and, on the other hand, more accurate than that of Aristotle in that its approximation to the facts is greater than that of Aristotle's. We therefore accept Galileo's and reject Aristotle's.

Second, Galileo's theory also provides an *explanation* for those facts, since in the equation expressing the motion of falling bodies, their mass does not function – meaning that all bodies fall to the Earth with equal speed, in contrast to the folk theory.

Furthermore, Galileo's theory also *explains more*. This theory also shows that falling bodies do not travel at a constant velocity, but rather with an acceleration (g), i.e. with a distance of 9.8 meters per second per second (or per s^2).

Galileo's theory is also more *productive*: it generates new explanations, for instance of the tides: on the basis of Galileo's theory, Newton would later be able to demonstrate that tides are intimately connected with gravity, in the same way as falling bodies are. Aristotle's theory cannot be used to explain tides. They even provide a powerful counterexample against his theory about a 'natural resting place' of things in the universe; tides show that the water in the oceans obviously has no such natural resting place!

Whenever one has a choice between theories about phenomena in reality, it is preferable to choose the theory that:

(1) does not contain (or produce) logical problems;
(2) is most in correspondence with what one may observe in reality;
(3) provides an explanation for the phenomena under consideration;
(4) is able to explain other (related) phenomena;
(5) is *semantically precise*, and hence allows measurement (this aspect will require further elaboration in a minute);
(6) generates new developments.

But again, even the best theories necessarily remain an *approximation* to reality.

To be more explicit about point number (5): Galileo's theory offers a high measure of *precision*. Its form allows the calculation of the distance (and speed) of falling bodies. For instance, it follows from the formula that after one second a falling body has traveled over a distance of 4.9 m, after 2 seconds 19.6 m and after 3 seconds a distance of 44.1 m. Such precision was totally absent from Aristotle's theory. The precision arrived at was only possible because Galileo measured time and distance; *measurement* is not a necessary ingredient of science: it is, nevertheless, one of its hallmarks. In this book, therefore, we will be dealing also with the question of how cultural matters can be measured.

Let us recapitulate: science starts from foundations and hypotheses that become internally linked and build up into a theory. That theory is subsequently subjected to a detailed and rigorous inspection. Such inspection may take two forms: a logical one or an empirical one.

(1) The first method makes use of methods of *logic* – that is, of rational reasoning (only): one sees to it that the theory does not contain any internal contradiction, or one checks whether any conclusions can be deduced from the

theory that are mutually contradictory. When such contradictions are spotted, the theory is said to be *incoherent*. Scientific theories should be *coherent*.

(2) The second method makes use of observations; we call such a method *empirical*. One checks whether the claims of the theory are in accordance with what may be observed in reality, to phenomena we can perceive. This is the *validity* of a theory: we say that a theory is *valid* when its claims correspond to what can be observed in real life. A theory that does not fulfill this requirement is not valid. It is false, or unfounded. Science attempts to make its theories as valid, as true and as founded as possible. Unfounded theories are suspect in science.

This, by the way, has not always been the case. The assertions in the previous paragraphs are themselves the result of centuries of historical development. In the course of that development, science has gradually freed itself from the direct intervention of religious and political powers. This was not attained without resistance. In fact, it took a long and painful process through which science overcame the manifold attempts at oppression from social forces. The figure of Galileo demonstrates this eminently. In 1633 the Catholic Church condemned both the man and his theory (that the Earth rotates around its axis, and that the sun does not revolve around the Earth, as the Catholic Church maintained). Galileo was threatened with physical torture, excommunication and possibly death at the stake. He was thus obliged to publicly renounce his views and put himself for the rest of his life under house arrest. His writings were listed on the infamous list of forbidden works, the *Index Librorum Prohibitorum*, which meant that no God-abiding person was allowed to read them. How deep this conflict between science and the Church ran may be derived from the fact that it took the Church 359 years (until October 31st, 1992) to admit that Galileo's theory was the correct one.

2.8. Critique

Since science considers incoherent or unfounded theories with suspicion, one would expect that it would avoid such an unpleasant verdict as long as possible. However, when we observe what scientists do, this is not the case at all: they are permanently in search of ways to denounce a current theory. In this respect, science distinguishes itself from most other human activities, in that it actively seeks to subvert all views that it has itself advanced. Rather than sparing or protecting them from harsh treatment, science inexorably submits its theories to a relentless form of *critique*. With never abating zeal, science looks for the weak chain in existing theories.

This may look paradoxical at first sight, because critique destroys what has been carefully constructed in the first place. However, science has no mercy with everyday views and expectations that do not stand up to the test of critical inspection. Thus, what are destroyed in science are unfounded knowledge, incoherent theories and false intuitions. Formulated positively, the road taken by science consists in *learning* from our mistakes (our unfounded views). The words 'criticism' and 'critique' stem from the Greek verb *krinein*, which means 'to judge'. This process, in which science learns from errors, is called scientific *progress*. The central and omnipresent apparatus needed to bring about this progress is criticism. Without unrestrained criticism there can be no science.

Crucial in this respect is not so much the fact that critique is exerted (since that happens in daily life as well), but rather that this critique is *ubiquitous, systematic* and *relentless*. Thus science has often become a fierce enemy of tradition. Paradoxically, this attitude has become so deeply ingrained in the way in which science operates, that it has itself become a tradition. It is the explicit aim of science to systematically subject all existing theories and explanations to a thorough critical investigation, so as to improve upon our present knowledge. This is what has been called the *critical tradition*, the practice that one always views current knowledge with a critical eye.

Let us illustrate this with an example from art history. Here is the problem: How to explain the changes that art undergoes in the course of time. Various answers to this question have been provided.

(1) Art history is merely a succession of masterpieces produced by humans of extraordinary talent (geniuses).
(2) History is a product of social forces.

Adherents of (2) criticize (1). They point out that reference to genius does not explain anything, since it merely shifts the problem, which now becomes: who is a genius and why history produces such talented people. Thus they argue that the Romantic view of history encoded in (1) does not work, because it:

- is not in correspondence with observable reality: also artists who are certainly no geniuses produce works that are preserved for posterity;
- does not explain anything (it merely asserts – post hoc – who is a genius);
- is semantically imprecise (it is not clear who belongs to the category of genius).

Against these weaknesses, proponents of (2) explain: art history is the result of social forces. Some French scholars at the end of the 19th century asserted that literary texts are the product of three such forces, which they called in French 'race', 'milieu' and 'moment'. These three factors (a writer's ethnical group, a writer's social environment and the historical moment in which an author writes) formed a sufficient explanation for the *French Positivists* (since that is what they were called) for the change one may observe in cultural history. Maybe their theory can explain more than that of the Romantics, who favored an explanation in terms of genius. The point is, however, that the critical tradition will not stop there. This somewhat better theory is criticized in its turn, for instance by the *Russian Formalists*, who claim that

(3) Positivists have nothing to say about the *form* of art works, while it is precisely the form that makes texts or objects into art works.

Hence the Russian Formalists formulated a new theory of literary history, which had little to do with the social forces that the Positivists were so interested in. Instead, they claim that the ever-ongoing innovation of artistic devices is the driving force behind cultural history. This led to interesting predictions about the impact of novelty as a driving force in the history of art, as we saw in the previous chapter. Although theory (3) is superior in many ways to theories (1) and (2) – as was corroborated by Martindale's many investigations referred to in Chapter 1, it was criticized in turn. And so history (of research) proceeds.

In sum, science never stands still: it is permanently under pressure to investigate old concepts and entrenched categories. Critique is the engine that drives this process.

2.9. White swans, black swans

The mechanism of critique described in the previous section has been elaborated further as the principle of *falsification*. This is the famous example of the black swans provided by Karl Popper, presumably the most important philosopher of science in the 20th century[1].

Popper started his career in the midst of a group called the Vienna Positivists, although he was never a member of this group. But even this loose association has led many (especially in the Humanities) to presume Popper to be a Positivist himself. Nothing, however, could be further from the truth; in fact,

---

[1] Just how influential Popper's ideas still are today could be anecdotally illustrated through a review by Colin McGinn in the *New York Review of Books* (NYRB), of 21.11.2002, pp. 46–50, titled 'Looking for a Black Swan', where four new books on the topic are reviewed.

Popper fought Positivism his whole life. You may be interested to hear that in many corners in the Humanities, the word 'Positivist' is actually a term of abuse. If you are called a Positivist, you are seen as a blockhead, someone silly enough to believe that all scientific work boils down to matters of numbers, observation and induction from such observations. Although we agree with Popper that Positivism has a wrong view of how science works, we invite you to refrain from such easy name-calling, even when you notice that it is practiced by notorious professors in your field. Our reason is a simple one: there is no merit, nor disrepute, in being a member of a particular group, whether it be Positivists, Feminists, Deconstructivists, Structuralists, Buddhists, Baptists, Jews, Muslims, or Communists. The value of scientific work lies in that work itself and its contribution to human knowledge and understanding, not in the label under which it (correctly or incorrectly) goes.

Now, suppose we have a 'theory' that all swans are white. How can we prove that it is correct? Easy, some say: you simply observe in nature swans' colors. You use your observations to *verify* your theory. This is the theoretical view that the Vienna Positivists defended: you try to find proof for your theory in the real world. And indeed you see that all swans are white. Thus, this approach is called *verification*. The Vienna Positivists believed that all scientific concepts could ultimately be reduced to forms of observable data. This is where Popper's views differ.

The problem is that verification is not fail-safe. How do you know that you have not missed out on a black swan in your verification? For so much is clear: your verification always remains partial. It is not really possible to verify *all* swans all over the Earth. But even if that were feasible, then you could still not be 100% sure that in the future a black swan will not break out of the egg. In short, it is not really possible to fully prove a theory by the method of verification. Moreover, it is an activity that is costly: it takes a lot of time and effort to check all swans!

Popper was the first philosopher to point out the *asymmetry* between verifying and refuting a theory. To refute a theory is much simpler (and considerably less time consuming): all you need is *one* counter-example. If I can point to one single non-white swan, then the theory that all swans are white is obviously false. The procedure to prove a theory false is called *falsification*. And as the example shows, it makes much more sense to try and *falsify* a theory than to attempt to verify it. Thus we are constantly searching for arguments *against* our theories.

2.10. A three-stage model

You may have noticed that this way of doing research actually consists of three stages. In the first stage, you have a problem: you stumble upon one, or it announces itself in the course of a discussion, or you are looking hard for one, because you surmise that there must be something wrong with a theory or an assumption upon which it is based. All these different forms of finding problems do not matter, as long as you find one. Remember: without problems there is no science. A good example of this can be seen in the life of John Dalton (the discoverer of 'Daltonism', a form of color-blindness). For 56 years of his life, Dalton went for walks out of Manchester every day to measure rainfall and temperature. Out of this mass of data, "nothing whatever came. But of the one searching, almost childlike question about the weights that enter the construction of these simple molecules [of water and carbon dioxide] – out of that came modern atomic theory [that Dalton first developed]. That is the essence of science: ask an impertinent question, and you are on the way to the pertinent answer" (Bronowski 1976: 153).

A second stage is entered when you try out different solutions for a problem. Maybe you try to solve it by a redefinition of terms (an easy way, but often not really a satisfactory one), or you try to solve it by identifying a hitherto unsuspected influence of another factor (a difficult way, but often a highly satisfactory one). Or you try many other ways, which is perfectly justifiable, since this is basically the stage of *trial and error*. Again, it does not really matter how you develop these solutions. Stages 1 and 2 have been identified by Popper as the *context of discovery*: here you are searching, trying out, looking into various possibilities. We know from the history of science that even a bit of luck, or accidentally stumbling upon something (Rosetta stone, a series of letters by a famous author, the archives of a past publisher) may play a significant role in generating problems and their solutions. This does not mean that these stages are wholly unscientific, but that there are no strict rules as to how to go about it. We can augment the chances of being successful, for instance through an non-authoritative learning environment for students, through the encouragement of genuine discussion and exploration, or through measures to increase young researchers' creativity, for instance in making them take an active part in research from early in their careers. All these measures increase the chances of finding interesting problems and their solutions, but they are not really 'rules' one should follow in order to have success.

This is not the case, however, in the third stage, in which you try to test which of the solutions serves your interest of solving the problem best. This is the stage of *error elimination*, which is crucial for a scientific solution. In this stage, how the test is conducted and administered, and how the results are interpreted, are highly relevant issues. Testing the proposed solutions really means trying to falsify them. And here we will show how you can do this.

Now suppose that the falsification is unsuccessful: you look very hard for any swan that is not white, but you cannot find one. Does that mean that the theory has thereby been proved 'right'? Not really, because it cannot be excluded that someone may find a black swan later. The only thing we can say is that so far the theory has withstood the effort at falsification successfully. Therefore, we must admit that it is not a bad theory, and we certainly do not wish to cast it overboard. Bear in mind that theories are made by human beings; so they are likely to be imperfect. Sooner or later, such imperfection may come to the surface.

Earlier in this chapter we said that it does not matter *how* you find a problem to investigate, or *how* you find potential solutions. But when you are testing (i.e. trying to falsify) your proposals, it matters very much *how* you do this. This distinction between the first two stages and the final stage relates to the famous difference between two 'contexts' in which research happens, framed by Popper as the context of *discovery* (for the first two stages) and the context of *justification* (for the third stage). Within the context of discovery, when you are trying to identify problems, or when you are trying to solve them, there are no real 'rules' for identifying problems: any method that will provide you with problems or solutions will do, whether it be opening a bottle of wine with good friends, running in the woods, looking out of the window, or discussing the issue with colleagues or friends. The only thing that counts is that you find a problem or a solution. In the context of *justification*, however, there are very strict rules on how to go about it. Here it matters a lot how you do the testing, and everyday knowledge is often not particularly helpful. Whether to decide that a theory has withstood an attempt at falsification well (or not) is subject to clear standards and procedures in science. That does not mean that scientists will never quibble over such issues as whether a theory should be accepted, but by and large, there is a strong consensus as to what counts as evidence in favor of (or against) a theory.

Together this consensus forms the bulk of what is called *methodology* in research. So how can you know about these rules, procedures and standards? Well, that is what this book is about: to make you acquainted with the most important issues of empirical methodology. Step by step, we will guide you through the various principles and techniques that will allow you to test whether your solutions to a problem are acceptable in scientific terms.

This does not mean, however, that we will skip the first two stages. Even when there are no strict rules for the identification of problems, you can nevertheless increase the chances that you will hit upon interesting ones. This is because in these stages, *creativity* plays a considerable role – and we know from creativity research that you can enhance the chances of coming up with creative problems and solutions. This is why science is not a mere mechanical thing, but involves a spiritual adventure. We know, for instance, that strict authoritarian relations between instructors and learners are *not* conducive to the emergence of such adventurous spirits, and hence do not promote a creative environment either. A creative atmosphere is also one of uncertainty, and many instructors unfortunately do not tolerate this state of not knowing exactly where to go; it will be clear that such instructors severely limit the chances of their students' becoming autonomous, creative and critical thinkers and researchers. That is why it is of utmost importance that learning to do research takes place in situations in which informal relations between lecturers and students allow for forms of communication that are as non-authoritarian and as collaborative as possible in institutions.

When it comes to the context of justification, it is helpful to keep these non-authoritarian forms of communication. Finding theories is one thing, but attempting to falsify them is another. The expertise of the lecturer in showing the what, the when, and the how of theory testing is going to be very important when providing both negative and positive feedback.

Our efforts at falsifying theories are therefore what we called before *error elimination*. When a theory has passed the most rigorous tests, we are dealing with a theory that obviously contains few errors. It is a good theory, in the sense that it is resistant against severe testing, and we will accept it for the time being, as long as no serious problems turn up. So even if you are never in a position to be absolutely certain of the correctness of your theories – a view that is called *fallibilism* (there are no ultimate foundations for human knowledge, although many try to solve this problem through *dogmatism*) this does not mean that we are totally helpless. What you can do is to look for the theory that has best withstood all rigorous attempts at falsification. You thus compare the merits of various theories and conclude which one you should prefer at this point in time, given the evidence that is available at the moment. Of course, this presupposes that theories are comparable: they must make claims about the same things in reality. This is the *ceteris paribus* principle outlined in the previous chapter, the principle that we compare the merits of various theories, *other things being equal*. You accept as 'true' a theory that, *ceteris paribus*, best withstood all attempts at falsification.

2.11. Immune theories

In this context, philosophers sometimes speak of an *evolutionary epistemology*. Epistemology means knowledge about knowledge. In other words, it is the study of the emergence, distribution, maintenance, increase, and reliability of human knowledge. Since knowledge changes constantly over time, you could also describe its *history*. Some philosophers go one step further, and see this history as an evolution. In the same way that we developed other traits typical of human beings, such as language, or being biped, science is an evolutionary product of the cognitive development that set in early in the history of the species. The great advantage of science is that we can, through the process of falsifying, let our hypotheses survive or die. Animals do not have this ability: if they do not adapt well to their changing environment, they will die. Human beings, on the contrary, can simulate reality, try out all sorts of scenarios, do away with those hypotheses that have no survival value – and prefer those that are resistant against such falsification.

There is one condition, however, for this process to succeed, and one which it has taken humans an extraordinary length of time to discover: you do not safeguard hypotheses that have been discarded once they have failed the test. Suppose you have invested a good deal of time, money and energy in developing a theory that explains a number of problems. You are evidently proud of your achievement. But now we run a falsification procedure to see whether your explanation will stand up to it. It turns out that it does not. What is your natural reaction? Not to believe the results. A mistake must have been made. Or a wrong method was chosen. Maybe the explanation was not properly understood and therefore the test was not valid. By natural inclination, we try to safeguard the theories in which we have invested time and energy.

Of course we can run more tests, with different methods, etc. If all these successive tests fail to provide support for the theory, are you now convinced that it is not a particularly good theory? Some people may, but experience shows that in many cases people are also prepared to go a long way to defend their cherished explanations. This may lead to a situation where a theory is conceived in such a way that it can no longer be disproved: whatever the outcome of a test, the results can always be interpreted in such a way that they support the theory in every case. Such a theory has been made *immune* (and the concomitant process of making it such is called *immunization*). A good example of this is provided by certain psychoanalytical theories. One of them is that you would like to sleep with your mother (if you are male), or with your father if you are female[2]. If you now tell psychoanalysts that you do not have such an inclination, they might turn your denial into support of their view, by pointing out that your vehement denial is precisely a proof of the fact that, deep

---

[2] "(…) an object-relation of a solely affectionate kind to his mother makes up the content of the simple positive Oedipus complex in a boy." (Freud 1984: 371); "the conclusion that in being in love with one's mother one is never concerned with her as she is in the present but with her youthful mnemic image carried over from childhood." (Freud 1975: 232–3); "The affections of the little girl are fixed on her father" (Freud 1979: 172).

down, this is your most sincere wish. In this way, it is no longer possible to disprove claims of psychoanalytic theory: anything you say or do can be used as evidence in favor of the theory. The theory seems victorious over all evidence against it: it has become totally immune against any attacks.

At first sight you might think that this is a good thing, for now your theory can no longer be attacked. It cannot be refuted, because all arguments and evidence against it can be turned round in corroboration of the theory. But in science, it works the other way: if a theory can in principle no longer be rejected on the basis of evidence, then it is left as mere speculation. This is Popper's famous *demarcation criterion*: only theories that can be rejected (falsified) on the basis of arguments and evidence can be accepted as scientific theories. Theories that do not live up to this criterion are not necessarily nonsense (though some may be), but they are certainly not scientific. Thus many religious questions may be interesting, but they can typically not be disproved by falsification procedures, and hence fall outside the realm of scientific research. This does not mean that we cannot discuss such issues, but only that a real scientific debate about them is impossible. They are of a different nature and function.

Against such speculative discussions, the scientific approach advises you to develop hypotheses that are simple and clear, that allow concrete predictions about the real world, predictions that can be tested against independent evidence. For all these reasons, it is important to develop hypotheses that are not trivial, but instead are *bold*, in the sense that unexpected hypotheses contain more information value than hypotheses with predictable outcomes. So, when you start out on your research, do not be afraid to be creative. The falsification procedures that you use in the context of justification will tell you which of your hypotheses is best, and which ones you can, in an evolutionary sense, allow to die. This is how the critical tradition came to the decision that Galileo's theory about moving bodies is to be preferred to Aristotle's. And this is how you yourself can discover whether your hypotheses hold scientifically or not.

2.12. The Truth?

Does all this mean that we must now change our former view that Galileo's theory about falling bodies is true and Aristotle's is not? Obviously, things are not that simple: if all our knowledge is fallible and if you can never be certain about the correctness of your theories, how can you then claim that a theory is true? Perhaps we should rather say that it is 'provisionally true'. But how can that be? 'Provisionally true' implies that truth can change over time.

That would mean that truth is something relative... Surely that cannot be what is meant here!

What we observe is that in making a true claim, one has not exhausted everything that can be said about the phenomenon in question. In that sense, even a true theory is incomplete, for instance, because its formulation lacks precision, or because measurements are (as they necessarily must be) incomplete. If you briefly look at the formula that describes falling bodies, as it was first developed by Galileo, you will notice that it allows you to precisely calculate in what time a falling body travels a particular distance. In a sense, this formula is 'true', but at the same time, it is incomplete. If you were to measure that time with high-precision instruments, you would find that the formula yields an approximately correct description, but that it never fits reality completely. This is because falling bodies are not only subject to gravity, but also to other forces besides, for instance, to resistance from air, or to the fact that the Earth rotates around its axis. Therefore we said before that theories are only an *approximation* to reality, and truth in this sense is never something absolute. Instead, it is defined as more or less approaching reality. And of course you prefer those theories that offer the best approximation!

This view leads to yet another requirement that science imposes upon itself, namely *modesty*. It follows from the insight that all our knowledge is incomplete and fallible. We must be modest about it, however successful we may have been in some respects. Scientific work continually confronts you with the limitations of human possibilities. This is the famous insight that Socrates develops in his *Apology*, his defense before drinking the poisonous cup:

> So when I went away, I thought to myself, "I am wiser than this man: neither of us probably knows anything that is really good, but he thinks that he has knowledge, when he does not, while I, having no knowledge, do not think that I have. I seem, at any rate, to be a little wiser than he is on this point: I do not think that I know what I do not know". (Plato. *The Trial and Death of Socrates*, 1906)

Socrates expresses here the principle of scientific *skepsis*: when you have too little information to make well-founded claims about a topic, you modestly refrain from uttering grand claims. The only thing you can say in such a situation is that you cannot (scientifically) say anything about it.

Maybe this is all fine, some critical reader may want to say at this point, but is it really the case that all scientists are indeed subject to this principle of criticism? What we have described so far is an ideal, not always found in that pure form in reality. Also in science one encounters cliques, envy, dishonesty, and rancor. And it is no exception to see scholars viciously criticizing the work of colleagues without tolerating criticism of their own work.

However, the fact that an ideal is not always practiced should not lead us to condemn or neglect the standards of that ideal. In practice, the bulk of scientific activities *is* built upon these high standards of critique. This again ensues from the notion of fallibility: because science is a human endeavor and humans being what they are, it is predictable that some will not stick to the rules. There will always be people to whom cheating looks attractive. But that does not make those rules meaningless. It may be, however, that there are significant differences between disciplines in this respect. Because there is less agreement on the standards with which to judge the merits of theories in the Humanities than in the Natural Sciences, it is to be expected that the picture we have painted above is adhered to more in the latter than in the former.

Another critical reader could come up with yet another fundamental question, namely whether Popper's view is not just one among many views, some of which may perhaps be more interesting or more important? But consider the following: how could Poppers' postulations be refuted? By showing that, for instance, other approaches are better able to solve existing scientific and philosophical problems. In other words: any superiority of other theories must result from a critical comparison with Popper's views. Hence, they must *falsify* Popper's views. But that is precisely what Popper's theory states! Thus it turns out that to refute Popper's theory one must make use of the fundamental insights of that theory. In that sense, Popper's theory has one important advantage over other theories, in that it contains basic insights that appear to be unavoidable in critical debate.

2.13. Research, an example

The previous sections provided some ideas about how science works. As will have become clear by now, science predominantly works as *problem solving*. The instruments we have at our disposal to solve problems go together under the general heading of 'research'. This book offers an introduction to research methodology. We hold the opinion that such an introduction should also contain exercises in research, since we believe that learning by doing is a better way of learning. That is why you will have to interact with us, trying out solutions to problems that we propose, so that you may develop into a cultural scientist yourself.

The task that we set you at the end of the previous chapter consisted of comparing a number of passages from the Gospel of Luke in the New Testament. The passages, you may remember, were given in a random order, and you were requested to find the equivalent passages in the Gospels by Mark and Luke.

To find out something about these passages, a useful method is to order them in a table or matrix, like the following one, ordered here as they occur in Luke (except for the final three passages. (Note: '……' means that there is no comparable passage in this Gospel.)

Mark	Matthew	Luke	Content
1: 1–8	3: 1–6	3: 3–6	John the Baptist
……	3: 7–9	3: 7–9	Generation of vipers
1: 9–11	3: 13–17	3: 21–22	Baptism of Jesus
……	4: 1–11	4: 1–13	Temptation in the desert
1: 16–20	4: 12–14	4:14	Jesus in Galilee
3: 13–19	10: 2–4	6: 12–19	The twelve apostles

Table 2.1. Matrix of quasi-identical text locations

Summarizing your observations by means of a figure, graph, matrix, or some other form of visual presentation brings considerable advantages, which can be seen at work immediately in Table 2.1 above: what before were mere loose observations are now displayed in a pattern. You see, for instance, that all passages in Mark have a counterpart in Matthew and Luke, but not the other way round: the passages named 'Generation of vipers' and 'Temptation in the desert' occur in the latter, but not in the former. This is a very clear pattern that becomes salient immediately when you arrange your observations in a visual form. We therefore advise you to always try to visualize your observations in such a way. Programs such as EXCEL, for instance, allow you to do this in a very straightforward and simple way. It may take you a little longer to do this than just write your observations on a piece of paper, but the gain is considerable, for it allows you to detect patterns which otherwise may have remained in the dark. In any case, the above table produced a clear and interesting hypothesis, which can be formulated as follows: always when a specific topic is treated in the Gospel of Mark, it will also turn up in the Gospels by Matthew and Luke, but not the other way round.

Now how do you go on from here? One clear possibility that offers itself is that you investigate the issue further, by making further checks of the hypothesis. You could systematically look up topics that are narrated in Mark and then check whether they also turn up in the other two gospels, and vice versa. What we do here is derive a concrete prediction from the hypothesis, and try to falsify it. Here are a few other examples of what such an investigation could yield:

Mark	Matthew	Luke	Content
......	5: 3–12	6: 20–26	The sermon on the Mount
14: 64	26: 65	22: 71	Accusation of blasphemy
......	7: 3–5	6: 39–42	Mote and beam
......	7: 16–20	6: 43–45	Tree and fruit
......	7: 24–27	6: 46–49	Two foundations
......	8: 5–13	7: 1–10	The centurion of Capernaum
......	6: 1–4	......	Giving alms
......	......	10: 38–42	Mary and Martha
......	6: 9–15	11: 2–4	Our Lord's Prayer
......	6: 16–18	......	Fasting
	7: 7–11	11: 9–12	Ask and it shall be given you
......	......	12: 13–21	The rich fool
......	6: 25–33	12: 22–34	Take no thought for your life
2: 18-22	9: 14–17	5: 33–39	Fasting
......	13: 36–43	......	Instruction of the disciples
......	13: 44–52	......	Parables

Table 2.2. Extended matrix of quasi-identical text locations

We see here that our initial hypothesis is corroborated: always when a particular topic is addressed in Mark, it turns up in Matthew and Luke, without a singular exception, as our prediction said. The other side of the hypothesis is likewise supported: some passages in Matthew and Luke are parallel, while there is no counterpart for them in Mark. We are now in a position to interpret as follows: this further check as a falsification procedure did not result in its rejection. We had framed a hypothesis on the basis of our initial observations. From this we derived a prediction, that if the hypothesis is correct, we must find similar cases if we scan all three texts. This prediction is borne out by the facts. Our hypothesis seems to be, at least for the time being, a good one.

Still, we would like to know what happens when we try this one more time and yet once more, and so on. Will we keep getting the same or similar results each time, or will we get something completely different on the third trial? This is a crucial methodological question. Maybe you have not thought about this before – if you have not, do not worry: even most lecturers and professors in the Humanities have not either! While it is still too early to give you clear answers to this question, one thing we can already reveal: with the help of (inference) statistics, we can solve this problem. That is, statistics can tell you how probable it is that you will find the same results if you repeat the investigation with other passages.

What is furthermore interesting in the above table is that some texts, although they are very central to the Christian belief system, like the Sermon on the Mount, or Our Lord's Prayer, do not turn up in all three Gospels. Therefore these differences are not negligible but they are not salient in reading the texts; they become so only through a systematic comparison in which the textual data are cast into a matrix.

Another striking thing that Table 2.2 reveals is that there are passages that occur only in Matthew *or* Luke. Whenever that is the case, such passages do not figure in Mark. At this point, it may be worth leaving the table aside for a minute and going back to the texts to have another good look at them. When you do this, you may hit upon a further observation: whenever there is no corresponding text location in Mark for a topic that is virtually identical in Matthew and Luke, the text is in direct speech – and always the words of Jesus himself. This is not the case, however, when there is a corresponding passage in Mark. Have a look at Table 2.1 once more, and look up the first text passage indicated: Mk 1–8. There it says: "The beginning of the gospel of Jesus Christ, the Son of God; As it is written in the prophets, behold, I send my messenger before thy face … I indeed have baptized you with water: but he shall baptize you with the Holy Ghost". Clearly the text narrates, and the direct speech at the end are not Jesus's words, but are those of John the Baptist. This passage is almost identical in Matthew (3: 1–6) and Luke (3: 3–6). But now read on in Matthew (3: 7–9), where it says: "But when he saw many of the Pharisees and Sadducees come to his baptism, he said unto them, O generation of vipers, who hath warned you to flee from the wrath to come?" Now the text has changed into direct speech, and the passage in Luke (3: 7–9) is almost identical, but we do not find anything of the kind in Mark. We can check this (again a falsification procedure!) for every single instance in Table 2.2 (or 2.1), and will come to the same conclusion in each case: identical passages in Matthew and Luke without counterpart in Mark are always the words of Jesus rendered in direct speech. What do we conclude from these observations?

First of all, the fact that all passages in Mark have counterparts in Matthew and Luke can be adequately explained when we assume that the texts by Matthew and Luke have been written *after* Mark's text, and that those authors made use of Mark's text in drafting their own Gospel. In this way it can be explained that the story lines in Matthew and Luke run parallel as long as they have corresponding passages in Mark, and can deviate from each other when they do not have such a corresponding passage in Mark. 'In this way' here means: from a scientific point of view. One can think of other explanations, for instance supernatural ones. However, supernatural explanations do not have a place in scientific research.

This does not explain, however, why Matthew and Luke display so many correspondences among themselves that do not have a counterpart in Mark. The most obvious way to explain this observation is to assume that the authors of these two Gospels had – next to the Gospel of Mark – yet another text at their disposal that they based their own versions on, a text that Mark himself did not use. We can characterize this assumption and the previous one (that a text of Mark was used by Matthew and Luke) as *hypotheses*: while it is difficult to imagine a better way to explain the observed regularities, this in itself does not prove that the hypotheses are right. Research on the New Testament has invested considerable effort in this question over the past century. The result is that so far the hypotheses have withstood all attempts at falsification rather well. Together with a great many other hypotheses (which will not be dealt with here) we can now speak of a conglomerate of hypotheses that have acquired the status of a *theory*.

But why are the quasi-identical passages in Matthew and Luke always in direct speech, rendering the words of Jesus? From this observation scholars derived the hypothesis that next to the gospel by Mark, the earliest Christians had at their disposal yet another text which consisted mainly of a collection of sayings of Jesus. This collection has become known as *The Book of Q* ('Q' for the German word 'Quelle', source – as the hypothesis was originally proposed by German scholars). This is the book upon which Matthew and Luke based their own texts (next to the Gospel by Mark) and one that Mark did not have at his disposal (or preferred not to use).

The theory that gradually developed can be graphically represented as follows:

Figure 2.1 The development of the three synoptic Gospels

In other words, in composing their Gospels, Matthew and Luke both had two texts at their disposal: the Gospel by Mark and the *Book of Q*, both of which they used in drafting their own texts. In this way all observations based on Tables 2.1 and 2.2 before can be meaningfully explained.

The investigation we carried out started from an implicit problem: the New Testament presents itself as one narrative, but in four variants. Our question was how these variants relate to each other[3]. Probing this question brought to light new and initially unsuspected problems. By systematically comparing the texts and eliminating possibilities we hit upon a theory that is able to adequately explain the observations made.

2.14. Conclusion

In this chapter we have reviewed a number of basic issues in the philosophy of science. We have also given two examples of how research works in practice. One of these examples came from the natural sciences: we showed how the notion of motion evolved from Aristotle's to Galileo's theory, and how in that historical process we can observe a number of fundamental features of scientific research. Second, we gave an example from the Humanities: how some textual oddities in the three synoptic Gospels gave rise to problem formation and the concomitant efforts at solving these, and the ultimate testing of the alternative solutions. We have chosen this latter example because it is rather typical for research carried out in the Humanities, and therefore you may already be familiar with such cases. This research is empirical in the sense that it is based on particular documents and carried out with the use of particular methods that can be checked by other researchers. To make this clearer still, we will review the methodology in a summary form in the following pages. By gradually working our way through text passages, and especially by casting them into a matrix summarizing all cases, we hit upon a pattern that led to the formation of hypotheses, the derivation of predictions, and the testing of these predictions. The hypotheses are coherent, in the sense that they do not contain contradictions or other logical problems – at least none have surfaced so far. The hypotheses also seem to rest on firm empirical grounds, in the sense that they are in accordance with facts, both to textual facts, and to historical facts relating to the time when Jesus lived in Palestine (known to New Testament scholars, but not discussed by us in this chapter). We have to be careful, though. Although the hypothesis resisted attempts at falsification relatively well, we should not forget that we are not absolutely sure of it: it is only an approximation to reality, but, admittedly, the best approximation we have so far. Compared to other views on the Gospels, this one is, scientifically speaking, the best, and hence the one to be preferred: it is able to explain the oddities initially

---

[3] Some readers may have wondered why we looked only at three of the four canonical Gospels, and left the fourth, by John, out. The reason has to do with the fact that the first three Gospels on the one hand show a large number of common characteristics, while at the same time distinguishing themselves from the Gospel of John, which was also written considerably later. Note that we have also, for similar reasons, left out other Gospels, like those by Peter, Thomas, and others, that are not in the canon of Christian scriptures.

observed clearly and precisely, in a logically coherent and empirically valid way, which – moreover – generated new insights and further developments. New Testament scholars nowadays, for instance, distinguish different stages in the development of the *Book of Q*, which they call Q_1, Q_2, Q_3, and so forth, adding further semantic precision to the description of the collection. This result is the product of critical discussion among those scholars, in which the amount of religious, political, or ideological commitment has been reduced as far as is possible. It has progressed steadily after the hypothesis of the *Book of Q* was first proposed, by learning from mistakes, that is, through error elimination. Such open discussion among New Testament scholars is characterized by non-authoritarian relations: all views and arguments deserve to be heard and analyzed. Dogmatism is banned, as it will stifle discussion and progress. Furthermore, the hypothesis is a bold one, but one that nevertheless is simple, transparent, and allows the formulation of very concrete predictions.

Of course, we are not dealing with precise measurement, as in the example from the Natural Sciences. This is why we chose those two examples in this chapter, to demonstrate two approaches that are very different from each other. Yet, underlying both are the principles of research as they have been formulated in the philosophy of science in the 20th century. In the rest of this book, you will be concerned neither with topics and methods from the Natural Sciences, nor with those from the (traditional) Humanities. Instead you will be studying something that lies somewhere 'in between', namely topics and methods from the Social Sciences. As we argued in Chapter 1, we will be using some methods from the Natural Sciences combined with some from the Humanities to enlighten ourselves with respect to the socio-cultural world. Let us now see how this works in practice. The following chapter introduces you to a range of methods that are used to this purpose.

CHAPTER THREE

TYPES OF RESEARCH METHODOLOGY AND RESEARCH DESIGN

3.1. Against monomethodology

At first glance, you may think 'monomethodology' is a difficult word. It consists of 'mono', from the Greek 'monos', meaning 'one', and 'methodology', the study of methods to carry out research. Thus monomethodology is the claim that there is only one method for scientific investigation. We think this claim is dangerous and it is one against which we must emphatically warn. We give reasons for this warning: first, methods vary along with scientific disciplines. For instance, astronomers use (among other things) telescopes. Data obtained with these instruments are highly complex and demand a special methodology that the budding astronomer is required to master. Biologists do not get such training, however, simply because they do not need it in their discipline. By contrast, they will be required to go through training in the methods to interpret data arrived at by looking through a microscope. Microscopes and telescopes are instruments that ground and shape a whole methodology that makes these two disciplines so different, besides the fact that they differ in terms of their research objects.

It is not just between disciplines that methods differ; within disciplines there is also considerable methodological variation. One astronomer will carry out observations through a telescope; another will tap the universe's radio signals through the use of a radio-telescope, while another will rely on spectral analyses of light. Some biologists may be heavily dependent on microscope work for their research, while others, like ethologists, may not be, because they observe animals in the wild. Still others may sit at their computers, studying non-linear algebraic equations that capture the distribution of predators and prey animals. Thus even within a single discipline the mere idea of a monomethodology is a chimera. But the picture looks even bleaker for the monomethodologist when we observe that one single research topic is often studied through a variety of methods. For instance, the fundamental structure of matter is studied by physicists with the help of highly different methods. Some approach it theoretically by using mathematical models, others observe natural phenomena such as neutrinos that pass through the Earth, while others create artificial collisions of atomic particles in super-colliders. All, however, want to gain insight into the fundamental structure of matter. Hence even when the research topic remains the same, the methodology may differ. The reason for this variation is simple: there is no single omnipotent research method. All methods have advantages as well as limitations. Not to acknowledge these limitations is the central flaw of monomethodology. Its opposite is called pluralism, that is, the idea that multiple methods may be employed in research.

The statement that there is not a single method to be hailed for all investigations, and that even a single research question may be studied through the use of highly diverse methods does not imply that 'anything goes' in methodology. The astronomer will still not resort to observing animals, and the biologist will not use radio-telescopes and their inherent methodology. It is true that there are discipline-overlapping 'methods', such as the use of particular forms of mathematics. For instance, calculus is used in a large variety of disciplines: physics, astronomy, biology, economics, sociology, and so forth. Some methods may even be useless in some disciplines. For example, the hallmark of scientific methods – the experiment – cannot be used in geology for the simple reason that one cannot 'experiment' with the Earth.

It has been hinted at before that this does not prevent one from emphasizing particular methods, for instance, as a result of a division of labor, or because particular questions require the use of certain methods more than others. This is also the case in the present book, for instance with respect to the distinction between quantitative and qualitative methods. As their name suggests, quantitative methods use numerical data, while qualitative methods do not, but instead try to analyze 'raw' data that have not been quantified, such as, for instance, people's utterances in an interview. We have put much more emphasis in this book on quantitative than on qualitative methods. Why?

One of the choices you are going to make sooner rather than later is that between qualitative and quantitative research. A considerable amount of ink has flown over the question of which of these two groups of research methods is to be preferred. Proponents of quantitative methods point out that on the basis of qualitative methods, generalizations are impossible, and research that does not lead to generalization is worthless. Qualitative researchers will counter by pointing out that quantitative investigations start from preconceived ideas that stem from the researcher's mind without having much of a foothold in the real world; qualitative investigations, by contrast, do not start from preconceptions, but instead look at the real world before making claims about it. Many such mutual reproaches have been made. In some corners, one may even observe outright skirmishes between supporters of these approaches. Of course, some researchers specialize in one or the other of these methods, and nothing speaks against this. However, whenever such emphasis implies looking down on the other approach, whenever someone claims the superiority of one, or it is suggested that one of them is better in itself, one should be on guard. In all probability, you are facing a monomethodologist!

Here is a brief summary of the pros and cons of each method:

- Qualitative methods are to be used whenever one is confronted with a field or topic that has hardly been investigated and where few theories or hypotheses exist.

- Quantitative methods are often appropriate where extensive literature about a field or topic exists. However, qualitative approaches may be employed in such a situation to explore hidden or unknown aspects of the topic further.

- Qualitative methods tend to be more appropriate to generate new insights and hypotheses. Quantitative methods are generally more geared toward testing existing theories or hypotheses.

- Qualitative methods are more difficult for beginners, contrary to what one might expect. Because quantitative methods involve number-crunching, they seem anathema to students in the humanities. Paradoxically, however, such methods are considerably easier (and often also more rewarding) for beginners.

- Qualitative methods require the researcher to be as explicit as possible about the various steps taken in the research, as is the case in most quantitative research. Here one must say that, alas, much research suffers from being sloppy. In all probability, it is such sloppiness that has given qualitative methods a bad reputation but sloppy use by some should not disqualify the methods as such.

- Qualitative methods are more dependent on actual real life experience than quantitative methods. They demand skills that are more difficult to acquire through the study of a book. You need more training 'in the field,' more background knowledge, more life experience, highly developed social and verbal skills, and so forth.

During your reading of this and the next two chapters you will have to determine which type of research will be suitable for your own research project. For your orientation, here are three basic categories:

1. **Explanatory research** allows you to test hypotheses of the type "If X then Y" (or "Y can be explained by X,"). Here are some examples. "Point-of-view can be used to enhance viewers' (or readers') feelings of suspense." "This exhibition audio-tour enhances visitors' perceptiveness to details in the paintings." When testing hypotheses of this type, it is advisable to choose an experimental research design (see Chapter 6).
2. **Explorative research** allows you to explore a new field, that is, a field of research where hardly anyone has ventured before. Here are some examples. "Would hospitalized patients benefit from reading particular kinds of literary texts?" "How do viewers' (or readers') backgrounds interact with their response to movies (or to novels)?" "Do lectures on art history (or literary theory) augment one's appreciation of art (or literary) works?" It should be noted, however, that there are few fields that theorists have not formulated hypotheses about. Also, do not be too quick to think that these are questions that no researcher ever thought of. The aim of explorative research approaches could be to formulate hypotheses for explanatory research. For a discussion of research methods suitable for explorative research you can turn to Chapter 4. How to find out what is known in research about a certain subject, turn to section 3.4 of the present chapter.
3. **Descriptive research** allows you to describe your research object. Here are some examples. "How many people of which educational level and socio-economic background go and visit avant-garde music concerts (or read a certain literary genre)?" "What are the characteristics of free indirect speech presentation?" For the appropriate methods you may turn to Chapter 4.

You must keep in mind that any type of research will have its advantages and disadvantages and will result in a different type of data. But also consider the possibility of combining research methods, either simultaneously, or one after the other. First, a questionnaire combining open and closed questions enables you to make generalizable claims on the one hand and on the other to look deeper into subjects' thoughts and find illustrations of what the figures show. As argued above, qualitative research can be used to generate hypotheses that subsequently can be put to the test in a quantitative approach. You could also consider conducting first an experiment or a survey to establish causal relations between certain variables, and subsequently performing interviews to shed some more light on these relations, to learn more about the structure of subjects' experiences. Rather than excluding each other, the approaches complement each other well. Thus, there are reasons enough to be against monomethodology.

3.2. Making a plan for research

Now we will take you step by step from forming an initial idea for a research project to choosing the appropriate method to conduct your study. What you need to do before you start reading this section is to think of some research problem from your own field of interest. That will help you to see the use of the steps that we will take you through.

- **Step 1**

First you should consider what the problem is that you want to investigate. It may be that you already have a clear idea of the theory and the hypotheses that you want to test; nevertheless, it is a good idea to start here: a first exploration of the research problem in the available literature. The purpose of this step is that, as a result, initial plans may be refined or adjusted by a) considering the scope of theories concerning the domain you are interested in and b) the research that has already been done.

Imagine you want to know about what causes emotional responses to literature. Then it may be a good idea to first learn a bit more about what emotions are, what is known about what causes them, how emotions develop, etc. The function of this step is twofold. First, it may inspire you to formulate or reformulate your research ideas, for instance by applying what you learned about emotions to your own field of interest, in this case, literature. Also, during your first excursion through what has already been written on the subject, you may stumble upon some (unfounded) empirical claims made by theorists that you think interesting to test. Second, this first investigation may also result in a further refinement of your plans. In most articles, especially in psychology, authors include self-criticism, which may inspire you to do things better; or they conclude with suggestions for further research, suggestions that you yourself may want to take up. We will discuss various possibilities for performing a literature search in Section 4.

- **Step 2**

The result of Step 1 is a more specific idea of what your research problem is going to be. In a second step you should think for a moment about the feasibility of the study: some ideas may be impossible for you to deal with, not simply because of the time and costs involved, but also in terms of the likelihood that you will actually be able to solve the problem, or that you will be able to come to a concrete conclusion. In short, Step 2 should be an evaluation of your plans in terms of feasibility. One way to do this is to ask for the opinion of others. Consult other students in your seminar group, but also your supervisor. His or her role here is, of course, not to make you change your mind, but to help estimate the likelihood of success.

- **Step 3**

    Step 3 should be a second literature search. Having decided upon a research problem, you need to conduct a more focused and in-depth study of the literature. It is advisable to make good notes or even keep a logbook of what you run into, and, importantly, also where you found your information! These notes may prove to be invaluable when writing up your final report. The aim of this step is to provide a solid basis for the next one. At this stage you may already start compiling your bibliography (thus saving precious time). Look into possibilities to have it automatically stored by WORD or other programs, like ENDNOTE, an extremely handy piece of bibliography software.

- **Step 4**

    In Step 4 you construct a conceptual model consisting of two or more elements between which you assume a causal relationship. Central to the model is a prediction in the form of "If X then Y." In this prediction X is the independent variable and Y the dependent variable. For example, "More experienced readers will be more flexible and imaginative in filling 'gaps' in a narrative (cf. Iser, 1975) than inexperienced readers." Here the level of reading experience is the independent variable and readers' response to 'gaps' in a story is the dependent variable (for further discussion, go to Chapter 4, where we will discuss Earthman (1992), who actually carried out this research).

    During Step 4, ways may part. In pure exploratory or descriptive research you may not want or be able to formulate hypotheses. But even in qualitative research it is important to stop and think about what you expect to find. It helps you to focus on certain aspects in your material and thus to make, to some extent, generalizing statements about it, as opposed to letting the reader of your report drown in details. Earthman's study (1992), as you will see later, is a qualitative study. So we recommend that you consider what, based on the literature search, your conceptual model looks like.

- **Step 5**

    One thing the study of the literature may reveal is that things are a little more complex than a one-dimensional causal link between X and Y, namely that

Y does not just depend on X but also on a number of other factors. Now there are two choices you can make. You may decide that:
(1) you want to include those factors as independent variables;
(2) even though you expect those factors to influence your dependent variable, you are not primarily interested in their effects. In this case, there are three options open to you:
(a) account for these factors by measuring them, and controlling for them in your statistical analysis (a simple procedure to be explained in Chapters 9 through 11);
(b) keeping that factor constant; for example, you suspect that readers' or viewers' age may influence their responses, and therefore you decide to focus on one age group (this has the disadvantage that generalization of your findings is limited);
(c) choosing other procedures, like randomization, which will be discussed later in Chapter 6.

Your conceptual model based on your literature search has now become more complex, more balanced, and more realistic. Of course you are free to include more factors than the literature study suggested. For instance, if you found no hints that gender might be of influence but common sense tells you it is plausible that results may be affected by subjects' sex, then you may register your subjects' sex. Controlling for any influence in the outcome of your study can easily demonstrate any effect due to gender.

An essential addition to the conceptual model is a precise definition of each of its terms (except the more obvious ones like sex and age). If you wish to investigate readers' (or spectators') identification with characters, what do you understand by 'identification'"? What definitions are there (see your second literature search) that come closest to what theorists had in mind when they made their empirical claims, and finally what do *you* decide 'identification' to mean? It is important here to keep in mind scientific relevance: it is always a good idea to adhere to the definitions of other researchers and theorists; in this way your results contribute directly to the debate among scholars.

3.3. Laying out your conceptual model

In some cases this may look simple, in the form of "if X then Y". But based on your literature study (or on common sense) you may now be able to make a list of variables that may play a role in the relation that you want to establish (in whatever form of research). On the next page are some of the forms that your conceptual model can take:

64   Chapter Three

X causes Y: e.g. seeing a character being humiliated on stage (X) will cause pity for this character (Y).

X and Y cause Z: e.g. X is the degree of suffering of the character; Y the degree of perceived similarity between viewer and character; Z the degree of pity.

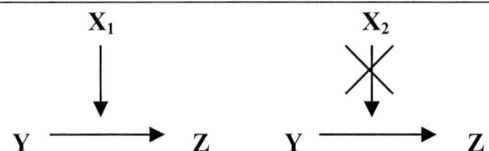

Only when X has a certain value, will Y have an effect on Z: e.g. only when the character is morally good (X_1) will his suffering (Y) cause pity (Z), but not when he is morally repulsive to viewers (X_2).

X ⟶ Q ⟶ Y
X has an indirect effect on Y, via Q: e.g. the suffering of the character (X) causes viewers to feel pity for him (Q) and this enhances their appreciation for the play as a whole.

X_1 ⟶ Y_1 ⟶ X_2 ⟶ Y_2

The effect X has on Y at time 1 affects X at time 2: e.g. hopes for a good story outcome (X_1) increase viewers' tension (Y_1), which increases hopes for a good story outcome (X_2), further enhancing their feeling of tension (Y_2), which again enhances hopes, etc.

Figure 3.1: Possible relations between variables

- **Step 6**

The next step follows closely what you did in the previous one: all the elements in your conceptual model should now be formulated in empirical terms. This is called operationalization. Having defined your terms, how are you going to measure them? At this point you are ready to make the next step: choose the appropriate research method. Read the next chapters keeping this in mind. However, first we want to tell you something more about the literature search. In each of the preceding steps, it may be that knowledge of the work of other researchers is essential for making the right choices in your own study.

3.4. A study of the literature

A literature search can serve several purposes, in different phases of your research project, but especially in Step 1. For example, as discussed earlier, it may help you to find or specify a research question. Also, it may help you to improve on what others did before you. Good sources of inspiration in this respect are the discussion sections of research articles. Here researchers often let you in on the restrictions they see themselves for the validity of their conclusions: can we generalize the finding to other populations than the one under examination? What are their alternative explanations for the results that were found? What possible criticism could fellow researchers have on the way the concepts were operationalized? Sometimes the authors make some suggestions for future research following their self-criticism. You may have come across such observations and found them trite and obligatory, but reflecting on how to do your own research you will often find them very valuable.

- **Make a plan**

The extent of your literature search must depend on what your aim is: do you want to make a complete inventory of research in a certain area (for instance for an MA thesis), or do you just want to report the main findings concerning your own research project? It is advisable to plan in advance in what detail you want to study the literature. You should first get a global overview (via abstracts of, for instance, an electronic database like *PsycINFO*) to find inspiration for a research question and then in a stepwise manner limit yourself to one very specific problem for your further study. Soon you will discover the importance of being specific, also in the formulation of the question for your literature search. Besides that, you may also want to determine in advance which sources you are going to draw from, and then go through them systematically, source by source.

These are the steps that you can take in your search of the literature:
⇒ **Question.** Formulate a general question, for example, "What do we know about the effects of humorous movies?" One potential problem is that your terminology will not always match that used by researchers,

let alone researchers in the area of psychology or sociology. Also, your research question may still be much too general in its formulation.

⇒ **Search terms.** Examine the terminology and concepts: find out which terms are used in the existing research, which terms are used for the phenomena you are interested in, use dictionaries, encyclopedias, introductory texts you find in handbooks: these are ways in which you can find out what search terms you need in your literature study. Write all these terms down. Make a hierarchy: decide which terms are closest to your own research problem, and which are further away. Especially for the terms central to your research you should think of as many synonyms as possible. Put synonyms of one term on the same level in your hierarchy. Also consider that along the way you will run into more synonyms. Write these down on your list, and search for these as well. If you have access to *Kinkade's Thesaurus* (1974), for instance, through the local library of the Psychology Department, make use of it in this phase.

⇒ **Collecting.** Do a search of the bibliographies of abstracts (e.g. *PsycINFO, Psychological Abstracts*), and the review journals (e.g. *Psychological Bulletin, Annual Review of Psychology, l'Année Psychologique, Advances in Child Development and Behavior, Review of Research in Education*), and in that order: make use as much as possible of the work of others. Always make notes of the sources you have screened. When this yields few references, maybe you should rethink the search terms: make them broader, or use related terms (e.g. instead of searching for 'humor in sitcoms', try and find references related to 'humor in television').

⇒ **Reading.** Make a selection of the material you have located and scan it. At first, do not read articles and chapters from beginning to end. Focus here, as far as available, on the domain of empirical studies of the arts and media. Select those articles (e.g. reviews), books, and book chapters that seem most pertinent to your research question. Start reading. In most cases the result will be a deeper insight not only into the problem area but also into what the research question of your literature study should be. You will gain an impression of which subjects receive a lot of attention from researchers, and what types of hypotheses are examined. You will also get an idea about the strength of the evidence in the field: is it just theory (one author's word against another's)? Are points proven with case studies only? Or are there also other types of studies, like experiments or surveys? All this information may help you adjust your own research question.

We recommend that you keep notes during your literature search. You may save files from the Internet or from other digital sources and note where you found what. Make complete references (author, title, journal or book title, year, page numbers). This will prove to be invaluable information later on: when you write your report you will need this information, or when you want to trace some sources, this information is also necessary. One way to do this is of course using pen and paper; a cleverer way is to use software like ENDNOTE. Also, your notes will provide you with an overview of what sources you already dealt with and what there is still to do. Instead of ENDNOTE you can also use cards to write references and abstracts on, but this will be much more time- and energy-consuming.

⇒ **Snowballing**. Sometimes reading one article will lead the way to other articles: scan the bibliography of the targeted articles/books you collected in the previous phase.

- **Look for sources**

We will now give you a brief overview of sources that you may consider in your literature search. We realize that some of the sources mentioned here may not be available to you. In any event, try your library and ask!

First there are the abstracts. If you are dealing with reactions or emotions, for instance, most important is *PsycINFO* (we will discuss that later); second there are the *Psychological Abstracts*, a valuable source dating back to 1927, that summarizes psychological publications worldwide. However, you will soon see an overrepresentation of English publications. For French publications you can check the monthly *Bulletin Signalétique*. More specific databases are *Child Development Abstracts and Bibliography* (since 1927 as well) and *Language and Language Behavior Abstracts*. The latter is a multidisciplinary journal (every three months) with abstracts related to language in its broadest sense. There is *Dissertation Abstracts International* (since 1938) with abstracts of American, Canadian, and European dissertations. Look for Section A, which covers Humanities and Social Sciences. Much of what you will find here is unpublished work. What you can do is copy the abstracts and refer to them in your report. Another more costly and time-consuming way is to order a copy of the entire manuscript via your library.

Second, there are the review articles. *Psychological Bulletin, Annual Review of Psychology*, and *Advances in Experimental Social Psychology* are often essential sources. The contributions in these journals summarize for the readers the enormous flow of publications. When you want to be up to date with developments in the domain of psychology, this is the place to start. Say you are interested in personality psychology; you can of course use old definitions of for example 'identity', but you may do better to read the recent developments in the field. Some of the references you will find in the bibliographies of the review articles may also be relevant in a more direct way and it may be worth your while to locate them in your library or obtain them via inter-library loan.

Sources often underestimated are MA theses. Realize that years and years of work are stacked away somewhere in your library and that some of it may be just what you have been looking for. Our impression is that there is a lot of good work done by students, work that disappears in the drawers of supervisors. Try and find out where you can locate the work of your predecessors and hopefully there is an easy (digitalized) way to find out whether there were theses written on your subject. Maybe one of the researchers of your own department or one at the Department of Psychology, or Media Studies, or Literature etc. supervised a thesis that is relevant to you. Imagine that a literature study was conducted just a year ago, and you can profit from that work. For dissertations, one can use the services of ProQuest, a firm that offers over 1,000,000 volumes. The cost for a dissertation (on microfilm or in PDF format) is around 30 US$. Many university libraries in Western countries will cover the costs. For further information, visit the ProQuest website at: http://il.proquest.com/products_umi/dissertations/.

In our field we often deal with pioneers' work. One implication is that we need to look at the most recent developments when conducting literature studies. Excellent sources for such information are *Proceedings*. In general, these are the collected papers presented at conferences or symposia. Here you may discover what is going on in certain domains at the moment not only in the empirical studies of literature, the arts, and media, but also in the sub-domains of psychology. Examples are the proceedings of the conferences of the International Society for the Empirical Study of Literature and Media, and those of the Poetics and Linguistics Association. For up to date work in psychology try those of the *Nebraska Symposium on Motivations* and the *American Psychologist*. You should realize that such publications are often inclusive: i.e. all the papers that were presented at those conferences are included; therefore you have to be wary of papers of a lesser standard.

Librarians often arrange books systematically or thematically. In your literature search you can make good use of that. Say you are interested in humor. You found a key publication on humor in the catalogue of your library; if the library has an open collection, go and find the location of the book in one of the rooms of the building. There is a good chance that on the same shelf or in the same bookcase you may find more on the subject. This is probably something you are already aware of but here we would like to emphasize that this provides yet another strategy for your literature search: check the 'surroundings' of key publications.

The Internet is also a valuable source of information. We will briefly discuss some relevant sites that you could check. A great many journals nowadays are also published electronically; see for an overview http://psych.hanover.edu/Krantz/journal.html. Many offer free abstracts and/or full texts of the articles, usually in PDF format. In some cases your library will offer you Internet access to ERIC, which indexes journal articles in the field of education, as well as documents published through the U.S. Department of Education, from 1966 to the present. Via the catalogue of your library you may also find access to *Current Contents and Social Sciences and Humanities Index.*

A very valuable source is *Social Sciences Citation Index.* In *Citation Indexes* you may find a reference you may think essential to the field of your interest. You can enter that reference and find a list of recent articles in which your reference was cited. At the time of writing this book, some libraries have switched to a more recent version called *Web of Knowledge*, which covers three citation indexes: *Arts & Humanities Citation Index, Science Citation Index Expanded* and *Social Sciences Citation Index.*

➤ *PsycINFO*

Almost any literature search in psychology will make use of *PsycINFO*. Hence we will go into the use of this source in a little bit more detail, as a means of illustration. In most cases you will find access to *PsycINFO* through your university library. It is a database of most publications (books, book chapters, journal articles) in psychology, complete with brief summaries. To make good use of this database, you first prepare a list of keywords related to your research problem (Step 3 in your plan). For instance, you could do this for humor, and find out that you could also look for laughter. A lot of research focuses on jokes and cartoons. When you are interested in responses to movies, you probably want to exclude terms like 'jokes' and 'cartoons' from your search. If you find only a few references, use more general and related terms such as 'emotional responses' or 'conditioned emotional responses'. Besides the term 'movie', you may want to use broader terms (e.g. 'motion pictures' or 'entertainment') or related terms (e.g. drama).

Next, select the publication years you are interested in. Recent publications are often to be preferred over older ones, because usually the authors have accumulated previous research before doing research themselves and report on their own literature study in their publication. However, if results of the *PsycINFO* search prove to be meager, one may consider widening the search, by selecting also older publications.

Start the search with individual keywords, preferably using the options offered by 'Advanced' (see Figure 3.2). It is advisable to do this one by one, checking the most essential ones first. If this results in a long list of, say, over

100 publications, you may want to refine your search by combining keywords. At the time of writing this book, the combination 'Movies and Humor' resulted in 19 hits. The *PsycINFO* Thesaurus (see 1 in Figure 3.2) advised the term 'MOTION PICTURES (ENTERTAINMENT)'. The search 'Motion pictures' and 'humor' yielded 272 hits. You may want a smaller result. To obtain fewer hits you could consider adding one more search term, or, for instance, limiting your search to articles published after 2000.

What you do when you have a 'reasonable' amount of hits is scan the results for relevance by first reading the titles. If this leads you to believe articles or book chapters are useful to you, also read the summaries to make sure. While reading through the results of your search, already check those articles that seem relevant to your research question (tick the box left of the hit number; see 2 in Figure 3.2). Often you will find that your plans need to be adjusted: reading the titles, summaries and the list of keywords used by *PsycINFO* itself (see the end of each file, for example in Figure 3.3) may make you decide to change your own list of search terms. For instance, you might decide to focus on sex differences in responses to humor.

During your search, check the publications you considered relevant, and select them for printing, saving, or mailing (see 3 in Figure 3.2; click on the icons on your screen and a new dialog box will appear where you can indicate which records you want (all records, a particular record number, or the ones you marked). Finally, check whether the publications are downloadable, or available (in your own library, in libraries nearby, or via your local inter-library loan system). For more possibilities of *PsycINFO* you can consult the *Database Guide* (see 4 in Figure 3.2).

Types of Research Methodology and Research Design 71

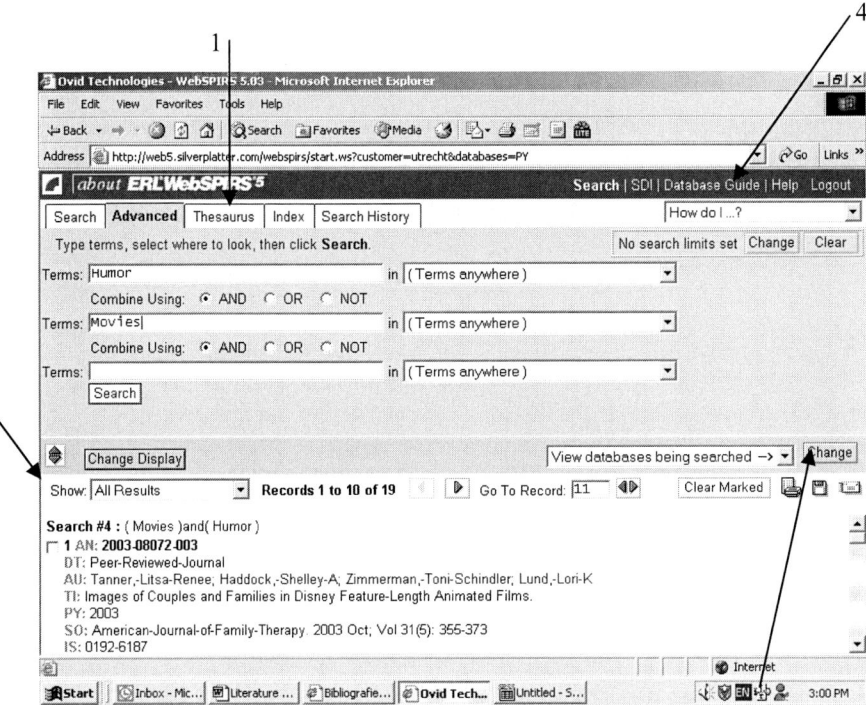

Figure 3.2: Example of a *PsycINFO* search result

```
6  AN: 2000-08071-001
   DT: Journal-Article
   AU: King,-Cynthia-M
   TI: Effects of humorous heroes and villains in violent action films.
   PY: 2000
   SO: Journal-of-Communication. 2000 Win; Vol 50(1): 5-24
   PB: England: Oxford Univ Press.
   IS: 0021-9916
   AB: This experimental investigation explores the use of humor in violent
   action films, focusing on the effects of wisecracking heroes and villains on
   audience distress. An action film was edited to create control film versions
   without wisecracking dialogue. The research revealed contrast effects.
   Among female viewers, hero wisecracks in an action film increased
   distress reactions to the film, but lessened distressful reactions to
   subsequent televised depictions of real, nonhumorous violence.
   Conversely, males exposed to hero humor found the film marginally less
   distressing, but rated depictions of real violence more distressing. For all
   viewers, effects of villain wisecracks tended to parallel females' reactions
   to hero wisecracks. Disposition theory is offered as a plausible explanation
   of study findings. ( PsycINFO  Database Record (c) 2002 APA, all rights
   reserved)
   DE: *Distress-; *Humor-; *Motion-Pictures-Entertainment;
   *Psychological-Reactance; *Violence-
   DE: Human-Sex-Differences
   FTXT:   Full-text via Homepage HighWire Journals
   WEBLH: Check UBU catalogue
   Complete Record  Document Delivery
```

Figure 3.3: Example of a *PsycINFO* file

Let us look at Figure 3.3 in somewhat more detail for a moment. Each file gives you the following information. First it tells you what kind of publication you are dealing with (DT): whether it is a journal article, or chapter, or book. Sometimes it is indicated that it is published in a so-called 'peer-reviewed journal'. This means that the journal uses higher standards in the selection of copy: authors have to tackle criticism from their fellow researchers before their articles can be published. When you want to know more about the journal itself, click on that name. It may be that you have a number of dissertation abstract in your search results. Remember that dissertations are often harder to obtain because many of them are not published. Second, *PsycINFO* tells you the name of the author

(AU). It is important that while you are reading through the results of your search, you pay attention to these names; maybe you notice that one particular name turns up a number of times in your search. Often this means that you are dealing with an important researcher in your field of interest, and that it may be worthwhile to use the name of that person as an extra search term or track the person through a search engine like Google, for instance. You can also simply click on the authors' names: this will result in an overview of their publications.

The abstract (AB) provides you with the most important information on the basis of which you make your selection. It will give you an impression of the kind of research you are dealing with. In Figure 3.3 we see an example of an article by King, 'Effects of humorous heroes and villains in violent films' (TI). The suggestion in the title (the word 'effects') is confirmed when we read the abstract: the author tries to establish a causal relationship by means of an experiment. During our search for studies on humor in motion pictures, we will also encounter an article by Brody (1976) entitled 'The Wonderful World of Disney: Its psychological appeal.' On the basis of the title we still do not know what methods the researcher applied, but the summary makes it clear:

> Analyzes the influence of Walt Disney and his creations—Silly Symphony, Mickey Mouse, Donald Duck, Disneyland, and Disney World, and his important feature-length movies, especially Pinocchio, Snow White, and Cinderella—and their value in shaping American culture. Disney's works are seen as essentially positive social influences in which "anal themes are used to lessen the anxiety of oral aggression," fears and anxieties are time limited, and castration anxiety is mastered as Disney's ingenious works plug into our unconscious. (*PsycINFO*: 1978-22675-001)

Clearly, the empirical claims made by this article cannot be as strong as those of King. Especially the terms castration anxiety and anal themes should make it clear to you that the author focuses on a Freudian interpretation of films rather than determining empirically what the appeal of these movies is.

Besides those discussed up to now, there are more or less obvious sources open to you. Here we only remind you briefly of them. You should do a regular literature search through your local library catalogue, preferably electronically, if possible. Other valuable sources are the publications you found in your first *PsycINFO* and catalogue search. You will find that most authors report on their literature study right after their introduction, or at the very beginning of their article. Having found articles that are really on target, it may be useful simply to read the bibliographies and make notes about references that seem useful to your own project. Your literature search may have resulted in a number of articles in one or two journals that seem particularly germane to your research interest. There is a good chance that they are to be found in one of the journals mentioned in Table 3.1. You may want to check the table of content of a few back-volumes for other relevant articles. Last but not least: ask people around you, in particular your supervisor or his/her colleagues for more literature tips.

Humanities	Social Sciences
Discourse Processes *Empirical Studies of the Arts* *Journal of Broadcasting and Electronic Media* *Language and Literature* *Poetics* *Poetics Today* *Reading Research Quarterly* *Research in the Teaching of English* *SPIEL*	*American Psychologist* *Child Development* *Cognition and Emotion* *Developmental Psychology* *European Journal of Social Psychology* *Imagination, Cognition and Personality* *Journal of Experimental Social Psychology* *Journal of Personality and Social Psychology* *Psychological Science*

Table 3.1: Relevant journals

- **Evaluation**

A final word on what you do, in the end, with all the literature you found. The quality of searches is not only determined by the thoroughness with which you went through all possible sources, nor just by the number of relevant books and articles you found. Quality is also determined by the way you discuss your findings. First, you should always keep in mind that you need to be explicit about the relation between your own study and those of others. Second, you need to discuss previous studies in a critical way. Do not be critical just to be critical, of course, and try to avoid merely listing summaries of what you have read. One way to be critical in a useful way is to examine the validity of the claims of the researchers. Are their conclusions as generalizable as they claim they are? What comments can you make about the way the researchers operationalized their concepts? Keep in mind that each approach or research tradition has its own set of criteria for quality research. In Chapter 6 we will discuss some guidelines for evaluating empirical studies. Using these guidelines will help you to determine what you can contribute to the field. Read on and see that you actually can.

CHAPTER FOUR

METHODS OF DATA COLLECTION

4.1. Introduction

In this chapter you will find an overview of some of the most frequently used research methods in the field of empirical studies of the arts and culture in general. We think it is important that you realize the full range of possibilities, that you see the advantages as well as the disadvantages of the different approaches, and what type of information each of these research methods produces. At the end of this chapter we hope you will be able to decide which method is most suitable for your own purposes. Also, you will see which methods require more interpretation of the data. You will also learn to distinguish between those that are better suited to generate hypotheses, and those that are more appropriate for testing.

This overview encompasses qualitative as well as quantitative methods. We already discussed the differences between them in Chapter 3 and it is useful to think of them when distinguishing between hypothesis-generating and hypothesis-testing methods. As discussed in Chapter 3, qualitative research is generally aimed at exploring phenomena, and can be used by researchers to formulate hypotheses about those phenomena. Typically, this type of research focuses on a narrative analysis of data collected, for instance, in interviews or observations. The data generated by qualitative approaches often inform us about people's experiences or perceptions. In order to do that, researchers interpret respondents' narratives or what the observed behavior tells them about people. In that sense, it is a more subjective approach, which leaves much room for researchers' interpretations. Quantitative research, on the other hand, concentrates on the analysis of observations that can be converted into numbers, which are subsequently analyzed according to the rules of statistical methods. In this way there is less leeway for subjective interpretations. In most cases they either confirm or reject a hypothesis.

Let us apply this distinction to an example. We could ask a number of readers in interviews how reading fiction affects their ideas about the world. A qualitative approach will not tell us whether fiction *does* affect readers' perception. It will tell us how readers experience the role of fiction in their view of the world around them. Interviewing, say, ten readers may be very informative about this experience, but we need to be careful when generalizing. Imagine that as many as six out of 10 say that they are sometimes confused as to whether they read some 'fact' in a novel or got it from a non-fiction source. Does this help us *explain* the influence of fiction in people's lives? Consider the possibility that our questions guided our respondents a little toward making statements about the possible influence of fiction on perception. The fact is that 10 respondents are not exactly representative of the general reading audience. What this study does tell us is that it *might* be that readers confuse 'fact' sources. This is an example of the hypothesis-generating function of qualitative research. Other researchers could pick up from here, such as Gerrig and Prentice (1991) did. They examined whether fiction could 'infiltrate' our memory and make it harder for us to decide whether something is true or not. If this hypothesis holds, it would take just a little longer for respondents to make that distinction. This is exactly what the researchers found. However, if they had found no difference they would have had to reject their hypothesis about the effect of fiction. The advantages of this study is that results were unaffected by the personal opinions or convictions of either the researchers or the respondents themselves (who were kept unaware of the purpose of the study).

However, as you will realize at the end of this book, statistical analyses also require some degree of interpretation. This occurs because you will have to figure out how the numbers relate to your theory. You have to bear in mind what the results of your experiment tell you about human response. Qualitative research might, likewise, lead to generalizations. For instance, think of the situation where you have the means and the time to conduct so many interviews that you can start generalizing your findings to a larger population. Or you can do your observations in a controlled environment, thus allowing you to draw conclusions about the effect of environment on behavior.

In Chapters 5 and 6 we will instruct you how to make a questionnaire and design an experiment. However, here we will give you a brief overview of many approaches that may be relevant to you. You may want to consider the possibility of combining research methods. So, this overview will help you estimate the value of studies that you found during your literature study, and the strength of the claims they can make. We start with a somewhat longer overview on observation research.

4.2. Observation research

The 'voice over' narrator in the movie *Amélie* (2001) introduces the main character by describing some of her favorite activities. One is observing people in the movie theaters of Paris. Rather than watching the movie herself, Amélie finds profound delight in observing the emotional reactions in the audience's faces. Many of us will readily identify with her innocent voyeurism, because we have had similar experiences. For instance, as we sit on a terrace and watch people walking by, we may make deductions about what they do for a living, what kind of relationships they have, what sort of person they are, and so forth. Similarly, some of us may have found out that studying museum visitors can be just as interesting as looking at the art objects. We may see that, for example, in (heterosexual) European couples it is often the man who points out something to the woman, seldom the other way round. Also, some of us might have had the experience that it can be very instructive, even amusing, simply to listen to how people talk about the novels they read instead of bringing our own (expert) opinion into the conversation. Observing others may not only be fun, but also very informative about human behavior, as for instance the work of Desmond Morris (1977) illustrates.

You may think that observation research is an easy way to gather data, but often you will find it a very elaborative method, partly because being a good observer requires training. One of the authors of this book is a passionate birdwatcher. Going out on his first field trip with the local birdwatchers' club resulted in most members spotting a wide variety of rare specimens, and him having seen a common black crow and one gull. Over the following months he found out that being a successful birdwatcher involves a lot of study and practice. You may have similar experience in your own field of interest. For example, as an advanced student in the Arts, you may have discovered that you 'instinctively' seem to recognize more relevant details in paintings, buildings, poems, movies, or music compositions than you did a few years before. Your training has resulted in an ability to *observe* much more precisely. The same holds for observing people: you have to learn what there is to observe, and you have to train yourself in doing so.

However, there is more that we want you to be aware of before launching a project based on behavioral observations. One practical problem is that, before you know it, you have more material than you can handle. Often observation research results in piles of paper with minute observations, or stacks of video- or audiotapes. You may find it hard to come to decide how to proceed from there.

Another thing you need to realize is that observation, like the other techniques discussed in this chapter, is primarily a descriptive method. This means that often you will not be able to make causal inferences. You may be able to see differences in behavior of, for instance, male and female museum visitors. You may find that in a discussion about literature some of the participants seem to quickly adjust their view as soon as one particular person in the group announces his or her opinion. The problem is, however, that you do not know *why* people behave differently. As to the latter example, it may be that people change their views because that particular person has claimed to be an authority and the others do not want to look stupid On the other hand, it may also be simply the power of his or her arguments that made them change their minds. On the basis of just your observations of the discussion it is impossible to decide what is the cause of the change.

4.2.1. Deciding on the type of observation research

In what follows, we offer a brief overview of the types of studies that observation research involves. We will look at advantages and disadvantages of each type and then focus on the type of studies that we think most of you may or will be involved in. Categorizing observation research is fundamental for making some important choices before you start working. Research in this field varies along two dimensions: first is the degree to which you structure your research; and second the degree to which you, as a researcher, participate in the behavior. (Note that some of the remarks here may also apply to other methods of research discussed in this chapter.)

One important choice to be made here is that between *structured* versus *unstructured* research. 'Structured' means that you manipulate or control (the setting of) your participants' behavior. It is important to consider whether you *can* structure your research, because the degree to which you do determines whether you will be able to make causal inferences.

In a field study there may be all sorts of aspects (i.e. environmental and subject variables) that influence the behavior of your participants, while you are interested in isolating just one. Let's take the example we mentioned above: studying the behavior of male–female couples in museums. In our study we define what is called a 'target behavior', that is, the behavior that we researchers are interested in, and that we want to register during our observations. We could define the target behavior of our study as follows: the pointing out with finger or hand of certain aspects of an art object to someone else. Whether the target behavior occurs may depend not only on whether the participant is male or female, but also on how many people are watching the paintings (our environment variable), or on whether one of them is more knowledgeable about art than the other (a subject variable). Such a *lack of control* is one of the most important and most frequently occurring weaknesses in the field of observation research.

Sometimes there *are* ways to structure your research. It is important, therefore, that before you start your study you first consider options to enhance your control of factors that may play a role, what we call 'potential variables'. One way to go about it is to use the method of observations to gather data about behavior, and combine it with the method of the experiment (for more details see Chapter 6). Zillmann and Bryant (1975), for instance, were interested in the role of moral beliefs in the appreciation of dramatic presentations. They made three videotapes of the same fairy tale, with only the last 30 seconds being different. The story was about a good prince and a bad prince. The bad prince tries to plot against the good one but fails. In one version of the last scene he is fairly punished, in one he is not and in a third he is punished too severely. Theories of developmental psychology (Piaget, 1948) predict that viewers younger than 7 years would appreciate the last version best. At that age children are found to believe that the more severe the punishment of a transgression the more just it is. After the age of 7, children believe punishment should be appropriate for the crime committed. In Zillmann and Bryant's study, two judges looked at 'candid camera' tapes of the participants, without sound so the judges would be unaware of what the participants responded to. They were also kept unaware of the purpose of the experiment. With both the participants and the judges being unaware of the conditions to which the participants were assigned, this is an example of a double-blind experiment (see below). The two judges were given a questionnaire with scales of 0–100 on which they were to indicate their observations. Each scale was numbered and marked at intervals of 10 points. Judges were asked, for instance, to rate the apparent appreciation of the last scene on a scale ranging from "gave no sign of liking" (0) to "appeared to like it very much" (100). These evaluations were entered only when both judges agreed in their assessment of the facial display. The results of the first observation are presented in Figure 4.1. In accordance with expectations we see a strong difference between the responses of the two age groups. The younger participants were inclined to like the stronger retaliation, while the older participants liked the version best in which the punishment was fairest.

In this study, the researchers chose to use several measures. Besides the observations they also interviewed their participants and asked them to fill out a questionnaire themselves. Observations are not always easy to interpret. With the help of supportive evidence (e.g. participants' self-reports), interpretation of, for instance, facial expressions becomes much more plausible. For example, Zillmann and Bryant also asked the older participants whether they thought the retaliation was appropriate. This once again confirmed their hypothesis, namely that participants did not like the version in which there was no punishment, nor the one in which the punishment was too extreme.

So, as you can see, it is not impossible to structure the behavior that you want to study. The example discussed here is typical of experimental designs that are the core of empirical research, and that allow you to make causal inferences.

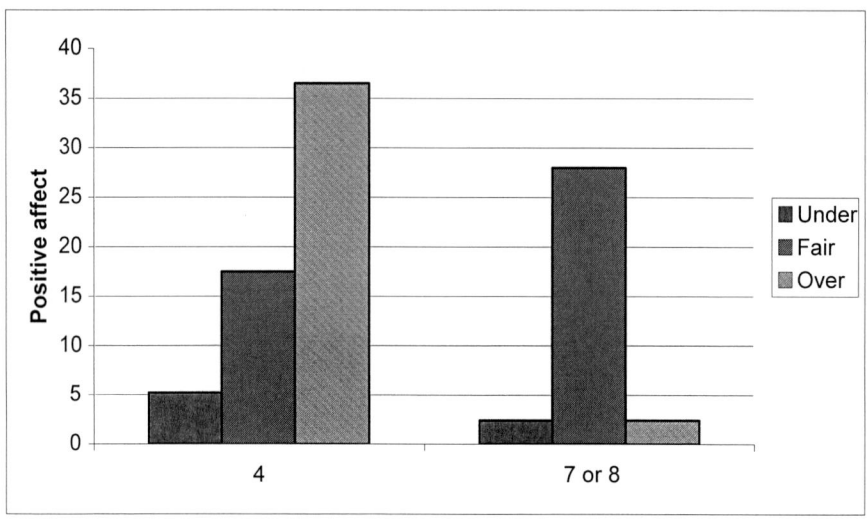

Figure 4.1- Candid camera observation of two age groups' responses to different degrees of retaliation for amoral character behavior (adopted from Zillmann and Bryant, 1975)

4.2.2. Degree of researcher involvement

Now let us discuss the second dimension on which you have to locate your study. There are different degrees to which observers are involved with their subject. In some studies researchers become part of the group they are studying. We call such studies *participatory research*. An advantage of such an approach is that you get an insider's perspective on the problem you are studying and that you may observe things that remain hidden to external observers. For example, when you are interested in how people outside the university interpret literature, you may consider becoming a member of a book club. Being a member of the book club turns you into one of your own participants but your participation itself may change the behavior of your participants. A more practical objection has to do with time: results in this type of research are often obtained over long stretches of time, and involve lengthy reports. A principal method in anthropology, researchers typically move in with their participants for a year or longer. In many cases, the time that you have for your own research project will not allow such an investment.

In what follows we will therefore focus on *naturalistic observations*. In these studies you observe how people behave in their everyday environment (e.g. a cinema) without being obtrusively present as a researcher. One of the advantages of such an approach is that you have a lower degree of *subject reactivity* than in participatory research. Subject reactivity means that the participants in your study may behave differently if they know that they are being observed. That there is such a chance was illustrated by Bechtel (1967). He found that visitors to a museum who knew they were being observed spent three times as much time looking at things than people who did not know (on average, 220 versus 71 seconds!). In psychology this phenomenon is referred to as the *Hawthorne effect*. Hawthorne (in Cook & Campbell, 1979) examined whether increasing the available lighting in a factory would enhance production. To his surprise, he found that control group participants (those without the extra lighting) also improved their productivity. This illustrates that just knowing that we are being studied may change our behavior. Is this a problem that we can solve? Some would say in principle we cannot. The idea is that there is nothing at all that can be measured without interfering with it in some way or another. We would like to argue, however, that there are *degrees* to this: one approach to your subjects may affect their behavior strongly, while with another approach they might hardly notice that they are being observed.

4.2.3. Reduce subject interactivity

There are ways to try to restrict the degree of possible subject interactivity. You can decide on *direct unobtrusive measures*, by means of which you observe the behavior directly but in a way that your presence is hardly noticeable. One way would be to work with a hidden video or audio recorder. You can also hide yourself. A good way would be through the use of a one-way mirror but few of you will have one available. Sometimes the problem is solved by the sheer number of people that you observe: you simply dissolve in the crowd, for instance, in a big movie theater. Of course this implies ethical issues, which will be dealt with later in this chapter.

What you need to remember with this type of measure is that you are making give-and-take decisions: the distance you create between you and your participants may decrease subject interactivity, but it may also result in loss of detail. Making recordings of, for instance, group conversations, you will find that it is impossible to catch everything on tape, and that some utterances are lost in the background noise.

There is one important note we have to add here. When trying to be as unobtrusive as possible, you may easily invade your participants' privacy. Also, when some measures to avoid participants' being aware that they are being observed are taken, we cannot meet the criterion of informed consent: participants have the right, previous to the study, to be informed that they will be observed, and they have to give you their consent. The American Psychological Association's website (www.apa.org) offers you more information on the rules you have to observe in this respect. For instance, in general it is accepted that you observe people in public places without informed consent but it is not allowed that you publish their pictures (unless you blot out the faces).

The second category of measures to avoid subject interactivity involves *indirect unobtrusive* ones. These measures are based on the outcomes that you assume have resulted from certain behavior. Here we find good examples of how research often requires us to be very creative. To come up with ways to observe behavior without even being present is sheer detective work. In one study the smudges on the glass casing of museums were used to measure the popularity of the art objects (and the height of the smudges allowed for inference about the age of the visitors!) (see Bechtel and Zeisel, 1987). Under the heading of these measures you could also place measures of reading speed as an indication of cognitive activity during reading. You can register surfing behavior. Data on library books borrowed could be a valuable source. We could even go further back in time, and reconstruct behavior of centuries ago. For example, Jonathan Rose (2001) studied what British working class people read in the 19th century, how they responded to classical music, what they thought of the Bible and the classics, and found, much to everyone's surprise, that laborers and laundresses, farm hands and domestic servants read and educated themselves auto-didactically in situations of poverty and deprivation.

As you see, we can minimize subject interactivity. It often takes some careful reflection, and indeed, some preliminary, explorative observations, to figure out which clues, or traces can help us to register behavior, without letting subjects know that they are being observed, let alone to what end. Do not think that we only need to avoid the influence of participants on research findings, however; how about the researchers themselves?

4.2.4. How to avoid observer bias

One of the advantages of naturalistic observation over participatory research is that you reduce the chances of an *observer bias* influencing your results. But even when you maintain a distance to your research subject, it cannot be avoided that in some way researchers' opinions and expectations may affect the results. Bandura et al. (1963) studied the influence of television violence on children's behavior. After exposure to a video showing an adult behaving aggressively, children were observed in a playroom through a one-way mirror. What researchers found was that boys were more violent than girls. But is it not possible that their expectations may have colored their observations? It could be that one particular behavior by a boy was scored as a violent act, while the same behavior in a girl was not. Can we avoid such bias?

Our view is that 'objectivity' is something we should be aiming for without being certain that we can ever attain it. What we need to do here is look for ways to reduce the influence of the observer as far as possible – and there *are* ways. One of the measures taken in the Bandura studies is to be very precise in the definition of the target behavior, or the particular behavior you are interested in. For instance, the adult in the movie sat on top of a big doll and punched it in the nose. This exact behavior had to be reproduced by the children for observers to register that imitative behavior had taken place. This exactness is important, first, because now we reduce the influence of observer bias; second, the results will now meet with one very important criterion: we could now replicate the results in another study using the same narrow definition. With loose definitions we would risk the possibility that slight differences between observers would cause completely different results. So what you need is a *behavior checklist*, that is, a list of target behaviors to be observed.

A second measure we already mentioned is called *double blind*. Neither the participants nor the observers should be aware of the conditions that they are under. For example, in the Bandura studies, participants did not know about the purpose of the study, and the observers did not know whether the participants had seen a video in which the adult was rewarded or punished, or whether the participants had seen a violent film at all. This should prevent them from forming expectations about imitative behavior. Better still is to not even inform the observers about the purpose of the experiment at all, but promise to let them in on it afterwards.

Observation research is often conducted using *several observers*. When you work with other observers, always report the *inter-observer reliability* (also called inter-rater reliability), i.e. the percentage of times that observers agree. Ideally this should be over 90%. In some studies raters are asked to sit around the table and discuss their differences. This can increase the degree of consensus. Keep in mind, however, that this consensus may come about through group dynamics among the observers that has little to do with objectivity. In addition, consider the possibility of videotaping subject behavior. This may help observers to view and analyze the behavior in greater detail and thus resolve their differences.

As we said in the introduction to this section, observing is something that you need to train yourself in. When you work with others it is very important that you *train your (co-)observers* in performing the observations of the target behavior as you have defined it. It will not always be possible to do a try-out, but it will result in more reliable data.

4.3. Stages in the research

Begin with some kind of *orientation*. A first step should be to go out and observe without any categories in mind. Do it casually, using all your senses, familiarize yourself with the environment, get an idea, an impression of what is going on, and generate from those impressions a plan for research: thus you may get an insight into the research question that you ultimately want to examine.

Next, develop a category system. Make a category system that deals with (1) the exact behavior that you want to measure and (2) the time factor. Make a precise definition of the behavior that you want to register: in such a way that someone else could do the observing for you. Describe where the behavior begins and where it ends. Describe in what detail you want the behavior registered. Basically, you can only observe behavior, but often one can infer intentions, ideas, and feelings from behavior. If I see my neighbor walking along with a ladder and a paintbrush, although I can only observe his behavior, I can at the same time infer from this that in all probability he is going to paint his house. Can we gain something about these inferences from behavior? Basically it is in part already there, for instance when from the smudges on the museum cases (signs of behavior) we infer that people were interested in the objects in these casings. Sometimes it is helpful to use a map of the environment, and let observers note what behavior takes place where. Before you start working on an elaborate system, it may be helpful to check whether there is already some category system developed by other researchers that you could use.

As to the time factor, you have to carefully consider the time intervals and the period over which you collect your data. Is there a time cycle in which the behavior you are interested in naturally occurs? Does it have a weekly cycle (e.g. is weekday behavior likely to be different from weekends?), or does it take a mere 24 hours before it starts repeating itself (e.g. will visitors to a museum behave differently in the morning than in the late afternoon?). Another problem is that often behavior is under the influence of the seasons: in most cases you will not be able to wait for a year! But on the other hand, it is not easy to decide what is the critical season; for instance, think of what you read during summer holidays, what you read on the beach, traveling, or on winter Sunday afternoons, or what you read during periods when you are busy at work. So, when planning your study, you have to consider time cycles in the behavior. Also, here is a much more practical consideration: often you simply cannot register every single unit of behavior! It would result in too much data to analyze. Also keep in mind that intense observation will wear out observers. In general we know that concentration does not last all that long. For example, the amount of information people remember of what was said during a lecture drops considerably after 20 minutes. Speakers are often recommended to throw in a joke to introduce a break in concentration, so as to increase the effect of their lectures. We see something similar for the effectiveness of observers. Research (cf. Baker & Wright, 1955) shows that their accuracy decreases after 20 minutes. Therefore, observation is often spaced: make a time interval schedule to allow observers to rest, and/or work in shifts. The schedule should be tested (if possible) to see if you miss any significant amount of data: work in two teams, one conducting integral observations, while the other team works with intervals.

4.4. Think-aloud protocols

In this method, subjects are asked to respond freely to some kind of cultural material. This method can be used, for instance, to examine emotional responses to movies and paintings to see how they develop over time during the viewing or reading. In a study by Davis and Andringa (1995) subjects were asked to think aloud and comment on a story, Faulkner's *A Rose for Emily*, which was presented in 13 segments. During the procedure, the interviewer interacted with the individual readers only through neutral questions like "What do you mean?" or "Could you say something more?" to stimulate the participants to express themselves. Afterwards the protocols were reviewed by the researchers to look for common themes, or common types of responses to the story. They decided on the following categories: (1) readers' reactions dealing with the reading process itself (e.g. aesthetic evaluation, their statements of curiosity, their anticipation of what was to come); (2) readers' emotional responses to the fictional world (that is, to the characters, the events, and atmosphere); (3) attribution of feelings directly to a character; (4) emotions that one character feels for another character. Looking at the distribution of these response categories over the segments of the story, the researchers were able to determine how readers' attitudes toward the story seemed to change over time. It was shown that readers started to read the story relying on feelings like expectations and judgments. Later, during their reading of the story, they came to express more specific emotional reactions to the characters and the setting, with a sharp increase near the end of the climax of the story.

In another study, Earthman (1992) describes the way readers create meaning from literary texts. In her study eight college freshmen and eight graduate students in literature participated in five sessions, in which four stories were read. Various content analyses (see Section 4.9 below) were carried out on the protocols of the think-aloud procedure. Earthman focused on the way readers dealt with 'gaps' (cf. Iser 1978): those things that are left unsaid, actions unexplained, true feelings not articulated. Her content analysis revealed that, while all readers fill gaps, graduate students attended more to gaps that were difficult to fill. While freshmen retained their initial view of a work, graduate students assumed varying perspectives. Generally, it was found that graduate students read in a more 'open' manner, using the text extensively and searching for alternatives. Freshmen's readings were much more 'closed,' remaining relatively unelaborated, and not often being revised.

One important advantage of this method is that you gain access to audiences' initial responses directly, from which their later response may grow. A downside to this method is that it is highly time consuming. Also, analyzing the protocols may require the researcher to go in for a lot of interpretation, making the results more subjective. Therefore, ideally, you need two or three *independent researchers* to agree on the way you categorize the responses of your subjects. Independent researchers should not be aware of the purpose of the study, nor of the conditions that are under examination. After having independently classified the responses, this may result in a consensus about what response belongs to which category. If not, you can decide to let the independent researchers discuss their differences to see whether they can then come to an agreement. Finally, it is often hard to say what caused the results. In Earthman's study, for instance, there is no control over the possible intervening variables at play. As she concludes, "A complex combination of developmental, intellectual, and instructional factors may account for these differences." (1992: 351).

4.5. Diary

At first sight, this looks like a method for lazy researchers: they do not have to do anything at all; just let their subjects write a diary (and then read these diaries afterwards). This is an illusion: the method of using diaries as research instruments demands detailed preparation and careful analysis (Bailey, 1990). The areas of interest, activities, events, or emotions that have to be recorded by subjects in their diaries must be clarified to them in advance. This requires not only the identification of such areas to be noted down, but also their precise relationship to the research aims set out. Without such a clear relation, the data collected by a diary are pretty worthless. This method is sometimes used to see, for instance how people spend their time on various cultural activities. For example, comparing reading time respondents report in questionnaires with the amount of reading time that appears in their diaries, researchers systematically conclude that in actuality the time spent on reading is overestimated in surveys (West et al., 1993: 36).

One area where diaries can be very useful tools is that of literary socialization. It is generally assumed that reading experiences during childhood form the basis of later motivation to read. However, we have little or no reliable information as to what reading experiences in childhood are significant. Here the diary method could be helpful. If children are asked to keep a diary in which they note which books they read at what time, how salient their reading experience was, which emotions they had while reading, what impression the book made on them, how pleasant they found the reading, one could build up a data base that would allow us to more accurately describe the role of childhood reading on the formation of later reading habits. As it is, there are in most cultures descriptions by well-known people (for instance respected authors) of their childhood readings, and such collections can be valuable up to a certain degree, but they have two major shortcomings. First, they tend to be anecdotal; diaries, however, are much more systematic, in that participants are asked to enter their experiences at regular intervals, so that any incident can be compared to the overall frequency and intensity of other reading experiences. Second, most such collections are written by adults, who reconstruct their childhood readings *as* an adult, making them vulnerable to memory slips, selective attention and other limits of human memory, tainting the reliability of the reports; diaries of the sort described before, on the other hand, are produced from the child's own perspective, not colored by the concerns that adults may have but children not.

Instructions to diary-keepers can be left general, so that subjects have only a general guideline as to when, what, and how to record in their diary. Alternatively, they can also be detailed, so that the diary resembles more a kind of questionnaire filled out. An example of the latter is the Audience Reaction Assessment (AURA) that presents respondents with all the possible programs they could have seen on television, per day and in the scheduled order, with each program bringing a six-point scale for the assessment of respondents' appreciation (Frost, 1969). In principle, it is also possible to instruct diary keepers when to enter their experiences, or in what format and detail, but the use of the diaries produced will largely depend on the verbal skills of the writer. It is therefore to be recommended to use this method only when subjects possess sufficient linguistic proficiency. The great advantage of the diary method lies in its authenticity: subjects report on their first hand experience in their own words, from their own perspective, and with their own emotional coloring. As such, data collected in this way have high validity and may open new vistas to the researcher that are not accessible through the closed questions that form the bulk of many other research methods. On the other hand, there are few controls the researcher can exert with respect to this authenticity. This may be especially dangerous with subjects who like to write and who know how to do it well: they may be 'lured' into writing fiction! With such diaries produced, there is no way of knowing whether the reports are authentic or fabricated, a fact that counter-indicates against relying on this method exclusively. Where the reports can be matched with other (independent) information, the diary method is a useful and appropriate one. In addition, the time lag that may occur between the entries may also be important when drawing conclusions. Time lapse may have been caused by lack of thoroughness; it is plausible, for instance that indoor activities (e.g. what people read at home) are reported more than outdoor activities (what people read away from home), simply for practical reasons. Time lapse may also have been the result of an understandable unwillingness to share everything respondents do during the day, simply for reasons of privacy, or because it is too tedious to report every little thing we do. But think of the consequences. Would diaries with time lapses allow us to conclude that the reported reading behavior in questionnaires does indeed differ from the 'real' reading behavior?

4.6. Interview

The first thing to say about interviews is that they are a highly personal form of research. The researcher and the informant work together. They look one another in the face and are dependent upon one another. This setting has several advantages. For informants it means that they can speak freely, that they can let their ideas run free, that they can unveil whatever they think may be of relevance to the topic at hand. For researchers, it means that they can ask freely, probe deeper, and can follow up on topics that they deem important for the research question at hand. There are also other reasons why the interview is an interesting research method. First of all, such an interview can happen in a natural setting, for instance a cafeteria or the informant's living room. In addition, the interviewer can create an informal atmosphere and so the interview may acquire the character of an everyday conversation in which the informant has few reservations to talking freely about the subject. That also allows the interviewer to intuitively check on the authenticity of the answers provided: because of the spatial proximity of both people, subtle verbal and non-verbal signals may show the interviewer how the interviewee feels. Things like hesitations, avoidance of eye contact, or muddled phrasing may be indicative of an informant's uncertainty, emotionality, or indeed dishonesty. More important, however, is the positive side of the matter, namely that there are few barriers to the informant providing the information sought, and perhaps even more. The interviewee, moreover, has considerable freedom in stressing or downplaying particular aspects, in elaborating or in avoiding other aspects, and has the freedom of formulation. All this then means that interviews are a rich source of information for research.

At the same time, whatever is an advantage from one particular vantage point automatically has disadvantages from an opposite perspective. For instance, the fact that the interview allows for some personal contact may in itself be threatening to some participants. Or they may object to the interviewer probing their personal living conditions. Similarly, the atmosphere of free expression of ideas and feelings may put stress on some informants – or on researchers who have difficulties with handling the emotional stress that may be involved. The interview demands a degree of sensitivity to one another that requires both skill and attention, something not everyone can offer. Also, the fact that the interview is recorded or filmed may de-naturalize the situation, and the interviewee may feel strained by it.

Some points in carrying out interviews are quite important. The major ones are:

- Explain to the informant what the purpose of the interview is, and make him/her comfortable.
- Ask the informant for permission to record the interview.
- Thank the informant for his/her willingness to spend time on the interview.
- Encourage the informant to speak freely about the issues at hand.
- Use your questions as you prepared them. Do not deviate from them, but address them in the flow of the conversation.
- If you have decided on a certain type of interview (see below), follow the order of the questions that you have prepared, in the same order for each participant.
- Do not skip questions.
- Do not be afraid of silence.
- Have informants elaborate on what they said. Ask them what they mean.

When it comes to describing the types of interview that can be used for research purposes, the distinction usually made is between *structured*, *semi-structured* and *unstructured* interviews. The former is, as its name indicates, largely in the hands of the interviewer, who has prepared the questions and their order beforehand and who steers the conversation in the direction in which he or she wants it to go. In the unstructured interview, by contrast, the control is much more in the hands of the interviewee and when the talk flows freely, the interviewer interferes as little as possible. Semi-structured interviews are a mixture of both. The interviewer has a set of questions but is free to allow for unplanned talk. Structured interviews can make use of a checklist, e.g. consisting of scaling techniques, so that this type of interview comes close to being an 'oral questionnaire'; for obvious reasons, the analysis of data collected through such interviews is much more straightforward and easy than is the case with the data collected through unstructured ones, though the shadow side of it is that such interviews demand considerably more time and energy to prepare than unstructured interviews, which, however, may have to be transcribed. Also, statistical testing is possible with structured interviews.

The distinction between structured, unstructured, or semi-structured interviews is not a categorical one, but rather one of kind. A better way to characterize these different types is to place *structured* and *unstructured* at two ends of a continuum. At one end (*unstructured*), the distinction with everyday conversation becomes (after an initial phase of introduction) negligible, while at the other (*structured*) end, we are dealing in fact with an oral version of a questionnaire, where the interviewer simply records the answers given by the informant. Between, there are all sorts of interviews that (if all goes well) are suited to the occasion. You may alternate structured and unstructured moments, depending on the topic, you may encourage the interviewee to speak freely or you may restrain him or her because you are only interested in particular aspects. In sum, you may do exactly the kind of thing that is needed to provide you with the information you are seeking. The point here is not that interviewing is a technique whereby 'anything goes', but rather that it is a method that can be tailored to the needs of the researcher. Among the required skills we can list: the ability to elicit responses, and especially the *kind* of response sought through the interview, the proficiency to motivate and guide the interviewee to the kinds of topic that are needed for the investigation, the mental resilience to play on opportunities for information gathering during the interview, or to create such opportunities. Since the questions in this type of interview are completely open-ended, the success of the information-gathering process is going to depend to a high degree on the social and verbal skills of interviewers in general, and on their concrete preparation and alertness in particular. It may seem simple enough to conduct unstructured interviews – after all, we can all run a conversation, can't we? This impression, however, is thoroughly misguided. As we have said before, you will need training. This does not mean that it cannot be done at all. Julia Lachenmann, a former student of one of the authors, ran a series of one-hour interviews, half of them with professional musicians, half with physicians. We list some of the things she did in her work, because it indicates the precautions taken to make the conditions for success in interviewing optimal:

- Sometimes it can be useful to have the interviewee 'prepare' the session; Lachenmann wanted to know about the importance of reading for life, so she asked her participants to have a look at their bookshelves the night before the interview.
- Carry out some interviews to find out what questions are useful and efficient; such interviews function as a 'pilot test'.
- Ask advice of professional interviewers you may happen to know, such as senior researchers, journalists, telephone advisers, people who work in marketing, etc.
- If your aim is to run open, unstructured interviews, you can end your questions with an invitation such as "And…?".
- Build in pauses after a question has been answered; maybe the interviewee wants to add or complete his/her response.
- To make the participants feel at ease, do not present yourself as an 'expert' in the domain about which you will be interviewing.
- Let the interviewees decide for themselves where they wish to be interviewed.
- Try to sit next to the interviewee rather than in front of him/her.

Interviews clearly show advantages over standardized questionnaires. For instance, in Lachenmann's case the purpose of the study was to find out more about the importance of reading in the professional and private lives of these two groups (Lachenmann, 1999). Several informants announced explicitly at the beginning of the interview that they did not read much and had not read much either earlier in their lives, and therefore might not qualify as the right respondents in this study. These utterances were later put into perspective. Sometimes informants were themselves surprised how much they had read and how deeply they had thought about their reading. Obviously this kind of information could not have been retrieved by a questionnaire; indeed, responses to a questionnaire by the same informants would have yielded completely different data.

You should never lose sight of the fact that the interview itself is not the purpose of the whole enterprise: which is that of gathering information that will allow you to better understand the problem you are studying. But that information is gone the moment the interview is over so you want to preserve it. One way to do this is by *taking notes*. It is a very imperfect solution though. For one thing, it is impossible to record everything the interviewee is saying, and the selection made on the spot may blend out information that on hindsight you would not have wished to dispose of. Then there is the problem that in taking notes you are distracted from the interaction with the informant, who might be de-motivated by it, or find your writing disturbing. That is why most interviews are *recorded*, either in audio or audio-visually. Of course one has to guarantee informants the anonymity of the research data and the fact that what they tell the interviewer is going to be used for research purposes only, so that none of their statements will be disseminated in any way. The best way to salvage the information provided by the informant is to both record it and take notes in which you concentrate on issues that will not show in the recording, such as, 'body language': sudden body movements, smiles, gaze direction, and so forth. Also interruptions (door bell, telephone, children entering the room, etc.) should be recorded.

Whether to make an audio or video recording depends in part on the research purposes and the technical facilities at hand. Suppose you are interested in the emotions called forward by video clips. In such a case, it will be wise to record the interview on video because facial expressions give away emotions much more readily than voice alone. If you can dispense with video images, it is advisable to make a simple audio recording, first because it is much easier, and second because a tape recorder is less intrusive than a video camera. On the other hand, the amount of intrusion of a video camera should not be exaggerated, especially not with longer interviews. People get used to a (fixed and unmanned) camera readily, and are usually no longer aware of it after a few minutes. Video recording also has another particular advantage: whenever the participants become aware of the camera, they *show* it by looking at it. In any case, make sure that you record the interview, in whatever form, so that the information is not lost and is made much richer than when you have to depend solely on note-taking.

However, what do you do with the richness of views, perspectives, and responses obtained? As long as the information remains in its recorded form, it is difficult to access (though digital recordings greatly facilitate retrieval). The usual procedure is to transcribe the interview. The degree of detail with which such transcription is made differs, especially when one is interested in sentences that are not 'grammaticalized'. For most research purposes that do not have a linguistic slant, it may be sufficient to render the content of what is said, and only bother about details of language behavior when there are good reasons to do so. Note, however, that it may be of importance to bring out salient features of language, because they may reflect emphasis, uncertainty or the general attitude of the respondent.

Interviews are a powerful technique for research purposes when combined with other techniques, such as (in the case of unstructured interviews) questionnaires or (quasi-)experiments, or (in the case of structured interviews) diaries or observations. They are also excellent for exploring areas about which little is as yet known or where highly personal experience plays an important role. As always, one has to be aware of both the power and the limitation of this research technique. Because of the time and energy required to prepare and hold interviews, but even more so when one considers the amount of time that has to be invested in the transcription and in the analysis of (especially unstructured) interviews, the number of such interviews is normally highly limited, usually not more than ten are carried out by a single researcher. One should not expect generalizations from such a limited sample but generalizations are not its aim. For developing new insights and generating new hypotheses, however, the interview – when carried out appropriately – has hardly any competitors [for some examples, see Holland (1975), Radway (1984), Miall (1990) and Aaftink (2004); for reflections on how to analyze your interview protocols, see Patton (1990) and Riessman (1993)].

Depending on the objective of your research and the context you are in, you can also use *telephone interviews*. These have particular advantages: they are easy to carry out, one does not have to look for respondents, and they do not take up much time. Of course, this presupposes that one has a well-prepared list of questions that are easy to answer: in contrast to the live interview, respondents are not prepared to talk at length over the telephone to someone they do not know. Thus the telephone interview must be brief, and the interviewer must prepare it in such a way that all relevant information is collected in only a few minutes' time. This means that this information will not be as personal, rich, or detailed as with the live interview. One shortcoming is that not every person you call will be prepared to cooperate and you may thus end up with a sample that is not really representative; it may even be the case that it is precisely the people who do not wish to cooperate who are the interesting ones for your study! If you are interested in the reasons why people blush, exactly those people who are prone to it might be reluctant to answer questions, because they feel exposed or embarrassed about their predicament. If you wish to find out how people react to 'scientific' information in science fiction, the chances are high that a telephone interview will canvass mainly SF fans, and not those readers who are not so keen on this genre. This sort of self-selection is a disadvantage that is difficult to avoid and is inherent in most survey techniques.

There are a couple of special situations in which you may wish to conduct an interview with a very limited scope and purpose, namely to generate materials that can be used later in a questionnaire. This is a highly recommendable practice. Suppose you wish to know what audiences think about a highly controversial play that is shown in town, for which purpose you will present people from the audience with a questionnaire using scales to which they can react. Of course you can think of a number of adjectives that you wish them to respond to, like 'shocking', 'disgraceful' or 'interesting'. Perhaps these will do, but the point is that you do not know: you do not know whether the categories you have selected are also the categories that the respondents in your sample will find appropriate to use in their responses. There is an easy way round this, in that you simply ask a small group of people (comparable to the ones in your sample, of course) what they would say about a controversial issue or a taboo subject. By using the terms provided by those respondents in the questionnaire you later develop, you can be certain that you are not using your own idiosyncratic categories. Card-sorting techniques have been developed to facilitate the development of such categories. Since these are both simple and also highly useful ways to help in constructing a questionnaire, we will briefly describe these techniques in Chapter 6.

4.7. Focus groups

There are times when quantitative research will not work, especially when you are interested in *understanding* attitudes rather than *measuring* them. Focus groups belong to the type of qualitative research that uses interactive methods to assess attitudes, opinions, feelings, and emotions. They are a powerful means to evaluate opinions, or try out new ideas. They are also excellent for the exploratory stages of a study, to generate hypotheses. Basically, focus groups are interviews, generally of six to ten people in a group. They are not discussions or problem-solving sessions. They try to explain *why* a group thinks, feels, or reacts the way it does. They can also help to solve the problem of having categories created by people other than the researcher, which can be used later in questionnaires for a quantitative investigation.

Although it has been under-used in social research, the idea of the focus group has a long history. During World War II it was initially applied by military propaganda to find out how the films they made influenced audiences. The use of this technique was so successful that marketing and advertising companies began employing researchers to find out consumer preferences. Nowadays, it is widely used as a marketing strategy. More recently, it has started to be used in medical research (Powell & Single, 1996). Focus groups are also very powerful for political polls.

The method comprises a kind of group interview with selected people, and is organized as a discussion, in which participants express their views based on personal experience. As defined by Morgan (1988: 12), it is the "explicit use of the group interaction to produce data and insights that would be less accessible without the interaction found in a group". There are no questions and responses between researcher and participants. Rather, the researcher acts as a mediator, with participants interacting around topics he or she provides. The main objective of focus groups "is to draw upon respondents' attitudes, feelings, beliefs, experiences and reactions in a way that would not be feasible using other methods, for example observation, one-to-one interviewing, or questionnaire surveys" (Gibbs, 2004). In contrast to the direct interview, in a focus group, the data result from this interaction. For instance, a student of ours mediated a focus group to find out how readers reacted to poems (Mattos & Mendes, 2002). She gave them five cards with different poems on each card and asked them to order the cards according to their preference. After this activity, participants had to justify their order. This led to a discussion on what they really thought literature was, what they found relevant, what insights they had gained from their courses, etc. There were no previous assumptions from the researcher. The session was recorded and then transcribed, allowing for the formulation of categories, which were later used in questionnaires. These categories she ended up with were derived from the discussion itself.

To organize focus groups, you will need planning and a relaxing, quiet, comfortable environment, without distractions that can draw participants' attention. Participants should concentrate on what they are doing and discussing. They should be invited to join the group depending on the goal you have. If you are interested in the reactions of adults and teenagers to the same film, two different groups should be organized: teenagers and adults. Then you may compare the way they talk about the movie and what kinds of topics are brought up during their interaction. Remember that getting participants together may also be difficult. You need to set a time that is convenient to all of them.

In a focus group, the moderator's role is essential. A moderator needs to be creative, have verbal and social skills, show tolerance, avoid any kind of intimidation, know how to listen and empathize, and to subtly control dominant voices. Running focus groups is not easy, but after doing it a couple of times you will learn what to expect from the group reactions and how to deal with them. For instance, moderators cannot put pressure on respondents or ask them questions that will lead them in a certain direction. They have to make sure that everybody feels comfortable. They need to keep the focus of the conversation, challenge participants, tease out details, make sure meanings are understood and shared… and still remain as much in the background as possible. A moderator should avoid approving or disapproving any opinions forwarded by participants. He or she should also shy away from contributing with their own thoughts.

There has been no agreement on how many respondents form a focus group. They can be from five to 12. Most studies, however, tend to concentrate on groups of six to eight, who gather for a 1ne to 2 hour session. Individual interviews are easier to control than focus groups, which are open-ended. However, in individual interviews, respondents might feel shy or unwilling to discuss more personal topics. In groups, not only do they feel encouraged, but ideas also spring up as the conversation develops and participants develop trust in each other.

One of the advantages of focus groups is that you can gain insight into multiple perspectives at the same time. They also allow insight into shared understandings and how people are influenced by others in a group situation. Here are some basics on how to conduct focus groups, as proposed by McNamara (2004). We follow his suggestions closely:

1. Preparing for the session:
A. Identify the major objective of the meeting.
B. Carefully develop five to six questions (see below).
C. Plan your session (see below).
D. Call potential members to invite them to the meeting. Send them a follow-up invitation with a proposed agenda, session time and list of questions the group will discuss. Plan to provide a copy of the report from the session to each of the members and let them know you will do this.
E. About 3 days before the session, call each of the members to remind them to attend.
F. One hour or so before the meeting, verify that the tape recorder (or video recorder) is working properly.

2. Developing questions:
A. Prepare five to six questions (remember that a session should last 1 to 1.5 hours).
B. Always keep in mind what the problem is so that you do not lose the focus yourself.

3. Planning the session:
A. Scheduling – plan meetings to be 1 to 1.5 hours long.
B. Setting and Refreshments – hold sessions in a conference room, or any other setting with adequate air flow and lighting. Configure chairs so that all members can see each other. Provide name tags for members as well. It is also interesting, depending on local culture, to provide sandwiches or refreshments for after the meeting.
C. Agenda – consider the following agenda: welcome, review of agenda, review of goal of the meeting, individual introductions of participants, questions and answers, wrap up.
D. Membership – focus groups are usually conducted with members who have something similar in nature, e.g. similar age group, status in a program, etc. Select members who are likely to be participative and reflective.

Attempt to select members who do not know each other.
E. Plan to record the session with either an audio or audio-video recorder. Do not count on your memory. If this is difficult, involve a co-facilitator who is there to take notes.

4. Facilitating the session:
A. The major goal of facilitation is to collect useful information to meet the goal of your study.
B. Introduce yourself and the co-facilitator (if any).
C. Explain how you intend to record the session.
D. Carry out the agenda.
E. Carefully word each question before that question is addressed by the group. Allow the group a few minutes for members to carefully think of their answers. Then, facilitate discussion around the answers to each question, one at a time.
F. After each question is answered, you may summarize what you heard (the co-facilitator may do this).
G. Ensure even participation. If one or two people are dominating the meeting, then call on others.

5. Closing the session:
A. Tell members that they will receive a copy of the report generated from their answers, thank them for coming, and adjourn the meeting.
B. Immediately after the session, make sure you understand all the notes taken during the session. If necessary, write them out fully. Make sure that the pages are numbered and that you have written down all the contextual information that is relevant to your research report, such as description of place, time, participants, etc.

You must realize that focus groups, like all methods, have limitations. The results cannot be extended to an entire population and they may not be representative of the target population. In addition, group dynamics may bias the answers you get. Also, there is always the risk of moderator bias, and it may be difficult at times to substantiate levels of data reliability. Having said that, focus groups can be a rich source of information, especially when combined with other methods.

4.8. Experiment

In research, an experiment is about the best way to demonstrate *causality*. In other words, it is the most appropriate method to see whether there is a *causal* relationship between two variables. To be able to speak of causality there are three requirements. For X to cause Y: (1) with a change in X we see a change in Y; (2) logically, X has to precede Y; (3) the relation between X and Y cannot be explained by any other variable.

To meet these conditions we need manipulation of the environment, measurement of input and outcome, and to control as many variables as possible. This is the reason why many experiments (though by no means all, and few of them in cultural studies) take place in laboratories where the manipulation, control and measurement of variables are maximized and in no way comparable to what can be done in everyday life. The laboratory is a controlled environment in which special instruments allow researchers to measure whatever they want to measure. And the tasks set respondents are manipulated in such a way that their reactions will provide decisive answers to the questions investigated.

Whenever it is possible to carry out an experiment to investigate a causal link, it is preferable over all other methods. However, there are some conditions that must be fulfilled to make an experiment desirable. Usually, setting up an experiment requires a theoretical explanation of the phenomena involved. In the absence of such a theoretical foundation, it may be premature to involve oneself in experimental research.

A few lines above we said that experiments are often carried out in laboratories. In Cultural Studies, however, this is often not possible, and not even desirable. In this respect, the *field experiment* becomes of paramount importance. A laboratory often fails to replicate the everyday conditions under which cultural phenomena occur, so that one needs to become engaged in real life experiments, wherever this is feasible and without harm to individuals or groups. A field experiment is a controlled investigation in its own right, but now taking place in real life. A study of the effect of a particular TV viewing diet answers most readily to this description: viewers are assigned to specific conditions and their reactions are measured through observations or questionnaires, so that one gets as close as one might toward manipulating, measuring and controlling as many variables as is possible. However, such experiments usually take time and require a high level of expertise to adequately control the experimental settings.

Often in the methodological literature there is talk of *quasi-experiments*. These are experiments in which the criterion of randomization (of participants in a sample, for instance) cannot be met, but in which there is a control group or other measures to allow maximal control without random selection. In this book, we will not make use of the distinction, as most experiments in cultural studies are in fact of a quasi-experimental design. Nevertheless, it is good to keep this distinction in mind when interpreting the results of 'experiments' in the cultural disciplines.

So, let us now see how an experimenter works. Let us explain by using an example. Say you are interested in the effects of the order in which narrative events are presented on identification with story characters. Intuition tells us that it makes a difference whether we first meet character A instead of character B; during the rest of the story we may focus a little more on character A's actions, take his point of view on story events, and identify with him. In a study by Bower (1978) this hypothesis was examined. He wrote a short story about three characters, Rich, Harry and Cindy. Cindy is to appear in a television commercial for a suntan lotion and she asks her friends Rich and Harry to help her. Harry has to drive a motorboat, and Rich is asked to play the water skier. During the shooting several mishaps occur, but the story is kept intentionally vague about the causes. The researcher wrote two versions of the story, one that starts with a lead-in of about 300 words about Harry, and another one having a similar lead-in about Rich. After reading the story participants were asked to fill out a questionnaire registering their recall of feelings of the three characters, their idea about the causes of the mishaps, their evaluation of the characters, and a sentence recognition test. The results showed that in the group that read the version in which Harry is introduced first, participants tended to locate themselves with Harry and had identified themselves with him. Also on a number of scales they rated Harry more positively than Rich. The little accidents that happened were attributed to Rich. However, in the other group with participants that had read about Rich first, the results were exactly the reverse.

In experiments we compare the effects of at least two conditions. In Bower's experiment there were indeed two: reading a story with a Harry lead-in was one, reading the version with the Rich lead-in was the second. Procedures of experimental research allow you to draw the conclusion that the differences that may occur between the groups can be contributed to the differences in treatment only. In this case the treatment was simply reading either version of the story. The idea of experimental research is to manipulate (or, change) only one aspect of the treatment, so that you know that differences in the responses of participants are the result of that manipulation. The manipulation is also called the *independent variable*; in Bower's case, the independent variable is the character appearing in the lead-in. The *dependent variable* here was, for instance, character identification. Before you can make causal claims about the relation between independent and dependent variables there are a number of things you have to consider. Most importantly, you have to make sure that only one variable is manipulated. If Bower had decided to change two aspects of the story then it would be impossible to determine which of these alternative changes caused the effects on identification.

This is important, because you must try to avoid alternative explanations. For this you have to look into ways to check the influence of *interfering variables*. For instance, if one story had started with a Harry lead-in, the other with a Cindy lead-in, you would not know whether any observed differences in response were due to the lead-in or to the character's sex. For this reason Bower chose the other male for the second version. Interfering variables can be divided into two categories: those that we can control, and those that we cannot. For instance, in Bower's study, considering that the two characters that are evaluated are male, one might think that female readers may respond differently from male readers. We can easily control for the influence of this interfering variable (we call them 'interfering' because we are not primarily, in this case, interested in the influence of gender). We simply include an item in the questionnaire asking participants whether they are male or female, and use a statistical procedure (to be explained later) to check whether participants' sex exerted any influence on their responses. Second, we see to it that the two groups have approximately the same number of women and men, or that women and men are more or less equally distributed over the two groups.

At this point, we must discuss an important issue. Perhaps you already thought of it yourself: besides gender there may be numerous other characteristics of the participants that may influence the results, from reading experience to a dislike for this type of story, or the mood participants are in. What if in the group that reads the Rich lead-in we had all participants who have a weakness for something that is said about Rich? Wouldn't that distort the results? What if in one group we find a disproportionate number of people who dislike the role of women in advertising? Or what if there is an accidentally higher proportion of homo- and bisexual men in one group? It will be clear that these are uncontrollable interfering variables; however much we would like to, there is no way we can control for all of these, because of the sheer number of them, and also because we may not even be aware of all the variables that may play a role.

One simple way to avoid this problem is *randomization*. What you do in this procedure is to distribute participants over the conditions in such a way that each participant has an equal chance of being assigned to one of the treatments. One particular way to do this is to make a numbered list of your participants and attribute every participant with an even number to one and every participant with an uneven number to the other condition. In this way the chances that one type of participant would be over-represented in one group are considerably reduced. Thus the responses of the groups can be safely compared. Note that randomization in principle does not get rid of the problem of interfering variables. It is still possible that by pure chance one of the groups contains a disproportionate number of participants with a given characteristic. What randomization does is to make such an outcome unlikely. And although possible in theory, we know (this is where statistics comes in) that an overrepresentation of several characteristics in one group at once is highly improbable. Randomization relieves you of the burden of having to think perennially about possible intervening variables by letting the odds work against them. That is why you should use randomization *whenever you can*.

Another method to avoid interfering variables is to take care that the groups are as *homogeneous* as possible. It is essential that the differences between participants within one group (as well as between groups, as discussed above) should be limited as much as possible. In an experiment like Bower's, we do not want, for instance, people's age to range from 15 to 80, or to include people of all sorts of educational backgrounds. Chances are that when you do not have homogeneous groups you will not find significant differences *between* the groups, because they are washed away by differences that already exist *within* the groups. This requirement does bring one disadvantage: using, for instance, only students of a certain age group makes it harder to generalize your findings; students' responses to Bower's stories may be different from those of working people.

Are you ready now to perform an experiment? Not quite yet! We refer you to Chapter 6 on experiments for more detailed instructions.

4.9. Content analysis

Content analysis is a research method that analyzes the content of communication by determining the frequencies of categories of thought, language, emotions, symbols, etc., either previously defined or extracted in the course of the analysis, and comparing these frequencies with respect to their potential meaning within a specific context. Though content analysis can in principle be done by hand, it is nowadays increasingly carried out with the help of computer programs.

One of the strengths of content analysis is that it combines qualitative and quantitative approaches. It has been called a 'hybrid method' (Schreier, 2001). It is qualitative in the sense that you may code data according to categories of your own making and quantitative because these categories can then be compared and quantified in a number of ways. For instance, we might want to know some readers' preferences for particular types of texts and relate these preferences to their reasons for deciding to study literature. We may categorize the answers to an open question instrument and compare these categories to those obtained in different contexts, like what students say about their preferences for reading in two different countries. We might also want to subject the transcripts of data obtained from focus groups to coding. In this case, categories emerge inductively as a result of the qualitative research process (CAQD, or computer-aided qualitative data analysis) and serve as a coding scheme for textual analysis. CAQD is a means of evaluating hypotheses generated from qualitative data. It offers strategies for building theories by employing networks of categories. To do so, it stores documents such as interview transcripts, which you may have coded, and helps you refine categories within your data (Kelle, 1995). The frequencies of the categories can then be computed and the groups can be compared by means of statistics.

To carry out content analysis, you should do the following:

1. Think of a research question, such as students' statements of affect when responding to literature.
2. Choose a sample, for instance, Biology and Humanities students.
3. Collect their written responses to a text (or transcriptions of verbal protocols).
4. Break these texts into units, trying to find out patterns for the expressions of like or dislike, indifference, enthusiasm, etc.
5. Code these patterns according to categories, either manually of by means of a computer program.
6. Count the frequencies of the patterns.
7. Analyze the sample in relation to the frequencies found and your research question.
8. Interpret your findings, always bearing in mind their context.
9. Derive general statements that may answer your initial research question.

When you do content analysis, there are two types of sampling you can choose from. The first one consists of concentrating on lexical and syntactical units as provided by concordance programs. The concordance allows you to find the words you have selected in their context of use and investigate what relations they build with the other words that surround them. This approach is called KWIC, or keyword in context (Sinclair, 1987; 1991). The second type of sampling consists of semantic units as provided by electronic semantic dictionaries, which classify words into concepts, removing them from their context. This is why this second approach is called KWOC, or keyword out of context. Nowadays, however, semantic dictionaries are also being developed to allow you to see the context from which a certain concept derived.

When you investigate a word in its context by means of content analysis, you may read much more than only between the lines: you can read 'through' and 'behind' them and see, for instance, the ideological mesh that sustains them. By looking at implied meanings, such as the way a society portrays men and women in fairy tales or car advertisements, content analysis allows you to understand how the text functions in context, how and why it is received and produced by a certain author, culture and society, and why it has the impact it does. As it resorts to replicable methods for making specific inferences, content analysis avoids the intuitive level of much work in, for instance, critical discourse analysis. By determining the presence and the frequency of certain words or concepts within a text, content analysis will allow you not only to substantiate your claims but also to notice further patterns that you would not otherwise have noticed.

You should bear in mind, however, some of the limitations of this method:

- it can be time-consuming;
- some texts can be difficult to automate or computerize;
- programs can be difficult to obtain and to master (but the Internet is getting more and more helpful here);

The advantages, however, are worth considering because content analysis can:

- help you learn how to look for relevant patterns and establish links between them;
- be easily tailored to your needs and wishes;
- handle large amounts of text;
- use naturally occurring authentic data;
- provide valuable historical/cultural insights over time;
- offer a view into complex models of human thought and language use.

Now you could also think of the possibilities of applying this method in combination with the other research methods discussed in this chapter: diaries and the protocols of focus groups can be content analyzed, interview and think-aloud protocols as well.

4.10. Survey

You use a survey when you want to ask a large group of people a great number of the same questions, about their opinions, attitudes behavior, etc. Survey research is best used for explorative research, and it is less suited for establishing causal relations. For example, one could ask people about their television-watching habits to see whether they watch a lot of violent action movies and series, and ask them about how they figure the rate of violent crime in their hometown. Researchers found that this results in a strong correlation: the more people are exposed to TV violence, the higher they estimate the rate of violent crime in their neighborhood. However, it is hard to determine what is cause and what is effect here. It might be that the exposure to TV violence affects people's perception, but it may also be that people with certain beliefs about the crime rate are more interested in crime on TV.

In some cases, however, survey research may be your best option. For instance, when you are interested in how often certain people go to the theatre, what they get from it, whether their theatre-going habits changed over the years, survey research is the most appropriate research method. The best way to say something about someone's behavior is, of course, to observe that behavior. But when you want to examine the behavior of a large number of people, behavior that took place in the past, or behavior that you simply cannot observe (for example, because it takes place in private), then, again, survey research is the best you have.

We will briefly discuss four types of research design with surveys: cross-section studies, panel studies, trend studies, and cohort studies. Not all this information will be of practical use to the readers of this book, but it is important that you know of these possibilities, if only to be able to understand the procedures when they are referred to in the literature.

4.10.1. Cross-section study

In a *cross-section study* you make a questionnaire and present it to a sample of informants. Using the appropriate sample size and procedure you may get representative results for a particular moment in time. One disadvantage of this type of design is that it gives you just that: information about one moment in time. You do not know what preceded it, nor do you know what happened afterwards. Thus, you will be unable to tell anything about developments or trends in your data, let alone causal relations. For example, you may find out how often people in your local town visit the cinema but you do not know whether that number is declining or rising. Moreover, you do not know what the relationship is between this frequency and for instance the weather, or other cultural activities in town, like festivals. For this you need to do more than one measurement, or in other words, do a longitudinal study: a panel, trend, or cohort study.

4.10.2. Panel study

In a *panel study* you put the same set of questions to a number of people on a number of occasions. In this way you can establish changes in, for instance, their television-watching behavior. The difficulty with this method, especially for beginners, is that if you want to measure at more than two moments in time, you need rather complex calculations to establish correlations.

With only two measures (A and B; for instance A for number of hours of television watching, and B the number of television channels available to the subjects; see Figure 4.2) and two moments in time (T_1 and T_2), the statistical procedures are rather simple. A correlation is calculated between A_1 and B_2 and A_2 and B_1; if the first correlation exceeds the second, one can assume that A 'caused' B. However, with more than two moments in time you need much more complicated Lisrel-analyses, not discussed in this book (see Saris & Stronkhorst 1984).

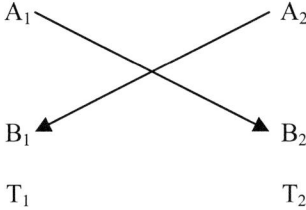

Figure 4.2: Two measures and two moments

Furthermore, panel studies have a number of other disadvantages. First, they can be very expensive, because the tests have to be administered several times. Second, a general problem is the increasing number of dropouts; because of the longer running time of the study there is more and more chance that participants will decide to withhold their cooperation. Third, there is a chance for 'panel effects': because informants answer the same questions a number of times they might start answering in a different way as compared to informants answering the same questions only once. They might also become more careless over time filling out the questionnaires, or they may become more aware of certain things related to the study and will change their behavior or attitude as a result of the study itself.

4.10.3. Trend studies

Trend studies are surveys conducted on a regular basis using samples of a certain population. An example is opinion polls for elections.

4.10.4. Cohort studies

Cohort studies, finally, are quite similar to panel studies. The difference is that, while panel studies select representative subjects from a certain group, cohort studies follow a certain group of people who have something in common over time. Here too, there are some disadvantages related to time. First, subjects of one cohort will become being less and less alike. Second, the problem of dropouts: the cohorts will become smaller and smaller over time. Third, with time so many other things change: one cannot distinguish between effects that are due to the cohort (namely a certain characteristic of that group) and changes due to the aging of the subjects and effects due to the changing environment of the subjects.

To summarize, most suitable to the readers of this book seems to be the cross-section studies (taking into account its disadvantages), or the panel studies (with two measurements).

4.11. What is next?

In this chapter you have been introduced to some research methods applied in empirical studies. You have also seen concrete examples of qualitative and quantitative research methods and realized that the distinction is sometimes not as sharp as the fierce battles fought in the Social Sciences between the two camps would suggest.

Next, we will focus on experiments. First however, we will tell you something about the ins and outs of designing a questionnaire. This research instrument can be used for both experiments and, of course, various other methods of investigation.

4.12. Other sources

4.12.1. Observations

- Shaughnessy and Zechmeister (1985)
- Bechtel & Zeisel (1987).
- See for an example of a category system of behavior: SYMLOG, by Bales & Cohen, 1979, p. 413).
- Kinographs: codes for facial expressions, used preferably for coding behavior recorded on film, because of the great number of behaviors going on simultaneously. (Birdwhistell, 1970, p. 260).

4.12.2. Electronic texts

There are many sites for downloading electronic texts. Here are a few:
- the project Gutenberg e-text wrnpc10.txt: http://promo.net/pg/
- e-books of the University of Adelaide Library: http://etext.library.adelaide.edu.au/t/t6

- public library and digital archives "ibiblio":
  http://www.ibilio.org/pha/events/index.html

4.12.3. Concordances

- *MICROCONCORD*, developed by Mike Scott & Tim Johns. Oxford University Press, 1993. (Oxford University Press, Electronic Publishing, Walton Street, Oxford OX2 6DP, UK)
- *MONOCONC for Windows* developed by Michael Barlow at Rice University (USA). Athelstn, 2476 Bolsover, Suite 464, Houston TX 77005, USA. E-mail: athel@nol.net
- TACT: Centre for Computing in the Humanities, Robarts Library, Room 1429A, University of Toronto, Toronto, Ontario, Canada M5S 1AS.
- *WORDSMITH*, developed by Mike Scott. Oxford University Press, 1996. Oxford University Press, Electronic Publishing, Walton Street, Oxford OX2 6DP, UK. A demo version can be downloaded electronically from the OUP web page.

4.12.4. Analyzing qualitative research material

- NUD*IST Software, N6, (www.qsr.com.au) that allows you to import and code textual data; retrieve, review and recode coded data; search for combinations of words in the text or patterns in your coding; and import data from and export data to quantitative analysis software.
- KWALITAN (see www.kwalitan.net) for the analysis of open, unstructured interviews, documents and reports, articles in newspapers, diaries and journals, and so on. But the qualitative, interpretative analysis is not restricted to written material, it also extends to objects like paintings, pictures, and video fragments. KWALITAN is a program that supports the researcher in performing this kind of analysis. It takes care of an efficient storage of the data and offers several features to analyze the qualitative material, such as coding, retrieving, categorization of codes, overviews of codes or words in the text, keywords in context, and writing memos. With the help of KWALITAN you can analyze text, pictures, audio fragments and video fragments.

CHAPTER FIVE

HOW TO CONSTRUCT A QUESTIONNAIRE

5.1. Introduction

This chapter is about asking questions: how to construct a workable questionnaire and collect data from people (interviewees, participants of experiments, or respondents in a survey study). Before getting to the practical aspects, we have to distinguish between types of questions. The first difference is that between open and closed questions (see Section 5.1). The second one has to do with the level of information that different types of questions allow you to assess (Section 5.2). We then present an overview of various techniques for eliciting information (Section 5.3), and hints on how to formulate questions (Section 5.4). Finally, we devote attention to the design (Section 5.5) and layout (Section 5.7) of questionnaires, as well as to instructional (Section 5.6) and procedural (Section 5.8) aspects.

First, let us see what the difference between open and closed questions entails. Imagine you are asked to do research for organizers of an exhibition in a museum. What they want to know is whether using music in their audio tour would enhance visitors' aesthetic experience of the objects, and if so, what type of music works best for what art works. How would you go about it? You could, of course, ask visitors "How did you enjoy the exhibition, and in what way do you think the music influenced your response to the paintings?" This is an *open* question: respondents can give any answer they wish. You analyze their answers, written or taped, to figure out whether you can draw some general conclusions about the use of music in the audio tour. You could also, like Limbert and Polzella (1998) did, use *closed* questions. In their experiment, the effect of music style on observers' perception of representational and abstract paintings was examined. Participants were randomly assigned to three groups: one where the music style matched that of the paintings, one where it did not, and one group where no music was played. Eight paintings were to be rated by visitors on so-called semantic differential scales, that is, rating scales composed of two adjectives with opposite meanings, as in the following example:

I find this painting							
Active	__	__	__	__	__	__	__ Passive
Ordered	__	__	__	__	__	__	__ Chaotic
Soft	__	__	__	__	__	__	__ Hard
Ugly	__	__	__	__	__	__	__ Beautiful

Figure 5.1: Closed question: a semantic differential (Limbert & Polzella, 1998).

These researchers found that ratings became more extreme when the paintings were accompanied by matching music. There was, however, a so-called main effect for impressionistic music: all paintings were rated less active and more beautiful as an effect of this music.

As discussed in Chapter 3, each research method has its pros and cons. When you are conducting exploratory research, open-ended questions are the appropriate way to collect data. It is fair to say that studying the influence of music on the aesthetic experience of paintings is pioneer research. However, we recommend using closed questions for many different reasons. First, they are much easier to answer, as well as to process and analyze. Second, open-ended questions bring with them what you could call a double interpretation problem. Respondents may understand the terms you use in a different way from you. Note that you may have this problem with closed questions, too. In addition, however, the responses to open questions demand supplementary interpretation by the researcher: how sure are you that you interpret correctly what respondents are saying? It is both hard and time consuming to determine whether the different wordings respondents use mean the same or whether their responses should be classified in different categories. This makes open responses less fit for computer analyses and it will be trickier to come to reliable conclusions. Also, you should consider that in many cases you do not want respondents to spend too much time on your questionnaire (people may have other plans after their visit to the museum). Closed questions are filled out much more quickly and more easily than open ones. But you can add one or two open questions to your questionnaire. The advantage here is that you can use these comments to check whether you have overlooked some important aspect of response. Or you may select some typical quotes from the responses to use them as illustration material in your report. Another advantage is that you have some extra control over the validity of your findings: you can use open responses to check whether respondents interpreted the closed questions correctly. Still, it is advisable, especially for beginners, to concentrate on closed questions. As Limbert and Polzella (1998) show, these may bring you faster and more reliable results, which can be revealing even when you are dealing with relatively unexplored territory.

Because of these advantages, we will concentrate on the techniques of closed questions here. To draw up a questionnaire, first consider what you want to measure. In addition, as discussed in Chapter 3, you also need to consider what different dimensions there are within those aspects that you want to assess. While making your questionnaire, keep track of which questions you think relate to which of your constructs or dimensions. This may help you to avoid confusion later on when you analyze your data. It may also prevent you from formulating more questions than you actually need. The questions you do include should provide you with information about those dependent and independent variables of which you want to examine the interrelations (check your conceptual model for this). In other words, the aim of the preparation of your questionnaire is to further refine your operational definitions: from more or less abstract concepts, you now move to concrete items.

Before you set out to build your own instrument for data collection, you should check whether there already is a test that you could use, either in full or in part. In the libraries of psychology departments there may be a section devoted to tests. Also, publications you may have come across during your literature search may include a questionnaire or reference to some test that you could adopt for (or adapt to) your own research. Remember that there is nothing against using other people's work, as long as you make the proper references in your report. This is also advantageous, as it allows comparison with earlier research. Moreover, in some cases, existing questionnaires will already have been tested for their validity, reliability (see Chapter 3), usability, and understandability.

5.2. Levels of measurement

A questionnaire measures things you want to know more about. Measuring is basically counting but the way this counting is done can vary. When we say that it is cold in Siberia, this is, in a sense, a measurement without a stated comparison. If we say that it is colder in Siberia than in Greece, that is also a kind of measurement, only one that contains more information than the first. Or, when we say that temperatures measured in Siberia and Greece yesterday were minus 34 and 5 degrees Celsius, respectively, that measurement contains even more information. These differences in the amount and precision of information provided by measurements are called 'levels of measurement'.

The level on which you conduct your measurements has important implications for the quality of the information you gather, the calculations that you carry out, the statistical tests that you can perform, and consequently the relevance of the conclusions you draw. Therefore, you have to consider on what level your measurements will take place: on a nominal, ordinal, interval or ratio level. Think of these levels in terms of a *taxonomy*: each level contains the information that any level below it also provides. Thus the ratio level contains all the information that the interval level contains, *plus* some more information.

The lowest level is that of *nominal* scales. Basically, this is merely counting. The best way to understand what this means is to remember that nominal scales register 'names' only. Imagine that you want to know respondents' gender, because you expect some differences between men and women in their responses to your questions. You ask them whether they are male or female, and thus you collect for every respondent the information you need for your analyses. What you can do with nominal measurement, for instance, is calculate a percentage of male and female respondents: 66.7% are female and 33.3% are male. You can also make a frequency distribution per experimental condition to show how many male and female respondents there were in each group. But it stops right here. For instance, you cannot make up what the 'middle measurement' is, the median, simply because the data are not arranged from low to high (and of course, in this case, also because there are only two sexes).

As we will learn later on, in some cases you can opt for a higher level of measurement, in which case you should. However, when assessing your respondents' places of residence, or their sex, or the name of the training program they are in, there is only one way: you use a nominal scale.

You can measure nominal levels by using open questions. Because you figure that you do not know all the possible cities, towns, and villages your respondents live in, you simply ask "Where do you live?" and leave some space open for their answers. Again, however, this can be confusing. Some people can refer to towns, others to cities; others might give you a detailed address. The question you should always bear in mind is: to what purpose am I asking this? Is it relevant to my research? Why? Therefore, it is better that you provide respondents with options that are exclusive and collectively exhaustive. In other words, the items should not overlap, and each respondent should only mark one option. Imagine you want to know which composers people attending a concert enjoy. For several evenings you ask a random sample of concert-goers to fill out a questionnaire. One question you ask your respondents is the following:

Which piece of music did you like best in the program tonight? That of...

__ Mozart
__ Haydn
__ Bartok
__ Schönberg

Figure 5.2: A nominal measure

The list of composers is complete (collectively exhaustive), and each respondent can only tick one of the options (there is only one they can like best). What you can do here is make a frequency count or calculate a percentage: for instance, you might consider calculating the percentage of your sample that liked the performance of Mozart best. You could also say which percentage liked those of the modern composers best and how large the percentage is that preferred the contemporary composers? If you do want to know this, you need more information: although you now know which piece of music was liked best by each of the respondents, you do not know anything about their evaluations of the performances of the other three composers. You just have one name. It might be that there are a number of respondents who liked Bartok second best, right after Mozart, or respondents who liked Schönberg just a little better than Mozart and therefore ticked his name. We do not know how many respondents liked the classical part of the program better than the contemporary.

To establish what the exact order is of respondents' preferences requires measurement on an *ordinal* level. This asks for a different format:

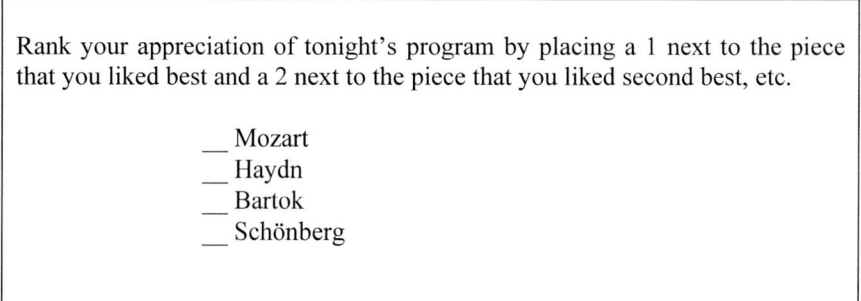

Rank your appreciation of tonight's program by placing a 1 next to the piece that you liked best and a 2 next to the piece that you liked second best, etc.

__ Mozart
__ Haydn
__ Bartok
__ Schönberg

Figure 5.3: An ordinal measure: the rank-order rating scale

Measurement on an ordinal level gives you more information than nominal measurement. Now we know for each respondent which performance was preferred over the other compositions. One visitor might respond as follows: 1 for Mozart, 2 for Haydn, 3 for Bartok, and 4 for Schönberg. With the previous formulation of our question we would only know she liked the Mozart best; now we also know that she preferred the Bartok to the Schönberg.

However, there is still some information missing. We do not know what the 'distance' is between Mozart and Haydn in each individual case. Was it a difficult choice the respondent had to make, or an easy one? Did she like the Mozart performance a lot better or only just a bit? As a result, again, we cannot do any mathematical calculations on the data the respondents gave us: we cannot add, subtract, multiply, or calculate an average.

Measuring on an *interval* or *ratio* level allows you to do just that. Now you can do more than just tell whether one respondent liked the Mozart performance more than the Haydn, we can also tell *how* much. Both interval and ratio scales have the same distance between each point of measurement. The only difference between the two is that ratio scales include an absolute zero point, and interval scales do not. A good example of an interval measure is degrees Celsius. It does have a zero point, you would think but it is arbitrarily defined as the freezing point of water, and consequently not absolute. As a result we cannot multiply measures on the Celsius scale. Therefore, we do know that the distance between 5 and 10 degrees Celsius is the same as between 10 and 15 degrees Celsius, but we cannot say that 15 degrees Celsius is three times as warm as 5 degrees Celsius.

Let us now contrast this with the possibilities that a *ratio* measurement gives us. Just like with an interval scale, we know the distances between any two points. In addition, it has a real, absolute zero point. In science temperature is often measured in degrees Kelvin. On this scale, the zero point (which equals minus 273.15 degrees Celsius) is the lowest possible temperature in the universe: it is the temperature where all electrons stand still, literally – therefore temperature can sink no further. In this sense, zero degree Kelvin represents an absolute zero point of the measurement. Age is another example of a ratio scale. Thus, we can say that someone who is 20 is twice as old as someone who is 10 (ratio of 10 to 20 is as that of 1 to 2, in other words 10 is one-half of 20). This is impossible for interval scales. It is not true that 10 degrees Celsius is twice as warm as 5 degrees Celsius, but 10 degrees Kelvin is twice as warm as 5 degrees Kelvin. So with measures on a ratio level we can do more than measures on an interval level: we can multiply and divide.

Let us look at two examples of question formats to make the distinction between interval and ratio clearer. Figure 5.4 would allow us to measure on an interval level how much our respondents liked the Bartok performance better than the Haydn.

I liked the Bartok performance much better than the Haydn.

Strongly disagree   Strongly agree
   –3   –2   –1   0   +1   +2   +3

Figure 5.4: An interval measure: the Likert scale

This scale enables us to calculate an average score and perform tests that give us much more information than those allowed for nominal and ordinal scales. This will be explained in more detail in Chapter 8. What you need to remember now is that the higher the measurement, the more mathematical calculations you can do on your data, and as a result, the more powerful the statistical analyses you can perform. For example, we could examine the interrelationship between the response to a musical performance and respondents' background variables, like their age or educational level. Note that the scale above includes zero. Nevertheless, one respondent who may have marked the 3 does not necessarily like the Mozart piece three times as much as one who may have scored a 1. Zero is chosen arbitrarily here; with other labels at the extremes, it would have been positioned elsewhere. A final observation about the format presented in Figure 5.4: a disadvantage here is that you have to ask participants to compare each composer with each of the other composers.

That means six comparisons. Maybe we can think of a more efficient way to obtain our data that will not cost participants that much work.

Figure 5.5 presents a so-called constant-sum rating scale, which results in data on a ratio level.

Please divide 100 points according to how much you liked each piece of music. (It is also possible to give zero points).
 __ Mozart
 __ Haydn
 __ Bartok
 __ Schönberg

Figure 5.5: A ratio measure: the constant-sum rating scale

5.3. Types of questions

Now let us discuss the formats that you can use for your questions. You will find that each has its advantages and disadvantages. It all depends really on the purpose of your study, the type of information you need and the level of measurement that you require.

5.3.1. Checklist

Imagine you want to know which television news bulletins respondents are familiar with, or which literary magazines they know, or which movie genres they see on a regular basis. In that case you can present them with a checklist of items in that category, and request them to tick those they are familiar with, or regularly watch, etc. Surely you want to make your list of items as complete as possible. This will make it easier for respondents to fill out your questionnaire, and easier for you to process the results: they just have to check the appropriate box; they do not have to think of alternatives themselves and write them down; and you can simply code the questionnaire, attributing numbers to each item and enter them in the computer for analyses. You can, of course, add an option "Other(s), namely…". The information that respondents give here, for instance in a pilot study, may help you to complete your checklist when you run the study with a larger group of respondents. It is important to add one last item that reads "None of the above" so that no uncertainty exists about respondents having or not having answered the questions.

There is one problem in using a checklist: it may guide respondents to certain answers that they would not have thought of themselves, and it is impossible to determine to what extent it does. The list may include items that respondents are not themselves familiar with, but which they now feel tempted to tick, for instance because they wish to make a positive impression on the researcher. There are ways to avoid this problem, demonstrated in a study by West *et al.* (1993). The researchers established a positive correlation between, on the one hand, 'exposure to print,' and, on the other, vocabulary knowledge and cultural knowledge: the higher the respondents scored on measures for reading, the more extensive was their vocabulary and the richer their cultural knowledge. These variables were assessed using checklists. Now, what we know about measures for reading is that respondents tend to report more reading than actually takes place. One could ask respondents to record their daily activities in a diary, which has been shown to be much more reliable than interviews or questionnaires (Carp & Carp, 1981). However, this method takes a lot of time, and thus it may be hard to find respondents willing to engage in such a long-term cooperation. West and his colleagues used a swifter method that, in addition, seems relatively immune against socially desirable responses. The respondents were given the *Author Recognition Test* and the *Magazine Recognition Test*, both checklists containing the names of real authors and real magazines next to foils (non-existent authors or magazine titles). The respondents were asked to scan the lists and check those names known to them (see Figure 5.6).

Below you will see a list of 25 names. Some of the people in the list are popular writers (of books, magazine articles, and/or newspaper columns) and some are not. Please read the names and put a check mark next to the names of those individuals who you know to be writers. Do not guess, but only check those who you know to be writers.

___ Isaac Asimov
___ *Isabel Beck*
___ *P.E. Bryant*
___ Barbara Cartland
___ James Clavell
___ *Gerald Duffy*
___ Ian Fleming
___ Stephen J. Gould
___ Andrew Greeley
___ *John Guthrie*
___ Dean Koontz
___ Judith Kranz
___ Louis L'Amour
___ *Isabelle Liberman*
___ James Michener
___ *Keith Rayner*
___ *Nancy Roser*
___ Sidney Sheldon
___ Danielle Steel
___ *Robert Tierney*
___ J.R.R. Tolkien
___ Richard Venezky
___ Irving Wallace
___ Joseph Wambaugh
___ Bob Woodward

Figure 5.6: Checklist (taken from West *et al.*, 1993)

In the list the names in italics are the foils – in the original format they were not, of course, in italics. The instruction used resulted in only a few foils being ticked. This means that almost all respondents did not mark as many names as possible to show how well-read they were, but only those writers they actually did know. In the scoring system, the proportion of foils ticked was subtracted from the proportion of correct items that were ticked.

Finally, when entering the data of a checklist you should realize that every item on your checklist must be treated as a separate dichotomous variable (more on this in Chapter 7). Asking respondents whether they are familiar with a number of literary magazines, each item on the list is a variable, and each variable can have two values: a score 1 for "yes", and a 0 for "no". This means, of course, that measurement through a checklist is on the nominal scale.

5.3.2. Multiple choice

Multiple-choice questions can have three forms: (1) a question followed by a number of answer options; (2) an incomplete sentence that respondents are asked to complete by marking one of the options; (3) a statement respondents are asked to respond to by choosing the options already provided.

The format of a multiple-choice question allows you, generally, to collect data on either a nominal or an ordinal level. An example of measurement on an ordinal level would be asking respondents how often they read poetry, and providing them with the following answers: (A) less than once a year; (B) once a month; (C) once a week; (D) more than once a week. An example of measurement on a nominal level can be found in a study by Andringa (1986). In her experiment she examined whether readers' sympathy and understanding for either one of two fictional characters in a story could be manipulated by narrative perspective (point of view). The story was about the conflict between a thief and a judge. In one group, the respondents read a version in which the thief was the I-narrator. In another group, the judge was the I-narrator. In a third version, the story was told by an external, neutral, narrator. The experiment was conducted with 14 to 15- and 16 to 17-year-old respondents, who were asked to read one of the three texts and answer questions like those in Figure 5.7.

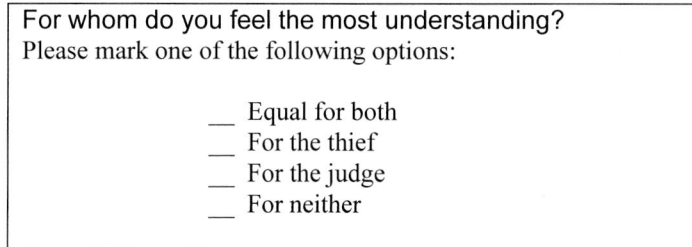

Figure 5.7: A non-ordinal multiple-choice question (Andringa, 1986)

Analysis of the data obtained showed that the manipulation did have an effect. Most of the time it was the character-I-narrator that received most of the respondents' understanding. It is, however, an overall effect that was demonstrated. With measurement on a nominal level it is sometimes hard to specify where exactly the differences between groups are significant: is the significant result due to the difference between the numbers of respondents who felt understanding for the thief? Or can the source be found when we look at the results for the judge? Moreover, maybe it is the differences between the two age groups that caused the significant result. We include the two figures representing the results below (Figures 5.8 and 5.9) just to show you how hard it is to interpret these results.

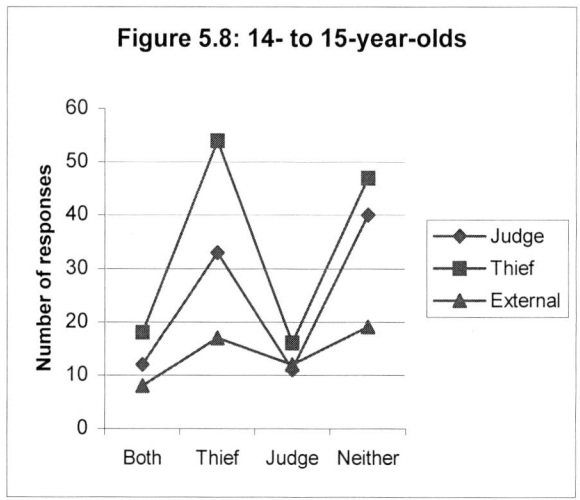

Figure 5.8: 14 to 15-year-olds

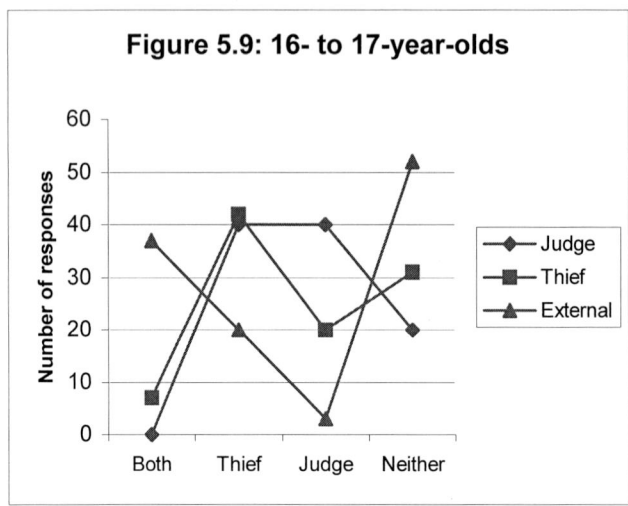

Figure 5.9: 16- to 17-year-olds

We do see all sorts of differences between the three versions (the three lines in the graphs), and differences between the two graphs, but how can we say anything about the differences between the two age groups that caused the result? You should remember this problem when designing your questionnaire.

Here are some more basic things you need to keep in mind when constructing multiple-choice questions:

- First, you should avoid asking more than one thing at a time. A question like "How often do you go to the theater or the opera?" might lead to confusion. What if one respondent goes to the opera twice a year, but almost every month to the theater? This question should therefore be split up into two separate questions.
- Also avoid double, let alone triple, negatives. Being asked to respond to a statement like "I do not think there is not enough opera on television" makes it hard for respondents to determine what they are actually saying when they mark either "Totally agree" or "Totally disagree."
- When asking people what their favorite pastime is, do not provide them with options like "Going to a music performance" next to "Going to the opera", or "Reading" next to "Reading poetry." The answers need to be mutually exclusive; in other words, avoid overlapping answers.

- Avoid guiding respondents by using evaluative wording. "Do you also think that the local concert hall should finally program more modern music?" This formulation makes it clear what the opinion of the researchers is and suggests that there has hardly been any modern music till now. Such questions are suggestive, and should be avoided at all cost. But you *can* include statements that express a value or standpoint and ask respondents to what extent they agree or disagree, such as: "There should be more opera on television." To avoid respondents thinking that it is the position of the researchers that is expressed, you can formulate the statement a little differently: "I think there should be more opera on television."
- The number of options should be determined by the aim of your study: How much detail do you need? Also, consider how much detail the respondents want. In general, the more complex the matter, the more detailed answers you want to provide. For many participants, responding to "I am against censorship by local library employees" might need a more refined set of answer options than "Have you visited the local library over the past week?"
- Sometimes it is important to avoid all respondents giving the same answer. Imagine you are interested in what your respondents think of censorship in their library. You expect most respondents in your sample to be against. You could give them two options (e.g. "I am in favor of censorship." and "I am against censorship.") but this will not give you much information. Maybe most of them (about 95%) will be against it. Depending on the purpose of your study, it may be more interesting to refine your options on the "against" side by including options like "I am against censorship, except in the case of outspoken racist material" or "I am against censorship, except when young children need to be protected against violent material." Note that here you should allow respondents to mark more than one answer, because one does not always exclude the other.
- Carefully consider whether you want to include a neutral position. In cases where you are sure that respondents have a strong opinion about something, do not provide them with options like "Don't know" or "Yes/No". On the other hand, retain such options when in real life a non-committed stand is a real possibility.

- Finally, place the options in a 'logical' order. So, "How often did you visit the local library over the past six months" should not be followed by "three times per month"; "once a week"; "never"; "twice a week".

5.3.3. Graphic rating scale

The format of a graphic rating scale requires respondents to mark a point on a continuum to indicate their attitude toward an object. If you are interested in what Dostoyevsky's readers think of the depth of the characters in his books, you could formulate a question like this:

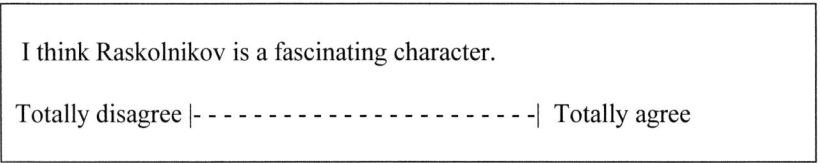

Figure 5.10: Graphic rating scale (non-comparative)

The advantage of such a scale is that you give respondents the possibility to choose from an infinite number of positions to express their own attitude toward the character. Also, the data that you collect allow you to do more complex tests and therefore draw more precise conclusions about what is going on in your data set. One disadvantage, however, is that it takes some more time to process the results: for every questionnaire you have to measure the distance from the left extreme with a measuring rod.

Graphic rating scales come in two variants: you can choose to make your scale comparative or non-comparative. With the latter, your respondents are asked to judge something (e.g. Raskolnikov) in an absolute sense. They are left free to compare it with anything. The danger here is, of course, that they may make comparisons that are not relevant to the study (and unknown to you). They could compare him, for example, with other characters in *Crime and Punishment*, with characters in other novels by Dostoyevsky, or with a character from a book by some other author they recently read. In a comparative rating scale you give respondents a point of reference:

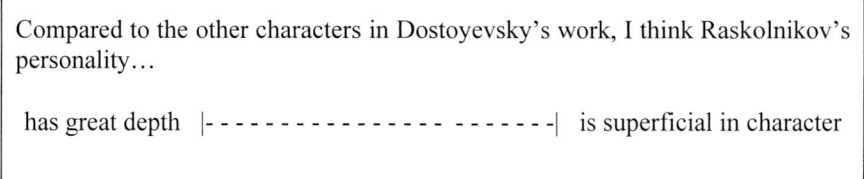

Figure 5.11: Graphic rating scale (comparative)

Carefully consider the labeling of the extremes. In some cases you may want to avoid making them too extreme because this could force your respondents into the center of the scale. In other situations, you should beware of making the end of the scales too mild, because it would then make respondents opt for the ends of the scale. It all depends on what you expect from your respondents, with your expectations preferably based on a pilot study (see Section 5.8). The reason you should avoid respondents all clustering together at either the center or at one of the extremes of your scale is that this results in loss of information. What you need is a sensitive instrument for differences in attitude that you expect from your respondents; and you do not want it to be ruined by a ceiling or floor effect (that is, with the lion share of respondents clustering either on the extreme left or right side).

Graphic rating scales produce data on an interval level of measurement. We may express the scores here in, for instance, centimeters, but remember that score 0 is an arbitrary zero point; it is not inconceivable that the measure continues beyond the point of "has great depth" (for instance "has extreme depth"). Hence, our measure in centimeters is not as absolute as it may seem at first sight.

5.3.4. Itemized rating scale

An itemized rating scale is much the same as a graphic rating scale, except that here you ask respondents to choose from a limited number of labeled categories. The format is somewhat related to multiple-choice questions, except that here you always measure at least on an ordinal level. As we have seen, with multiple-choice questions this is not always the case. Imagine you want to know how the audience of a play evaluated the performance:

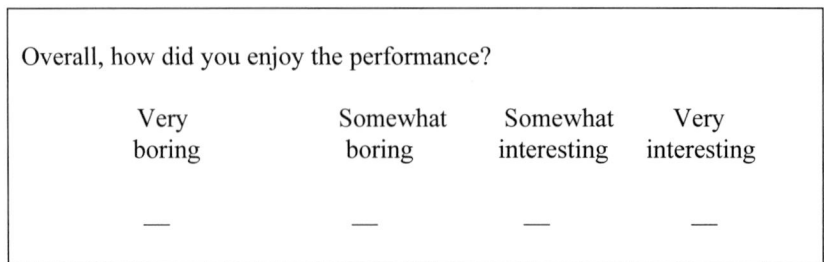

Figure 5.12: Itemized rating scale

There are a number of things we can note here. First of all we need to emphasize that we are dealing with a scale rather than a multiple-choice question. The format suggests to your respondents that they are dealing with a continuum. Second, as you can see, in this particular example of an itemized rating scale there is no middle ('neutral') position. With an even number of options you force respondents to make a choice. As we discussed before, in some cases this is perfectly legitimate, for instance, when you are sure your respondents do have an opinion about the issue at hand. However, in some situations there is a chance that some of them are unfamiliar with the object of your scale; in such a case you should leave them the possibility to answer "no opinion." Think of the danger that some will simply come up with an answer even though they have no opinion, or simply skip the question, in which case you do not know whether they were unwilling or unable to answer the question.

Another consideration is whether you want to describe the items with words (e.g. "Totally disagree", "Disagree", "Neutral", "Agree", "Totally agree") or simply indicate them with numbers. In a study by Gibson *et al.* (2000) the questionnaire presented below was used (Figure 5.13). The purpose of the study was to examine the relation between people's inner states and their preference for music. For instance, when we are sad, do we seek out music that matches our feelings or do we prefer happy music to avoid becoming even more depressed? In this experiment researchers focused on the effect of romantic deprivation on musical preferences. Their respondents, high-school students, were subdivided into people with high scores on a (standard) test for loneliness and those with low scores on that test. They were shown a number of video clips, some classified as love-celebrating music, and some as love-lamenting. Right after viewing the clips they were asked to rate them on these scales:

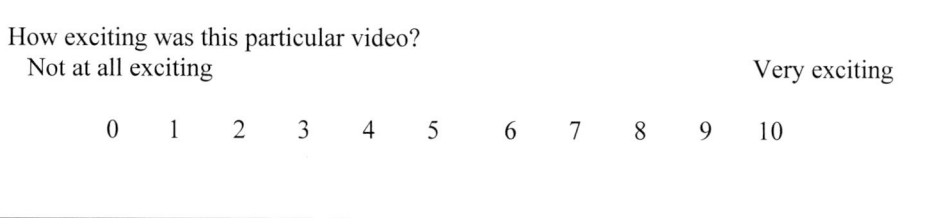

Figure 5.13: Itemized rating scale (numbered) (from Gibson et al., 2000)

Now the other items are presented in exactly the same format: (b) How good was this music video? (c) How good did it make you feel? (d) How enjoyable were the visual images in this video? (e) How good was the singing in this music video? (f) How good were the lyrics in this music video? (g) How good was the band in this performance? (h) How much do you like this group or performer in general? The purpose of questions (a) to (c) was to assess a general response; (d) to (g) focus on specific components; and (h) measures respondents' liking of the performers beyond the particular music video that was shown. It was found that loneliness had no effect on respondents' enjoyment of love-lamenting songs. On the other hand, love-celebrating songs were less enjoyed by highly lonely males as compared to less lonely males. Females responded the other way round: highly lonely female respondents enjoyed the love-celebrating music clips more than their less lonely counterparts.

The advantage with verbalized items ("Totally disagree", etc.) is that respondents know rather precisely what each option means; having worded the options it will be easier for your respondents to make a choice. On the other hand, numbers allow you to treat your measure as an interval scale: it is clear that the distance between 1 and 2 is equal to that between 7 and 8. Thus, in the experiment by Gibson and colleagues, more powerful analyses could be conducted, so as to find out the difference in responses between male and female respondents, highly lonely and less lonely ones, to love-lamenting and love-celebrating music video clips. Such conclusions as were drawn by these researchers are only possible with measures of an interval or higher level of measurement.

In constructing an itemized rating scale, you can choose between a balanced and an unbalanced scale: with an equal number of favorable and unfavorable items you have a balanced scale; with more items on one of the two ends of the scales you have an unbalanced scale (see Figure 5.14). You may want to choose this in case you expect the overall majority of respondents to be on one side. In that case it is important to make that part more refined so as to enable any differences that may exist among your respondents.

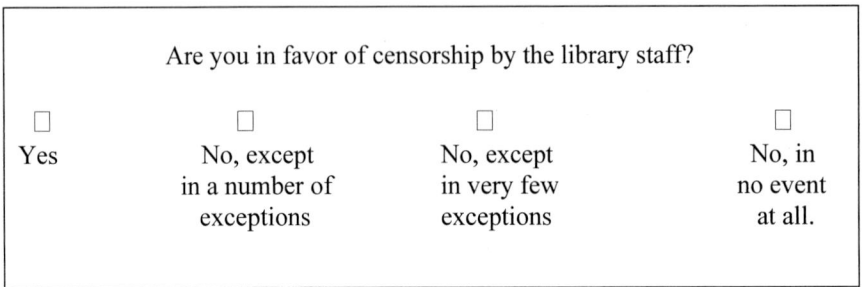

Figure 5.14: Itemized rating scale: unbalanced

There is no general rule to decide how many points a scale should have. In attitude measurement, researchers generally choose either a five-point or a seven-point scale. The advantage of seven over five points is that it is more precise: the more points a scale has the more exact the information respondents can give you. On the other hand, this only holds up to a certain extent: keep adding points and sooner or later the extra precision will become an illusion. Are respondents really able to distinguish what a score 10 means on a 15-point scale as compared to a score 9 or 11? Also, in some cases you may not even need so much precision: with a question like "Do you want to finish reading the story?" a two-point scale would suffice: Yes/No.

5.3.5. Rank-order rating scale

With this type of question, respondents are asked to place a number of items in a certain order. They compare them, using a criterion you may have given them and decide on the hierarchy. We discussed an example of such a scale earlier in this chapter (Figure 5.3). Respondents are, for instance, asked to rate their favorite music piece by placing a 1 next to the piece they liked best, a 2 next to the piece they liked second best, etc. It is important not to include too many items; otherwise it may become too hard for respondents to handle. Another requirement is that all respondents should be well acquainted with all the items presented.

5.3.6. Constant-sum rating scale and fractionation rating scale

Using a constant-sum rating scale, you ask your respondents to allocate a set number of points according to some criterion to some cultural entity, e.g. operas. We have already seen this type of scale in Figure 5.5. A fractionation rating scale also allows you to treat the results on a ratio level. You ask respondents to compare something (e.g. an author) with a reference object. Compare the fractionation rating scale below with the constant sum format used in Figure 5.5.

If Flaubert is assumed to score 100 points in terms of being important for world literature, how would you compare each of the following authors?

Flaubert	100 points
Sterne	... points
Dostoyevsky	... points
Stendhal	... points
Dickens	... points

Figure 5.15: Fractionation rating scale

A disadvantage of this measure is the possibility that, using another point of reference, you would find different results. Also, some respondents may exaggerate their preference for one of the authors, for example, attributing 500 points to Dickens. Such extreme values bias averages.

5.3.7. Likert scale

With Likert scales, participants are asked to respond to a statement, indicating the degree to which they agree or disagree with it. This is one of the most frequently used techniques in attitude measurement. In principle, it results in an ordinal scale; but, in practice, it is treated as an interval scale. In any event, make sure that the boxes to tick are at equal distance from each other; otherwise you cannot treat the results as interval measurements. To build a Likert scale, you first generate a great number of favorable and unfavorable statements about, for instance, a story character. You should really try to write down as many as you can think of. They should be statements that are to some extent disputable; do not make statements that refer to facts: Likert scales are used to test attitudes, not knowledge. We saw an example of a Likert scale earlier in this chapter (Figure 5.4).

In the introduction to a Likert scale, you can instruct respondents what the numbers refer to:

Strongly agree	=	+2
Agree	=	+1
Neutral	=	0
Disagree	=	−1
Strongly disagree	=	−2

In a pilot study you could eliminate those items on which almost all subjects score the same. Again, as we discussed previously, we want an instrument that discriminates best between respondents' attitudes toward an object.

Before we move on, we would like to make two observations here about the processing of data. Imagine you have ten questions concerning viewers' attitudes toward a movie character, five of which refer to negative attitudes and five to positive ones. The purpose of your study requires that you calculate an overall attitude score. When processing the data you have to make sure that you reverse the scores on the unfavorable statements so that all negative scores mean a negative attitude and all positive scores a positive one. Also, when calculating an overall score, you should divide by the number of items that you use, so the average score is still on a scale from +2 to −2. This helps both you and your readers to interpret the results. How to perform these actions will be discussed later in Chapter 7.

5.3.8. Semantic differential scales

Here respondents are asked to express their feelings toward an object by selecting a position on a scale of bipolar adjectives or phrases (see Figure 5.1). Imagine you want to examine responses to modern dance, and you focus on respondents' reactions to two dance performances: A and B. Using semantic differential items you could draw up a profile analysis of the two events (after the scales have been redirected, so that they all point in the same direction): it shows you on which adjectives the performances were comparable, and where they differed. The graph below shows what a profile analysis would look like with the marked adjectives (*) indicating significant differences.

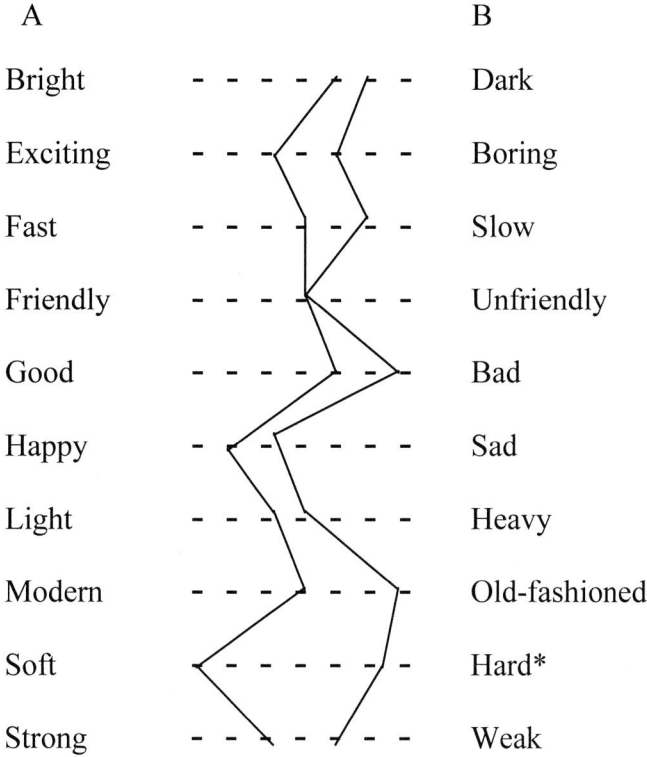

Figure 5.16: Profiles of two dance performances (A and B)

It is important to make the poles real opposites of each other: an item like "Impressive – Silly" may be hard for respondents to interpret because two dimensions are mixed here. As you can see, not all of the adjectives used in this semantic differential seem to apply directly to a dance performance; nevertheless, asking respondents to compare performances on such abstract adjectives may be very revealing. Sometimes, it can also be advantageous to include 'irrelevant' adjectives, for instance when you wish to hide the purpose of the study from participants: such adjective pairs make it more difficult for respondents to imagine what you are after.

5.4. How to formulate a question?

Now that we know how important it is to be aware of the level of measurement, let us think about how to get appropriate answers to your questions. Basically, that is what the rest of this chapter will be concerned with.

Some variables are easy to measure. Answering questions about age or gender will not cause respondents too much trouble. Others, however, may lead to misunderstandings. Suppose you want to know to what extent people identified with a movie character. What identification means to you, however, may not be the same as what your respondents understand it to be. One may think it to mean "feels sympathy for", or "imagine myself in the position of the character", or "feeling similar to the character." Maybe you want your measure to include all these possible aspects of responses to the character. In some cases, however, you may want to distinguish between them, because you want to know exactly which concept of identification respondents had in mind. Also, you may yourself have reasons to measure just one of these interpretations of the word 'identify', for instance, because you do not want to include sympathy, but just "imagining myself in the position of the character". In sum, with abstract variables you need to consider more carefully what you mean exactly and how respondents may define your terms themselves.

We should note, however, that between the realm of concrete variables (e.g. age, gender) and abstract variables (e.g. identification, happiness, enjoyment) there is a large gray area. Even terms you expect to be crystal-clear might be understood in various ways. This can be illustrated by the results of a study by Conrad and Schrober (2000). They examined to what extent respondents and questionnaire makers actually understand each other. In their study they employed a standard questionnaire used for government surveys. They compared two ways to submit questions to their respondents. With one part of their sample, they conducted standardized interviews in which the interpretation of the questions was left entirely to the respondents. This is how these questionnaires are normally administered. In the second half of their sample, a conversational interview technique was applied: interacting with their respondents, the interviewers made sure that they would understand the concepts the questions referred to in the same way as the US Government defines them. And, guess what? On seemingly straightforward questions like "How many people live in your house," "How many rooms are there in your house" and "Do you smoke" researchers found some stunning contrasts between the two groups. One respondent might have thought that his or her partner smoking half a cigarette did not count, or that smoking tobacco in a joint did not amount to being a smoker. The US Government thinks differently.

Given the time frame you need to complete your study in, conversational interviews may not always be an option. However, there are other, less time-consuming, ways to avoid miscommunication between you and your respondents. One is to specify your questions by adding some examples that the respondents would understand. For instance, when you want to know what movie genres respondents like to watch, the option "Romantic comedy" might be accompanied with some well-known titles of what you consider prototypical examples of this genre. It is important, however, to restrict such additions to a minimum. Anyway, keep in mind that respondents may not always read questionnaires very carefully.

If there is one thing that has become clear from Conrad and Schrober's study, it is that we need to take into account that respondents might not share our frame of reference. So, when preparing your questionnaire, you need to put yourself as much as possible in the position of your respondents. Never use the jargon that you may have picked up during your literature search. That means, for instance, that you want to avoid asking for people's 'attitude' toward an object, but circumscribing what you want to know in laymen's terms. Also, consider what knowledge respondents can readily have – neither you nor your respondents want to lose too much time over it. Finally, think what questions they would be willing to answer. Putting yourself in the position of your respondents might also bring to light questions experienced as threatening or sensitive. Some other questions may evoke socially desirable responses. For example, the amount of time people spend on reading is systematically overrated (see, for instance, Zill and Winglee, 1990). Think of ways to formulate your questions in such a way as to make respondents at ease and make them answer as honestly as possible.

5.5. Questionnaire design

We have discussed a number of formats for formulating closed questions. When you have made your choice and have composed a list of questions, it is time to consider the structure of your questionnaire. In which order will you present the questions? Making this decision you should think of the questionnaire as something that could function as a replacement of having a normal conversation with your respondents. Here are some things you should keep in mind:

- Order the questions according to subject. Do not switch from one subject to another and then back again, unless there is a very good reason to do so. There is one exception: in case you want to ask

one question several times but in different wording (e.g. one time positive, one time negative, to enhance the reliability of your results, or to check whether your respondents are consistent in their answers), it is advisable not to let the one follow the other.
- Explain after one group of questions what comes next, and if possible, what the relation of the issue is to the purpose of the study. Do not give too much away, but do tell your respondents something.
- Generally it is a good idea to set out with general questions before you move to more specific ones. Some recommend that you ask for personal details (e.g. sex and age) at the end of the questionnaire. You may also order your questions so that the most central, non-threatening questions are at the beginning, and the more difficult and threatening ones turn up later on.
- Putting your questions in a logical or chronological order may enhance respondents' memory. Not doing this may cause irritation. For instance, when you are interested in respondents' history as readers, you could ask questions about their youth, followed by adolescence, and adulthood.
- Thank participants for their cooperation. Participants are often promised results of the study as a way to thank them for their help. We recommend that you do this in the following way: request participants to let you have their email address. The best way to do this is to have them write this down on a separate sheet of paper, or – better still – on a list with the addresses of other participants, so as not to threaten participants' anonymity. When the analysis of the data is ready and your report has been written, make a short summary (half to one page in length) stating what the aims of the study were, what the results showed, and what conclusions you draw from the analysis. Do this in everyday language so that participants, who will almost certainly not be acquainted with your academic discipline, will understand. Finally, thank them again for their time and help.

Apart from these considerations, there is also another way to control the way respondents 'go' through the questions. With filter questions you can select those respondents whose answers you are really interested in. Suppose you want to know what visitors of a certain theater think of the programming and services installed six months before by the new management of that theater; you may want to exclude respondents who had not been to the theater before the changes were implemented [e.g. let the question "1. Have you visited this theater in the past six months?" be followed by two options: "(a) Yes (please go to the next question)" and "(b) No (please go to question 10)" – where 10 and subsequent questions may provide you with information you want from all your respondents]. You may even want to focus just on those respondents who have been to the theater both before and after the new policy was implemented. In the design of the questionnaire you may want to refer those respondents who did not witness the changes and compare them to others who did.

5.6. Instruction

We are ready for the next step now: writing an instruction. Its function is to motivate respondents to participate in your study and conscientiously fill out the questionnaire.

Here are some things you may want to include in the introduction to your study:

- Describe the purpose of the questionnaire. Be careful here not to give too much away; in some cases, like in experiments, it is crucial that respondents are unaware of the true purpose of the study. This information is only given to them at the end of the study, in a 'debriefing.' Nevertheless, respondents need to know something about the aim of the study and why they would want to participate in it. When formulating the purpose of the questionnaire, you may consider making clear to respondents, briefly, what the personal relevance of the study could be for them.
- Make clear who gave the assignment to the study (e.g. your professor or the company at which you have an internship), who the researcher is and to which institution or organization he/she belongs; this is first a matter of courtesy, but it may also enhance trust.
- Tell respondents what will be done with the results. This is more than a matter of courtesy, but of ethics; respondents have a right to know this.
- Make clear why the questionnaire is anonymous, or why it is not. In some research it is necessary that data are personalized, for instance because the researchers want to follow respondents over a longer period of time. In any event, ensure your respondents that

the results will be used for research purposes only and that their presentation will be anonymous.
- If necessary, give instructions about how to fill out the form; for instance, if the questionnaire consists of standard Likert scales you can set out what the codes –2 to +2 stand for (as in section 5.3.8).
- If necessary, give instructions about how to send the questionnaire back.
- Add the name, address, and phone number of the researcher; this may also enhance trust: it is not some anonymous and mysterious institute that asks questions, but a person with whom participants can get into contact.

5.7. Layout

Before you start to make a layout of the questionnaire you should evaluate the questions that you have. Ask yourself whether all the questions you included in the questionnaire are really necessary. Will you use them all in your analyses, for instance to establish a relation between dependent and independent variables? Also, consider again whether respondents will be able or willing to give the information you ask for. Do this first; otherwise you may have to do your layout twice.

The success of your study is in part determined by the degree to which you are able to motivate your respondents to participate and finish the questionnaire. A professional layout may stimulate them to take your research seriously. A uniform format for your questions helps to make the layout look good, and will make it easier for them to fill out the questionnaire. Also, make the answers to the questions as uniform as possible: ask them to circle a number, or blacken a square, or tick a square or circle; do not mix these options without good reason.

Put all the sheets of paper of your questionnaire in a (stapled) booklet so that none of the sheets will get lost. Finally, here is a checklist of things you may want to consider:

- Use enough space; some respondents may be a bit hasty or not as precise as you would like them to be when they mark their answers; consequently it is sometimes hard to see, for instance, which box they ticked. Using enough space helps to avoid this problem.
- Use a large enough font (recommended: 14); respondents will be less likely to read your instructions when it is a smaller print.

- Emphasize important information.
- Number all questions and sub-questions. Give numbers to all answer options: this will ease the data processing for you later, and will help you to avoid making mistakes when doing so.
- Carefully check the filter questions: do they refer respondents to the right questions and will they not skip any question that they should answer?
- Take care that none of questions run over to the following page.
- Use a different font for instructions, e.g. bold or italics, or change fonts (from Times New Roman to Arial, for instance).
- Thank your respondents at the end of the questionnaire for their participation.

5.8. Procedure

There is still one more thing you should do before you can collect your data. It is advisable that you do a try-out or a *pilot study*. For this you select respondents (say around 10) who are comparable to the population you have in mind for the actual study. If it is not possible to get respondents from the intended population, then ask people not involved in the study to answer the questions.

There are two good reasons to conduct a pilot study. The first concerns the time it takes to fill out the questionnaire, and the second concerns the comprehensibility of the questions. Because you compiled the test, you are the least likely person to judge fairly these two aspects of your instrument.

In the pilot study you check how long it takes for respondents to fill out the questionnaire. In many cases you have a limited amount of time within which to collect your data. Respondents may, for instance, only be available to you for the duration of one class or they may be willing to spend only a limited amount of time voluntarily.

Second, you want to know whether respondents have trouble with the wording of some of the questions, or with understanding what is actually asked of them. There are two ways to find this out. You could specifically instruct them to add their comments and questions in the margin of the questionnaire. Or you ask respondents to think aloud while they fill out the questionnaires. They can then mention what is unclear to them, and possible changes can then be discussed with them directly. This is, of course, more time consuming because the tests cannot be administered in a group but it will provide you with more valuable and more detailed information. Also, the number of respondents in the pilot test is very low so this is not very time consuming and hence certainly to be preferred.

After the pilot study you are now ready to collect your data. If you collect your data in an educational setting, which is a quick way to gather a lot of data, respondents may pay better attention to their task when the questionnaires are administered in smaller groups than classrooms, or even better, when they are filled out individually, separate from the others, e.g. by the wall of a booth or even in a separate room.

It is important to realize that there are many other settings in which you can collect your data. Take for instance the study of West *et al.*, in which travelers at an airport terminal were asked to participate while they were waiting for their connecting flight. Other options are hospitals, prisons, waiting rooms, audiences, or stations. It should be pointed out that finding ways to collect data also requires creativity. One student of ours, Simone Kohl, was interested in people's reactions to 'sound poems' of the kind written by Ernst Jandl and others. She recorded the poems on a CD and went to the English Garden in Munich, where during the summer months thousands of people relax. She asked people whether they were interested in listening to some performances on her disc-man as part of an experiment, and had many responses. Other students (Barros, 2003) waited at the exit doors of a movie house to get respondents to answer a questionnaire about scenes in that film.

Another possibility is that you send out your questionnaires. This is a much more expensive way to collect data. Think of the postage for sending the material to your respondents. In addition, to stimulate respondents to send the questionnaire back to you, you may want to include a stamped envelope. But even then you may risk running in to some non-response: the likelihood of getting all your questionnaires returned is rather slim. Even when respondents are willing to participate in your study, they may still forget to fill out or send back the questionnaire.

If you conduct an experiment, remember to randomize the questionnaires for the different groups. Here it is important to realize how long it takes to finish each questionnaire. It is to be preferred that each test takes approximately the same amount of time. If not, be sure to ask respondents not to start talking when they finished their test but to do something for themselves till everybody is ready. In a study by one of our students, Elise Nuhoff, the participants (children) were asked to keep themselves busy with coloring a picture distributed by the researcher after they were ready with the questionnaire; it worked like a charm. For older respondents, you may want to consider another approach.

In sum, these are the steps you take to get ready for the actual data collection. First you determine the aim of the questionnaire. Write down what information it is exactly that you need. When you have done this, you check whether there is already a test available that you could use. If not, you sit down and write down all the questions that you can think of. Next you determine the format in which you want to put the questions to your respondents. Then you determine the order in which you want to present the questions. You make the layout and photocopy a number of questionnaires to be tested on friends and colleagues so that you can ask for feedback. After adjusting the questionnaire, you can run a pilot study. When you have again made the necessary revisions you are ready to conduct the actual study.

CHAPTER SIX

EXPERIMENT

6.1. Introduction

Performing experiments is one of the core methods in Social Sciences. This chapter introduces you to its key concepts and helps you to design your own experiment. In Chapter 3 we discussed the basis of each empirical study, that is, the conceptual model that describes your hypotheses in terms of the interrelations between variables. Here we look at a suitable approach to test your ideas about the relation between the elements of your model: the relation between the independent and the dependent variable. In Section 6.2, you will see how one influences the other. Sections 6.3 through 6.5 will guide you through the choices you have to make when you design your experiment. We will show you not only how each choice has its advantages and disadvantages, but also how you can minimize the effects of the latter. Section 6.6 describes the methodological problems you need to be aware of while designing your study and also when drawing your conclusions. Moreover, this section will be helpful when you are evaluating previous studies. What it all basically comes down to is this: how certain can you be that your results tell you something about the relation between independent and dependent variables? In other words, how sure can you be that one thing influences the other? What does this tell you about the world outside our experiment? Can you generalize your findings beyond the participants of your study?

6.2. Independent and dependent variables

One of the main objectives of an experiment is to establish causal relations. You want to examine the effect of one variable (X) on another (Y). Does narrative perspective in a story (variable X) affect readers' identification (variable Y)? Does watching a horror movie with other people (X) cause more excitement (Y) than watching it alone? Will art education (X) enhance appreciation for abstract painting (Y)? Will awareness of linguistic patterns (X) increase textual appreciation (Y)? In all these examples, X is what we call the *independent variable* and Y the *dependent variable*. Degree of identification with a story character, for example, is assumed to *depend* on narrative perspective. The independent variable is the factor that you, as experimenter, manipulate. Hence it is sometimes called the *manipulated factor*. In experiments you always try to manipulate some factor to see whether this causes changes in the dependent variable. For instance, you write two stories to verify the effect on narrative perspective, your dependent variable. In one you have an external narrator, and in the other an internal narrator. In this case your manipulated factor (or independent variable) is narrative perspective, that is, two stories written from two different perspectives. Another synonym for independent variables is *conditions*. In each experiment you need a minimum of two conditions so that you can compare. For instance, you may have one group that reads a story with external perspective, and one that reads the story with an internal perspective. Or you may have one group of subjects that watches a horror movie in a group, and one that watches the movie individually. Sometimes conditions are referred to as *levels*. In the last example, the first level is watching the movie in a group, the second is watching the movie individually. Whether a participant in this experiment is in one group or the other is the independent variable.

To help you realize the range of possible manipulations we will briefly discuss three categories of independent variables: the situation, the task, and the instructions. (1) In the first you manipulate the situation. An example of such a *situation variable* would be having the participants watch a movie in a group or individually. (2) The second type of independent variables concerns the tasks you give your participants. Hence, this type is called *task variables*. An example would be that one group of participants is asked to watch one movie, and another group is asked to watch another. (3) The third type is *instruction variables*. Participants in one condition are asked to conduct a certain task in one way, and those in a second condition are asked to do the same task in another way. In Chapter 2 you were already introduced to the study conducted by Zwaan (1991), in which some participants were told they were to read a newspaper article while others were given the same text, but they were told they were to read a literary text. Zwaan assumed that the different instructions (the independent variable) would lead to different reading styles (the dependent variable), that is, either casually skimming the text like most readers of newspaper articles do, or more carefully paying attention to the exact wording of the text like readers of literary texts often do. He found that instructing readers that they were to read literary texts did indeed make them read more slowly and remember more of the surface structure of the texts than the participants in the other group who read the same texts thinking they were newspaper articles. As you can imagine, in this design it is essential that Zwaan's participants were unaware that they *were* instructed to do their tasks in different ways.

In some cases you may want to combine different types of independent variables. In a study by Bourg et al. (1993), for instance, one instruction variable and one task variable were examined. Participants were asked to read either story A or story B (a task variable), and were asked to try to put themselves in the shoes of the story characters while reading or they were given no specific reading instruction (instruction variable).

In the examples we discussed so far, all independent variables were manipulated. Of course, you may say, that is the definition of independent variables. However, in some cases you may want to examine the influence of variables that you *cannot* manipulate yourself. For instance, you want to compare female and male responses to particular television series in which women are the heroines. In your experiment you have a group of men and a group of women watch an episode of, for instance, *Sex in the City*, the New York sitcom. What you are examining in this study is a *subject variable* rather than a manipulated variable. The same holds for developmental studies in which the influence of age is examined. When do children start to realize what is real and what is fiction in television programs? To test this you may want to examine three groups: groups of 3-year-olds, 6-year-olds and 9-year-olds. Age is not a factor that you can manipulate. It is another example of a subject variable.

The distinction between manipulated variables and subject variables is an important one. Studies in which you manipulate a factor are called *true* experiments. Results of such studies allow you to draw conclusions about cause and effect. However, when examining subject variables you cannot. Suppose you find that men identify less with the problems that the sitcom brings up than women do. What *causes* this difference? Is it that men dislike women to be the leading protagonist, the one who saves the day? Or is it that they find it altogether harder to identify with characters of the opposite sex? Or is it that they, in general, identify less intensely with characters irrespective of gender? The problem illustrated here is that subject variables do not allow you to control for all variables that may play a role in your finding. Imagine you are comparing children of several age groups watching, for instance, *Finding Nemo* and you do find a difference. The 9-year-olds can distinguish reality from fiction, while the 3-year olds cannot. Is this because of a wider experience with television shows, or because of some cognitive development in the older children?

So using subject variables makes it harder to generate causal inferences. Nevertheless, often you will want to compare different groups of participants. The thing to remember is, then, to be careful in your conclusions.

What you can say is that the groups you studied differed in their scores on the dependent variable. What you cannot say is that this difference was caused by the subject variable.

What about the dependent variables? In Chapter 5 we discussed questionnaire design: measurement of mainly dependent variables. Of course your questionnaire will often do both: assess age, gender, maybe experimental group, but also, for instance, the degree to which participants identified with characters, what they recalled from the text they read, etc. The main thing to remember about dependent variables, as we emphasized in Chapter 5, is to strive for the highest possible level of measurement. We also discussed already what options there are to do so. Now let us look at procedures to establish causal relations between independent and dependent variables.

6.3. Designs

In this section we will discuss ways to design your study. An experimental design refers to the sort of comparison you will be making. In some studies you compare two (or more) groups of participants. For example, to one group you give participants the instruction that they will see a frightening scene; to another you do not warn participants. To assess the effects of forewarning, you ask every participant afterwards how scary they thought the scene was. This is called a *between-subjects design*. You make the comparison *between groups* of participants (or subjects): on the one hand, the group of subjects who received the forewarning, on the other hand the group of subjects who did not. You are interested to find out whether there is, on the whole, a difference *between* these groups. It will be clear that in this type of research design it is essential that every person participates in one group only. Otherwise, you will not be able to examine the effect of forewarning. In the case of Zwaan's study (Zwaan, 1991) mentioned earlier, we also saw that it was necessary that participants were part of one group only. They could not both be told that the text they were to read was a literary text, *and* be told it was a newspaper article. In these examples, it is necessary to have *naïve participants*, that is to say, participants who are unaware of the experimental procedure. When you examine subject variables, you also have no other choice than to have a between-subjects design. For example, comparing the responses of two age groups, participants are by definition part of just one group.

The second type of design is called the *within-subjects design*. Sometimes participants can be submitted to more than one condition. For instance, you have everybody judge 10 paintings. After viewing each painting participants are asked to rate it on a number of scales. In your analysis you compare the evaluation of each individual participant of each individual painting. Hence the term within-subject: you compare two or more measurements within each individual case. Another term for this type of study is a *repeated-measures* design, because you repeatedly measure participants' evaluations (10 times in the example). Other examples of within-subjects designs are studies that have *pre-tests* and *post-tests*. Vincent van der Velde, one of our students, asked his participants to rate the reliability of the television news bulletin before and after they saw a documentary on the personal biases of television journalists. In his analysis he compared the scores of each individual participant – within each case – to see whether there were differences between the pre-test and the post-test, hence a *within-subjects design*. To his surprise, he was unable to register an effect of the documentary on participants' evaluation of news bulletins in terms of objectivity and reliability. The choice you make here determines later, in the analyses of your data, which statistical tests you can run (see Chapters 9–11).

Do you need to make a choice between the two types of design, or could you combine the two? Think for example of a study in which you have a within-subjects design that you use in different countries. However, the important thing here is that you determine which design fits your research question. Having made your choice you must now consider some of the problems involving the design of your choice. We will first look at what issues you should consider when using between-subjects designs.

6.3.1. Between-subjects designs

The first thing to remember is that between-subjects designs require equivalent groups. Let us consider the example of the study examining the effects of forewarning on arousal. You have a group of participants who are told they will see some frightening images, and one group is not. This is exactly what Cantor (1984) did. On the one hand you might expect that being warned means being prepared and, consequently, the person will be less frightened or shocked. The assumption here is that the unexpectedness of frightening images may cause more arousal. On the other hand, maybe the anticipation of something frightening may cause more tension, which, when unleashed, causes more arousal than in a situation without the anticipation. What the author found was that forewarning increases arousal. She concluded that anticipating scary images causes more fear than unexpected scary images. Or does it? Is there any reason to doubt this conclusion? Maybe in the first group the researchers had a disproportionate number of people who were not used to seeing frightening movies, and by coincidence all the horror movie fans in the sample were in the second group. Would this not affect results? We are not saying that Cantor was not mindful of this problem, but let us consider a hypothetical situation in which she was not. Table 6.1 presents what the results of such a study might look like:

Forewarning

Without		With	
Participant	Score	Participant	Score
P1	5	P11	6
P2	4	P12	7
P3	6	P13	1
P4	7	P14	3
P5	4	P15	4
P6	4	P16	7
P7	1	P17	6
P8	2	P18	5
P9	3	P19	5
P10	1	P20	3
Average:	3.7	Average:	4.7

1 = 'not scary at all', and 10 = 'extremely scary'; *italics* = horror fans

Table 6.1: Scariness scores

Clearly, the unequal distribution of the horror fans (scores in bold) makes it hard to compare the two groups. Not having equivalent groups affected average group results. The (hypothetical) data represented in Tables 6.2a and 6.2b suggest that being a horror fan decreases the scores considerably. Also notice that this is just one of the many possible confounding factors. Maybe age plays a role, or gender, or anxiety level before the experiment. We do not know.

One way to reduce the effect of known and unknown confounding factors is *randomization*: participants are assigned to the groups on the basis of coincidence. If you randomly assign participants to the two groups, there is only a very small chance that the distribution of horror fans is as unfortunate as shown in Table 6.1. However, randomization is not an absolute guarantee that an equal number of fans will be in group 1 and group 2. The smaller the number of participants in each group, the larger the chance that randomization does not result in equivalent groups. Suppose that in one study we have 10 participants and in a second 40. In the first there are two fans, and in the second there are eight (notice that we keep the ratio of fans to non-fans the same as in the example above, namely 1 : 5). We use a randomization procedure in the hope of obtaining an equal distribution of fans across two experimental conditions. In spite of this procedure, the chance that in the first study both fans end up in the same condition is far larger than the chance that all eight fans in the second study end up in one, or even seven or six fans; this is simply a matter of probability calculus.

A second way to create equivalent groups is called *matching*. In this procedure participants are paired together on some trait known to the researcher before the experiment. An example would be that you have good reasons to believe, for instance, based on previous research, that frequency of previous exposure to horror movies influences whether people are frightened by scary movies. Imagine you want to create two equivalent groups, again to examine the effects of forewarning. You have participants rate how often they see movies featuring either chain saw killers, haunted houses, or space monsters. On each of these items they score from 1 to 10 and the average of the three is their horror experience score. Subsequently, participants with highly similar scores are 'matched'. Here in Table 6.2a and 6.2b are the hypothetical results for 20 participants.

Table 6.2a Calculate the scores for preference for scary movies

Table 6.2b. Arrange in ascending order; pair participants and form two new groups

Group 1		Group 2		Group 1		Group 2	
P1	3.6	P11	1.3	P3	1.3	P11	1.3
P2	4.7	P12	1.7	P12	1.7	P17	2.3
P3	1.3	P13	5.2	P15	3.1	P1	3.6
P4	7.3	P14	4.5	P18	3.8	P20	4.3
P5	5.6	P15	3.1	P14	4.5	P2	4.7
P6	6.8	P16	7.3	P13	5.2	P5	5.6
P7	*8.1*	P17	2.3	P6	6.8	P19	6.9
P8	*9*	P18	3.8	P4	7.3	P16	7.3
P9	*8.4*	P19	6.9	*P7*	*8.1*	*P9*	*8.4*
P10	*8.8*	P20	4.3	*P10*	*8.8*	*P8*	*9*
Average	6.36	Average	4.04	Average	5.06	Average	5.34

Table 6.2: Paired matching for preference for scary movies

Again the data for the four horror movie fans are printed in italics. As we saw in Table 6.1, the unequal distribution of fans over the two groups biased the results of the study. Here is what a matching procedure could do to avoid this from happening. In Table 6.2a we can see what scores might look like for the two groups represented earlier in Table 6.1. As you can see, average scores on our scale for experience with horror is higher for the first than for the second group – it may be that this difference explains the difference we saw in Table 6.1. These are the steps you take to form equivalent groups. First you arrange all the scores in ascending order. In the example this would result in the following order: P3, P11, P12, P17, P15, P1, P18, P20, P14, P2, P13, P5, P6, P19, P4, P16, P7, P9, P10, P8. Second you pair the first in your list with the second (in the example, P3 with P11), the third (P12) with the fourth (P17), and so forth. Now you can create two new groups (see Table 6.2b): the first of each pair is placed in Group 1, and the second in Group 2. As you can see, the horror fans are now equally distributed over the two groups, and the average scary movies preference score is now more or less equal for the two groups (5.06 and 5.34, a mean difference of 0.28). The two groups are now, as to this one variable, more comparable than before (a mean difference of 2.32). Having created two equivalent groups we can now run our experiment testing the effects of forewarning, knowing that our results are not influenced by participants' experience with horror movies.

As you can see, the method of matching is more elaborate than that of randomization. It is the preferred way of creating equivalent groups, however, when the number of participants you are working with is small. Remember that randomization may not be effective when working with small samples. Also, use matching when the variable you want to match participants on affects scores in a predictable way, for example, the number of academic courses on literature that participants completed and their ability to detect intertextual references, or children's age and the sophistication of the way they recount stories from shows seen on television. Finally, of course you can only use matching when there is a possibility to measure the matching variable. Practical or organizational reasons may prohibit you from using matching.

6.3.2. Within-subjects designs

A within-subjects design requires control for order effects. When you have few participants at your disposal and when the tasks that you have in mind for them cost little time, then repeated-measures designs are a suitable way to conduct your research. Within-subjects designs also avoid the equivalent group problem that between-subjects designs have. Your results will not be influenced here by individual differences among the participants. For instance, you want to find out whether actors perform better before a large audience than a small one. You ask the actors themselves after their act to rate their performance while independent researchers rate their performance from footage that does not reveal the size of the audience. It may be that you find only a few actors who are willing to participate. In this case it would be necessary to use a within-subjects design: measure the quality of the actors' performances before several audiences of different sizes. Each actor participates in each of the conditions. Therefore the groups in each condition are the very same persons. Hence, there is no need for randomization or matching procedures. Because you measure more than once, this procedure is also called repeated-measures design. Another example would be a study in which you want to find out whether texts describing landscapes are read faster or slower than those describing action. In this case too you can let your subjects participate in more than one condition: you ask them to read several passages and measure their reading pace. Three describe landscapes, and three describe action. You could also have two groups, using a between-subject design, with one group reading the landscape passages and another group the action passages. However, in this setup you have to make sure your groups are equivalent. Also, you will need a considerable number of participants. However, in a within-subjects design you would not have to worry about differences that may already exist between the participants, for the simple reason that the participants in all conditions are exactly the same persons: and for each of them we compare their reading pace in the two conditions.

Or are they not the same? After having read, say, five passages participants may be getting tired of your experiment and read faster anyway, irrespective of the content. As to the other example mentioned earlier, those actors who expressed their dissatisfaction with their performance the one night may be more eager to do better the next, irrespective of whether the audience is small or large.

These are called *order* or *sequence effects*. To give you an idea of the kind of effects that you could run into when using a repeated-measures design, here are a few examples. First, a *carry-over effect* occurs when the effect of one treatment is still present as the next is administered. What we call a *latent effect* occurs when the dormant effect of one treatment is activated by the next. *Learning effects* occur when participants score better on a test merely because of the repetition. The problem is that we do not know in advance whether such effects will occur, what their direction will be, or to what extent they will influence the results. In the case of the reading study, maybe participants will read the sixth passage slower because they are tired, or maybe they will read faster because by then they will have fully 'warmed-up'.

As you can see, every choice in research has its advantages and disadvantages. Every choice is a matter of give and take. Sometimes your 'choices' are dictated by the purpose of your study or the situation in which you conduct your research. For instance, when you have very few participants, the choice for a within-subjects design is the most obvious one. However, in that case you have to do everything possible to avoid sequence effects influencing the outcome of your study. There are several measures that you can take.

The first is called *complete counterbalancing*. In this procedure every sequence is used only once. Suppose you want your actors to perform before three different audiences: (A) one of 20, (B) one of 60, and (C) one of 180 spectators. Because you are not sure how sequence affects the performances and because you want your results only to reflect the effect of audience size, and because there are three audience sizes, you need 3! or 6 actors. The symbol ! stands for the mathematical calculation called factorial, in which the number preceding the symbol is multiplied by every number smaller to it until you reach the number 1. 3! for instance is $3 \times 2 \times 1 = 6$. In the example, participants would be assigned randomly to one of the following orders:

1. ABC
2. ACB
3. BCA
4. BAC
5. CAB
6. CBA

It may be that actors perform better each consecutive night, as a result of more training, and irrespective of audience size. Using just one order, say ABC, this would result in the best scores in audience C, leading you to the dubious conclusion that actors perform better before large audiences. Using all six orders, you know that the order will not play a role in your final conclusion: the extra effect of training will contribute equally to all three audience sizes. It could also be that actors perform worse in the second, and even worse in the third performance, maybe because of boredom with their tasks. Again, counterbalancing will eliminate the possibility that this effect interferes with the purpose of your study: finding out the effect of audience size on actor performance. Notice that counterbalancing has an advantage comparable to that of randomization: we do not need to know which factors may cause an order effect; neither do we need to know the direction of this effect. The effect will be 'cancelled out' because it will favor each of the conditions to the same degree.

Now consider what happens when you want to use complete counterbalancing for the study in which six passages are read. Remember that you need one participant for each of the sequences. How many actors would you need? $6! = 6 \times 5 \times 4 \times 3 \times 2 \times 1 = 720$ (!!!) Obviously, when you can only get a few participants, total counterbalancing is out – it is only suitable for experiments with a very small number of conditions. When you have too many conditions to allow for complete counterbalancing, you can use a subset of the total number of possible sequences. This is called *partial counterbalancing*.[1] What you do is take a random sample of all possibilities.

In the present section we have discussed two major categories of research designs. In *between-subjects designs* participants are exposed to one condition only. We have seen that this type of design requires you to take measures to make equivalent groups. In *within-subjects designs*, participants are exposed to more than one condition. Here you need to consider the danger of order effects. Having made your choice for either form of design you need to make some more. What elements in your design are required to make your conclusions valid? In other words, which elements are necessary (or desirable) to infer causal relations between independent and dependent variables?

6.4 Building an experimental design

The best way to make your design is to compare the purpose of your own study with what is called a *pre-test post-test control group design*. An important thing to understand about this so-called classical experimental design is that we do not always need it, that it sometimes is not possible or even desirable to apply it, and finally that sometimes we need to extend on it. For every research question there is at least one design that is most suitable. The purpose of this section is to help you find out which one fits yours best. One way to explore your own possibilities and the methodological requirements of your own study is to see what you do and do not need from the classical experimental design and also to consider that maybe something is missing in your own plan.

In classical design participants are randomized into two groups: one experimental group and one control group. Randomization is represented by the dotted line in Figure 6.1. First both groups make a *pre-test* of some kind, represented by O_1 for the experimental group and O_3 for the control group. For the experimental group the *pre-test* is followed by the treatment (X). They are asked, for instance, to perform some task like reading a story, seeing a movie, or going to a play. Next they are asked to do the *post-test*, which measures the same variables as the pre-test (O_2). The control group is not exposed to any treatment but does do the same post-test (O_4). In the analysis of the results we compare the difference between O_1 and O_2 with that between O_3 and O_4. The advantage of this design is that there is no reason to assume that *extra experimental factors* influence the results. For example, you examine the effects of a video of a political debate on voters' behavior: between viewing the video

---

[1] There are other ways to avoid the problems of complete counterbalancing (reverse and block randomization). These do not fall within the scope of this book (see Goodwin 2002).

(the *treatment*) and the elections, however, many other factors may influence your participants. These extra-experimental factors might affect the results of the tests, but there is a fair chance that they will affect both the control group and the experimental group scores (see also Section 6.6). That is why having a control group presents such an enormous advantage: because both O_2 and O_4 are likewise influenced by extra-experimental factors, any difference between them may be ascribed to X, the experimental treatment.

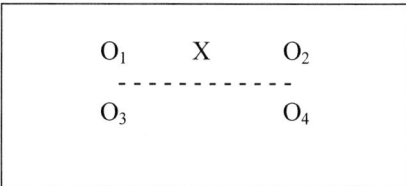

Figure 6.1: Pre-test post-test control group design

As we emphasized earlier, you do not always need the full pre-test post-test control group design. Let us explain this by using an example. Say we are interested in the effects of the order in which narrative events are presented to readers on their identification with story characters. Intuition may tell us that it makes a difference whether we first meet character A instead of character B; during the rest of the story we may focus a little more on character A's actions, take his or her point of view on story events, and identify with him or her. In a study by Bower (1978) this hypothesis was examined (see Chapter 4). Just to remind our readers of this study, Bower wrote a short story about three characters, Rich, Harry and Cindy. Cindy is to appear in a television commercial for a suntan lotion and she asks her friends Rich and Harry to help her. Harry has to drive a speedboat, and Rich is asked to play the water skier. During the shooting several mishaps occur, but the story is kept intentionally vague about the causes. The researcher wrote two versions of the story, one that starts with a lead-in of about 300 words about Harry, and one of equal length about Rich. After reading one version of the story participants were asked to fill out a questionnaire registering their recall of feelings for the three characters, their idea about the causes of the mishaps, and their evaluation of the characters. It turned out that in the group that read the version in which they first met Harry, participants tended to locate themselves with Harry and had identified themselves with him. Also on a number of scales they rated Harry more positively than Rich. The accidents were attributed to Rich's clumsiness. However, in the other group with participants who first read about Rich, the results were exactly the reverse.

In this experimental design we do not see a control group or a pre-test. Why not? Well, it is not necessary and not even possible to have either a control group or a pre-test. Before the experiment participants will not be able to judge the characters, simply because they have not read the story yet; participants in the control group will not have read the story at all, so how can *they* say anything about the characters? Hence, when comparing the conditions, you will have to settle for post-tests only.

6.4.1. Extending on the classical experimental design

In your research you may want to compare several experimental conditions. In that case you simply add extra experimental groups to the design. Say you want to compare two conditions. The experimental design would look like this:

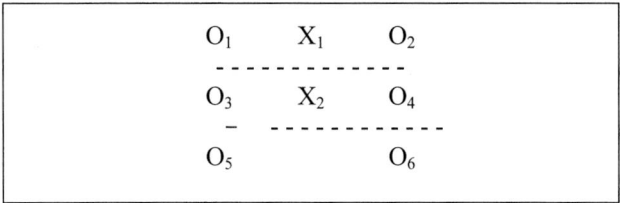

Figure 6.2: Pre-test post-test control group design with two experimental conditions

By now you will understand what the figure represents: participants are randomly assigned to one of three groups (note the dotted lines); in the first group participants make a pre-test (O_1), are exposed to a treatment (X_1) and then they do a post-test (O_2). Something similar happens in the second experimental group, except that participants are exposed to a different treatment (X_2). In the third group no treatment is administered. However, participants are asked to take the two tests. Let us look at an example to make this all less abstract. When you want to investigate long-term effects of a treatment one can add a *post-post-test* (or *delayed post-test*). For instance, Flerx et al. (1976) were interested in the possibility of using stories or films to change children's ideas about how males and females should behave, in other words, their sex-role concept. In one experimental condition they *read* five *stories* representing egalitarian roles for male and female characters to a group of 5-year-old readers (X_1). In another group children *saw* five egalitarian *films* (X_2). A third group participated in the normal school curriculum and was not exposed to either the stories or the films.

All participants responded to a test measuring their attitudes toward sex-roles before and after the experiment. Using this pre-test post-test –control group design, researchers found that both treatments had an effect on participants' sex-role concepts. To establish whether these effects were lasting, they conducted the same post-test 1 week after the experiment (so, a *delayed post-test*). Even though the difference between the control group and the experimental groups became slightly smaller after the 7-day period, the effects of both treatments were still strong. Considering all the possible influences that the children may well have experienced between post-test and delayed post-test, this is a remarkable finding. Maybe it may be worthwhile to include such a delayed post-test in your study too. Often researchers are satisfied with establishing effects with measures administered right after the treatment but in some cases theoretical claims pertain to long-term effects!

To examine particular research questions you may need a design more complicated than the pre-test post-test control group. For instance, you want to know which of two nature documentaries makes students more aware of environmental problems. Your independent variable, or experimental factor, is exposure to one of the two documentaries. But because you are planning to use the documentaries in an educational setting you want to find out in which grades which of the two would work best: does it make a difference whether viewers are high-school students, undergraduates or graduates? It may be that one has more effect on younger viewers (e.g. footage of endangered species, with an emphasis on cute baby animals) and the other may prove to be fitter for senior students (e.g. focusing on the effect of economic growth on the quality of water and air). To examine this you need to compare three age groups. This is your second experimental factor. You will need six (3 × 2) groups: three groups per documentary. The design you are using is called a *factorial design*, and this particular type of factorial design is called a *two-way design*: There are two factors of interest that are examined: first the treatment (one of the two documentaries or the control condition) and second, the participants' age.

One can make things even more complex by adding more factors. In a study by Bourg et al. (1993), briefly mentioned in section 6.2, we find an example of a *three-way design.* In their experiment they examined the effects of empathy on narrative text comprehension. Participants either received an empathy-building instruction (they were asked to try to put themselves in the shoes of story characters), or no specific reading instruction (factor one). They read one of two stories (factor two). Using a standardized test, the researchers distinguished three levels of reading comprehension (factor number three). After reading the story several tests to measure story comprehension were administered. It was found that the empathy-building reading strategy did indeed enhance comprehension, but only in one story, and that this reading instruction helped subjects with low comprehension levels more than it did subjects who had high scores on reading comprehension to begin with. With one manipulation causing different effects under different conditions we have what is called an *interaction effect*. *Main effects* are effects of individual factors (or, variables). We speak of an interaction effect when the effects of one experimental factor differ with levels of another experimental factor. The procedure of factorial designs may be the same as for the design we discussed before, but the analyses are slightly more complex. This will be explained in Chapter 11.

6.4.2. Doing the 'next best thing'

In some cases it is better to choose a *non-equivalent control group design*. As has been argued earlier, a randomization procedure allows us to assume that the groups are more or less comparable, so that any differences in test results are the result of the treatment and not of differences between the groups that already existed. On the other hand, a randomization may not always be possible. In *field experiments* (that is, an experiment not conducted in a controlled environment like a 'laboratory') one may be forced to work with intact groups, like classrooms. Moreover, it can be argued that working with intact groups enhances the 'naturalness' of the situation. One problem with experiments is that they often occur in 'laboratories', and it is sometimes contested whether results that are assessed in these situations can be generalized to real-world situations. Students who are taken out of their classroom environment may become aware of the test situation and respond differently to when they would all have simply been left in their class. In large experiments the problem of not being able to randomize subjects can be solved by working with a number of intact groups, then randomizing these over the conditions and treating them in the analysis as individual cases as you would with individual participants. However, realize that you then need a large number of participants!

6.5. Control groups

The value of experimental research is partly determined by the level of control you have over all sorts of factors that may (or may not!) have played a role in behavioral differences (often 'behavior' is simply the participants' response to questions) you find between groups. We have seen this in studies that compare participants on subject variables. Because of the lack of control in these studies, we have to be careful when drawing up our conclusions (see Section 6.2). Also in studies examining the effects of some types of treatment we have to be aware of alternative explanations for the effect found. Imagine you want to know what effects television advertisements have on people's self-esteem. You have a series of television advertisements representing beautiful and successful people, and you expect that watching these advertisements makes viewers aware of their own shortcomings (not being slim, not having a car, etc.). Or, say, you want to see what effects reading sessions in the local library have on children's reading behavior. You expect that being read stories by the librarian once a week for a given time will stimulate children to borrow books in the year after the treatment. In this type of study it is often desirable to have at least two conditions: one in which the treatment is administered, and one in which it is not. As you realize by now, the first is the experimental group and the second the control group. These groups are identical in all but one respect: one watches the advertisements, the other does not; one sits in on the reading sessions, the other does not. The control group provides you with a baseline measure against which you can compare the experimental group. The advantage is that now you can make causal inferences. The difference you find between the groups can only be attributed to the fact that one group did receive a treatment and the other group did not. In other words, there are no alternative explanations. This is exactly what you should aim for when you want to establish a causal relation.

We can distinguish four types of control groups. It is important to consider the choices you have, the advantages of each, and when to apply them. The first is the *straight control group*. We have already seen examples of the use of straight control groups in the previous example. Participants assigned to the control condition simply do not receive any treatment. It may be worthwhile for you to consider other possibilities, for example, the so-called *placebo control group*, the second type of control group. In medicine, the term *placebo* refers to a substance patients believe to have some effect, but which, in fact, is inactive. Imagine you want to find out whether alcohol affects the degree to which an audience enjoys a comedy show. Your prediction is that alcohol will make the audience laugh louder. However, you also expect that just *thinking* that you have drunk alcohol will make you louder. You want to distinguish *this* effect from the *real* effect of alcohol. What you could do is have three groups: one that does not drink alcohol (the straight control group), a second group that is given a certain amount of beer (the experimental group), and a third group that is given alcohol-free beer (the placebo group). Every participant is then equipped with a small device to measure sound output in decibels. Figure 6.3 presents your (fictitious) results. Maybe these data may convince you of the use of a placebo group.

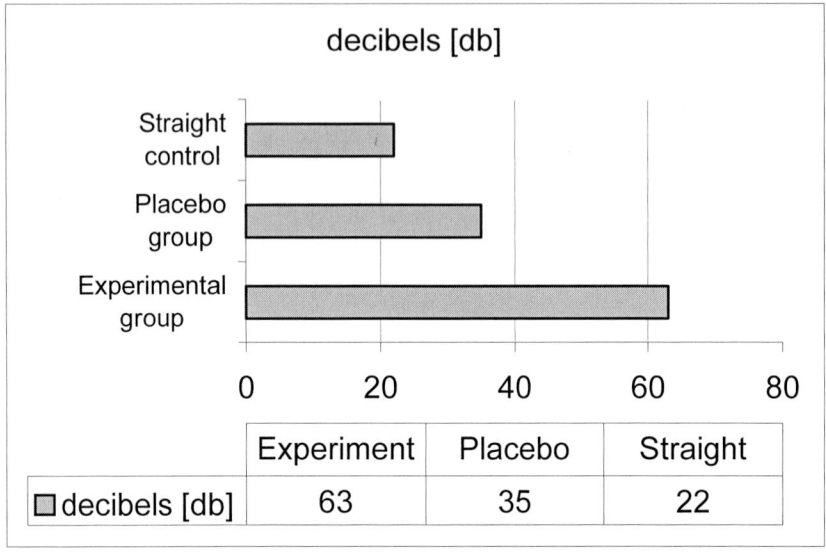

Figure 6.3: Alcohol at the Comedy Club

Participants who were unaware that they drank alcohol-free beer were louder than the group that drank soft drinks only. What this tells you is that what participants expect about the effects of drinking alcohol already adds to their noisiness (from 22 db to 35 db). However, as you can see, drinking alcohol had an effect that went beyond participants' expectations about the effects of alcohol (35 db to 63 db). In short, a placebo control group helps you to distinguish the true effect your manipulated variable has from mere suggestion.

The third type of control group is called *waiting list control group*. Such control groups are often found in studies evaluating some types of program. Participants who have not entered the program yet can function as the baseline in the assessment of the effects of the program. An example would be that you want to examine the effects of poetry reading on students who suffer from anxiety. You post the program in your school and 40 students register as participants. You run the program twice: once for the first 20 students, and the second time for the other 20. Both groups fill out the anxiety test before the experiment starts. Only the first group, however, enters the actual program immediately, while the second group, the control group, waits its turn. After running the program for the first time, and before the second group enters the program, both groups are again assessed for their anxiety levels. What is the advantage of doing your experiment this way? To assess the effects of the program you could also use students of your school who did not enter the program. However, these may not be suffering from anxiety. They may also not have any interest in poetry. Therefore they are less suitable as control group participants. It is better to have the second group of students as a waiting list control group, because you can assume they suffer from the same problems as the first group, and also have the same interest in participating in a program involving reading poetry.

The fourth type of control group is the *yoked control group*. In such a control group every participant is paired with (or 'yoked' to) a participant in the experimental condition. Imagine you are interested in learning with the help of computer games. You study a game for small children to tell the time. What you are interested in is whether program-generated compliments or reprimands enhance users' learning or not. To examine this you have one straight control group. In this group no program is used. In the experimental group the participants play the game, and are complimented when they tell the time correctly, and they are reprimanded when they make mistakes. If you find a difference between the results of the control group and those of the experimental group, you cannot be sure whether this is the result of the rewards and reprimands. It may just as well be because of other aspects of the game that helped participants to learn. It may simply be its exercises, or the crystal-clear explanation of the principles of telling the time. Therefore you need to pair every participant of the experimental group with a participant who uses a version of the same game *without* the compliments and reprimands. Now you will be able to verify what this factor contributed to the learning effects of the game. For example, let us say the experimental and the yoked control groups both score higher on a test for telling the time than the straight control group, and the experimental group also scores higher than the yoked control group. The difference between the experimental and yoked control groups reveals what compliments and reprimands *add* to the effect of the game.

Ending this overview of types of control group, now you need to decide which would serve the purpose of your study best. The examples discussed here give you an indication of which type fits which sort of situations. You have seen that the strength of the claims that you can make on the basis of your results depends to some degree on your choice. Still there are a number of other factors that may contribute to the validity of your conclusions, or that may pose a threat to them.

6.6. Estimating validity

In every type of research it is important to estimate to what degree the conclusions are *valid*. Validity, in the present context, refers to the degree to which your study allows you to make claims about the relation between X and Y. Will it be possible for other researchers to propose alternative explanations for the results that you claim show that X causes Y? Could there be a factor Z that is actually responsible for Y? Does your test really measure Y and not something else? Does X *always* cause Y? You can see that it is essential that you address these and similar questions. In the present section we will give you an overview of possible *threats to validity*, some of general importance, and some specific to evaluating experimental research. This overview can be used in two ways. First, it may function as a checklist when you are designing your own study. Use it to examine whether the threats apply to your study, and, if so, whether there are ways to avoid them. Second, this overview can play an important role in your literature study. As argued before in Chapter 3, reviewing the literature will often result in adjusting and refining your hypotheses. Your literature study will reveal what is actually known about a certain research problem. To do this, you need to critically examine claims made by previous researchers about what their findings mean. Do they offer a solid and acceptable basis for their interpretation? Did they take care of the validity threats sufficiently? To enable you to estimate whether these claims are valid, you obviously need to be aware of what possible threats there are to validity. Frequently your literature study will also give you an idea about what the value of your own contribution to the field can be. Again, one of the factors that you can pay attention to here is to how your study can improve on what has been done before.

6.6.1. Internal validity

We distinguish two kinds of threats to validity: those to internal validity and those to external validity (see Section 6.6.2). *Internal validity* means that the relation you found between your independent and dependent variable cannot be explained by any other variable. We can be sure that the results are not due to the interference of some uncontrolled factor. In some cases researchers do not use a control group, or only conduct a post-test, or do not apply a randomization procedure. When using such incomplete experimental designs, it is impossible to determine whether differences between groups are due to the treatment, or to some other difference that was already there. Take for example this research design.

Figure 6.4: Case study

Here only one group undergoes a treatment. We want to know whether a film-studies education program has an effect on students' motivation to go to see more art-house movies than standard Hollywood productions. Students are enrolled in the program and afterwards we ask them about their attitudes toward different movie genres. Scores indicate a positive attitude toward art-house movies. What does this tell us? Very little, indeed. We do not know whether the score is the result of the effect of the treatment or not. What we need is a means to compare our results with participants' attitudes before the program (see Figure 6.5).

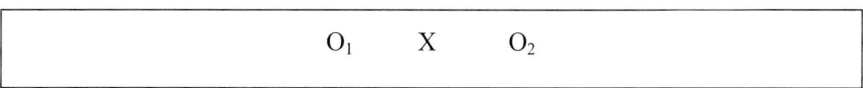

Figure 6.5: One-group pre-test post-test design

Imagine we find an increase in scores from O_1 to O_2. This design does not allow us to conclude whether that increase is caused by the program either. Maybe something else happened during the period of the experiment. Maybe an art-house movie became very popular, like occurred with *Being John Malkovich* (1999). We do not know whether scores were influenced by these *extra-experimental factors*. It could be that we would have registered a more positive attitude even without the program. Again the internal validity is threatened. To test this we could use the design represented in Figure 6.6.

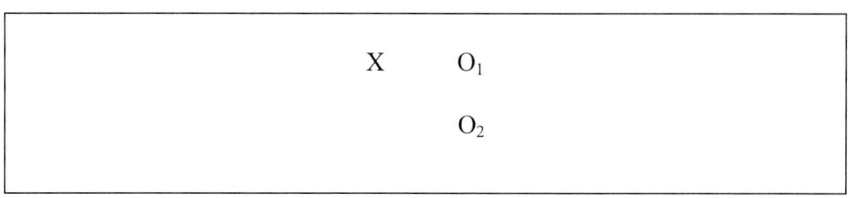

Figure 6.6: Afterwards comparisons of existing groups

Suppose that we find a more positive attitude in O_1 than in O_2. How valid is our conclusion that our treatment is responsible for this difference? A little more than before; now we can tell whether the score of the experimental group is high or not: we now have a reference point, that is, we can compare scores on O_1 with those on O_2. However, we still do not know whether the findings are the result of a difference that already existed between the groups. Maybe participants in the program differ in some essential respect from our control group participants. They may have a teacher who is particularly interested in art cinema. Perhaps, then, there is a general difference between the curriculum of the experimental group and that of the control group (which threatens the validity of the study). To test for such differences we need to conduct pre-tests:

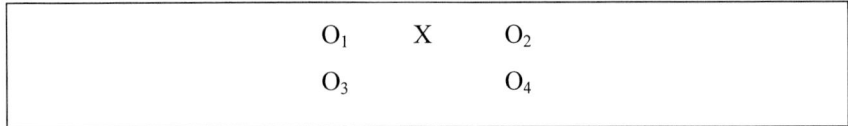

Figure 6.7: Non-equivalent control group design

As you may have noticed, we are now closer to the classical experimental design represented in Figure 6.1, except that Figure 6.7 does not include a randomization procedure. Again we have increased our control over possible intervening variables, and hence the validity. We now know what the scores of the two groups were before the experiment and we can compare them with those obtained after the treatment. However, remember our argument on the importance of randomization. Assigning your participants randomly to either experimental or control group will increase your control over the relation between independent and dependent variables. There may be potential variables that may influence the results. We may not be aware of all of these variables. As discussed earlier, randomization may help to avoid this threat to internal validity. As you can see, an incomplete experimental design might cause lack of control and hence pose a threat to validity, but also remember that in some cases it is impossible to have a perfect design.

Having found ways to restrict the possible influence of one threat to internal validity (extra-experimental factors), there are other threats to be considered. First there are the so-called *test effects* or *testing*. Test effects can occur when the pre-test sensitizes participants to some aspect of the treatment. Asking participants to fill out a questionnaire on their opinions about environmental policy before showing them a nature documentary will probably make them aware of the purpose of the study, and make them focus on aspects in the documentary related to the questionnaire.

In some studies test effects are avoided by administering two different tests, hoping that results of both tests can be compared in that they both measure the same variable. In psychology this is sometimes done with a *Form A* and a *Form B* of the same test in which the questions in *Form B* are put in a different way from *Form A*. These tests have, ideally, been calibrated in advance, and have also been checked for whether they actually do show the same results for a particular population. However, if the two forms have not been tested in advance, it is possible that participants respond differently to the wording of the second test, so that a difference in responses between pre- and post-test cannot be attributed to the treatment but instead is the result of different formulations in *Form A* and *Form B*.

The best way to evaluate the interaction between the pre-test and the treatment is the Solomon design.

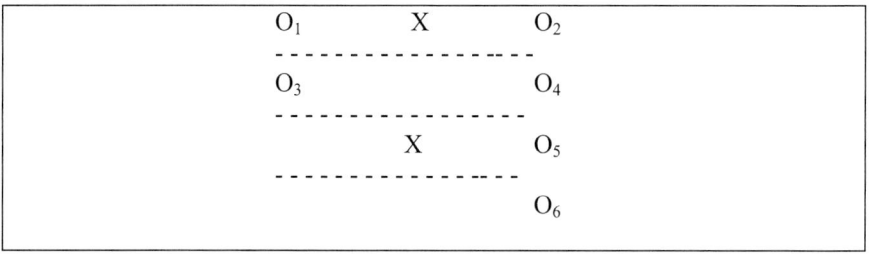

Figure 6.8: Solomon design

We see four groups here: one that first does a pre-test (O_1), then is exposed to a treatment, and does a post-test (O_2); a second group that does both the pre-test (O_3) and the post-test (O_4), but skips the treatment; the third group does not do the pre-test, but is exposed to the treatment and makes the post-test (O_5); finally, we have a group that only does the post-test (O_6). In this design comparing the differences between O_2 and O_4 on the one hand, and O_5 and O_6 on the other will tell us whether conducting a pre-test influenced the results. To explain this, let us again look at a fictitious example. In Figure 6.9a and b we present the results of two experiments, both using a Solomon design. In the first we see what results would look like when there is no effect of the pre-test on the results of the post-test. Let us say participants score on a Likert scale that runs from −5 to +5. In the figures we see the averages scores per group, on the different tests that are administered. For example, looking at the first figure, we see that the first experimental group made a pre-test (O_1) with an average score of −3, then was exposed to some treatment (X) and then made a post-test (O_2) with an average of 2.

(a) Pre-test		Post-test	(b) Pre-test		Post-test
$-3\ (O_1)$	X	$2\ (O_2)$	$-3\ (O_1)$	X	$2\ (O_2)$
$-3\ (O_3)$		$-3\ (O_4)$	$-3\ (O_3)$		$2\ (O_4)$
	X	$2\ (O_5)$		X	$-3\ (O_5)$
		$-3\ (O_6)$			$-3\ (O_6)$

Figure 6.9: (a) No pre-test effect and (b) effect of pre-test

Let us look at Figure 6.9a first. Comparing the differences between O_2 and O_4 and O_5 and O_6 we can conclude that conducting a pre-test did *not* affect the scores on post-test: whether a pre-test was administered or not, the treatment X resulted in a score 2 on the post-test, while the two control groups scored −3, *also* irrespective of whether they were administered a pre-test. In the results presented in Figure 6.9b, however, we see that filling out a pre-test must have influenced scores on the post-test. Without the pre-test, the experimental group scores −3 (average group score on O_5) on the post-test, while the experimental group *with* the pre-test scores an average of 2 on post-test O_2. Since participants were randomized across the four groups, what else could this mean than that the pre-test influenced the responses of the post-test? In short, the Solomon design gives you the possibility of estimating the internal validity of your study. However, do realize that the procedure involves more participants.

When we use pre-tests and post-tests, the threat of testing is just one of our worries. In experiments with a time lapse between pre-test and post-test there is the potential problem of *maturation*. Maturation refers to the fact that people change anyway, with or without your treatment. Imagine you want to measure the effects of a 1-year literature program on children's moral development. It is likely, however, that children will develop a more advanced reasoning about moral issues even without the literature program. This problem is, again, best solved by adding a control group to your design.

Another problem is formed by the so-called *ceiling or floor effects*. Imagine you want to measure the effects of an advertisement campaign against unsafe sex. In your test you ask "Do you think it is important to use a condom when you are having sex with a new partner?" Participants who saw the ad and control group participants answer this question by indicating their opinion on a five-point scale.

No, absolutely not   Yes, absolutely
   1   2   3   4   5

In both control group and experimental group you find extremely high average scores on this scale, say for instance 4.6 and 4.8 respectively. These findings do not tell you that the treatment had no effect. It is more likely that, since the control group also scored high on the test, little could be improved of participants' opinions in the first place. Because scores could hardly get any higher we speak of a *ceiling* effect (the reverse, with scores not being able to get any lower, is called a *floor* effect). A way to avoid this is to formulate your questions differently, so that you do get a sensitive instrument to gauge any change that might occur as a result of the treatment. Or you could enhance the sensitivity of the scale by making it run from 1 to 10 or even 100. Also, it is always a good idea to test your instrument in a *pilot study*, to see whether the answers to the test could help you distinguish between people with different opinions on the subject at hand (see Chapter 5).

One problem with experiments involving pre-tests and post-tests is *dropouts* (other terms used in the literature are *mortality* and *attrition*). It may happen that between pre-test and post-test some people may decide to stop participating. If this group of dropouts is a random one this will not be a threat to internal validity. But there is a chance that you are dealing with a specific group of participants. For instance, it may be that some of your participants do not like the story or film that you presented and decide not to take the post-test. In experiments where an ability of some kind is measured it may be that participants who fear they will score low want to quit.

A last form of internal validity is a special one: statistical validity. It means that you have chosen the right test for the right data. Remember the levels of measurement discussed in Chapter 5.2? As we announced there, some tests require a certain level of measurement: running a test on data measured at an ordinal level when the test requires ratio measurement can result in wrong conclusions. How to make the correct choice will be discussed in Chapter 11.

6.6.2. External validity

External validity means that we have good reasons to believe that our results can be generalized to the real world. Here we estimate whether our conclusions are valid for the whole population, that is, for all samples from that population, in other environments and at other times. Earlier we considered whether there was indeed a causal relationship between the manipulated (independent) variable and the variable you measured (dependent variable) within the experiment. Now we take matters of generalizability into account: is the causal relationship we found something that we will meet in the world outside the experiment as well? Will experiments with other participants (for instance of a different age group) result in the same conclusion? Often the steps we take to obtain internal validity result in threats to external validity. Experiments are conducted with a selection of people, for instance because we are striving for group homogeneity. Also, we conduct experiments preferably in controlled environments. As a result, the situation into which we bring participants is often an artificial one. These measures impair the degree to which findings can be generalized. Again, we see that conducting experimental research involves giving and taking. Let us see what forms of threats to external validity we can run into.

First there is the possibility of an *interaction between selection and treatment/measure*: it might be that the group of participants you selected responds differently to the treatment or test than another group. How? You don't know. Neither do you know whether this threat does actually occur but clearly it poses a problem to the generalizability of your study. One solution would be to include other groups in a (factorial) design. For instance, you are interested in how people respond to complexity in paintings. You ask art students to rate, say, eight selected paintings that you show them in random order. Before the experiment you asked experts to rate the paintings on 'complexity.' Thus you can arrange them from low complexity (#1) to high (#8). What you might find is that the higher the complexity of the paintings, the higher your participants' aesthetic appreciation. But at some point you may see that aesthetic appreciation declines with increasing complexity (as illustrated by the graph below). What is described here in this fictitious example is a recurring result in studies conducted by Berlyne and other researchers (see Chapters 1 and 2).

It may well be, however, that your results would be different if your respondents had been math students. The degree of education in art is a likely intervening variable. What you could do is vary both complexity of the painting and the degree of art education of your participants by including, for instance, math students, college freshmen and graduates in art history. This would certainly enhance the external validity or generalizability of your findings.

A second threat to external validity is the *specific situation in which the treatment and tests are administered*, which might cause an interaction. For instance, it may be that conducting an experiment in a school, your participants may consider the questionnaire you handed out as a test. It is possible that in another context they may respond differently. In other words, here you have a problem generalizing your findings to other situations.

The same holds for events that occur outside the 'laboratory'. This third threat to external validity refers to an interaction between treatment and the circumstances outside the experimental situation. Imagine you are interested in the effects of a documentary on Islam on viewers' attitudes toward Muslims. But while you are conducting your research, a dramatic situation occurs in world or local politics that makes participants extra sensitive to your treatment.

It seems likely that in this case you have to be careful when generalizing your findings.

Note the similarity between this case and the threat to internal validity mentioned above, that of extra-experimental events. As you may remember, there is a difference: internal validity refers to the degree to which you can attribute the differences you found between observations to the treatment; external validity refers to the possibility of generalization of your conclusions to the outside world.

A fourth threat is an interaction between measurement and treatment. It may be that an effect of treatment only occurred because you administered a pre-test. One way to avoid this is the Solomon four groups design (see above), which helps you to determine what exactly caused the effect you registered.

A fifth threat is that the number of your participants is too small for you to draw any conclusion at all, let alone generalize your findings to a larger population. How many participants do you need? That crucially depends on the type of research you are doing. For a survey (see Chapter 4, Section 10), you need a representative sample. That means that every individual in the population must have equal chances of ending up in your sample. In other words, all possible characteristics of participants must be represented in your sample: people living in large cities and in provincial towns, as well as those living in the countryside, people with high, middle and low education, people with high, middle and low income, and so forth. It will be evident that such types of research are complex and also expensive, and that we will not normally be dealing with such research here.

Fortunately, the situation is much less complex when we are dealing with (quasi-) experimental research, i.e. research in which we wish to test a particular hypothesis – which is what most of us will be doing, unless we are involved in qualitative research, of course. In this case, we will be involved in *generating* hypotheses. For (quasi-)experimental investigations, the rule of thumb is that you need 30 participants per cell in your design matrix. For instance, if you wish to compare reactions of male and female viewers, you have two cells, and you need 30 male and 30 female (60 in total) participants. Suppose you also wish to compare two age groups, for instance, 20–30 and 50–60. You now have four cells in your matrix: young males, young females, old males, and old females. For each of these cells you again need 30 subjects, hence 120 in total. You see that the number of participants rises quickly when you add more conditions to your research, which is one reason why you should keep the design of your study simple.

What if you do not have 30 participants per cell? It is a bit difficult to give a clear answer to that question because the answer presupposes that you understand some basic concepts of statistics, which we will see in Chapters 9,

10, and 11. Basically this has to do with the power of generalization of our findings. In themselves, the results of our research do not interest us: they are of interest insofar as we can draw generalizations from them. If only those 30 men and women behave the way they do, our research is not so interesting. We need to find general patterns. The concept that is used in statistics to express this possibility of generalizing is *significance*: we hope to find *significant* results, that is, those that apply equally well to other groups of comparable people. The point now is that by lowering the number of participants in your research, you will also lower the chances of finding *significance*, that is, generalizable results. Hence, the size of your sample should be seen on a scale: with 25 participants per cell you may still be fine and come across significant results but the chances are lower than with 30. With 20 participants, you lower even further your chances of obtaining significant results, and so on. The ideal number is 30 because, as experience (and statistics) shows, with this number chances are ideal. You may, of course, canvass more participants if you wish to do so and have the ability to do it, but you should realize that this is going to be more work, which basically is not needed, because the chances of significant results are optimal with a sample size of 30 per cell.

Construct validity, a special form of external validity, is the last factor that you need to consider. It is here that researchers make contestable choices. Therefore it is important to examine this possible threat to validity critically, so as to find out in what way your study can improve on previous work. Also, in your own study, consider how you yourself 'translate' the concepts central to your theory into measurable variables (see notes on operationalization in Chapter 4). Imagine you want to find out what the relation is between the degree of literary socialization and appreciation for literary texts. For this of course you first have to define 'literary socialization' and subsequently, how you would measure the degree of literary socialization. Would you ask people how much time they spend reading, or how many books they read? Wouldn't you want to know *what* they read? Of course you want to focus on how much *literature* they read, and not the time they spent reading newspapers or comic books. Does it matter what type of literature? And, what *is* literature? Does reading bestsellers like Dan Brown's *The Da Vinci Code* qualify? Do you for instance let participants decide themselves whether and how much 'literature' they read? The problem is that respondents' definitions of literature differ from yours. Moreover, maybe you think that simply *reading* many literary texts does not add to literary socialization. So maybe it is an idea to test participants' knowledge about literature. But what questions would be suitable for such a quiz? Do *you* decide which questions should be included? Maybe you are modest enough to see that you do not have the authority to make decisions like that. One idea is to leave things to others: seek the advice of experts, ask them what knowledge they consider indicative of a high level of literary socialization. But is knowledge really what your construct 'literary socialization' is about? As you can see, many decisions have to be made, and where you make decisions, you may find that others have objections.

In sum, in this chapter you have learned how to develop experiments, and be in a position to evaluate their weaknesses and strengths. Now it is time for you to run your experiment, collect your data and enter them into the computer program SPSS (in the next chapter you will learn how to do this). Then you need to know how to draw conclusions from your data. First you will find out how to explore the data. This requires descriptive statistics (see Chapter 8). For instance, you may want to know what the group mean scores on certain variables are. Are they different? If so, does this difference tally with our expectations? Often we will need to do more than that and draw conclusions about causality. For this you need inferential statistics (Chapters 9–11). Finally, in Chapter 12, you will be instructed on how to communicate your results to fellow researchers in a way that they may find useful and interesting.

Chapter Seven

How to Enter and Manipulate Data in SPSS

In this chapter, and in the following ones, we will introduce you to the computer program for statistical analyses, SPSS. Familiarizing yourself with this program will open up a whole range of possibilities for your research that will enhance the power of your analyses. Hence we will concentrate first on how to enter your data in SPSS once you have collected them. The chapter will also consider how you can manipulate these data when you have entered them for analyses.

7.1. Why use a computer program?

Before you can analyze data, you must first collect them. When you have your data, one way to analyze them is by browsing through them, read through the participants' responses, make notes here and there, compare the responses of one participant to those of another one, and so forth. Now suppose you had 55 participants in your study and you asked them to respond to 20 questions. You then have to deal with 1,100 answers. Finding a pattern in those 1,100 replies is going to be a lot of work. Of course you can do it by hand, if you wish, but it is going to eat up an inordinate amount of your time. Better to use a computer program to do so. The program has several advantages over a manual analysis: it is much faster, it makes no mistakes (as you are apt to if you do it by hand), and it allows you to generate tables and graphs that may clarify the patterns that you found. Moreover, it offers you the opportunity to do statistical analyses that sometimes are very important.

These advantages also tell you that it is not always necessary or even desirable to use SPSS. If you have only a couple of questions answered by a small group of people, then you might as well calculate the average by hand. Or when your observations are all in the nominal scale of measurement and you do not really need tables or graphs, it can often be as efficient to do everything by hand. Remember that entering data into SPSS requires time as well. That time must bring extra rewards afterwards and in most cases this will indeed also be the case.

There are only three requirements for the use of SPSS. First, you must have access to the program; most universities have a campus license on offer for students at reasonably cheap rates. Second, you must be acquainted with the program and you must be able to interpret the results that the program produces. That is what you will learn in Chapters 8 through 11. Third, you first have to enter the data in the program. That is what you will learn in the present chapter. The program we have chosen is SPSS, an abbreviation for Statistical Package for the Social Sciences. It is one of the most widely used programs for statistical analysis, not merely in the social sciences but also in many other disciplines. We will use the Windows version of the program – version 12.0 (but we may make occasional comments when things were different in the previous version). In order to make it clear when we mean commands in the program rather than the everyday word, we will use a different font. Thus CANCEL means: go to or click on the button that says 'cancel'.

The first thing you must know is how to enter the data you have collected into the program. That is a relatively simple thing to do, but also a bit boring. It requires a high amount of concentration (to avoid making mistakes) while there is little intellectual challenge in the task. However, we will try to enliven it by using an existing data set of a piece of research that is familiar to you from Chapter 1. We will guide you step by step through how to enter these data in SPSS. You may then use this procedure as an example when you will later have to enter data on your own.

7.2. Start SPSS

SPSS runs both on PCs and on MacIntosh. In this book we refer to the PC version but there is no difference whatsoever from the Mac version. To activate SPSS, click on the START button in Windows, go to PROGRAMS, then to SPSS 12.0 FOR WINDOWS. A window will now appear on your screen.

Chapter Seven

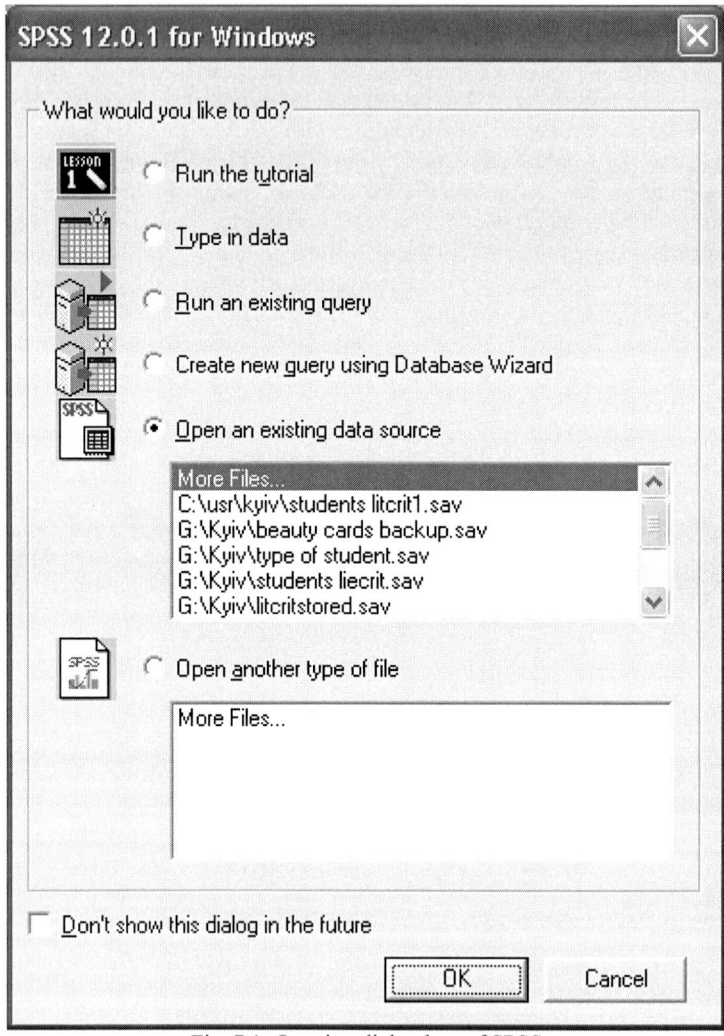

Fig. 7.1: Opening dialog box of SPSS

It is obvious that at this stage the second option (TYPE IN DATA) is what you want. Choose that option, or click on CANCEL. (You can also, if you wish, run the tutorial at a later stage, to further familiarize yourself with the program.) You will now see on the top of your screen UNTITLED - SPSS DATA EDITOR.

How to Enter and Manipulate Data in SPSS 169

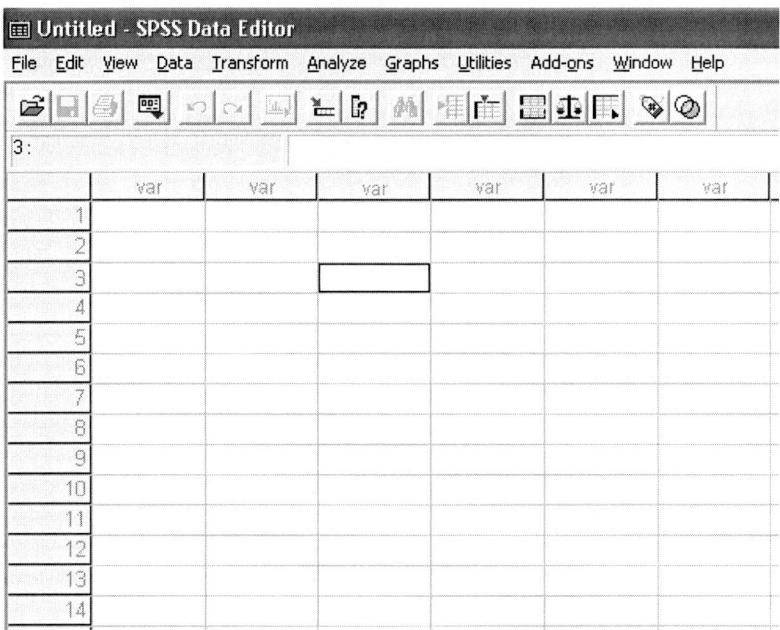

Figure 7.2: SPSS Data Editor

Below that you see a series of words like **FILE, EDIT, VIEW**, etc. These are the menu items. Under them, you see a toolbar containing a number of icons, some of which, like the diskette or the printer, you will recognize because they also appear in other Windows programs. The largest part of the screen is filled by a matrix of cells. The columns contain the variables of your research, hence the row of boxes all containing **VAR** on top of each column. The rows represent the observations you have made, these are numbered, hence the numbers 1, 2, 3, and so forth to the left of the rows. Basically, in most research, the rows are the different participants, while the columns are the different questions you asked them. Hence the matrix contains as many cells as the product of the number of participants and the number of questions you asked them. This should be absolutely clear to you before you go on: rows are cases (these could be participants, text characteristics, and so forth), columns are variables (i.e. the categories into which you have divided your observations).

Under this matrix, in the left-hand corner, you will see two tabs, one saying **DATA VIEW**, the other **VARIABLE VIEW**. Clicking on these tabs takes you to two different kinds of information that your data will contain. The former (**DATA VIEW**) will show you the matrix as you now see it on the screen with all the numerical values entered. Clicking on **VARIABLE VIEW** will show you all the information about how the matrix is composed, so that you can interpret it in case you have forgotten what the numbers mean. It is here that we will start our work: before you can enter your data into the program, you must set up the format, so that SPSS is ready to receive your data. Therefore, now click on the **VARIABLE VIEW** tab. The screen now changes and you will see on top of the matrix **NAME, TYPE, WIDTH**, etc.

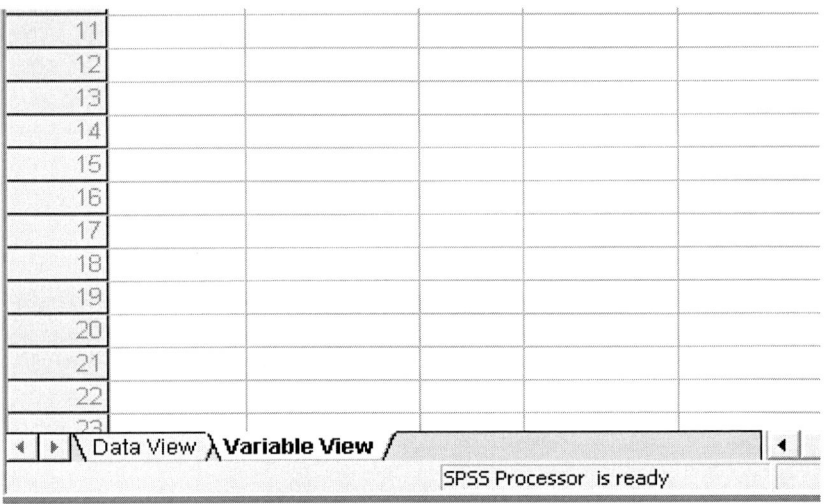

Figure 7.3: SPSS Variable View

The meaning of these terms is simple: in the cell with **NAME** we are going to enter the name of the variable, in **TYPE** we will tell SPSS what type of variable it is, whether they are numbers ('numerical') or words ('string'). The first thing to do now is to look at your data. To this end, we will now first describe the data we collected in our research.

In Chapter 1 we described an experiment in which readers rated eight identical lines of a poem, each 'I love you not' on a scale, one after the other, for the degree to which they considered the poem beautiful, with the ninth line, 'I love you notwithstanding' deviating from the pattern (van Peer, Zyngier & Hakemulder, 2007). Below you see a filled out version of this questionnaire.

How to Enter and Manipulate Data in SPSS 171

−5	−4	−3	−2	−1	0	+1	+2	+3	+4	+5
−5	−4	−3	−2	−1	0	+1	+2	+3	+4	+5
−5	−4	−3	−2	−1	0	+1	+2	+3	+4	+5
−5	−4	−3	−2	−1	0	+1	+2	+3	+4	+5
−5	−4	−3	−2	−1	0	+1	+2	+3	+4	+5
−5	−4	−3	−2	−1	0	+1	+2	+3	+4	+5
−5	−4	−3	−2	−1	0	+1	+2	+3	+4	+5
−5	−4	−3	−2	−1	0	+1	+2	+3	+4	+5
−5	−4	−3	−2	−1	0	+1	+2	+3	+4	+5

(Boxed responses, top to bottom: +4, +1, −1, −2, −2, −3, −3, −4, +5)

Figure 7.4: Example of a filled-out questionnaire

This questionnaire is extremely simple, and this is one of the reasons why we are using it to teach you how to enter data in SPSS. Basically, there are nine variables, i.e. the nine lines of the poem. But we ran the questionnaire in different countries, so that is another variable (**NATION**). Also, in some countries we had different groups (**GROUP**) respond to it, or we noted the gender (**SEX**) of the participants. Those are three more variables, so that together with the nine lines we have a total of 12 variables. How to enter these in SPSS?

The best way to do this is by preparing a list with the dependent and independent variables (see Chapter 6) in the order you would like to enter them into the program. Then, give each questionnaire an individual number; write that number on top of the questionnaire in a striking color. The order itself is irrelevant because these numbers serve only for the potential identification of the original questionnaires. It may be, for instance, that in the analysis later you hit upon something strange in the data of Participant 46. Because you have entered the data in the order you have determined by the numbers, you can then go back to the questionnaire and check if you have not made a mistake when entering the data – for instance, you typed in '33' instead of '3', or the participant gave '25' as a response to the question how many hours a day she read.

Now let us look at the answers. Participants gave us their opinion on the 'beauty' of each line by marking a scale which went from −5 via 0 to +5. It would be a bit cumbersome to have to write the pluses and minuses each time – better to rearrange. One simple way is by taking the –5 as the number 1, –4 as 2, –3 as 3, and so forth. The +5 then becomes 11, we have an 11-point scale here. In order to prevent making mistakes when entering the data in this converted way in the program, write the appropriate number in red next to each of the scales. This takes some time, it is true, but will allow you to enter data much faster – and with considerably less likelihood of mistakes when you finally enter them. When you have done that, we are ready to instruct SPSS how to deal with our data. We begin by preparing the **VARIABLE VIEW**.

7.3. Preparing the VARIABLE VIEW

Maybe to beginners there is something annoying about SPSS in that in the **DATA VIEW** the columns represent the variables but in the **VARIABLE VIEW**, it is the other way round: here it is the rows that contain the variables! However, you will soon see that this is in itself logical – and in any case you will get used to it immediately you start using the program. So what are the columns here? They contain diverse pieces of information about each separate variable. For instance, since the two questionnaires above belong to different groups of participants, i.e. two different nationalities, we want to be able to distinguish their data once they have been entered in SPSS. A first important difference between the respondents is their nationality. This could therefore be our first variable. (Which variable is the first, which the second, etc. is not really of importance; what is usually done is that the variables entered follow, more or less, the order of the questions in the questionnaire.) Let us call the variable 'nationality', so type this word in the first cell of the **VARIABLE VIEW**, and press **ENTER**. SPSS allows you to use a maximum of 65 characters as a **NAME** [1] – whereby the first character must be a letter. It is to be recommended, however, that you limit yourself to a name with a maximum of 18 characters, because in any output SPSS will break off the name of a variable after this. When you have typed 'nationality' in the first cell and then pressed **ENTER**, this is what your computer screen will look like:

---

[1] In all versions of SPSS before version 12.0, a maximum of only eight characters (and no punctuation signs) is allowed. When you use one of these versions, you will have to think of an abbreviation as a name. Here we could choose 'nation', which is less than eight characters. You can, however, make up for this deficiency in this version, by giving a more extended name (of up to 256 characters under **LABEL**).

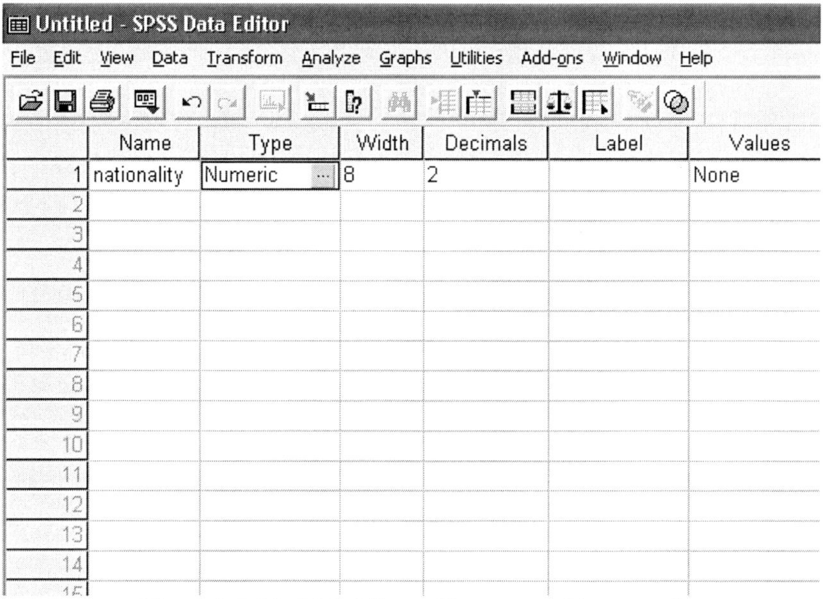

Figure 7.5: Variable View with one variable entered

Did you notice that now the other cells in this row have been automatically filled with information? For instance, under **TYPE** you see 'numeric', under **WIDTH** '8', etc. All this is not very important to most of the types of research we refer to and use in this book. In the column **LABEL**, however, there is still nothing; why is that? Here you can provide a longer name for your variable, or – which is often a good idea – type in the full question that you asked the participants (if you used a questionnaire). It may be that you do not remember the correct formulation of the question while you are working in **DATA VIEW** or that when you are doing an analysis together with another person, he or she may not be as familiar with the questions you asked, so having the questions here will help. You may use up to 255 characters here, and all keys on your keyboard may be used. Again, however, it may be wise to limit yourself to the 18 characters that will be kept by SPSS in any output file. You may want to do some further analysis a couple of months after you did the research, and you may have forgotten what exactly the variable name stood for. Here you can type in the information necessary to refresh your memory. So here you could enter, for instance, 'nationality of participants'. Always remember that when you want to inspect your data later, the **VARIABLE VIEW** menu allows you to check crucial information about your variables. Hence it is important at

174   Chapter Seven

this stage that you are meticulous about what information should be entered here.

How will SPSS recognize the nationality of the participants? We could type in the nationality in this cell for each of the participants. This would mean a lot of work, however, and you might make typos, causing trouble later, which is why SPSS offers you a much simpler solution. To that end, click on the cell under **VALUES**, and then on the shaded area to the right in this cell, containing three dots. A new window, **VALUE LABELS**, now pops up.

Figure 7.6: Value Labels dialog box

Now enter '1' for the first group of nationals in the box **VALUE**, for instance, then enter 'Brazilian' in the box **VALUE LABEL**, then click on **ADD**. You will now see that in the box below an entry "1.00 = 'Brazilian'" has been added. (Do not worry that your '1' has been changed into '1.00' – SPSS does this automatically, but it has no meaning here. If you wish, you can change this by going to the **VARIABLE VIEW** and in the relevant row click on **DECIMALS**: you can now, using the arrows, set the decimals to zero for this variable – or indeed for any other variable where you wish to get rid of the decimals.) Now enter '2' in the box **VALUE** for the second group, e.g. the Ukrainian group, then type 'Ukrainian' in **VALUE LABEL**, click on **ADD**, and proceed for any remaining groups. In this way we will later save an enormous amount of time when we enter the data. If we had not defined nationality in this way, we would have to type in 'Brazilian' or 'Ukrainian' etc. for each single participant.

Now in the Brazilian group there were both teachers and students. We want to be able to distinguish these, so we determine this by creating a variable for it. So do the same as you did for nationality. In the second row, under **NAME** type in 'group'. Then, in VALUES, assign the number 1 for students and the number 2 for teachers.

Since we have no other independent variables to define, we can now begin by entering the responses of the scales. Take the pile of questionnaires. In the third row (1 was for nationality, 2 for group), under NAME, type in 'line1' and press ENTER, and type 'line 1' under LABEL. There is no need to determine the values here, as these are the numbers on the questionnaire, ranging from 1 through 11. Do the same for the eight following lines. In VARIABLE VIEW, you see that as the 12th variable you find sex. In some groups we asked participants for their gender. (We use these two words as synonyms in this book; note that in some research fields, they may mean different things!) When you double-click on the grey area in VALUE LABEL, you will see that '1' has been allocated to female participants, '2' to male participants.

As with the coding of the group variable, we assign a number to each of the sexes, and the exact order is, of course, irrelevant. It is also possible to make a more meaningful assignment, such as F for female and M for male. To do that, click on the button in the cell TYPE (in the row for sex). In the box VARIABLE TYPE that now appears, set the variable's type to STRING and click on OK. Now click on the cell VALUES and again on the button in this cell. Now type in 'F' in the box VALUE and 'female' in the box VALUE LABEL, then click on ADD. You will see that in the main box it now says "F = 'female'". Repeat for male. (Take care, though: value labels are case sensitive, so 'M' does not equal 'm'!)

We have now defined the variables for this little experiment. All dependent variables were scored on scales. However, in the chapter on how to make questionnaires, we also reviewed other types of questions that were not of a scalar nature. How do we enter these in SPSS? We look first at nominal data, for instance in a checklist. You presented participants with a list of things, events, or activities and requested them to tick the things they knew, did, liked, etc. Suppose we had included a question about poetry-reading habits in this research, because we suspected that such habits may influence their responses. For instance, we could have asked them the following question:

I read poetry
   ....   by German poets
   ....   by English poets
   ....   by Russian poets
   ....   by poets from non-Western countries

In such a case, it is best to enter each of the alternative answers as a separate (sub)variable. So if this question was named variable 8, you can name the first answer variable 8a, the second 8b, and so forth. If a participant ticked the first alternative, then enter '1' as the score, and enter nothing for the other alternatives. If a participant ticked more alternatives, then enter '1' for each of these.

What if you asked participants to indicate their preference by ticking alternatives? Look at the following example (see Chapter 5):

Which reading activity do you like most?
    .... Novels
    .... Poetry
    .... Short-stories
    .... Fairy tales
    .... Detective novels

You can code this in the same way as the previous example (i.e. treat each of the answers as sub-variables, and enter a 1 if it has been ticked), but it is also possible to treat this question as one variable only, and in **VALUES** define the alternative answers as follows: '1' = Novels, '2' = Poetry, etc. In this way we can simply type in '2' as the response of a participant who ticked 'poetry' as his/her response to this question. Alternatively, you can also enter the full variable names, like 'novels', 'poetry', etc. One obvious advantage of this method is that when you are doing statistical analyses later, you will have the names of the variables on the screen, instead of numbers, which you may have to check each time. A disadvantage is that you will have to do some more typing while entering the data.

Now suppose you had asked your respondents to rank order these types of reading activities (see Chapter 5, Section 5.2) by placing a number 1 next to the genre they like reading most, a number 2 by the one they like second best, etc. In this case it is again best to enter each of the alternatives as a separate (sub)variable. As data, you can then enter the number given by each respondent for each of the (sub)variables.

We are now ready: we have defined all the variables, so that SPSS is ready to receive the data. Before doing so, however, it is recommended that you first save your work! Click on **FILE** and on **SAVE AS**, then give the file a name, for instance "complexity". By default, SPSS will save the file in an SPSS folder, but it is also possible to specify another directory, or to save the file on a disk. Always keep multiple copies of your data, for instance one copy on your hard disk and two on separate floppy-disks, CDs, or USB-memory sticks. And do not forget to update them when you make any changes!

7.4. Entering the data in DATA VIEW

There are various methods for entering data. One is to do it together with a colleague of friend: while one reads the data aloud, the other types them in. This is faster and of course also more fun than having to go through the whole thing by yourself. Also, you can change places when you become tired. In that way you will avoid making mistakes.

Now click on DATA VIEW at the bottom left-hand corner of your screen. You will now see that the name of your first variable, 'nation' has appeared at the top of the first column. The numbers to the left of the DATA VIEW screen, i.e. the rows, are the participants. Hence each participant is allocated one row, in which his/her data are entered. We begin with the first participant. You are now ready to enter the data, so type in the value '1' (meaning: this is the questionnaire of a participant belonging to the group of Brazilians) in the first cell. Because you are looking at the data of the students (not the teachers, that is a different pile – if you think it necessary, mark this on the questionnaires too), you enter '1' in the second column, 'group'. Then you see that you have written '2' next to the scale for the first line, because the participant had responded with minus 4. So, type in '2' in the third column, which says 'line1' at the top. Enter the values for the other scales in the following columns. Then take questionnaire 2 and work through it in the same way, until all the questionnaires from the students' pile have been entered. (By the way, do NOT forget to periodically save the document, to prevent loss in case of a power cut or a computer crash or any other accident that may happen!) Then do the same for the teachers' questionnaires, but of course you now enter '2' for GROUP. Then you go to the pile of Ukrainian questionnaires, and enter '2' for NATION. Repeat for the German, Egyptian, and Dutch piles.

As you can surmise, entering the data can be time consuming, especially if you had many participants and there were many questions to be answered. It is therefore good to plan time to enter data beforehand. For the kind of research that you will be dealing with, an afternoon or two will usually suffice. There is one remaining point that is important here. The analysis of the data that you will carry out later can only be as good as the data themselves. So if you make mistakes in entering the data, this may seriously flaw your whole research project. It is therefore of the utmost importance that you avoid mistakes in entering the data. Unfortunately, there is no failsafe way to guarantee this, so a lot is going to depend on your concentration. Most people are prone to make mistakes. One consequence of this is that it is much better to spread out the task over different short sessions than one long one. Although there is no method of avoiding mistakes that is totally foolproof, there are a number of things you can do to increase the likelihood that no errors have been made.

A question that will pop up sooner or later is what you do when a participant has forgotten (or refused) to answer a certain question. These are what are called in SPSS 'missing values' and you do not have to worry too much about them. You just leave that cell empty, and SPSS will see to it that it is treated as a 'missing value'. (For instance, it may tell you in the descriptive statistics how many missing values there were.) The same applies to situations where a participant has overlooked to fill in his/her gender, age, etc. Just skip these cells. Certainly do not start 'guessing' whether this person was male or female. Another situation where missing values turn up is when you cannot clearly read the answer a respondent has entered, for instance because of poor handwriting or because of unclear ticking or circling of answers on the questionnaire. In such a case it is wise to first consult with someone else – maybe a friend of yours is better at deciphering handwritings, or has an interpretation that sounds highly plausible. However, in all cases where you cannot reach a clear conclusion, refrain from guessing, and leave the cell in question open. It is better to have a missing value than a wrong value!

One thing you can do is, as already pointed out, work together with someone. The one who reads the data can also occasionally cast a glance at the screen to check whether everything is going all right. Another thing you can do is to regularly check on the screen whether the data you are typing in are entered in the right column. For instance, for the questionnaire we are using here, you could type in the numbers grouped in threes. Thus after typing three numbers, look up at the screen and check whether the data for the second group of three starts in the column that has 'line4' above it. Still another measure to prevent mistakes is to enter the data one participant at a time, so typing in the rows first. If you work by the columns, typing in the group for all participants, then the next variable, etc., you are much more likely to make mistakes. You can also check the numbers on the screen for oddities. If you see the number 126 in a cell for age, you can be pretty sure that someone has made a mistake. Also watch the end of the row: if the last value you entered is a column too far compared to the other rows, something has gone amiss. Here is yet another trick: it is possible in SPSS to order the values in your columns in ascending/descending order. You do this by clicking on the name of the variable at the top of a column; the column will now be highlighted in black. Now right-hand click the mouse and a menu will open: below you will see the possibilities SORT ASCENDING and SORT DESCENDING. When you inspect the data in this column again when they have been sorted, the odd entries will be much easier to spot.

When your data have been entered and checked, they are now ready for analysis. However, it may be the case that you need some more work before you can actually start the analytic work. Perhaps you want to look at some of the variables together, because you assume that the individual questions taken together make a variable as a whole, thus collapsing several questions into a single variable. You may for instance want to know what the attitude of your respondents towards a television program is. At, say, four different places in your questionnaire you have included a question concerning participants' appreciation of information content. It may be that you have good reasons to believe that all these questions actually measure just one aspect of participants' response toward the program. The goal of statistical analyses is often to summarize the data, so here you may not want to present the results of all four questions but just one average for all four together. Now how can you analyze these responses in one go? These and other questions will be answered in the next section.

7.5. Manipulating data

You have entered all the data, and meticulously checked your SPSS data set for mistakes. In most cases this will take hours and hours! Take it from us that you will now have some difficulty in suppressing the almost irresistible urge to find out immediately what the outcome of your study is. This is one of the moments when you will experience how exciting empirical work can be. However, often you may first need to 'manipulate' your data. Discard any associations you may have here with corrupt scientists who manipulate their data so as to make them fit their theory; it is often essential that you do prepare the 'raw' data for final analyses, i.e. the kind of statistical test that you will encounter in the next chapters. Let us now look at some of those situations where more preparatory work is necessary one by one.

7.5.1. Compute: making new variables based on your data

In some cases you want to create new variables using existing ones. We already gave you an example at the end of the previous section. Let us look at a second example. Imagine you are interested in whether the context in which an audience sees a play influences its reception. A performance in a traditional theater hall sets the audience's expectations perhaps in a different way to one in an ex-factory hall or a school auditorium. In the school auditorium people may expect an amateur performance. Here the audience may be more willing to accept imperfections in acting, lighting etc. In the traditional theater audience standards are perhaps set a little higher. In your study you randomly assign participants to three groups. They all see the same show by one drama group, but one group is invited to a theater in the city center, the second to an ex-factory hall, and the third to a school auditorium. After the show participants are asked to answer 10 questions with which you intend to measure their

180   Chapter Seven

appreciation of the performance. You give them 10 statements they can respond to by indicating the degree to which they agree with those statements on seven-point scales.

Since you consider the 10 questions as one variable (i.e. 'appreciation') you may want to summarize the results for those variables (that you simply entered as, say, var1, var2, var3, etc.). As a general rule, in statistics you want on the one hand to summarize your data as much as possible (to see whether there is an overall pattern), on the other you are also interested in the responses to the individual scales. In the latter case, however, you will have to avoid capitalizing on chance, something we will return to in Chapter 9 when we introduce you to the way in which to draw inferences about populations from statistical analyses.

How do you compute this new variable using the 10 old variables that you already entered? Click on **TRANSFORM**. This opens a menu. In this menu select **COMPUTE** and click. This opens the dialog box as seen below in Figure 7.7. On the left you see the variable list: all the variables that you entered: **CASE, GENDER, AGE, VAR1**, etc. With the transport button you can bring variables you select from the variable list to the field labeled **NUMERIC EXPRESSION**. As an example, let us enter in the **NUMERIC EXPRESSION** the variables **VAR1** through **VAR10**. For each respondent you want to add the scores on the 10n appreciation questions. But this is not all. The scores for each question are on a seven-point scale. Simply adding the scores would increase the scale to 70 points. This may be confusing for you and for the readers of your research report. It is often preferable to stick to the original scale: this makes the interpretation of the results more transparent for you and for the readers of your final report. Therefore, here we not only add the scores but also divide by the number of variables we added up (10 in the example). This will bring your results (for instance, average scores for the two groups) back on to seven-point scales.

How to Enter and Manipulate Data in SPSS 181

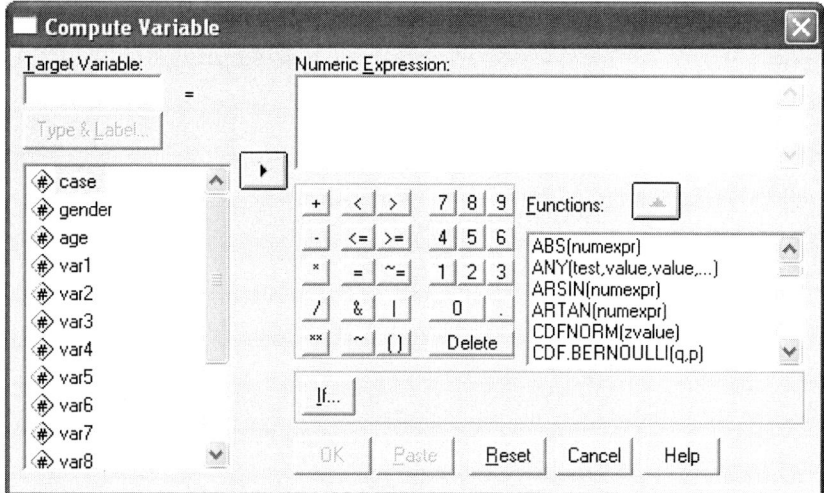

Figure 7.7: Compute Variable dialog box

To compute a new variable, you do the following:

1. Enter a new name for the variable you want to create, for instance 'evaluate' in the box **TARGET VARIABLE**.
2. Next, you define the new variable by entering the formula as presented in the field for **NUMERIC EXPRESSION** in Figure 7.7 ('/' stands for: divide). You can do this by typing the expression. You can also use the transport button with which you can select variables from the variable list and the control panel with which you can add the (), + and / sign; this avoids making typing mistakes.
3. Finally you click on **OK**. Now SPSS adds a new variable for each respondent that filled out all the three questions. (Check how this worked out by going to **DATA VIEW**: you will find the new variable at the right-hand end of your data matrix.)

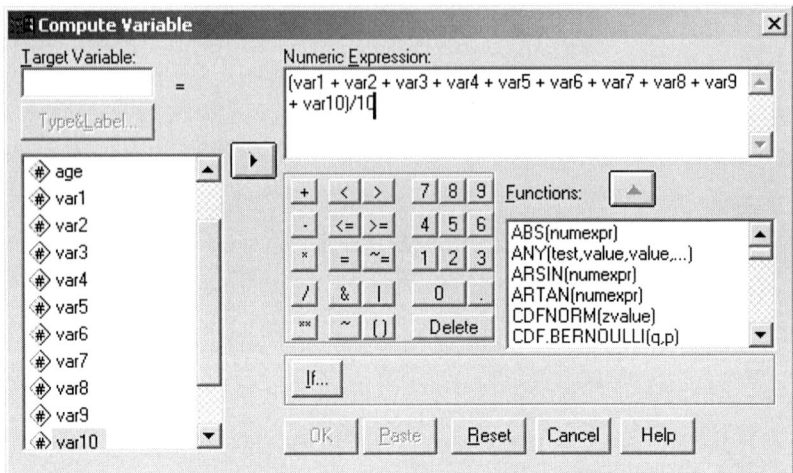

Figure 7.8: Compute Variable: example

Basically the new variable is the average score for each respondent on **VAR1** through **VAR10** put together.

But how do you know that these 10 questions measure the same kind of evaluative response? If they do not, then you should not create one variable out of them – adding teddy bears and airplanes together will not make any sense. To answer this question, refer to Chapter 8, where we will answer it when we talk about 'reliability analyses'.

Here is a problem: what if one of the statements does not exactly express a positive evaluation of the performance and is formulated as follows?

I found the performance of low quality.
True   1   2   3   4   5   6   7   Not true

Adding up participants' scores on this scale with responses to positive statements (e.g. "I enjoyed this performance enormously") would seriously distort the results of your research. You want to enter your data so that the answers are pointing in the same direction, either positive or negative. To avoid a problem of this kind, you either have to change the direction of the scales before entering the data (which can be useful, but needs attention and concentration) or you can enter the data as given on the original questionnaires and then later recode the scores on this one statement, so as to make sure that the scores on each scale mean the same: i.e. a score 1 stands for low appreciation and a score 7 stands for a high appreciation of the show. We will now discuss how to do this.

7.5.2. RECODE: changing the values of your variables

To change the values of your variables you go to the TRANSFORM menu. You click on RECODE. Now you see you have two options: recoding into (1) the same variable and (2) a different variable. Choosing the first will overwrite your data set. For example, you decide to change the values of the responses to the statements in a way that will make high scores for all variables correspond with a positive evaluation. In the case of the responses to the statement "I found the performance of low quality" you want to reverse the scoring by changing 1 into 7, 2 into 6, 3 into 5, etc. Thus the scale does not measure the degree of negative evaluation anymore, but like the other scales in your instrument, it measures positive appreciation. Of course, in subsequent analyses that you may do, it is important that you remember that you recoded the responses. (Maybe consider making a note in the data set itself, under LABEL).

In this case the recoding is not as permanent as it may be in other situations. If you need the old data again, you simply reverse the scores again (again by changing 1 into 7, 2 into 6, etc). There are, however, situations in which you will lose information permanently. For instance, you decide to cluster responses. Say you had a scale running from 0 to 100, and you want to reduce it to a four-point scale to be able to do certain statistical analyses, to be explained later in Chapter 9. All answers running from 0 to 25 you change into 1, 26 to 50 into 2 etc. The procedure RECODING INTO SAME VARIABLES will now cause you to lose information permanently – you will not be able to retrieve the original finer scale when you need it.

In such situations it is better to opt for RECODING INTO DIFFERENT VARIABLES: this will leave the original variable intact and simply add a new one with a scale from 1 to 4 instead of 0 to 100.

Let us now see how the procedure works. Clicking on RECODING INTO SAME VARIABLES will open the dialog box presented in Figure 7.9.

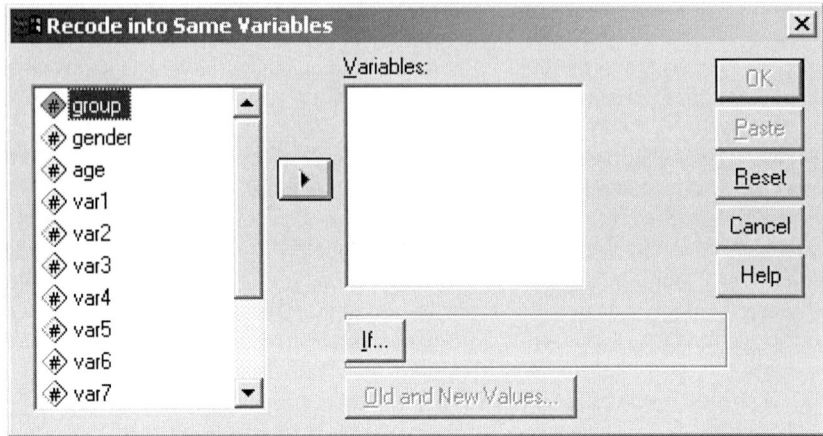

Figure 7.9: Recode into Same Variables dialog box

What you see here is again a field with a variable list. What you do is select the variable (e.g. **VAR1**) that needs recoding, and transport it to the field on the right-hand side. As soon as you do this the button **OLD AND NEW VALUES** turns black, which means it is activated. You click on this button and the next dialog box, presented in Figure 7.10, opens. To start recoding you type under **OLD VALUE** a 1, and under **NEW VALUE** a 7. When both values are entered the **ADD** button is activated. With this button you can now transport the old–new pair 1–7 to the field labeled **OLD** → **NEW**. You follow the same procedure up to the last pair: 7–1 (see Figure 7.10). When this last pair is transported to the field on the right-hand side using the **ADD** button, you can click on **CONTINUE**. You now return to the previous dialog box. Here you can click on **OK** and now SPSS will automatically change all the values: 1 into 7, 2 into 6, etc. for all your respondents.

How to Enter and Manipulate Data in SPSS 185

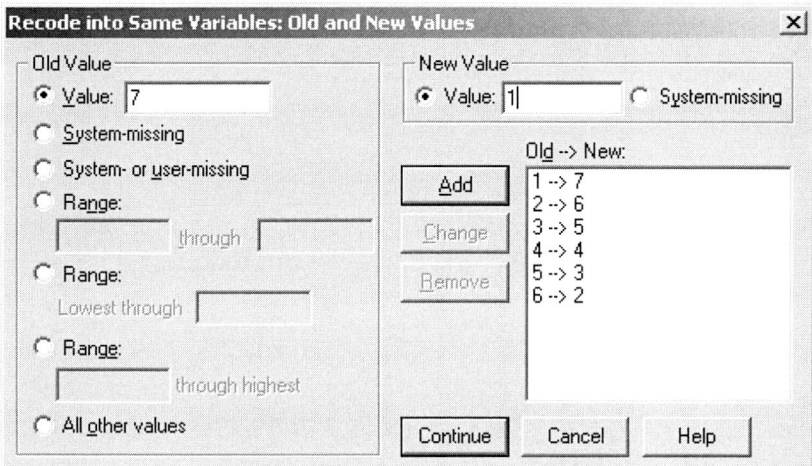

Figure 7.10: Old and New Values dialog box

The procedure for **RECODE INTO DIFFERENT VARIABLES** is only slightly different. Go to the **TRANSFORM** menu and select **RECODE** and then **RECODE INTO DIFFERENT VARIABLES**. Now the following dialog box is opened.

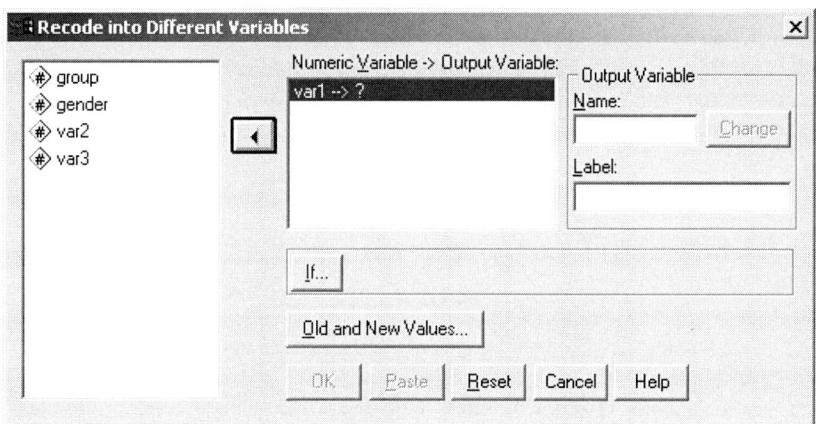

Figure 7.11: Recode into Different Variables dialog box

Here you again select **VAR1** and transport it to the center field labeled **NUMERIC VARIABLE → OUTPUT VARIABLE**. Under **OUTPUT VARIABLE** you can enter the name for the new variable. It is advisable to choose a name that reveals the relation between the old and the new variable, for instance **VAR1**a. When you have entered the name for the output variable, click on **CHANGE**.

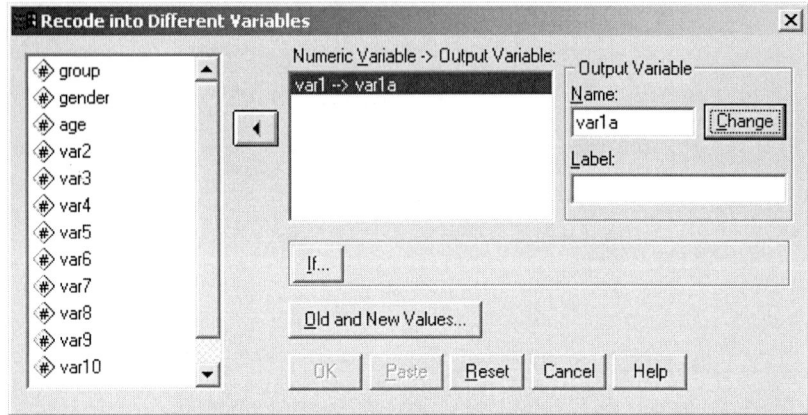

Figure 7.12: Recode into Different Variables: example

From here on, the procedure is the same as for **RECODING INTO THE SAME VARIABLE**. You click on **OLD AND NEW VALUES**. This opens a dialog box similar to Figure 7.10. Here you can again make a list of old and new value pairs. Click on **CONTINUE** and on **OK** in the next dialog box (as seen in Figure 7.11). SPSS will now add a new variable to your data set instead of overwriting your original data. The new variable with the adjusted scoring is shown at the very end of your spreadsheet on the right-hand side.

7.5.3. SELECT CASES: doing analyses for a subset of your data

In some situations you may want to perform an analysis on just a subset of your data. For instance, you found out that some participants were very young and others were much older. To avoid this distorting your results you make a selection of participants older than 20 and younger than 40. Another example would be that you fear that in one of the experimental groups results are flawed because of some external reason (the interviews were not conducted in the same way as in the other groups; there was a power failure in the theatre hall; the audience was particularly noisy and uncooperative; etc.). In your analyses you decide to leave that one group out. In that case you can select all other groups before you run statistical tests on the data.

How to obtain such selections? For this you go to the menu **DATA**. You now scroll down to the option **SELECT CASES**. When you click, the dialog box presented in Figure 7.13 opens.

How to Enter and Manipulate Data in SPSS   187

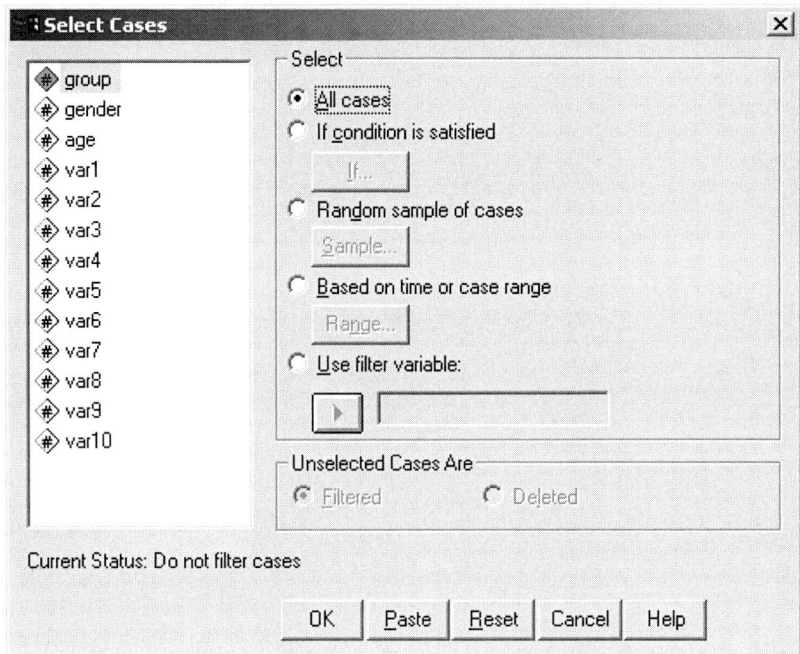

Figure 7.13: Select Cases dialog box

As usual you see a field listing your variables. On the right-hand side you see a number of options. Right now there is just one option relevant for you. You click the button for **IF CONDITION IS SATISFIED**. Next you click on the button marked **IF...**This opens the dialog box presented in Figure 7.14.

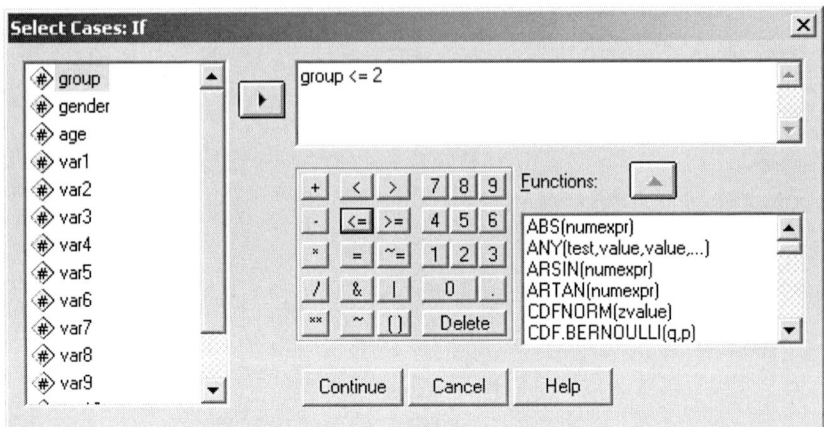

Figure 7.14: Select Cases If dialog box: example

Again you see a variable list: all the variables of your data set. On the top right-hand side you find a field in which you can enter a formula for your data selection. Entering a formula here does not require you to be a mathematician; a 'formula' is simply a selection criterion that you ask SPSS to use for the time being. It is important that you realize that the selection does not mean you lose the data: the change will not be permanent.

Like before, there is a control panel that you can use to avoid typos and other mistakes. Let us look at an example. In case you want to restrict the analyses to the results of groups one and two (the theater and the ex-factory) you can transport the name of the relevant variable (group) to the formula field. With the control panel you can then formulate the selection criterion, "GROUP <=2" (group number is smaller or equal to two) or "GROUP < 3" (group number is smaller than three). This will select all cases in group 1 and 2 and exclude groups with a higher number. When you want to limit your analyses to a certain age group, for instance all respondents between 20 and 40 you could enter a formula like "AGE > 19 AND AGE < 41".

During subsequent analyses it is important to remember that you activated a filter. SPSS reminds you by marking the cases that you excluded for analyses: in your spreadsheet you will see a diagonal line through the row numbers. Another reminder is the note that you find on your right-hand side at the bottom of your screen (**FILTER ON**). To undo the filter you go back to the **DATA** menu, click on **SELECT CASES**. This opens the dialog box as seen in Figure 7.13. Now you can click the radio button for **ALL CASES**, click on **OK** and your filter is turned off.

In this final section we discussed three basic ways to manipulate your data to prepare them for analyses. We learned that **COMPUTE** can be used to make new variables using your original data set. **RECODE** is a simple procedure that enables you to change the values of your variables and **SELECT CASES** makes it possible to define a data subset that you want to analyze. As you may have guessed looking at the dialog boxes, there are numerous other possibilities for the manipulation of your data. The ones discussed here are the ones that we expect researchers who are beginners will need most. For the others we would like to refer you to SPSS handbooks.

We are now ready to look into statistical procedures that will enable you to analyze your research hypotheses. These will be discussed in the next three chapters.

7.6. Closing SPSS

Finally, when you have finished working in SPSS, save all your documents (and make back-ups!), then leave the program as follows: click on **FILE**, then on **EXIT**, and it will shut down by it itself.

CHAPTER EIGHT

DESCRIPTIVE STATISTICS

In this chapter we start from the assumption that you have collected empirical data, and have entered these into SPSS. What, now, do you do with your data? Basically, two things. The first is that you go through them to see what answers the data provide to your research questions, that is, whether your hypotheses are confirmed or not. In a second stage, you will also investigate whether these results can be generalized. This will be discussed in Chapters 9 through 11. In the present chapter we are first and foremost dealing with the question: to what degree do the data provide (clear) answers to our questions. That, basically, is what descriptive statistics is all about: it helps you to interpret the mass of data that you have collected. That mass can be considerable. Think again of the example we saw at the beginning of Chapter 7: if you are dealing with 1,100 answers, it may be difficult to come up with any intuitive grasp of what the data tell you about your topic. That is where you need descriptive statistics.

8.1. Two measures of descriptive statistics

There are two things we are interested in when inspecting data from a descriptive point of view. On the one hand, we are interested in what the overall tendency of the responses was. At the same time, however, we are interested in individuals' reactions, or better: we wish to know to what extent any general tendencies detected are shared by all, or by what proportion of the responses. For instance: when we do a content analysis of two authors, investigating to what extent they use metaphors of the 'heart', we wish to know how often such metaphors occur in the works of each of these authors. If one of them has written many more works than the other, we want to find out the frequency of such metaphors relative to the total output of both authors. This could be expressed in percentages of metaphors per 1,000 words, for instance. Such a measure gives us an idea of a general tendency in the data. At the same time, we are interested to know whether the occurrences of the metaphors are spread out evenly across all works, or whether there are certain works, or chapters, or passages, that are 'thick' with such metaphors. To indicate this, we will have to detect how the occurrences are distributed. Both measures belong to the techniques of descriptive statistics that you will learn about in this chapter.

Each of these measures creates its own focus of interest, and corresponds to one branch of descriptive statistics. Group tendencies or general patterns in the data are investigated by inspecting measures of central tendency, while the relation of individuals to such tendencies is revealed by measures of dispersion. The first of these measures you will be already in part familiar with, as it deals with averages, such as means, something you have learned about in school. The second measure describes the bandwidth of the various responses as they cluster around the average. This may be new territory for you. Apart from those two measures, there are also other aspects you can investigate, such as whether the responses to two or more variables display similarities. This will be discussed in Sections 8.3 and 8.4 of this chapter, where we will discuss correlations and reliability analysis. But first let us look at measures of central tendency and measures of dispersion.

8.2. Measures of central tendency

There are three major measures of central tendency that are used in descriptive statistics: the mean, median and mode. Let us consider each of these in turn.

The arithmetic mean (often represented by the Greek letter μ, sometimes also by an x with a bar above it) is no doubt the most widely used measure of central tendency in daily life. It is the average of all responses. Suppose you had asked five people their age – they are 28, 29, 30, 31 and 32. You obtain the arithmetic mean of this by adding these numbers together (28 + 29 + 30 + 31 + 32 = 150) and dividing the sum by the number of people you asked, i.e. 5. Thus, 150/5 = 30. We say that the mean age here is 30. It is a measure of central tendency in the sense that this value represents some central value, around which the other observations are clustered. The mean informs us of the overall response that we can find in the data. This number is informative, because it adds something that the simple series of numbers does not tell us: 28, 29, 30, 31 and 32 are just individual numbers that in themselves do not tell us very much. We now know, however, that 'in general' the observations are organized around a central value, which is 30. In this sense, descriptive statistics adds information that is not there in the mere numbers themselves. The general purpose of such measures of descriptive statistics is to summarize large amounts of data into more meaningful information.

You hear about such averages in daily life, or read about them in the newspapers. But now let us look in somewhat more detail at the arithmetic mean. Suppose you again had carried out observations on five people, whose ages were: 10, 20, 30, 40, and 50. What is their average age? Again, it is 30, though the actual ages are very different from those in the previous example. Or look at a third example. The ages of people involved in our observations are now: 2, 6, 10, 28, and 104. What is their average age? Again, it is 30! Surely you had not expected this by looking at the sheer numbers. Here you see the value of descriptive statistics: it allows you to pick up tendencies in the data that you could not have detected intuitively, not even in such a simple and short series of five numbers. Hopefully this persuades you how much more important such measures of central tendency become when you are dealing with hundreds, or thousands, of cases: in such a situation you must compress the data for them to become meaningful to you.

On the other hand, is there not something unsettling about the fact that three very differently composed groups all reveal the same mean age? If the average is the same for such divergent numbers, is that not a sign that the arithmetic mean is really not very informative, or perhaps even misleading? That is right. There are two reasons for that. One is that measures of central tendency do not reveal anything about the measure of dispersion. The second type of descriptive statistics we mentioned above, and about which you are about to read more in the next section, will clarify this further. To be really useful, both measures should be combined, as we will argue. There is also something wrong with the arithmetic mean (as a measure of central tendency) in that it is strongly influenced by extreme values. Let us look again at the third series of numbers: 2, 6, 10, 28, and 104. If we had calculated the average for the first four numbers only, it would have been 11.5, and that would have made much more sense. The much higher average of 30 was brought about by the extreme number of 104. This one number in the series made the average jump to a value more than twice as large! Such values are called outliers in descriptive statistics and they are corrosive to the informative value of the arithmetic mean because they bias it toward values that are somehow not 'realistic' for the observations under scrutiny. As a thought experiment, just imagine that you have the scores for a game 2, 6, 10, 28, and the fifth value had been 1,688,435 – what would the arithmetic mean have been in this case? In such a case it becomes intuitively clear that outliers create averages that are somehow not true to the overall pattern of observations – they do not convey a realistic picture of the real numbers involved. So the mean as an expression of central tendency is vulnerable to outliers. That is why a second measure of central tendency is important: the median.

The median is the value that lies exactly in the middle of all observations when they have been rank-ordered. In the former series of 28, 29, 30, 31 and 32 the median was 30: this value separates the data so that 50% of the observations lie to the left of it, 50% to the right of it. We see that in this case the median equals the mean, as it also does in the other series of 10, 20, 30, 40, 50. But in the series 2, 6, 10, 28, 104 the median is very different from the mean – which was 30 – it is 10, which gives a much more realistic picture of where the 'real' average of most of the observations lie. You see that the median, in contrast to the mean, is much less influenced by outliers, because outliers are counted as just one more observation next to the others, and their numerical deviation from the other observations is not taken into account.

There is still another, third, measure of central tendency: the mode is the value that is encountered most often in the data. For instance in the number series 2, 4, 18, 3, 4, 20, 7, 19, 4, 3 the mode is 4, because it occurs three times compared with 3,which only occurs twice). How can you obtain the mode? Rank order all observations (as with the median, it does not matter whether you do this in increasing or decreasing order) and count how often each observation occurs – the value that you count most often is the mode. As will be clear from the example, the mode is rather useless in small samples. Only when there are hundreds or thousands of observations pertaining to one single variable can the mode be of informative value. That is why we will not devote any further attention to it here.

The previous examples may have given you the impression that you will have to do a lot of calculations. You will not, do not worry: SPSS will do all that work for you.

8.3. Measures of dispersion

There are three measures of dispersion: the range, standard deviation, and variance. Let us start with the simplest one, the range.

The range is simply the difference between the maximum and the minimum values in your data. Hence in the series 28, 29, 30, 31, 32 the range was: $32 - 28 = 4$. In the symmetrical series of 10, 20, 30, 40, 50, however, the range was: $50 - 10 = 40$. Here we see immediately why the combination of the two measures (of central tendency, and of dispersion) creates a much more informative picture than the mean (or even median) could have provided on their own. Had we known the range of the series before, we would have had a much clearer picture of the series than on the basis of the mean or median values of 30 alone! The range is a measure of dispersion, because it tells you how the various observations are grouped round the average. In the case of the first series it shows that the difference between the numbers left and right of the average run to a total of not more than 4, so they are clustered narrowly around the mean. In the second case the range is much wider, namely 40, so that there is a much wider spread of the data.

With the second measure of dispersion we may leave well-trodden roads. Indeed, the formula for calculating the standard deviation (symbol σ, often also abbreviated as **SD**) may seem daunting at first sight:

$$SD = \sqrt{\sum (x - \mu)^2 / N}$$

That is: subtract the arithmetic mean (μ) from every single observation (x) and square the difference, sum all these numbers ($\sum$), then divide by the total number of observations (N) and take the square root from this number. (You already see here that this can be a time-consuming exercise, which is why it is much wiser to simply have SPSS calculate it!)

This insight now has some consequences. For one, it means that the smaller the **SD** is, the more the data are clustered close to the average. A lower **SD** means concentration around the average. In other words, a small **SD** indicates a high degree of agreement among the participants, a high **SD** is indicative of considerable disagreement between the answers respondents gave. You could say that a high **SD** marks a high amount of variation among participants' responses. We can now define a standard deviation as the 'average distance from the mean': how far are all individual observations, on average, from the mean of the data? The temptation is strong to equate this kind of variation between informants with variance, the third measure of dispersion that we announced before. There is a sense in which this is true, yet the term variance has a more technical meaning within statistics: it is the square of the **SD**. Do you remember the formula for calculating the **SD**? If you do, then you will recall that it is a square root from a number. If you want to square the **SD**, that is simple: drop the square root! If you do, you get the formula to obtain the variance:

$$\sum (x - \mu)^2 / N$$

Now if you realize that the **SD** is a linear measure, indicating the average distance from the mean, then it follows that the square of this measure must be two-dimensional (as against the one-dimensionality of the **SD**). The consequence of this is easy: the variance is (part of) the surface of the distribution of your data. If you report the **SD** next to a measure of central tendency in your research report, there is no need to report the variance too, as it can be calculated easily enough from the value of the **SD**, i.e. by squaring it. The most common reference to variance in research reports is in the use of a particular statistical test, the 'analysis of variance' (ANOVA), to which we will turn in Chapter 11. Also you will come across phrases like 'x% of variance explained". This simply means that a specific factor can account for that percentage of the variance observed in the distribution of your data; the higher that percentage is, the more convincing your findings.

There also another way to explain what variance is[1]. Suppose we asked six students how many books they had read over the past month. Suppose the answers were: 1, 3, 4, 5, 7, and 10. The mean is 5. But among the answers given by the students this number is rare: it occurs only once. In other words, the mean is a hypothetical construct. We could say that it is a model predicting values in reality. Is it a good model? One way to test the model is to see how much each individual answer deviates from the value predicted by the model. We can do that by plotting the various answers in a graph. This is called a scatterplot: on the horizontal axis we indicate the different responses (or students, if you want, because each of them gave only one response), on the vertical axis we plot the number of books read. The scatterplot of the various responses now yields a picture like the one in shown Figure 8.1, with the mean of 5 indicated by the line in the middle. Now for each singular response, we can calculate the deviation from the mean. That deviation is an error: the model predicts some value, but in actual practice the observed value is different, hence the model is in error on this score. Thus for the first participant, the model is quite in error: it predicts five books, while only one book has been read. Because this value falls below the predicted value, it is wrong by –4 points. Participant 6, by contrast deviates 5 points from the predicted value, but this time, the deviation is above the line of the mean, so that the error here is +5. Now add up all the deviations above and below the line of the mean: (–4) + (–2) + (–1) + (0) + (2) + (5) = 0.

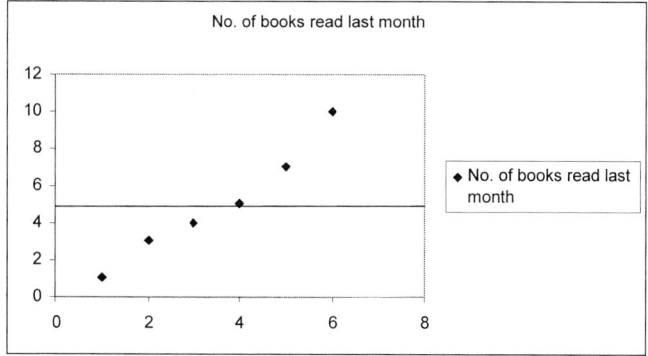

Figure 8.1: Scatterplot of differences between individual observations and the mean

---

[1] This explanation owes a lot to the highly recommendable book by Andy Field, *Discovering Statistics Using SPSS for Windows*. London: Sage, 2005, especially pp. 4 ff.

This means that the total error of the model equals zero, meaning that the 'fit' between the model and the real data could not have been better. So, although individual responses deviate from the model (and in these cases the model is in error), overall there is the lowest possible difference between the model and the actual responses given.

So the model is perfect? In no way, because there were considerable errors! That the overall error is zero is only because negative and positive values cancel each other out. To estimate how large the discrepancy between model and reality is, we need a way to get rid of the pluses and minuses. One easy way to do this is to square each individual error, and add these together: you will remember that multiplying a negative number by itself yields a positive number. If we do this, we get $(-4)^2 + (-2)^2 + (-1)^2 + (0)^2 + (2)^2 + (5)^2 = 50$. This is called the sum of squared errors (**SS**). This sum of squared errors is a good indication of how well the model works. But there is something wrong with it: the more observations we make, the higher the **SS** will become. Therefore, we have to divide **SS** by the number of observations, here the number of people we questioned. (In doing this, however, we usually – for reasons that will not be explained here – divide by the number of observations minus one.) In this case, we divide 50 by $(6 - 1) = 10$. This measure, the sum of squared deviations divided by $N - 1$ is called the variance! Hence for the answers to our small questionnaire the mean is 5 and the variance is 10. However, because the variance is expressed in units squared, it is not particularly insightful: it does not use the same measurement scale that we used in eliciting the answers from our respondents. Transforming the variance to the same scale is easy enough in itself: take the square root of the variance – that brings in the old measurement scale again. The square root of 10 is: 3.16. You now know what this figure means: it is nothing else than the standard deviation, the average deviation, or error, from the mean.

It is not the calculation of the standard deviation, however, that interests us: it is what it means! As the range, the standard deviation is a measure of 'spread'. It tells you how the data are formed around the measure of central tendency. In contrast to the range, however, the standard deviation has a very specific meaning, and therefore is highly informative. To understand this meaning, you must first acquaint yourself with the notion of the normal distribution.

8.4. The normal distribution

The normal distribution is sometimes also called the Gauss curve, because it was discovered by the Carl Friedrich Gauss (1777–1855), one of the greatest mathematicians of all times. Sometimes it is also called the bell curve, because its shape indeed resembles that of a church bell, as can be seen in the following illustration:

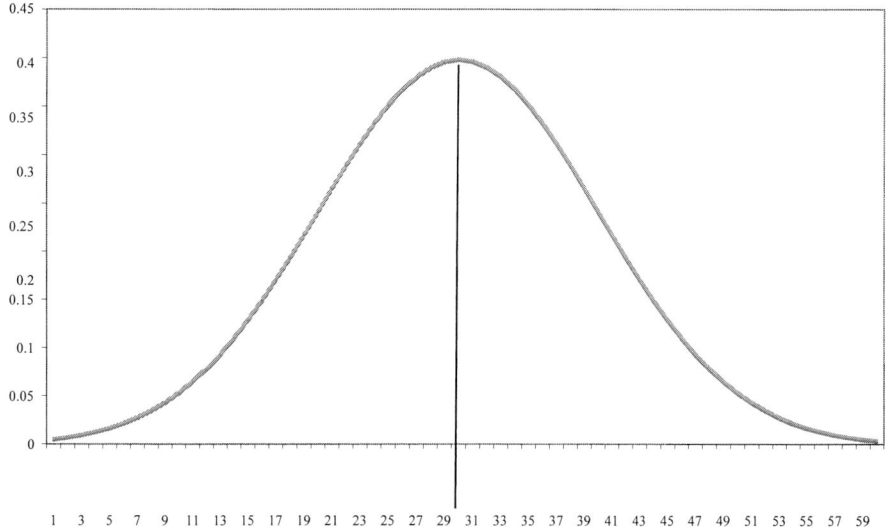

Figure 8.2: Example of a normal distribution

What you see in this figure is the distribution (hence the name!) of data around the average, which is here represented by the vertical line in the middle. When you go from the average to the left on the horizontal axis, values gradually decrease, while they increase when you go to the right of the average. While this grouping of values around the means is set on the horizontal axis, the vertical axis contains the number of observations. Thus you see that the highest number of observations is found in the immediate vicinity of the average, and decline as you move to the left or to the right of it.

An example may illustrate this better than a lengthy explanation. Body height is usually normally distributed within a population. Suppose within a given adult population (say that of Germany) the average height is 1.75 meters, so more people will be around that height than around any other height. As you move to the left of that value of 1.75, the height decreases, to 1.74, 1.73, etc., while the height increases (to 1.76, 1.77, etc.) when you move to the right of the average. Now you can see that the number of people for these heights diminishes gradually as they become farther and farther removed from the average. Surely this tallies with our intuitions: once you get to values such as

1.20 m, there are going to be very few people of that height found in the adult population, in the same way as there are going to be very few people measuring 2.05 m. That is why the curve flattens out at the edges.

This shape is found in many areas. You would basically get the same shape if you plotted the distribution of shoe size in a population, also intelligence (as measured by intelligence tests), musical ability, the time for running the 800 m, or the numbers of books read. It would intuitively even appear to apply to, yes, beauty. Most of us are not particularly beautiful, but not particularly ugly either. That is why the great majority of people cluster around the average. If you go left of that, the Gauss curve tells us you will gradually find fewer people who are gradually becoming less pretty. But the opposite is true too: as you move gradually away from the average to the right, beauty will increase, but you will find increasingly fewer pretty people. That is why the two ends (called the tails), representing very ugly and very beautiful people, are very flat, meaning that very few people in the population are really very beautiful (unfortunately), but also very few people are very ugly. In a sense the normal distribution therefore offers comfort to all of us who want to be more beautiful (or intelligent, or musical, sportive, or whatever): most human beings are average in all these respects, and the offshoots to the right of the average are rare, but also (there's a comfort!) the ones to the left. Thus knowledge about the normal distribution can also be a source of modesty and relief.

The figure above illustrates the basic shape of an ideal normal distribution. Why is it 'ideal'? Because, in reality, it is very rare to find this shape. This follows from the *central limit theorem*, which says that the more observations you carry out, the closer the approximation to the ideal normal distribution will become. If you have only a small sample of people whose body height you have measured, the distribution will be very ragged (or skewed). As the number of measurements increases, the more the shape of your distribution will become like that of the figure above.

What are the characteristics of this distribution? You need to know two parameters for that: the mean (μ, which in an ideal normal distribution is the same as the median and the mode) and the standard deviation (σ). Look at the normal distribution again:

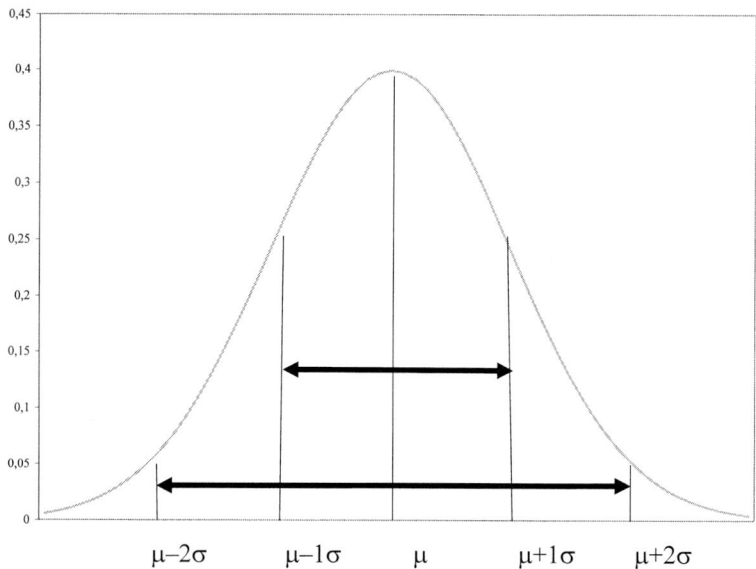

Figure 8.3: Standard deviations within the normal distribution

The vertical line in the middle represents the arithmetic mean. The distribution has now been divided by four more vertical lines. The first two lines left and right of the mean indicate one standard deviation, and the area of the distribution covered by it is indicated by the horizontal arrow between the two lines. The point where the left hand line starts is labeled $\mu-1\sigma$, σ being the symbol of the standard deviation. The point where the right hand line starts is labeled: $\mu+1\sigma$, for obvious reasons. Interesting for your work is that you know that this area always consists of the largest part of your observations, namely 68.3%. Within 2 standard deviations (indicated by the second horizontal arrow, and labeled $\mu-2\sigma$ and $\mu+2\sigma$ respectively and between the next two vertical lines in the distribution), lie 95.5% of all your data. The part that is added by a third standard deviation, finally, adds little, since within 3 **SD**s lie 99.7% of all your observations. When you know this, you know a lot more about your data than when you just know the average response. That is why it is imperative to always report the **SD** next to the mean or median.

8. 5. Two distributions

Now consider what we do most in empirical research: we compare the observations of two (or more) groups, for instance the evaluations given by male and female spectators to a group of paintings in an exhibition. We plot the distributions of these observations and put them on the same scale. The result (this is a fictitious example only) could look like the following:

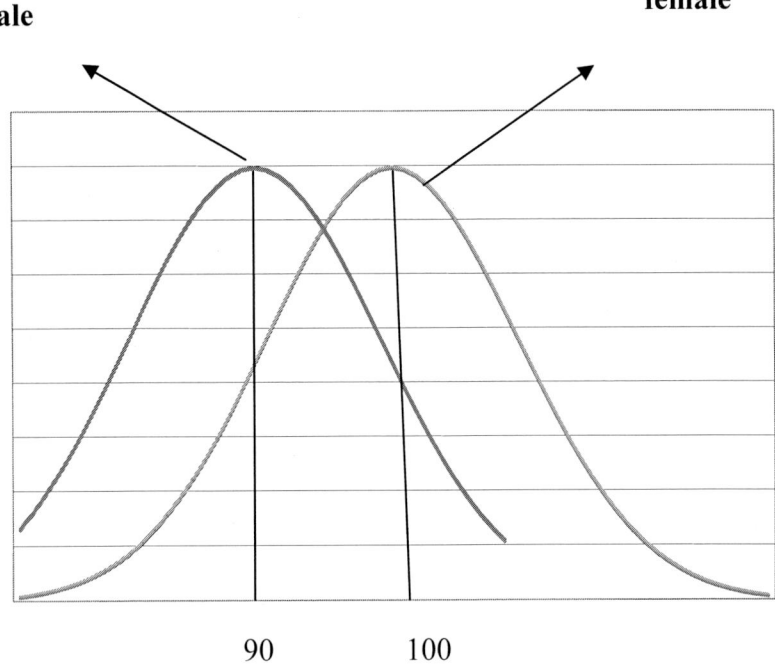

Figure 8.4: Two overlapping distributions

The vertical axis contains the number of people, the horizontal one their performance. We readily see that the averages for both groups are different. It turns out that the right-hand curve, which has 100 as the mean score, is the one for the female participants in your sample, the left-hand curve, which has 90 as an average score, is that of the male participants. You can see that both curves have an area where opinions of female respondents can be found while no men entertained such an idea, and vice versa: at the very left-hand side of the left-hand curve there is an area where men expressed evaluative responses that were not shared by any of the women in your sample. In the middle, however, there is an area of overlap: this is part of the variance where opinions are shared by both men and women.

In such situations, two fundamental questions always crop up. One question is whether the area of overlap is small enough for you to accept that the two groups reacted essentially differently, or whether that area is so large that the difference between the reactions of both groups is negligible. You see here very clearly that it is not just differences in average response between the two groups that count, but also the differences in variance. The other question is whether the difference here is one to be observed only with these informants, or whether it can be generalized to all participants of this kind. The latter goes under the name of *significance* – you ask whether the observed difference is 'significant' – which means that you will find such a difference again if you repeat the same research with other respondents from the same population. This question of significance is the subject matter of Chapter 9.

The other question, however, whether the difference is large enough to be accepted by us, has nothing to do with significance, but goes under the name of *effect size*. By this we mean the observed average difference between two groups, either between subjects or within subjects (see Chapter 6). You wish to know whether the effect size of the difference is large enough for you to accept it as meaningful. Who can tell you? Nobody. Maybe you are puzzled by this blunt answer. Maybe you expect there to be some methodological rule to distinguish 'acceptable' from 'non-acceptable' differences, but the simple truth is that there are no such rules. In fact you may be the person who knows best to judge the case because you know the area of research perhaps better than most people. Of course there may be more extreme cases, where judgment would be easier. Imagine that you observed a difference of 10% in the mean, with a considerable overlap in answers between both distribution graphs. If the difference had been 2 or 3% of the mean, and the overlap even wider, most people would perhaps agree that it was too small to be considered as a serious gender difference. Alternatively, if the mean response had differed by 80%, with only a thin strip of overlap, most people would come to the conclusion that the men and women did indeed differ considerably in their judgment of the paintings. These are the easy cases, where the effect size is either very small or very large, allowing relatively straightforward decisions on the part of the researcher. It is the cases in between that are difficult, however, and where you may be hard pressed for good reasons to accept or to reject the difference as relevant. (All this presupposes, of course, that the difference is 'significant', i.e. generalizable. If it is not, then all discussions about effect size become rather theoretical. But if the difference is significant, this does not necessarily mean that it is also relevant: in that case, the effect size must first be considered before any conclusions can be drawn.)

8. 6. Descriptive Statistics with SPSS

The above elaborations were necessary to have a good grasp of the underlying mechanisms of measures of central tendency and measures of dispersion. How does one make SPSS calculate such numbers? This is the topic of the current section. In it, we will show you how to go about generating the numbers that allow you to check what your data have to say about your research question: whether they confirm your expectations or not.

Suppose we want to know the ages of visitors to the local library, and that we observe the ages as before: 28, 29, 30, 31, 32. Open SPSS, define the variable as **AGE1** (we may make more observations later) and enter the data in the following way:

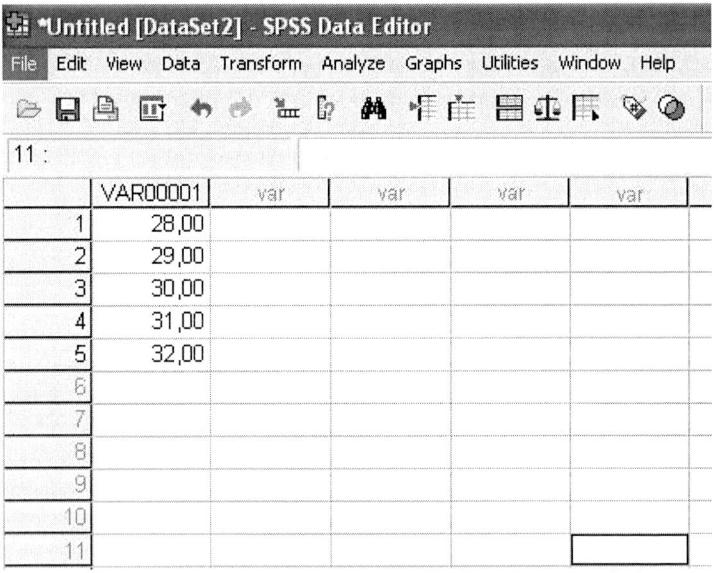

Figure 8.5: Enter frequencies to obtain descriptive statistics

We enter them all in one column, because they all represent observations of one variable, age – the rows are the persons of whom we noted down the age. Now suppose you wish to know some measures of central tendency and of dispersion. To obtain these descriptive statistics for these data, click on **ANALYZE**, then on

DESCRIPTIVE STATISTICS, finally on FREQUENCIES. The following window opens:

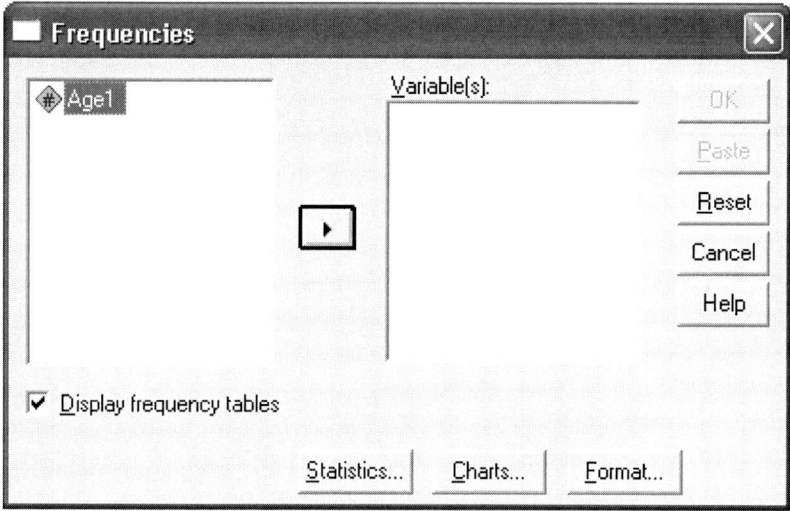

Figure 8.6: Dialog box to obtain frequencies

Click on the name of the variable, **AGE1**, and then on the arrow between the two windows. **AGE1** is now transported to the right hand window, called Variable(s). Then click on **STATISTICS**, and the following dialog box opens:

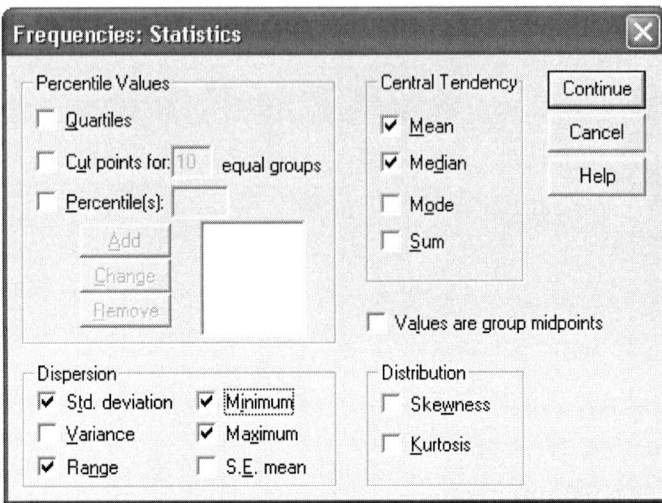

Figure 8.7: Dialog box to request statistics

Click on mean, median, standard deviation, range, minimum, and maximum, then on CONTINUE. You are now returned to the previous dialog box, where you click on OK. Wait a few seconds for SPSS to process your request. The output you will now see on your screen is:

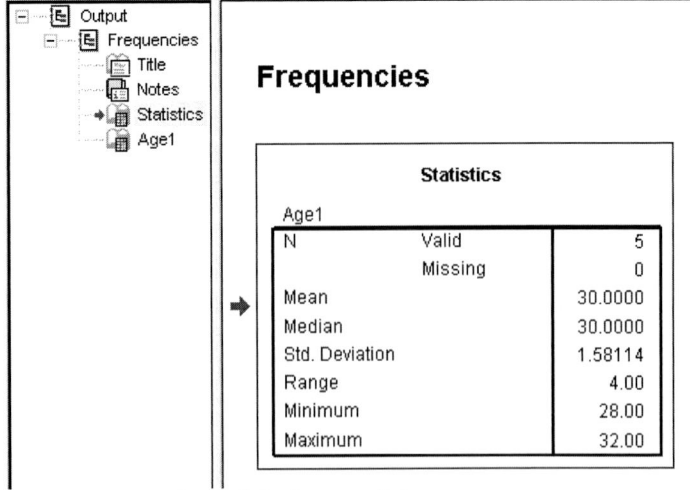

Figure 8.8: Output of FREQUENCIES

What interests us is the table at the top, where the results of the frequency calculations are displayed. As you can see, the output lists 30 as both the mean and the median, 1.58 as the standard deviation (usually we cut off after two decimals), meaning that (because the value of the SD is low) the ages are all clustered close to the mean. Furthermore the minimum is 28, the maximum 32, and the range (maximum minus minimum) is 4. All this is pretty straightforward, and would not have been worth calculating using a computer program because it is so simple. The great advantage of programs such as SPSS, however, is that they can handle much more complex calculations, and many at a time. Suppose, for instance, that we also wish to have these descriptive statistics for the two other groups, whose ages were 10, 20, 30, 40 and 50 on the one hand, and 2, 6, 10, 28, and 104 on the other. We can enter each of these groups in SPSS at the same time in the following way:

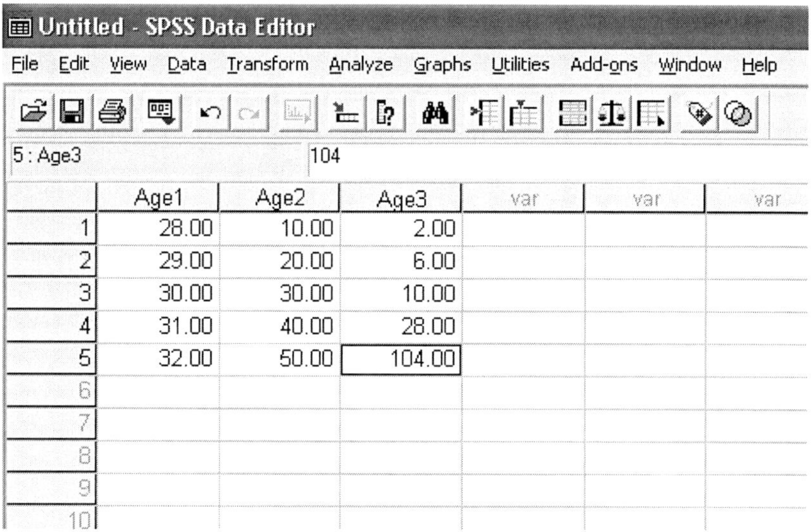

Figure 8.9: Enter several variables for descriptive statistics

Go through the same steps as indicated above, and you will get the following output:

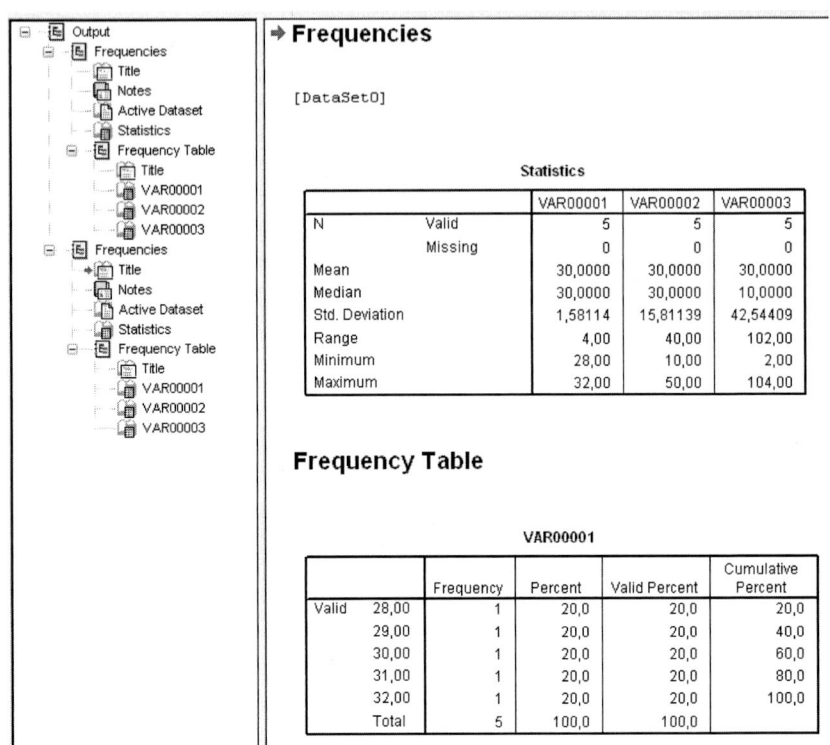

Figure 8.10: Output of **FREQUENCIES** of several variables

We now see that the mean is the same for all three variables, but the median differs for the third group, and of course the standard deviations, the range and also the minimum and maximum differ for all three. In this way, SPSS can handle large bulks of complex data, and produce clear tables containing the descriptive statistics for you.

A further note on entering data is needed here. Although theoretically there is nothing wrong with the way we have entered the ages of the three groups above, this is not usually how data are treated. Much more economically, of course, would be to have only one variable for age, and to define the groups. Suppose the first group was observed on a Saturday, the second group on a Sunday morning, and the third group on a Wednesday afternoon. We may be interested in finding out whether different times attract different age groups (for instance, visiting the library), so we define one variable for age and one for group:

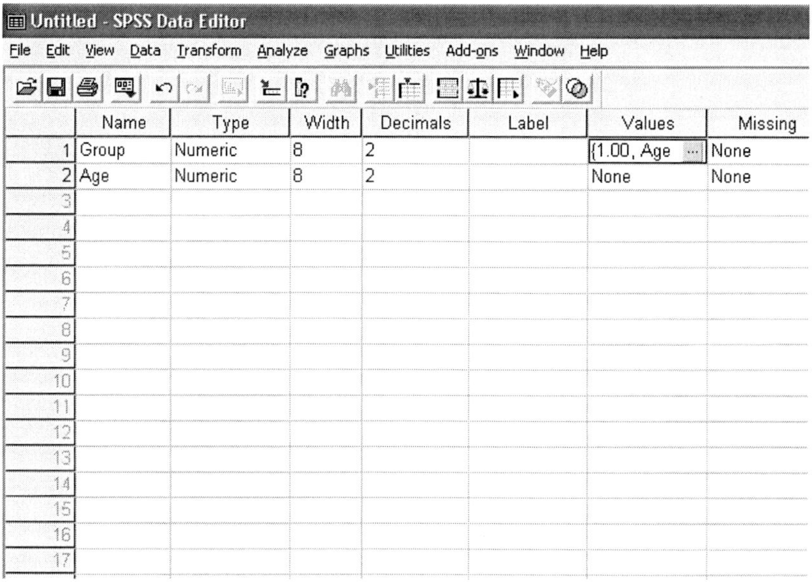

Descriptive Statistics 207

Figure 8.11: Output of descriptive statistics of several variables

We then define the groups as such, and **VALUE LABELS**:

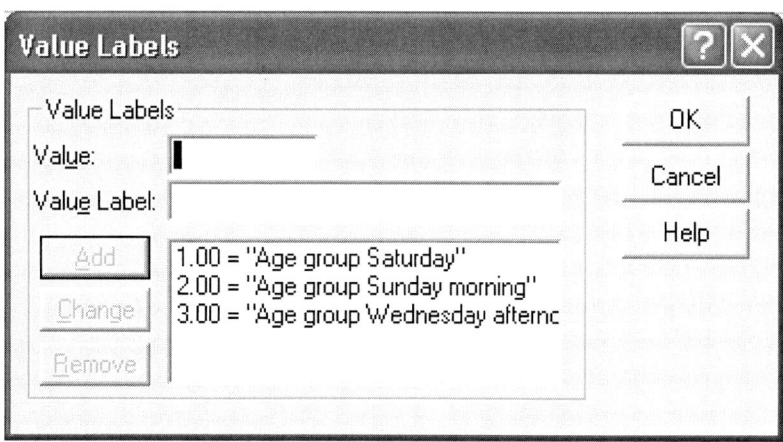

Figure 8.12: Defining different groups in **VALUE LABELS**

208   Chapter Eight

In entering the data now, you enter the number for the group in the first column, then the observed ages in the second column (or vice versa, that does not really matter), in the following way:

	VAR00001	VAR00002
1	1,00	28,00
2	1,00	29,00
3	1,00	30,00
4	1,00	31,00
5	1,00	32,00
6	2,00	10,00
7	2,00	20,00
8	2,00	30,00
9	2,00	40,00
10	2,00	50,00
11	3,00	2,00
12	3,00	6,00
13	3,00	10,00
14	3,00	28,00
15	3,00	104,00

Figure 8.13: Entering data as defined by group

To obtain descriptive statistics, now click on **ANALYZE**, then on **TABLES**, then on **BASIC TABLES**, and the following dialog box will appear (the variables have been entered into the appropriate boxes already):

Descriptive Statistics

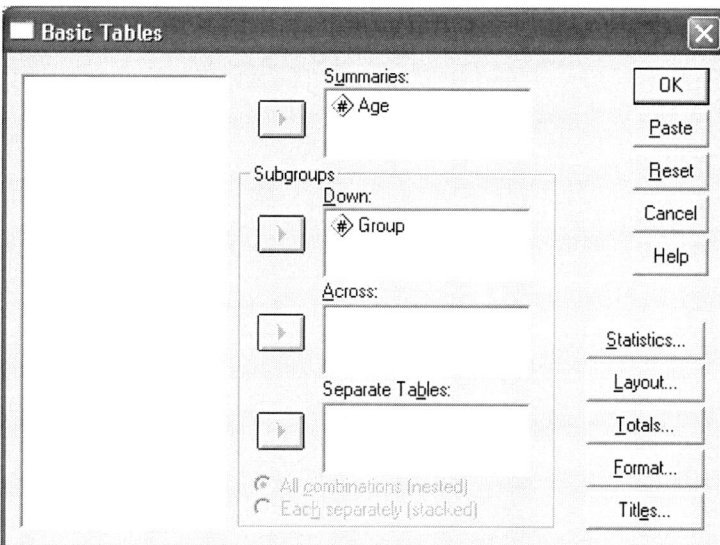

Table 8.14: **BASIC TABLES** dialog box

Now click on **STATISTICS**, and you will see the following:

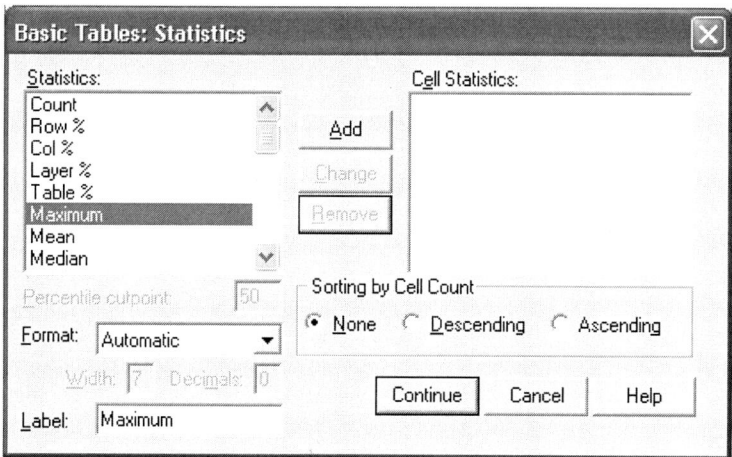

Table 8.15: Statistics selection in **BASIC TABLES**

The format is, as you see, a little different here. Click on the statistics measures you wish to obtain, for instance **MAXIMUM, MEAN, MEDIAN**, and so forth (you can scroll down in the window for further measures), and by clicking on **ADD** each time, the measure is selected and entered into the window **CELL STATISTICS**. When ready, click on **CONTINUE**, then on **OK**, and the following output will be displayed:

Tables

➡ [DataSet1]

	Maximum	Mean	Median	Minimum	Range
Age group Saturday	32,00	30,00	30,00	28,00	4,00
Age group Sunday	50,00	30,00	30,00	10,00	40,00
Age group Wedneday	104,00	30,00	10,00	2,00	102,00

Figure 8.16: Output of **BASIC TABLES**

The result is self-evident: all descriptive statistics requested are presented in a table, split out according to the three groups we had defined before.

Once you have these descriptive statistics on your screen, you may wish to save them for further use in the future. This can be done easily enough by using the **SAVE** function of most other computer programs. If you are working from a computer in a university facility (or elsewhere), you may save the output on a CD or a USB-stick. If you are working at home, you may save the output to your hard disk, but we recommend that you also keep copies on CD or USB-stick. Make sure you gave the file a clear name, so that you can easily recognize it later. You may also wish to incorporate the output in a document you are writing, for instance in your research report, in a seminar essay, an M.A. or Ph.D. thesis. This is easy enough: click on the table, then press **CTRL-C**, switch to your word processing program, put the cursor in the place where you wish the table to appear, and click **CTRL-V**. The table will now show in that location. You can give it a number and a title, and you can change its shape by the usual procedures for handling tables and graphs in your program. However, always reflect whether the table is necessary, whether you cannot just as well list the appropriate results (and *only* these!) in your ongoing text – this is most often the case with tables. With graphs, things are different, because often a visual display can compress a considerable amount of information that would be cumbersome to describe in words.

8.7. Cronbach's α

In Chapter 7 we discussed a way to compute new scales using your original variables. When several items (read: original variables) are assumed to measure the same construct, for instance 'complexity', 'interest', or 'pleasantness', there could be a statistical relation between respondents' scores on these items. It could be the case, for instance, that dependent variables such as 'smooth', 'merry', 'amusing', and 'radiant' all tap some general quality of 'pleasure.' If so, it is meaningful to conflate such variables. A prerequisite for making such a new scale, however, is that respondents scoring high on the one item also score high on the others. Similarly, respondents scoring low on the one item should also score low on the others. In sum, the variables have to correlate.

In this paragraph we will discuss when you may conflate scales. A suitable SPSS-procedure is Cronbach's α. Following this procedure, you can test whether the scales you had in mind meet statistical standards for homogeneity. Say you decided to construct a new scale summarizing a number of the text qualification variables (interesting, stimulating, etc.). Before you start a COMPUTE procedure (see Chapter 7), and then compare group means on the newly produced scale, you first run a reliability analysis, like Cronbach's α.

Now let us see how to obtain such a reliability analysis. Open the ANALYZE menu and select SCALE, and then RELIABILITY ANALYSIS. This opens a dialog box like the one presented in Figure 8.17. You select the variables you want to put together in a new scale, and transport them to the field marked ITEMS. Imagine you want to focus on text 1, for instance to compare Brazilians and Egyptians on a new scale called 'PROFOUND1', defined as complex text 1 + deep text 1 + intense text 1 + rich text 1 + power text 1.

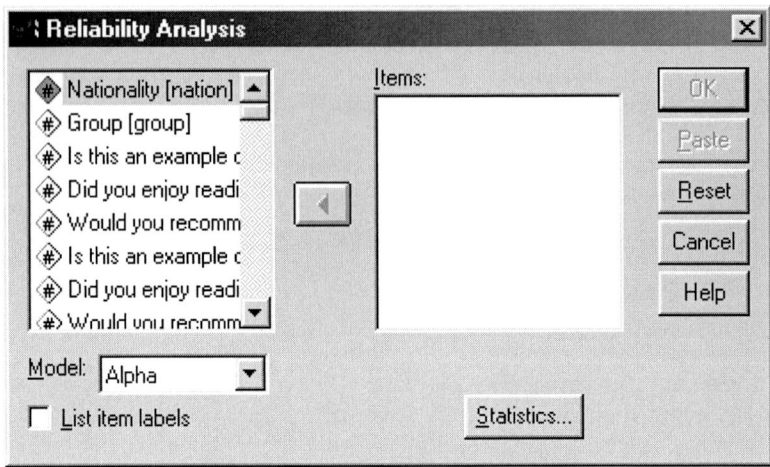

Figure 8.17: Dialog box for Reliability Analysis

To do this you need to instruct SPSS to calculate per item what its part is in the reliability of the new scale: does it enhance or decrease its homogeneity? Click on **STATISTICS**. This opens the following dialog box.

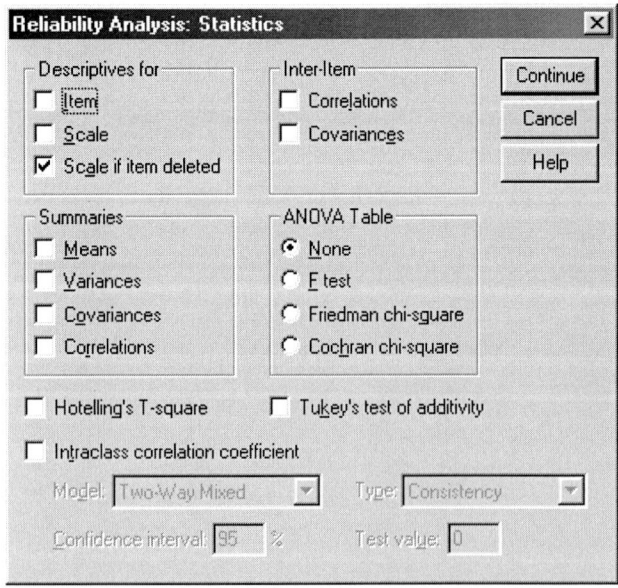

Figure 8.18: Dialog box for Reliability Analysis: **STATISTICS**

For our purposes you need to check only one of the many options given: SCALE IF ITEM DELETED. Click on CONTINUE, and you will return to the dialog box presented in Figure 8.15.

Now you are ready to run the test: click on OK. SPSS will now open a new window for the output. The results are presented below.

```
R E L I A B I L I T Y   A N A L Y S I S  -  S C A L E   (A L P H A)
Item-total Statistics

            Scale      Scale      Corrected
            Mean       Variance   Item-        Alpha
            if Item    if Item    Total        if Item
            Deleted    Deleted    Correlation  Deleted

COMPLEX1    14.1724    46.2839    .3224        .8662
DEEP1       13.2644    35.1967    .7402        .7599
INTENS1     12.6782    36.7324    .6474        .7878
RICH1       13.0460    36.2072    .6738        .7799
POWERF1     12.9080    34.3170    .7520        .7553
```

Figure 8.19: Output of reliability analysis (Cronbach's α)

Let us see how we should interpret these results. Basically, you need to do two things. First you look at the value of α. This is the result of the Cronbach's α reliability test. If this measure lies between 0.65 and 0.90 you may use the scale for further statistical tests. Second, you need to check whether the item-total correlation for each item is equal to, or larger than 0.30. This measure indicates the degree to which an item correlates with the total of the rest of the scale. In this case the results meet both criteria.

In some cases it will be important to check what happens when you delete one of the items. For this you look at the last column marked "Alpha if item deleted". When Cronbach's α increases considerably (e.g. from 0.62 to 0.85) when you remove one of the items from your scale, you may want to consider doing so. However, if you have good reasons to include that particular item you can decide to keep it in. Say you want to construct similar scales for text 2 and 3, but you find that for text 3 α increases greatly if you delete 'powerful'. This makes it impossible to compare group mean scores on the new variable you are trying to create (PROFOUND1, PROFOUND2, PROFOUND3) because they would not have similar variables 'powerful' would be missing in PROFOUND3. In this situation you may want to decide to have one relatively low α for PROFOUND3. Another good reason to include an item that keeps α down could be that you want to compare your results to a previous study in which that particular item *was* used. Still another reason may be found in your theoretical framework: it may be that one of the items is essential for testing your hypothesis.

In sum, it should be stressed that it is important not only to check statistical criteria but also to consider the content of the items. In addition to the reasons already mentioned, it may be that looking at the statistics alone, the items fit perfectly, but when you look at content some of them do not make much sense!

However, in our example both content criteria and statistical criteria are met. In your research report you do not have to include the entire SPSS output. You do mention how you constructed the new scale (that is, of what items it consists) and how you motivated your choice. Furthermore, you report the value of α (e.g. Cronbach's $\alpha = 0.83$ – two decimal places is sufficient, the third you can round up).

What to do if the criteria for homogeneity are not met? Imagine, for the sake of the argument, that you wanted to include 'boring' in your scale. This would lead to the following results.

```
R E L I A B I L I T Y    A N A L Y S I S - S C A L E (ALPHA)
Item-total Statistics
             Scale          Scale                        Corrected
             Mean           Variance        Item         alpha
             if Item        if Item         total        if Item
             deleted        deleted         correlation  deleted

COMPLEX1     17.1264        42.6931         .4214        .6473
DEEP1        16.2184        34.7541         .6912        .5484
INTENS1      15.6322        35.7003         .6289        .5708
RICH1        16.0000        37.5349         .5390        .6039
POWERF1      15.8621        35.6319         .6147        .5748
BORING1      16.5172        56.5549        -.1930        .8285

Reliability Coefficients
N of Cases = 87.0; N of Items = 6
ALPHA = 0.6872
```

Figure 8.20: Interpreting Cronbach's alpha

As you can see, the results meet only one of the two statistical criteria (ignore the content criteria for the time being): α is larger than 0.60, but in the third column we see that the item-total correlation of one of your items is smaller than 0.30. In fact, it is a negative number. This means that you cannot construct the scale as planned. However, the output helps you to correct your scale. The last column shows that the value of α increases considerably when you delete **BORING1** (as we might have expected, of course). This also happens to be the one item with a low scale correlation. In this case you run the test again, but this time without this troublesome item.

8.8. Graphs

Often it is of great value to represent your data not merely through numbers (as we have done when we talked about means, median, standard deviation, and the like), but better still to represent them visually. In many cases a graph may render particular patterns in your data much clearer than any lengthy description could do. In this section we show you how to generate such graphs in SPSS. We will limit ourselves to three of the most widely used and most interesting graphs: bar charts, line graphs, and boxplots.

8.8.1. Bar charts

In this section we will look at ways to depict descriptive statistics graphically. Open the **GRAPHS** menu. Here you see a number of options from which to choose. We will discuss the one that is most frequently used, namely bar charts. Click on **BAR** and SPSS opens the dialog box presented below:

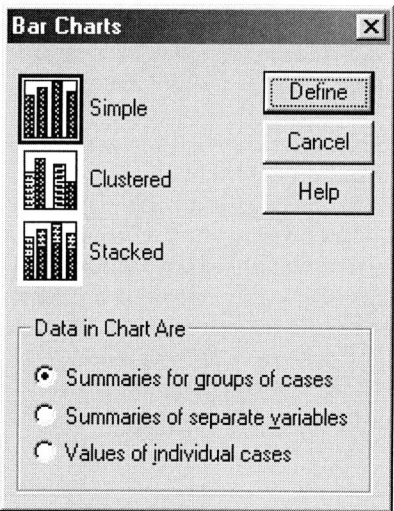

Figure 8.21: Dialog box for Bar Charts

Let us start with the simplest option: creating a bar chart for groups of cases. Click on the first option you are presented with (**SIMPLE**), check the first radio button under **DATA IN CHART ARE** (default), and click on the **DEFINE** button. The following dialog box opens:

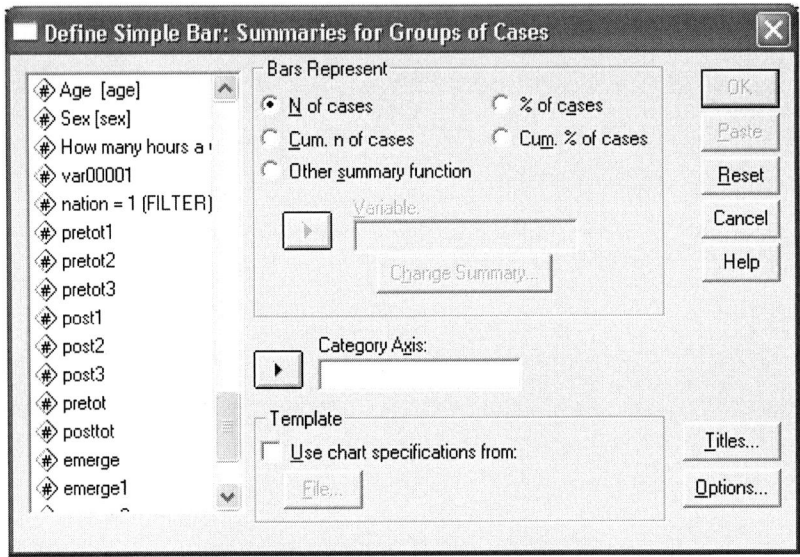

Figure 8.22: Dialog box for Define Simple Bar: Summaries for Groups of Cases

Here you can select the variable in which you are interested, for example **SEX**. First, click on **SEX** in your variable list (down below in the field on the left-hand side) and transport it to the field marked **CATEGORY AXIS**. Second, you choose the way in which you want to represent your data. Two options that are given are relevant to you. You can choose to represent the number of male and female respondents, but you may also want to represent the percentages. In the example we choose percentage and tick the relevant radio button. Third, click on **TITLES** and SPSS opens a window in which you can enter titles (for instance "Respondents' Gender"), subtitles and footnotes to your graph. When you have done so, click on **CONTINUE** and you return to the dialog box presented in Figure 8.22. Finally, click on **OK** and SPSS will produce the following graph in its output window:

Descriptive Statistics 217

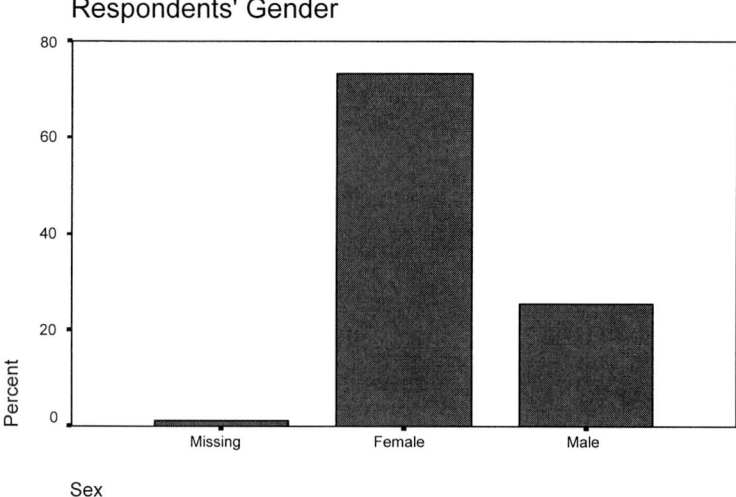

Figure 8.23: Example: Bar chart for respondents' gender

As you can see the percentage of female respondents is more than twice the percentage of male respondents. Also, some cases are 'missing': apparently some respondents did not answer this question. You may want to exclude missing cases in your graph. To do this you need to click on the OPTIONS button in the dialog box represented in Figure 8.22. This will open a dialog box (not represented here) where you will find that SPSS includes missing values by default. Simply correct this by removing the tick. Click on CONTINUE. You return to the dialog box you see in Figure 8.22. Click on OK and SPSS will produce a graph similar to the one in Figure 8.23, but this time without the missing cases.

To include parts of SPSS output, such as graphs, in your written report, you select the relevant part by a click of your left mouse button. SPSS will mark the part you have selected. Click on the right mouse button and select COPY. Now you can paste the graph (or any other part of the SPSS output you selected) into your report. Marking the graph with a click of your left-hand mouse button allows you to adjust the size of your graph. For other alterations it is advisable to use SPSS rather than Word. In the SPSS output, double click on the graph and a window opens that offers you a great number of options: adjusting colours, adding patterns, changing label style or bar style, omitting one of the bars, etc. When you are done with your alterations, then copy and paste your graph into a Word document.

Let us now turn to a somewhat more complicated graph. Still using the example we have been referring to throughout this chapter, you want to compare results of the pre- and post-test for both students and teachers in the Brazilian group. First, select only the Brazilian participants. (If you have forgotten, then refer to Chapter 7, Section 7.5.3.) In that case you are working with separate variables (i.e. pre-test and post-test results). In the dialog box represented in Figure 8.21 you need to choose that option (SUMMARIES OF SEPARATE VARIABLES). Second, you need to select the second graph option: CLUSTERED. When you have done that, click on the DEFINE button. This opens a dialog box as presented in Figure 8.24. Here you select the two variables of which you want to represent the group means in a graph.

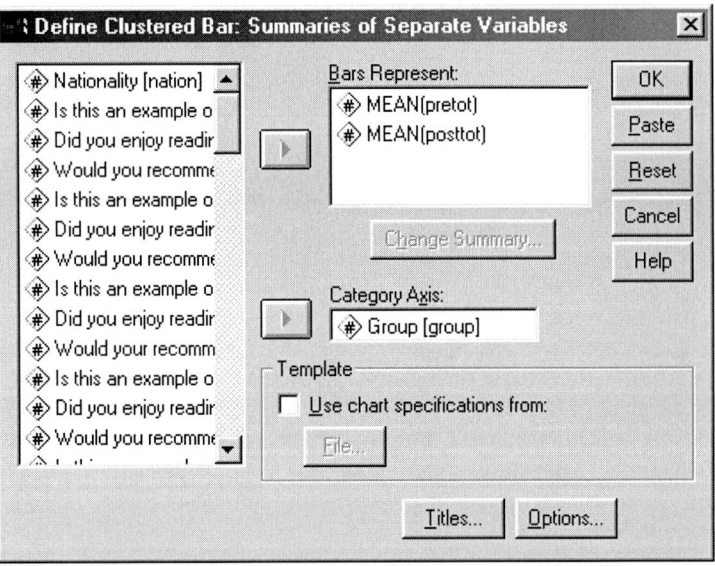

Figure 8.24: Dialog Box. Define Clustered Bar: Summary of Separate Variables

The variables PRETOT and POSTOT are new variables we had created, summarizing all (TOT, for 'total') the responses in the pre-test and post-test, respectively. Transport both these variables from your variable list to the field under BARS REPRESENT. Second, transport the variable that should separate the teachers' reactions from those of the students. That was the variable we had called GROUP. (If you had forgotten, you can, of course, as always, check in the VARIABLE VIEW.) Thus, enter GROUP into the field CATEGORY AXIS. As in the previous example you can again enter a title for your figure by clicking on TITLES. When you have done so, click on OK. SPSS produces the graph as seen on the left in Figure 8.25.

Descriptive Statistics

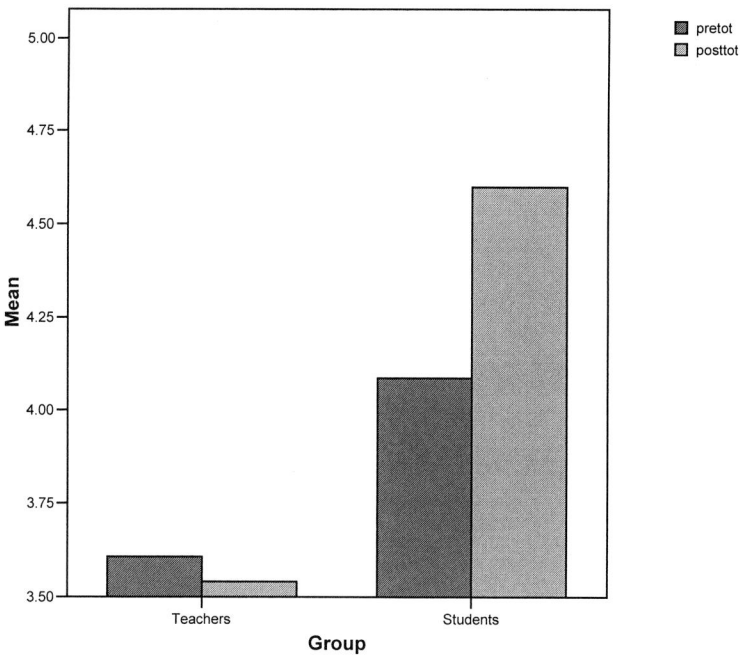

Figure 8.25: SPSS output: Bar charts for separate variables

As you can see, the expected effect seems to occur for students: students score higher after the second reading (**POSTOT**) than after the first reading (**PRETOT**) of the texts. This difference does not occur for teachers: whose scores on the second reading were even a little lower than on the first reading. Also, the graph shows that the scores of the students are generally higher than those of the teachers.

However, and importantly, you see that the scale of the vertical or y-axis runs from 3.4 to 4.8. (We have done this by defining the y-axis to run from 3.50 through 5.00.). This depiction of the results exaggerates the differences between mean scores. Of course this could help you and the readers of your report to detect the differences more easily. On the other hand, it biases the results, by magnifying the differences, something that is often done in journalistic presentations of research results, but which needs careful scrutiny. For this reason, you may wish to choose the original scale; this would result in a more truthful representation of what the differences between the groups look like. To do this go to the graph in the SPSS output viewer and double click on the graph axis. (You can change virtually any aspect of your graph this way!).

This opens the following window. (Note that SPSS now opened a new feature called SPSS **CHART EDITOR**.)

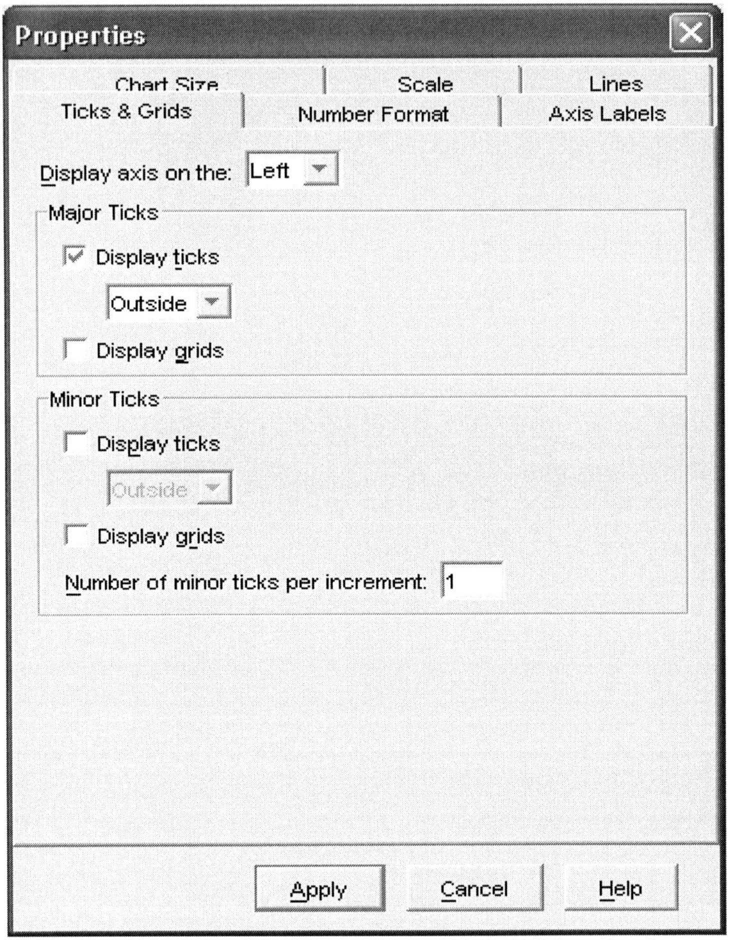

Figure 8.26: Dialog Box for Scale Axis in Editing Graph

Descriptive Statistics 221

Then click on **SCALE**. The following dialog box opens:

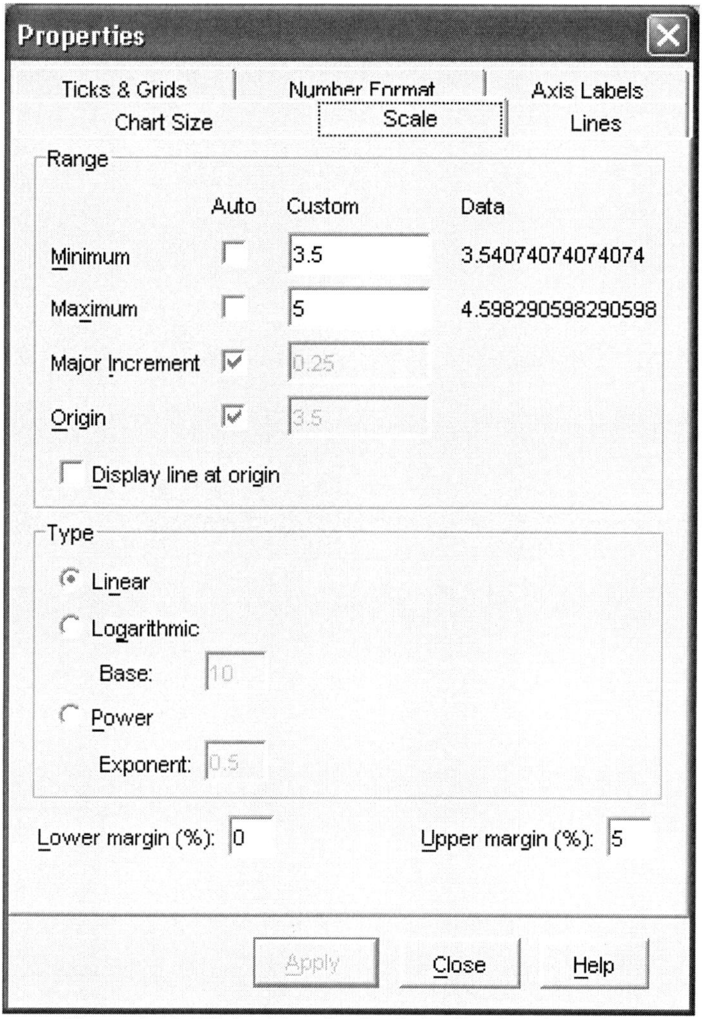

Figure 8.27: Dialog Box for Scale in Graph Adaptation

You can now see (in the **MINIMUM** and **MAXIMUM** boxes) that the scores run from 3.5 to 5. So, under **MINIMUM** you enter 1, and under **MAXIMUM** 7. Now you have your graph as seen on the right-hand side in Figure 8.28.

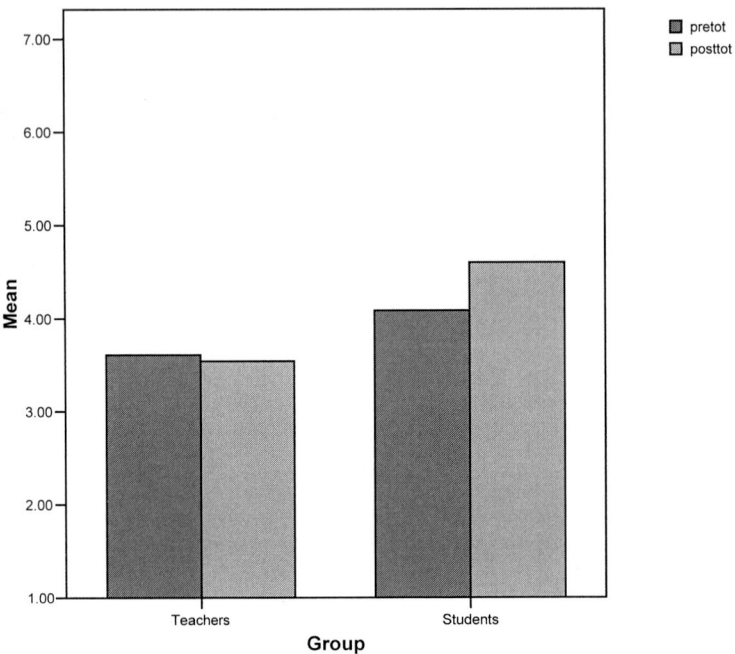

Figure 8.28: Bar chart on original scale

As you can see, the picture now shows that there is hardly any difference between the pre- and post-test for the teachers, and that for the students, the difference is in the predicted direction, but the effect is small. Be careful in reading research reports generally for biases of the kind illustrated above.

Note that when you want to import your graph into another (Word) document, you may need to save it as a JPEG file; sometimes editors of journals or books request that you to hand in graphs as JPEG files as well. To do this, click in the graph, then right-hand click, select **EXPORT**, then **CHARTS ONLY**, then **OK**.

8.8.2. Line graph

Bar charts are a good way to present general patterns in the data, but they are not well suited to trace the development of something over time. To this end, line graphs are much better: they visualize how particular changes occur in the course of an event. We have already presented you with an example of such a line graph in Chapter 1, where we showed the results of an investigation probing the relationship between novelty and beauty. Let us now see how to produce such a line graph. Go to GRAPHS, then LINE, then click on SUMMARIES OF SEPARATE VARIABLES (because that is what we wish to see: how each of the individual verse lines, which acted as variables, was responded to). Then click on DEFINE, and transport the names of LINE1 through LINE9 into the right-hand box, then click on OK. The result is the graph you saw in Figure 1.3 in Chapter 1.

8.8.3. Boxplots

A boxplot is a highly informative way to summarize your data in a graph. It presents descriptive statistics for the central tendency as well as for the distribution of the data around the median. It shows the median, the 25th percentile, the 75th percentile, and values that are far removed from the rest. Let us first run through an example and then explain how to interpret the results.

Open the GRAPH menu and select BOXPLOT. This opens the window presented in Figure 8.29. You select SIMPLE and SUMMARY FOR GROUPS OF CASES (both default in SPSS) and then click on the DEFINE button.

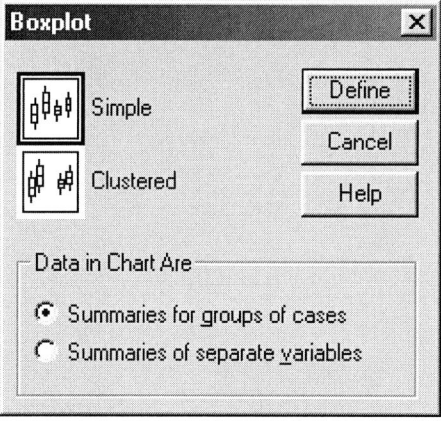

Figure 8.29: Dialog Box for Boxplot

Say you want to present the results for "How many hours a week do you read for pleasure" per nationality. This may reveal that the distribution varies between Egyptians and Brazilians (see previous discussions in this chapter). As you clicked the DEFINE button the dialog box as shown in Figure 8.30 opens:

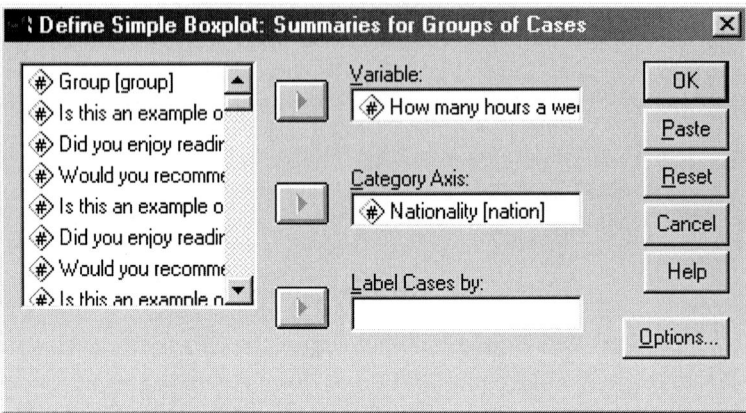

Figure 8.30: Dialog Box. Define Simple Boxplot: Summaries for Groups of Cases

You now transport the **READ** variable from your variable list to the field labelled VARIABLE, and the NATION variable to the field labelled CATEGORY AXIS. Now click the **OK** button, and SPSS makes a Boxplot as seen in Figure 8.31.

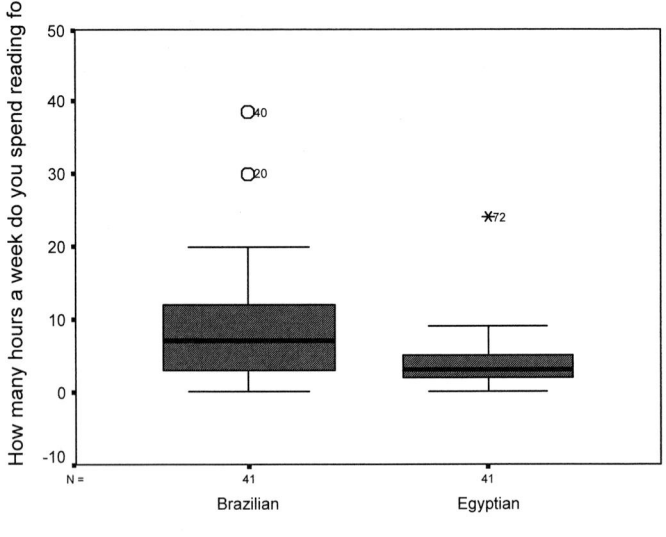

Figure 8.31: Output of Boxplot

Let us see what information we can extract from this graph. The lower boundary of the boxplot is the 25th percentile of your data, while the upper boundary represents the 75th percentile. The horizontal line inside the box is the median. The box as a whole represents 50% of your cases. As discussed before in this chapter, the median indicates the central tendency in your data. You see that the median of the two groups does not differ much, but that the central tendency among the Brazilian data is slightly higher than among the Egyptian data. The length of the box can be interpreted as an indication for spread or variability of your data: variability among the Brazilian respondents is larger than among the Egyptians. If the median is not in the center of the box, this indicates that your data are skewed. When the median is closer to the top this tells you that the distribution is negatively skewed. Closer to the bottom means the data are positively skewed; when you look at the data for the Egyptians you can see an example of this.

Finally, we would like to draw you attention to the two dots and the asterisk in the graph. These represent values that are far removed from the boundaries of the 25th and, in this case, the 75th percentiles. SPSS prints the number of these cases. For the Brazilians it is case 20 and 40; for the Egyptians it is case 72. The dots indicate cases that scored values more than 1.5 box-lengths removed from the 75th percentile; these are called outliers. The asterisk indicates a value more than three box-lengths removed from the 75th percentile; this we call an extreme.

As has been illustrated in this paragraph, boxplots are highly useful way not only to present your data but also to explore them. Based on these findings you may want to decide, for instance to exclude the outliers and the one extreme. It may be that case 72 slightly exaggerated her reading for pleasure time (24 versus a median of 3 hours a week). This may make your analyses a little more reliable.

In this section we have shown you a few possibilities to represent your results by means of diagrams: bar charts, line graphs, and boxplots. Of course these do not come close to exhausting the various possibilities that SPSS offers you for producing graphs from your data. Other such possibilities are, for instance, scatterplot, pie charts, or area charts. We advise you to be careful with the selection of the graphs, however, and always reflect whether the graph you choose is the clearest way to present your results. If in doubt, consult with friends, colleagues, or your supervisor.

8.9. Final words

This chapter has introduced a number of measures of descriptive statistics. We have introduced both measures of central tendency and of dispersion, correlation, and reliability analysis, and we have seen how to produce three different kinds of graphs to represent your data. Needless to say, this is a mere introduction, and by no means is it all there is to say about descriptive statistics. Many more measures are at hand, such as, for instance, factor analysis or regression analysis. These are more sophisticated techniques to interpret your data. Although these other techniques can be quite helpful, we believe that with the present introduction you can go a long way, and can present most of your data in an elegant and adequate way. For further techniques, we refer you to other works on statistics that you find in the bibliography.

All these measures of descriptive statistics are, however, confined to your own observations. That is in some sense a problem, because in research we are not just interested in the responses of these individuals; instead we wish to know whether people in general would also give such (or similar) responses. To know this, you need so-called inference statistics: these measures will allow you to make inferences about the likelihood that other respondents will give similar answers. That will be dealt with in the following three chapters.

CHAPTER NINE

INFERENCE STATISTICS: PRELIMINARIES

9.1. Introduction

The previous chapter has shown you how to describe patterns in the results you obtained. However beautiful and convincing such patterns may be, they have one major shortcoming: they are only patterns that you observed in the data provided by your informants! You do not know whether other informants might not have provided you with data revealing different patterns. This is where inference statistics comes in: these techniques allow you to estimate how likely it is that you would have obtained similar answers from other informants. Obviously, this is an enormous gain over descriptive statistics: you will now be in a position to conclude not only that the patterns you observed in your data are such and such, but also how much confidence you may have that these patterns apply not only to your informants, but to the world in general. Another more technical way of putting this is that this form of (inference) statistics allows you to *generalize* from your limited observations to the general population. You may be surprised, perhaps, that it is possible to infer from a small set of data how people will behave in general, but that is precisely what statistics is all about. This makes inference statistics one of the most powerful tools of scientific analysis and explanation. Without applying inferential statistics, your data remain relatively worthless because they are bound to this particular group of respondents. With inference statistics, you can now make pronouncements on how things look in the world at large.

Using inference statistics does not necessarily presuppose that you have a profound grasp of the underlying mathematics involved in the various tests, although such knowledge is obviously conducive to understanding things at a deeper level. So if you have the time, the possibility, and the resources to take courses in statistics, we encourage you to enroll in them: a fascinating world will open itself to you, and we guarantee that you will discover a whole new way of looking at things, and develop a whole new understanding of the world around you. This is not a course book on statistics, however. Instead, we will review some of the basic principles of inference statistics that you *must* understand to apply the various techniques that SPSS allows you to perform to estimate the possibility of generalizing from your data. Beyond that we will simply familiarize you with the various techniques, what rules there are for preferring a particular technique over others, how to carry it out in SPSS, and how to interpret and report the output of such statistical tests.

9.2. Errors

In observing the world, we are bound to make errors. One source of errors is our limited capacity: we do not have unlimited time to make observations. Take the number π, a number you need in order to calculate the circumference of a circle. You may have learned in school that the value of π is 3.14. But that is an approximation. A more precise choice is 3.14159. Since the numbers after the decimal point are infinite, you can never be sure to measure the circumference of a circle in its fullest and most precise way. This may not be a problem for everyday purposes, but once you get into scientific issues, matters are no longer that simple.

Take the influence of watching soap operas on people's perception of the world. We may intuitively expect that there is such an influence, because these experiences contribute to our knowledge about how people behave in some circumstances, how different kinds of people react to certain challenges, or what kind of possibilities exist to cope with specific difficulties in life. To investigate whether such contributions to our beliefs also structure our lives, we must carry out observations. Ideally, we should observe a representative group of soap fans over a considerable number of years. We would have to chart their experiences, monitor their attitudinal changes, observe their behavior, and so forth, over a period of some 20 years or so. The example already makes clear that this is not going to be possible. Also, not enough people will be ready to accommodate such prolonged investigation into their private lives. On top of that, no researcher has enough time and/or money to carry out such longitudinal research. Thus we will have to be content with occasional glances at restricted groups of people for a very limited period of time. This limitation may be a fundamental source of error. We can never be certain that other groups of informants will not think or behave differently, and we can never be sure that after we had observed them, respondents thought or did things differently from when we cast an eye on them.

There is also a second source of error: we are bound to make mistakes. We can see this in the fact that we may make an error in calculating, in putting a wrong name-tag on a sample, or in forgetting to enter an observation when preparing a data matrix. As humans, we are fallible, and hence cannot rule out mistakes. This is the notion of fallibility proposed by Karl Popper that we discussed in Chapter 2. Of course we can take measures to prevent such errors as much as possible, and we can also do our very best to concentrate, and eliminate mistakes that have been made but that will not eliminate all of them.

In methodology, a distinction is made between two such types of errors, *constant* and *random* errors. Let us have a look at both types. Constant errors are such that we have introduced a source of error that will systematically bias results. For instance, a researcher in the Ukraine is interested in whether children's self-esteem profits from a literature program. So she runs a program in Kiev and has a control group in Odessa. After 6 weeks, she compares the self-esteem of the two groups, and finds a difference. Can she conclude that the program was successful? By no means, as the design of this study conflated two variables. On the one hand there is the literature program, on the other there is the geographic location of the two towns. It is quite possible that there are other factors that have to do with the local culture of those two cities that may have influenced the results. This is a *constant* error: it introduces errors of a systematic nature, potentially biasing the results and making the outcome impossible to interpret.

This example may be clear enough in itself, but sometimes it may be quite difficult to detect constant errors. For instance, in the heyday of behaviorist research, it was usual to reward research animals with food. Thus rats finding their way through a maze would be given food as a form of reward during a set time period. What the researchers were unaware of at the time was that different individual rats are able to ingest different quantities of food in the same amount of time. Depending on food as a method to reward animals thereby introduced a constant error, namely that some animals could eat their fill (and thus were fully rewarded), while others were left half-hungry (and thus were not fully rewarded), thereby creating differences between the animals, not on the basis of their performance in the maze, but on the basis of their ability to take in food. This is called an *intervening*, or *confounding*, variable. In research, we try to avoid as much as we can such confounding variables, which count as constant errors. This may sound obvious enough in hindsight, but often it is difficult to be aware of such slight errors. When this insight emerged, researchers switched to allocating successful animals only a given portion of food, so that the quantity of the reward was the same for all animals. What the example shows is that constant errors must, and can, be controlled. Such control does not eliminate errors completely but it transforms them into *random* errors. It is a profound insight of methodology that whatever we do in designing and executing our research, *random errors will not go*! Is this reason for despair? Not at all. It simply means that we must always be on the look-out for potential sources of errors. The insight also has a very important consequence: when in spite of these random errors we do find an effect of the independent variable on the dependent variable, the effect must be a strong one, because it still shows, in spite of the skewing influence of the random errors. We call such an effect *robust*, as it was unimpeded by the confounding influence of all random errors – which we know are there all the time!

Hence we must estimate how great the probability is that the observed effect came about through random errors, i.e. how probable is it that only the unavoidable random errors created the observed effect of the independent variable? When this is not particularly probable, we decide that the independent variable had an effect on the dependent variable. But when do we judge something 'not particularly probable'? Let us look at an example first that may clarify the issue in a concrete way, after which we can abstract from it. Maybe you have observed the strange form of behavior in readers, or viewers, that they often indulge in sad endings of movies, stories, novels, plays, etc. On the other hand, people also like happy endings of such films, television series, or tales. We would like to know which ending people prefer in general. So we set out investigating whether reading a story with a sad ending is judged more rewarding than reading a story with a 'happy end'. Imagine I started out informally by asking eight people in my environment what they would prefer, seven of whom said they preferred the sad version, and only one the happy version. How probable is such a result?

To investigate this, let us start from the fact that every informant had two possible choices (prefer 'sad', or prefer 'happy'), both therefore having a probability of 50%. So much we know from everyday experience. Let us render all potential choices that two people have schematically as such (whereby + means 'prefers sad ending' and − means 'does not prefer sad ending' – or the other way round, that does not really matter):

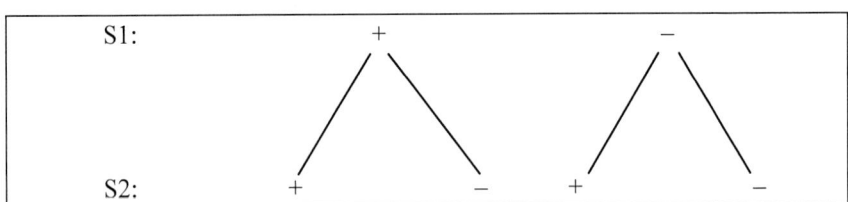

Figure 9.1: Distribution of preferences for story outcome with two participants

Inference Statistics: Preliminaries   231

Hence with two informants (S1 and S2) we get four possible results (2^2):
- S1 chooses +, S2 chooses +
- S1 chooses +, S2 chooses –
- S1 chooses –, S2 chooses +
- S1 chooses –, S2 chooses –

Out of these four possible combinations, a + occurs at the same time for both informants, i.e. once in four. In other words, the probability that both informants both choose + is 1 in four, i.e. 0.25 (or 25%). Now let us observe how often it occurs that a + actually is preferred by the two informants: this happens twice, so two times in four. That is, the two informants can only prefer a sad ending (+) once each. The probability of this event is easy enough to estimate: it is two times out of four, or half of all occurrences, thus 0.50 (or 50%). Similarly, zero times + occurs once as well, namely in the case when none of the two informants prefers the sad ending. The probability that this happens, therefore, is once in four, i.e. 0.25 (or 25%).

Now let us investigate the combination of the distribution of choices across four informants. Schematically, this appears as follows:

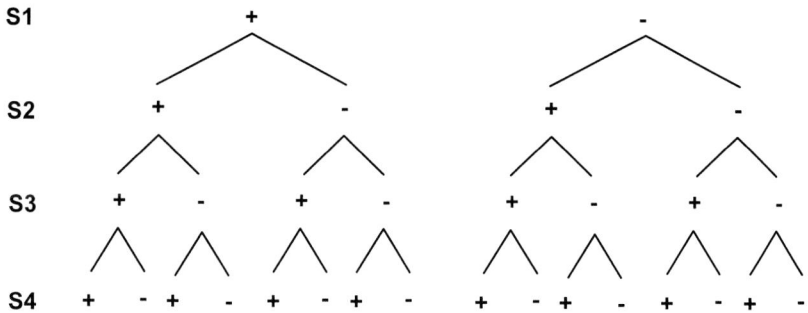

Figure 9.2: Distribution of preferences for story outcome with four participants

If you count how many possible combinations there are now, you will find that there are 16 (2^4) in all. These 16 possibilities of + occurring are distributed as follows:

No of participants choosing +	Fraction	Probability
4	1/16	0.0625
3	4/16	0.2500
2	6/16	0.3750
1	4/16	0.2500
0	1/16	0.0625

Table 9.1: Table of outcomes of preferences for story outcome with four participants

In other words, the probability that all four informants prefer + (i.e. a sad ending) is 1/16, which equals (if you divide one by sixteen) 0.0625 (or 6.25%), while the probability that + is chosen twice is 6/16 = 0.3750 (or 37.50%).

Now let us increase the number of informants to eight instead of four. There are now 256 possibilities (2^8) that all participants will choose +. The possibilities of choice are distributed as follows:

No. of participants choosing +	Fraction	Probability
8	1/256	0.004
7 →	8/256	0.031
6	28/256	0.110
5	56/256	0.220
4	70/256	0.270
3	56/256	0.220
2	28/256	0.110
1	8/256	0.031
0	1/256	0.004

Table 9.2: Table of outcomes of preferences for story outcome with eight participants

If seven of my eight informants said they preferred the sad version (which we indicated by a +), we now see that the probability of this choice occurring is 8/256 = 0.031 (or 3.1%) (see arrow in figure).

Probabilities are expressed numerically in statistics as varying between zero and one. Zero probability means 'NEVER happens', while one means 'ALWAYS happens'. Placing the decimal point two places to the right yields a percentage, as we have seen systematically in the examples above. Hence $p = 0.031$ means: this event has a probability of occurrence of 3.1%. This, in other words, is the probability that this result may come about by pure chance. Another way of saying this is that there is a 3.1% chance that this outcome occurred by pure chance. In other words, there is a 3.1% chance that it occurs by random errors. On the other hand, the probability that all eight informants will choose + is highly unlikely. As a matter of fact, there is only one possibility in 256 that this situation will occur. So, there is a probability of 0.004, or 0.4% chance, it may happen. The possibility of error is here highly reduced.

Because random errors will *never* go away, we check how likely it is that a particular outcome could have been caused by such random errors. By drawing tree structures of the kind we have just done, we are able to disentangle the various chances of their probability of occurrence. The problem, as Figure 9.2 implies, is that such tree structures become difficult to manage manually once the number of informants increases. It is, among other things, on the basis of such structures and their concomitant estimates of occurrence that statisticians are able to provide evidence for the probabilities of certain events. Such probabilities are indicated by the letter *p*. In the case of our little experiment, as we showed above, the *p*-value indicates the probability that seven out of eight people preferring the sad ending is not due to chance. The probability of chance (random error) is very low: 0.031, or 3.1%. In other words, it is *un*likely that pure chance caused this outcome. But if it was not chance, what was it? Well, a provisional conclusion for our little 'theory' would be that it is a general characteristic of people to prefer stories with a sad end. In this perspective, *p* represents the probability that we *falsely* conclude that the independent variable had an effect on the dependent variable. The independent variable, remember, is the kind of story ending, the dependent variable is the preference for either kind expressed by the respondents. The *p*-values, in other words, indicate the likelihood that we made a mistake. Therefore, the lower they are, the surer we can be that our results stand. The *p-values* indicate the probability that our results are caused by random errors. They are a measure of our uncertainty. How certain are we therefore? If our uncertainty is 3.1% then our confidence in the results is: $100 - 3.1 = 96.9\%$. Another way of saying this is: when we repeat this experiment 100 times, we will on average find the same results 96.9 times. In such a situation it is allowable to say that the ending of a story has an effect on readers' preference.

9.3. Region of rejection

Now let us see how these preferences for sad endings (+) are distributed graphically. Suppose we set out the possibilities on a coordinate system in which the number of + participants are set out on the horizontal axis, and the number of occurrences of + preferences is on the vertical one. The result for eight informants can be seen in the following figure.

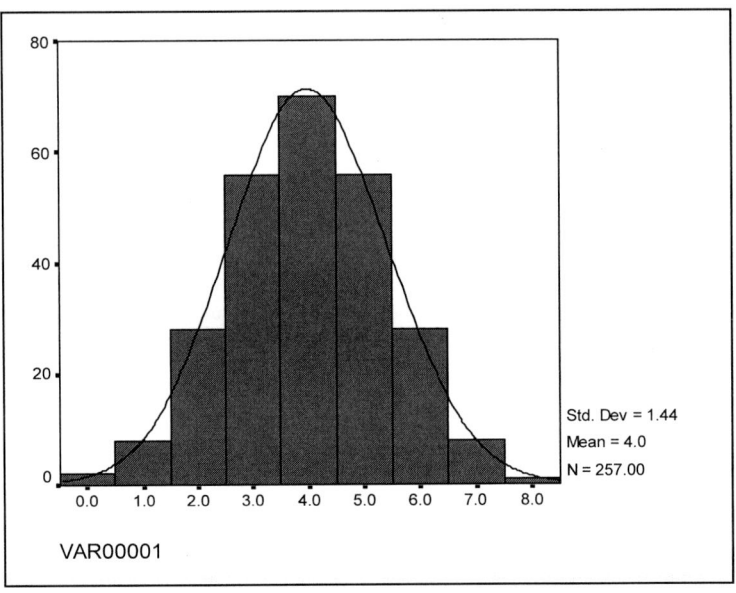

You can see that a kind of rough normal distribution emerges, in which both zero and eight participants choosing + are situated at both ends ('tails') of the distributions. You also notice that their occurrences are very low, i.e. 2 × 0.004 = 0.008, or 0.08%, as we saw in Table 9.2. (Please note that we must multiply the value of 0.004 by 2 because there are two such possibilities, namely the case where one person prefers + and that where eight persons prefer +.) Also 1 + and 7 + are relatively rare, i.e. together 2 × 0.031 = 0.062, or 6.2%. The main question here is, of course, how 'rare' such an event must be before we decide that we accept it as low enough for us to accept our little theory. This is generally discussed under the name of the 'region of rejection'.

Basically, what we are doing is testing a hypothesis, usually a hypothesis of *difference* (between groups). We call this the 'alternative' hypothesis (usually abbreviated as H_a). The logical opposite is the hypothesis of *no difference*, called the 'null' hypothesis (abbreviated as H_0). Remember what we said about falsification in Chapter 2, when we spoke about Karl Popper's introduction of the asymmetry between verifying and falsifying a hypothesis? What we do is to try to reject H_a. If we cannot reject the alternative hypothesis, we have no other choice than to reject its logical opposite, which is the *null hypothesis* (H_0). We then reject the hypothesis that there is no difference between the groups, and we accept the hypothesis that there *is* a difference. If we *are* successful in rejecting the alternative hypothesis, then we accept the null hypothesis, that there is no difference between the groups. In deciding whether to reject either of these possibilities, we take into account the probability of the event. We saw that the probability that seven out of eight informants chose the sad ending by pure chance is 3.1%. Is this high or low enough?

Theoretically speaking, there is no hard and fast answer to this question, because random errors always remain, so we cannot fully eliminate them. Must we say that 3% error probability is low enough? Or 0.3%? Or 0.0003%? We are dealing here with a gliding scale, on which each of these numbers gives us information on the likelihood of error. There is no indication in the numbers themselves as to when to decide that the error probability is low enough. However, statisticians have developed some kind of convention for making decisions in this respect. Basically, it works like this: you 'choose' a level of error probability that you are prepared to accept as reasonable. In some cases this level may be higher than in others. For instance, when you are at the very beginning of exploring a new domain, about which there is hardly any literature to be found, and no research is available yet, you may want to be rather lenient, and accept an error probability of 10%. In other situations, where you can base your work on a considerable body of previous research, you may wish to be much sterner, and accept only data that have an error probability of 1%. This level, which you can choose more or less freely (depending on the kind of research you are doing) is called the *significance level*, and it is indicated by the symbol α. You put α at the level of 10%, 1%, 0.1%, etc., depending on how much you want to accept in terms of errors. Any *p*-value below this chosen α is then 'significant'.

Now an important consequence of such a decision is the kind of risk you run in drawing false conclusions. If α is very high, there is a high probability that you will come to the conclusion that you observed an effect of the independent variable on the dependent variable, while in reality this so-called effect is merely due to chance. Because you are ready to accept a high level of error probability, you thereby run the risk of including too many errors in your conclusion. That is self-evident. This is called a *type 1 error*: you conclude that the independent variable had an effect on the dependent variable, when in reality it did not, but was the result of an error, or of chance (which is more or less the same in methodology). The opposite is true too, of course: if you choose a very low level for α, this may also lead to a false conclusion, but the opposite one, namely that you miss out on effects of the independent variable on the dependent variable which do occur, but with a higher probability than your α has allowed. Your low α prevents you from 'catching' the effects you are looking for, because they are rejected as above the significance level, hence not worth considering. This is called a *type 2 error*: you reject the alternative hypothesis, and accordingly accept H_0 although it is wrong, and the alternative hypothesis is, in fact, right. You blinded yourself from seeing it by filtering out numerous occurrences of it through a very low α. These considerations lead to the conclusion that you must somehow get a balanced α, neither too high nor too low.

The relationship between rejecting the H_0 and the different types of error can be cast in a decision matrix of the following kind:

	H_0 is true	H_0 is false
Fail to reject H_0	Correct decision	Type 2 error
Reject H_0	Type 1 error	Correct decision

Table 9.3: Decision matrix for error types

Experimenting with various levels of α in research has led to some form of standard practice, whereby α is set at the level of 0.05, i.e. 5%. This significance level thus entails that we are prepared to accept a risk of 5% error probability. Some methodologists consider this too high, because it means that for every 20 investigations carried out, one may lead to erroneous conclusions! However, it is still the case that the conventional significance level of 0.05 is widely accepted. So in this book we will go along with this practice, that is: accepting a 5% error probability. In practice, this means that we accept results as generalizable when they have an error probability of 5%. Such results are called *significant*. This means that they can be generalized beyond the sample (though it is always good to reflect on how to define the population from which the sample had been drawn). Whenever the *p*-value drops below 0.01 the results are called very significant, below 0.001 they are called highly significant. Some will say that the qualifications make no sense, because it is the significance or non-significance that is relevant. This is to misunderstand the nature of probability. It makes little sense to say that a result with a *p*-value just above the 5% level (say 0.052) is not significant, while one with a *p*-value just below (say 0.048) *is* significant! It is precisely the graded version of *p*-values that makes them so informative: these two results with *p*-values near to the significance level have almost identical error probabilities, so it makes little sense to say that one may be generalized and the other not. Hence we would like to warn against a *mechanical* use of the significance level, and instead plead for a *reasoned* use.

The acceptance of a conventional level of significance leads to a separation between an area in the distribution of the data where only random errors had an effect, and an area where the independent variable had an effect on the dependent variable. Graphically, this area appears as follows:

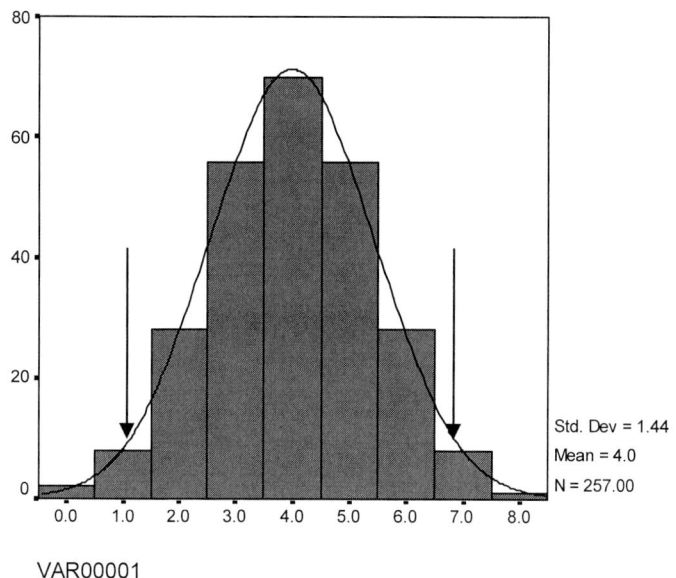

Figure 9.4: Region of rejection at both ends of the curve

On the horizontal axis we find the number of respondents who have expressed their preference for the sad ending. We have seen that both 0 and 1 times, as well as 7 and 8 times have probabilities lower than 0.05: this, then is the *region of rejection*. In this area of the distribution we accept that the independent variable had an influence on the dependent variable. Do we know for sure? Not at all! But the likelihood that we are mistaken here is low enough, we presume, to accept this conclusion.

What exactly is that conclusion? Remember I asked eight friends whether they preferred stories with a sad or happy ending. These eight people are but a small sample of people in my environment, of course. That seven out of eight preferred the sad version we now know is a rather unlikely event. We know it can happen by chance and that chance is 6.2 in one hundred (see above). This *p*-value tells us that if I ask another eight people from among my friends, the chance that I will get a similar response is almost 94% (100 – 6.2). This is what inference statistics is all about: it tells us how confident we can be in generalizing from a sample to a group at large. Without such information, our claims remain vague and uninformative. Inference statistics makes such claims more precise, more reliable, and more realistic.

In asking my friends about their preference for the sad or the happy ending, I had no inkling what would come out of it but I *was* testing a hypothesis, namely the H_a, namely *that* there would be a difference in reaction to the two versions. It turns out that I have to reject this alternative hypothesis, because the probability associated with it, i.e. 0.062, was higher than α (i.e. 0.05). Consequently, I have to accept the H_0; however, note that the likelihood (*p*) that this difference came about through chance is very close to α: the difference is a mere 0.012 (or 1.2%). Here a pure mechanistic application of α would conclude in favor of H_0; a more informed conclusion, however, would specify that with such a small sample of informants, the *p*-value is very close to the critical value for me to accept it as relating to the difference in content between the two story-endings. A conventional way of saying this in research reports is that there is a *tendency toward* significance.

However, I have tested only the hypothesis *that* there is a difference between those two endings. This is called a two-tailed test: if you look back to Figure 9.4, this means that the region of rejection lies at both ends of the curve: either the sad endings are preferred more (one end – or *tail*, as it is called, hence the name 'two-tailed' test), or the happy endings are chosen more often. The alternative hypothesis is a *non-directional* one: it predicts a difference, but without claiming the direction of the difference. I could, however, also have specified this direction, for instance if I had specified (in advance) that the sad (not the happy) endings would have been preferred more often. In such a case the H_a is a *directional* one: it predicts not only a difference, but also the direction of the difference. In such a case the test is a *one-tailed* one: the probability of the distribution lies only at *one* end of the tails of the curve in Figure. 9.4. SPSS, however, as a rule, calculates *p*-values for two-tailed tests, that is, for non-directional hypotheses. So what do you do in the case where you have a directional hypothesis? Simply divide the *p*-value by 2! You can now see that in such a case there would have been no doubt as to the significance of the results, as 0.062 divided by 2 yields 0.031, and this *p*-value is lower than 0.05! Some readers may at this point surmise that therefore a clever move would be to resort to a directional hypothesis when it turns out that the *p*-value is on the borderline. This, however, is methodologically not allowed: one has to specify *in advance* whether the hypothesis tested is a directional or a non-directional one. All else is capitalizing on chance, and that is against everything that scientific research is about: we are not interested in low *p*-values per se, we are interested in learning to understand how the world is structured.

Now that we know how inference statistics works in theory, let us turn to some examples of how things work in practice. To this end, we will concentrate on a number of tests that compare two or more groups of respondents to test the possibility of generalizing any observed differences. If you can, follow the instructions in SPSS on your computer screen.

9.4. Correlations

In statistics, we can consider whether certain variables in our data show a particular relation to each other. In Chapter 8, for instance, we spoke about the normal distribution of body height and of shoe size. But obviously these two have something in common: generally tall people have larger shoe sizes than short people. Of course this is not the case for every single individual: there are certainly tall people with small feet and some short people may have proportionally large shoe size. In general, however, the relationship holds that shoe size and body height are related to each other. This is the kind of relation that is called a *correlation* in statistics. Another way of saying this is that there is a *similarity* between those two variables. This similarity is expressed in statistics as a numerical value between -1 and $+1$. A correlation coefficient (r) of $+1$ indicates that the two patterns of observation match each other perfectly positively. The word 'positively' here means that when the values of one variable increase, those of the other will too – and vice versa: if the values of one of the variables decrease, so will the other. This is called a negative correlation. When $r = -1$ this means again a perfect match, but now something different is the case: whenever variable X increases, the values for Y go down – and vice versa: when the values of Y go up, those of X decrease. This is what we call a *negative correlation*. What if $r = 0$? This means that there is absolutely no similarity between the two variables. An example: reading frequency correlates positively with educational level. Thus, if we plot the number of books read on the horizontal axis and the highest level of education that person has had on the vertical axis, the pattern one gets is shown in Figure 9.5.

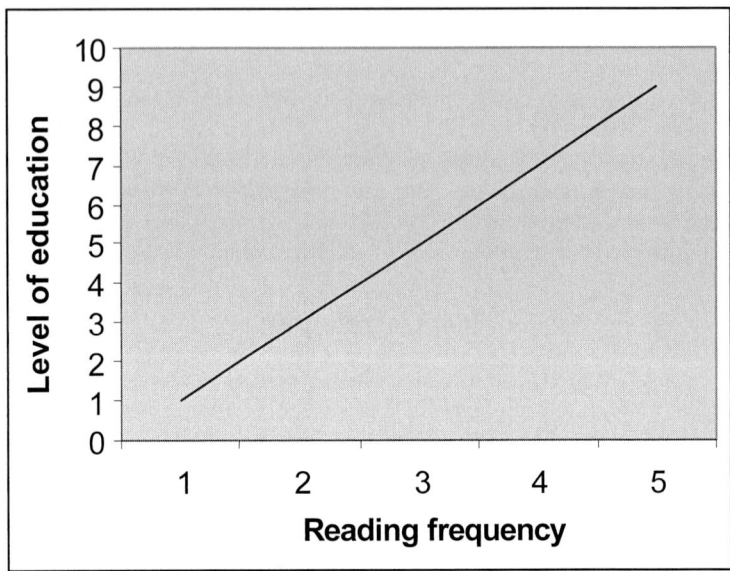

Figure 9.5: Example of a positive correlation

The relation between both variables (reading frequency on the one hand, and educational level on the other) is indicated by a straight line, starting in the lower left-hand corner and going up to the upper right-hand corner, which indicates a positive correlation. You see that whenever the variable on the horizontal axis has a low value, the one on the vertical axis has a low value too. And vice versa: high values on the vertical axis have their counterpart in high values on the horizontal axis too. Correlation can also be negative, though: in this case they show an *inverse* pattern of relation. This means that a low value on the horizontal axis corresponds to a high value on the vertical axis – and again, of course, vice versa. A good example of such a negative correlation is between children's reading frequency and the amount of time they spend watching television, as is illustrated in the following graph:

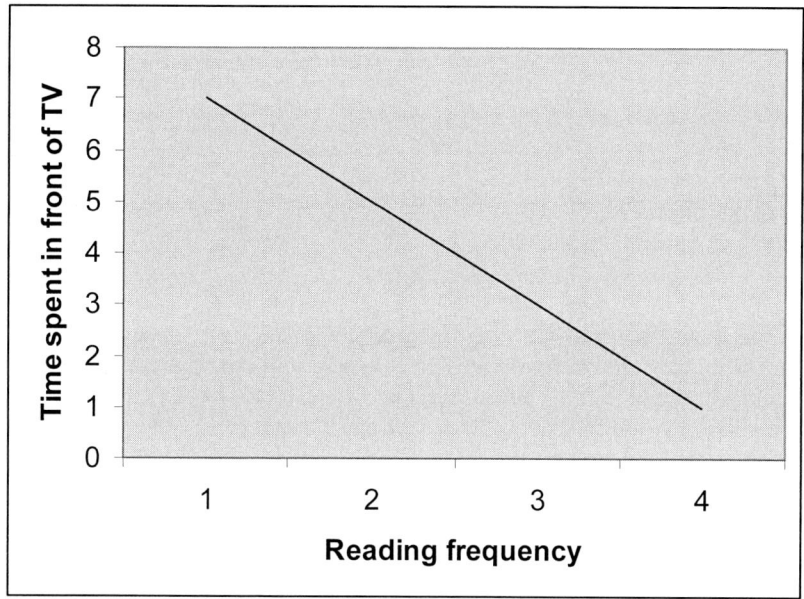

Figure 9.6: Example of a negative correlation

Thus, if we set out the number of hours a child watches TV in a week on the horizontal axis and the number of books this child reads plus the number of hours he or she spends watching television on the vertical axis (or the other way round, that really does not matter), one gets the typical patterns of a negative correlation: a straight line starting in the upper left-hand corner going down to the lower right-hand corner.

The example shows how treacherous correlations can be. Many people (especially journalists) tend to interpret this negative correlation as 'proof' that a high diet of TV watching is bad for one's reading appetite – hence that one should not let children watch television too much. Independent of the question whether this is a good educational measure, this certainly does not follow from the negative correlation. A correlation only indicates a similarity between two sets of data, not causality. It may be the case that heavy TV watching drives children away from books, but the opposite may be the case too: children who happen to be not so good at reading prefer watching TV as a leisure activity. We are not saying that this is the case, only that this is just as possible on the basis of the correlation. There are other potential causal chains as well. Given what we said before about a positive correlation between educational level and reading frequency, it may be the case that in families with lower educational levels, watching television is the preferred pastime, and children read less. There is no direct causal link between reading and watching. Instead, both are caused by a third (often invisible) variable, here educational level. Generally, correlations can be interpreted in four ways:

- X causes Y
- Y causes X
- Q causes both X and Y
- the correlation is pure coincidence.

We have discussed the first three possibilities above. The fourth makes clear that in the complex world we live in, where millions of characteristics may be related to millions of other characteristics, there are bound to be such correlations by pure accident, devoid of any meaning. So how do you know whether a correlation you have found is purely accidental or not? The problem is, you do not. Here interpretation of your results, and comparison with other, independent, data, becomes indispensable. Interpretation, here, however, is not something arbitrary. For instance, there is a relation between the probability of such coincidences and the number of comparisons carried out. With a small number of correlations, very low probabilities are highly unlikely, so these may well not be coincidences. If they are still difficult to explain, you can think hard of how these things may correlate. You can also repeat the study and see whether similar things come out of it.

Let us now see how to calculate correlations with the help of SPSS. Often it is highly instructive to look at your data before actually calculating the correlation. This can be done with a so-called scatterplot. Remember the experiment we described in Chapter 1, where we asked readers to rate eight consecutive lines of a poem ('I love you not') on an 11-point scale for beauty, while the ninth line deviated from it ('I love you notwithstanding'). We are using the data from this experiment to illustrate how this works. Click on **GRAPHS**, then on **SCATTER**, then on **SIMPLE**, then on **DEFINE**. You then transport the two variables you wish to correlate in the boxes for x-axis and y-axis, then click on **OK**. SPSS will then produce the following output:

Inference Statistics: Preliminaries 243

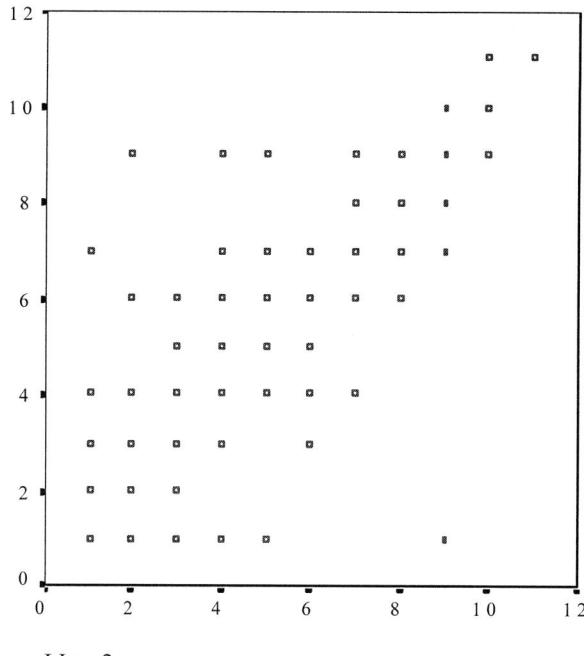

LIne 2

Figure 9.7: Scatterplot showing a positive correlation

The dots (or squares, or whatever) you see here are the individual observations. What you see here corresponds to the general trend you saw in Figure 9.5: a movement starting in the lower left-hand corner diagonally moving to the top right-hand corner, hence a positive correlation. Whenever the values allocated to one of the lines is low, the other is low too. Whenever one is high, the other is high as well. Thus a scatterplot allows you to see whether there is a pattern at all, and whether it is positive (as above) or whether it is negative, as in Figure 9.6 (showing the reverse pattern, namely coming down from the top right-hand corner to the bottom of the left-hand corner). In the following figure, there is no pattern at all to be seen:

244   Chapter Nine

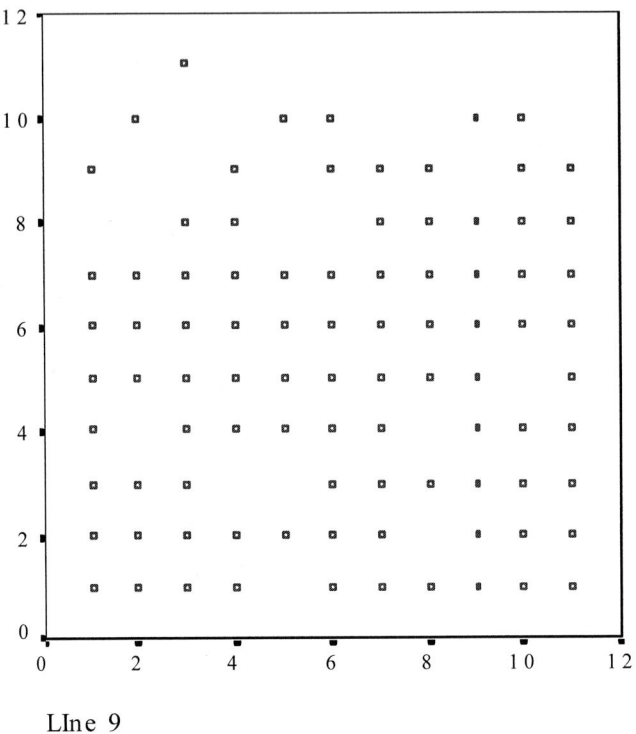

Figure 9.8: Scatterplot showing no correlation

Perhaps you find it easier to interpret such graphs if they have a straight line, as in Figure 9.5 and Figure 9.6. You can have such a line, which represents the 'best fit' between all the individual dots in the graph, and is called the *regression fit line*. To obtain it, click on **GRAPHS**, then on **INTERACTIVE**, then on **SCATTERPLOT**. A new window opens, in which you see a vertical and a horizontal arrow, each containing a box. They represent the vertical and horizontal axes of the scatterplot. Assign a variable to each, for instance LINE 1 to the vertical arrow and LINE 2 to the horizontal arrow. The click on **FIT**: you will now see a pull-down menu box in the top left. Click on it, then on **REGRESSION**, and finally on **OK**. The result is the following:

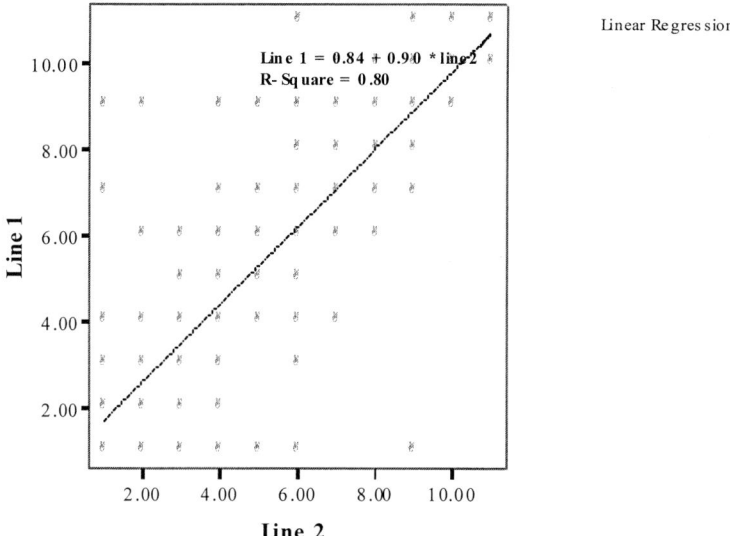

Figure 9.9: Scatterplot with regression fit line and R-square

The scatterplot is much easier to interpret now because the regression line clearly marks the overall trend. Moreover, SPSS has also calculated and included in the graph the *R-square* measure. This is a very useful measure to help you interpret correlations. It indicates the variability in one of the variables that is explained by the other variable. When we are dealing with human beings and their reactions, we must include very many factors that may influence their behavior, like their age, their educational background, the mood they are in, their inclination toward a particular kind of event, and so forth. What R-square expresses is the degree to which the variability in the one variable of our scatterplot can be explained by the other variable. You see that in Figure 9.9, R-square is 0.80. Applying the 'percentage' perspective to this, by shifting the decimal point two places to the right, it means that in this scatterplot 80% of LINE 1 accounts for the variability in the response to LINE 2. That leaves 20% of the variability that must be accounted for in terms of other variables (which we do not know, of course). In this way R-square helps us to interpret correlations. However, please note, as we explicitly stated above, that correlations do not necessarily entail causality, and that view is not challenged by using R-square. Nevertheless, it is a useful measure to better grasp the strength of the correlation.

As we have seen, scatterplots are very useful in interpreting your data when you are interested whether two or more variables correlate. However, they do not give you the numerical value of the correlation, nor the *p*-values associated with them. This is what we will have SPSS do for us now.

First, open SPSS, click on **ANALYZE**, then on **CORRELATE**, then on **BIVARIATE** ('BI' because you are going to compare two variables at a time). Now a new window opens up:

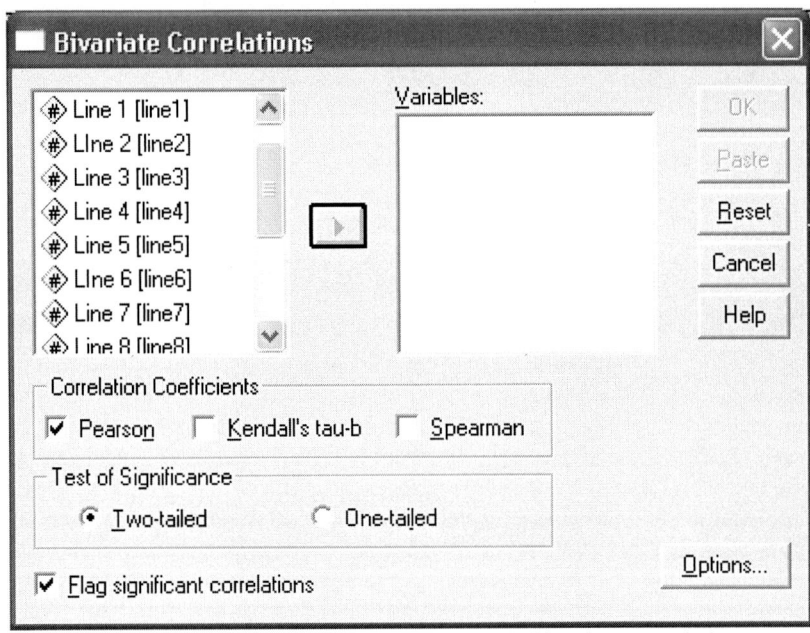

Figure 9.10: Dialog box to obtain Pearson's bivariate correlations

In the dialog box to the left, you see a list of the variables, such as the nationality of participants, and, of course, the nine lines. Transport the variables **LINE1** through **LINE9** into the right-hand window, by first clicking on them, and then on the arrow in the middle between the two windows. Under **CORRELATION COEFFICIENTS** you see that the box **PEARSON** has been ticked: this is indeed the default value for correlations. For most usual applications, leave the default value as it is. (If, however, your data are not in the interval measurement, but instead are of ordinal level, then you have to choose the **SPEARMAN CORRELATION COEFFICIENT**.) In the box below, you see that the 'two-tailed' type of significance testing has been set as the default value in

Inference Statistics: Preliminaries 247

SPSS. As we have said before, this is so in *all* applications in SPSS. Now click on **OK**. The result that SPSS produces is the figure below:

		Line 1	Line 2	Line 3	Line 4	Line 5	Line 6	Line 7	Line 8	Line 9
Line 1	Pears. Corr	1	0.862 (**)	0.709 (**)	0.589 (**)	0.470 (**)	0.403 (**)	0.278 (**)	0.228 (**)	-0.083
	Sig.		0.000	0.000	0.000	0.000	0.000	0.000	0.000	0.188
	N	254	254	254	254	253	253	254	252	254
Line 2	Pears. Corr	0.862 (**)	1	0.842 (**)	0.723 (**)	0.556 (**)	0.481 (**)	0.330 (**)	0.276 (**)	0.013
	Sig.	0.000		0.000	0.000	0.000	0.000	0.000	0.000	0.834
	N	254	255	255	255	254	254	255	253	255
Line 3	Pears. Corr	0.709 (**)	0.842 (**)	1	0.858 (**)	0.725 (**)	0.627 (**)	0.481 (**)	0.415 (**)	0.031
	Sig.	0.000	0.000		0.000	0.000	0.000	0.000	0.000	0.623
	N	254	255	255	255	254	254	255	253	255
Line 4	Pears.	0.589 (**)	0.723 (**)	0.858 (**)	1	0.887 (**)	0.791 (**)	0.638 (**)	0.539 (**)	0.074
	Sig.	0.000	0.000	0.000		0.000	0.000	0.000	0.000	0.238
	N	254	255	255	255	254	254	255	253	255
Line 5	Pears. Corr	0.470 (**)	0.556 (**)	0.725 (**)	0.887 (**)	1	0.922 (**)	0.796 (**)	0.696 (**)	0.129 (*)
	Sig. (two-tailed)	0.000	0.000	0.000	0.000		0.000	0.000	0.000	0.040
	N	253	254	254	254	254	253	254	252	254
Line 6	Pears. Corr	0.403 (**)	0.481 (**)	0.627 (**)	0.791 (**)	0.922 (**)	1	0.889 (**)	0.818 (**)	0.158 (*)
	Sig.	0.000	0.000	0.000	0.000	0.000		0.000	0.000	0.012
	N	253	254	254	254	253	254	254	252	254
Line 7	Pears. Corr	0.278 (**)	0.330 (**)	0.481 (**)	0.638 (**)	0.796 (**)	0.889 (**)	1	0.951 (**)	0.235 (**)
	Sig.	0.000	0.000	0.000	0.000	0.000	0.000		0.000	0.000
	N	254	255	255	255	254	254	255	253	255
Line 8	Pears. Corr	0.228 (**)	0.276 (**)	0.415 (**)	0.539 (**)	0.696 (**)	0.818 (**)	0.951 (**)	1	0.266 (**)
	Sig.	0.000	0.000	0.000	0.000	0.000	0.000	0.000		0.000
	N	252	253	253	253	252	252	253	253	253
Line 9	Pears. Corr	-0.083	0.013	0.031	0.074	0.129 (*)	0.158 (*)	0.235 (**)	0.266 (**)	1
	Sig.	0.188	0.834	0.623	0.238	0.040	0.012	0.000	0.000	
	N	254	255	255	255	254	254	255	253	255

Pears. Corr., Pearson correlation; Sig., significance (two-tailed test)
*Correlation is significant at the 0.05 level (two-tailed).
**Correlation is significant at the 0.01 level (two-tailed).

Table 9.4: Output of Spearman rank correlations

Let us see how to interpret it. You see the names of the nine variables turn up in nine columns as well as in nine rows. Now watch the diagonal that runs from the upper left-hand corner down to the right-hand bottom corner. You will notice that the number 1 appears up nine times, 'dividing' the table into two triangles. If you look at the number 1 in each case, you will understand what has happened: SPSS has correlated each of the nine variables to each of the other nine, hence also correlating each variable with itself, and this is – of course – a perfect match, expressed by 1!

The first line, also correlates 0.862(**) with the second line, and 0.709(**) with the third line. These are very high correlations, as they approach the value of 1. This means that there is a strong association between the ways our readers rated each of the lines. When the rating for line 1 was low, it was also low for lines 2 and 3, when it was high for 1; it was also high for 2 and 3. As a matter of fact, as you read on in the first row, you will notice that line 1 correlates strongly with all other lines, except one: line 9. There, the correlation is not only low (0.083), it is also negative: –0.083. This means that there is an *inverse* relation between the ratings of line 1 and line 9: when ratings for line 1 are low, they are high for line 9, and vice versa: when they are low for line 9, they are low for line 1. This is the only instance of a negative correlation in the matrix above. Further inspection reveals that virtually all correlations in the matrix are very high, with only a few exceptions, all of them with respect to line 9, very much in line with what the theory of novelty, as expounded in Chapter 1, predicted.

There is one other thing that has to be explained in the matrix above: most of the coefficients are accompanied by asterisks, mostly two. This is explained below the table, where it reads: "** Correlation is significant at the 0.01 level (two-tailed)" We now know what this means. It means that the chances that such a correlation came about by chance are lower than one in a hundred. One asterisk means that this chance is lower than five in a hundred (0.05 level). Another way of saying this is that when we repeat this research with similar respondents a hundred times, the chance of not finding the same correlation is less than one in hundred. Such low levels of significance mean then, that we may generalize the findings beyond the sample of informants who took part in our experiment. Considering that students were our informants, we can say with a high degree of probability, that other students from these universities will give us the same answers (as a group). As we can see in the matrix above, nearly all correlations between lines are significant or highly significant, except for line 9, as predicted by the theory.

A limitation of Pearson correlation is that it can only be used with data on the interval and ratio level of measurement. When you wish to investigate a relation between groups of nominal or ordinal data, use the Spearman's *Rho*. This is a so-called *non*-parametric test, which can be used in all cases where the level of measurement is lower than the interval. To obtain it, follow the same path as before: click on **ANALYZE**, then on **CORRELATE**, then on **BIVARIATE**. Now undo the option for the Pearson correlation, and instead tick the box **SPEARMAN**, as has been done in the illustration below:

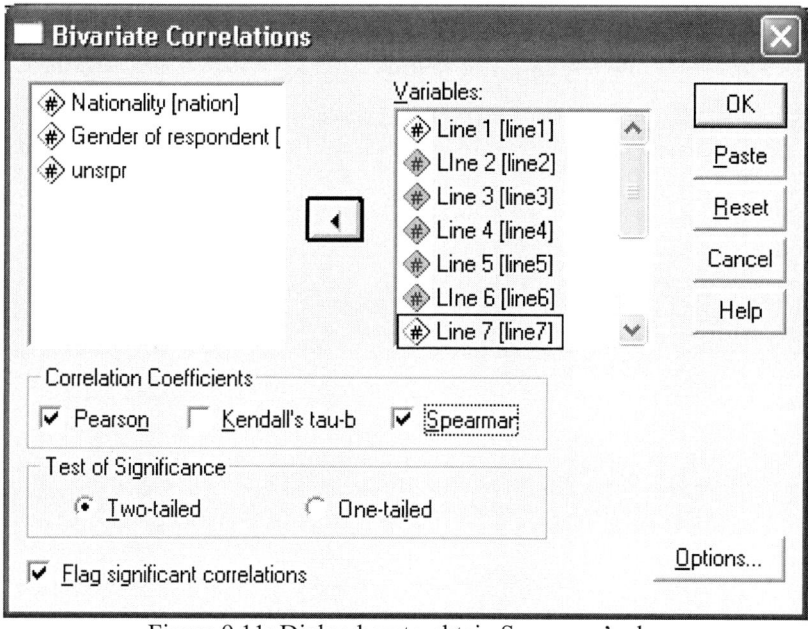

Figure 9.11: Dialog box to obtain Spearman's rho

Then click on **OK** to get the following result:

	Line 1	Line 2	Line 3	Line 4	Line 5	Line 6	Line 7	Line 8	Line 9
Line 1									
Corr Coeff	1.000	0.858 (**)	0.712 (**)	0.592 (**)	0.472 (**)	0.405 (**)	0.306 (**)	0.247 (**)	-0.074
Sig.		0.000	0.000	0.000	0.000	0.000	0.000	0.000	0.238
N	254	254	254	254	253	253	254	252	254
Line 2									
Corr Coeff	0.858 (**)	1.000	0.845 (**)	0.729 (**)	0.577 (**)	0.510 (**)	0.381 (**)	0.319 (**)	0.003
Sig.	0.000		0.000	0.000	0.000	0.000	0.000	0.000	0.960
N	254	255	255	255	254	254	255	253	255
Line 3									
Corr Coeff	0.712 (**)	0.845 (**)	1.000	0.875 (**)	0.754 (**)	0.657 (**)	0.531 (**)	0.459 (**)	0.012
Sig.	0.000	0.000		0.000	0.000	0.000	0.000	0.000	0.848
N	254	255	255	255	254	254	255	253	255
Line 4									
Corr Coeff	0.592 (**)	0.729 (**)	0.875 (**)	1.000	0.894 (**)	0.820 (**)	0.676 (**)	0.580 (**)	0.050
Sig.	0.000	0.000	0.000	.	0.000	0.000	0.000	0.000	0.423
N	254	255	255	255	254	254	255	253	255
Line 5									
Corr Coeff	0.472 (**)	0.577 (**)	0.754 (**)	0.894 (**)	1.000	0.920 (**)	0.802 (**)	0.708 (**)	0.110
Sig.)	0.000	0.000	0.000	0.000		0.000	0.000	0.000	0.080
N	253	254	254	254	254	253	254	252	254
Line 6									
Corr Coeff	0.405 (**)	0.510 (**)	0.657 (**)	0.820 (**)	0.920 (**)	1.000	0.897 (**)	0.825 (**)	0.138 (*)
Sig.	0.000	0.000	0.000	0.000	0.000		0.000	0.000	0.028
N	253	254	254	254	253	254	254	252	254
Line 7									
Corr Coeff	0.306 (**)	0.381 (**)	0.531 (**)	0.676 (**)	0.802 (**)	0.897 (**)	1.000	0.945 (**)	0.215 (**)
Sig.	0.000	0.000	0.000	0.000	0.000	0.000		0.000	0.001
N	254	255	255	255	254	254	255	253	255
Line 8									
Corr Coeff	0.247 (**)	0.319 (**)	0.459 (**)	0.580 (**)	0.708 (**)	0.825 (**)	0.945 (**)	1.000	0.238 (**)
Sig.	0.000	0.000	0.000	0.000	0.000	0.000	0.000	.	0.000

N Line 9	252	253	253	253	252	252	253	253	253
Corr Coeff	-0.074	0.003	0.012	0.050	0.110	0.138 (*)	0.215 (**)	0.238 (**)	1.000
Sig.	0.238	0.960	0.848	0.423	0.080	0.028	0.001	0.000	
N	254	255	255	255	254	254	255	253	255

Corr Coeff;, correlation coefficient; Sig., significance on two-tailed test.
**Correlation is significant at the 0.01 level (two-tailed).
*Correlation is significant at the 0.05 level (two-tailed).

Table 9.5: Output of Spearman's rho

Spearman's *rho* has now been calculated for each of the nine lines with each of the others. You see that again the same pattern of correlations can be observed: very high and highly significant correlations between most lines, with the exception of line 9. Parametric tests are as a rule more powerful, i.e. they can detect significances better than non-parametric tests, which have to make up for the fact the data are not normally distributed.

There is also a third kind of correlation test, which should be used especially in those cases where you have a small number of observations and a lot of *ties*. These are measurements that are the same in both conditions and will therefore get equal ranks if we rank order all data. For instance, only five persons in only three groups, with several ties, Kendall's τ was the most appropriate correlation to be applied. To obtain it, go through the same steps as for the other correlation test, but now tick the box Kendall's τ, and do not forget to deselect the Pearson and/or Spearman tests.

9.5. Outlook

In this chapter we have studied the foundations of probability upon which significance testing is based. We then applied this knowledge to correlations between variables. Now that we know how such correlations work and how we can have them calculated by SPSS, we turn to the situation where we are less interested in the correspondence than in the difference between variables. Wherever we observe such a difference, the question for test statistics is whether these differences are to be found only in the sample of observations we have made, or can be generalized to a larger population. That is what will keep us busy in the next chapter.

CHAPTER TEN

INFERENCE STATISTICS: TEST SELECTION, *t*-TEST AND NON-PARAMETRIC EQUIVALENTS

When you do empirical research, you are not really interested in individual responses. However unique (and therefore interesting) an individual's reactions may be, for science they are only interesting insofar as they tell us something about the world in general. The Latin phrase *de singularibus non est scientia* summarizes this aptly: about the single individual there is no science. We are always looking for comparisons: to find out in what way individual responses are similar and to what extent they differ from each other. But those similarities and differences that we then discover do not interest us as such. We are far more interested in knowing whether these similarities and differences can also be applied to other, comparable, individuals and groups. For instance, in gender studies we will try to find out whether differences in female and male behavior that we have observed in a group are differences between women and men *in general*. How can you know this? That is exactly what inference statistics does – so we need to be introduced to it. There are a number of statistical tests that allow you to estimate how probable it is that the differences you have observed are general characteristics. How does this work? By taking into account the different aspects of the observation, such as the number of observations, the way in which they were collected, the level of measurement they are in, etc. For instance, it will be intuitively clear that if I have informally observed different behavior of men and women in a small, informal group of 10 people, the probability that these observations can be generalized are much lower than had I made rigorous observations of 100 men and women. Hence the rigor of observation and the number of people observed are two parameters that will enter the concrete statistical tests to estimate the generalizability of findings.

10.1. Which test(s) to choose?

One problem for the novice is to know which (type of) statistical test to use in which situation. In this section we acquaint you with this. We present this as a decision chart, in which you successively go through a number of steps that ultimately lead to the selection of the appropriate statistical test. Such decisions depend on a number of issues, the most important of which are: whether your data are normally distributed, whether your samples are dependent or independent, what scale of measurements you used, and how many dependent and independent variables are at stake in your design.

A first major distinction to be made here is between *parametric* and *non-parametric* tests. The *t*-test, analysis of variance (ANOVA) and general linear model (GLM) are examples of the former, the Wilcoxon, Chi-square, and Mann–Whitney tests are examples of the latter. One of the major presuppositions on which the use of the parametric tests is based is that your data are normally distributed. (Do you remember what a normal distribution is? If you have forgotten, then refer back to Chapter 8!) But how do you know whether your data are normally distributed? A first and quick approximate answer to this question can be provided if you look at the *histograms* of your data.

We will use the same data as the previous chapter, i.e. respondents' reactions to the nine lines of the 'poem' we fabricated. To obtain these, click on ANALYZE, then on DESCRIPTIVE STATISTICS, then FREQUENCIES. A new window will open (Figure 10.1).

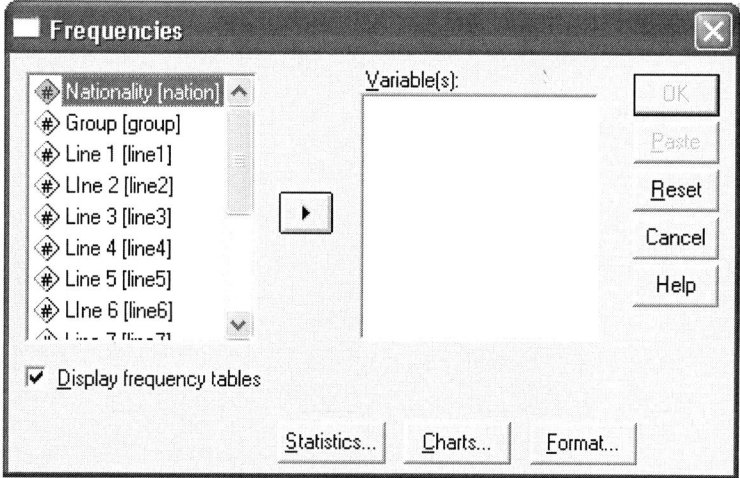

Figure 10.1: Dialog box to obtain histograms

In this window, click on **CHARTS**. You may wish to click on **STATISTICS** as well, of course. Then enter the **DEPENDENT VARIABLE** (e.g. lines of poem) in the right-hand box, after which the following window opens:

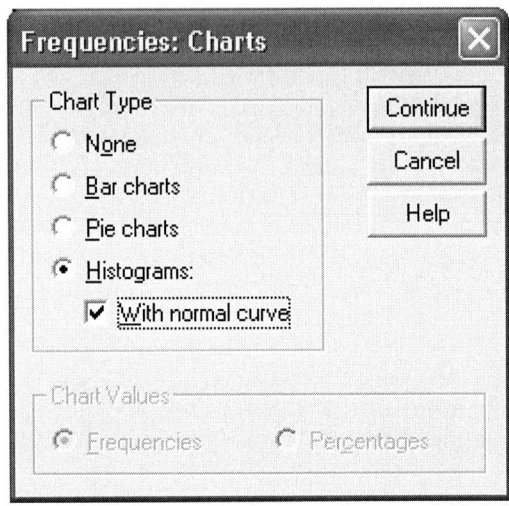

Figure 10.2: Dialog box to obtain normal curves with histograms

Click here on **HISTOGRAMS**, then on **WITH NORMAL CURVE**, then on **CONTINUE**. As an example of the output that is provided by SPSS, let us look at the result for line 1 of the poem:

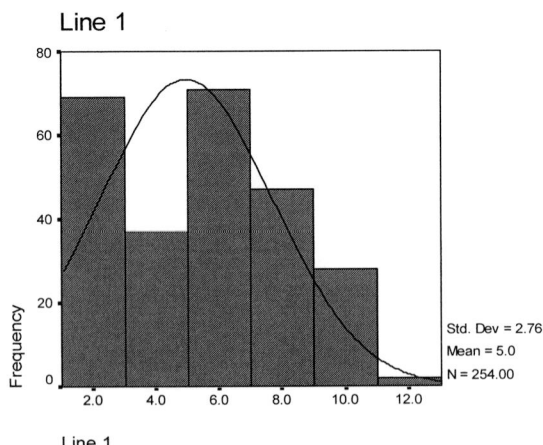

Figure 10.3: Histogram for Line 1

The horizontal axis contains the evaluative points on the scale (from 1 through 11), the vertical axis represents the number of respondents who chose this point on the scale. You see that the curve that has been drawn by SPSS across the bar charts is not normally distributed because its highest point is not in the middle of the scale, but somewhat more to the left. Such a distribution is described as *skewed* (left-skewed in this case). Let us look now at the results of for line 9.

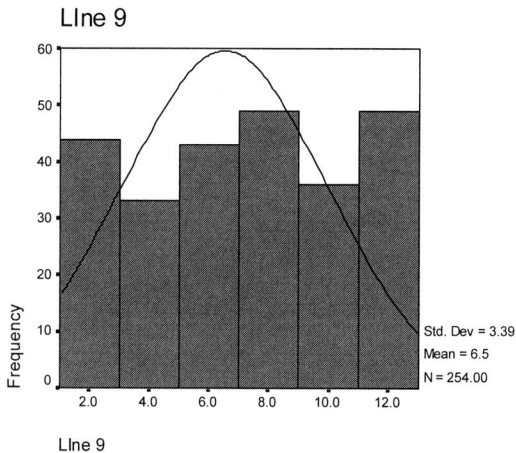

Figure 10.4: Histogram with normal curve for line 9

In this case the curve indicates a more or less normal distribution, although the bar chart shows something quite contrary to this, namely that the tails at both ends are far too high for this distribution to be taken as normal! What this shows is that such histograms are open to interpretation, and thus allow subjective decisions to be made. Maybe to one researcher the distribution looks like an acceptable normal distribution, while another one might dispute this. You want a more objective criterion on which to base your decisions, of course.

Such a objective decisions can be reached using the Kolmogorov–Smirnov test. This compares the scores in your sample to a normally distributed set of scores with the same mean and SD as your own data. If the test turns out to be non-significant ($p > 0.05$), your distribution is not significantly different from a normal distribution, i.e. it is normally distributed and you can use parametric tests. If, by contrast, the test is significant ($p < 0.05$), this means that your data are significantly different from a normal distribution, hence they are probably *not* normally distributed. To carry out this test, click on **ANALYZE**, then on **DESCRIPTIVE STATISTICS**, then on **EXPLORE**.

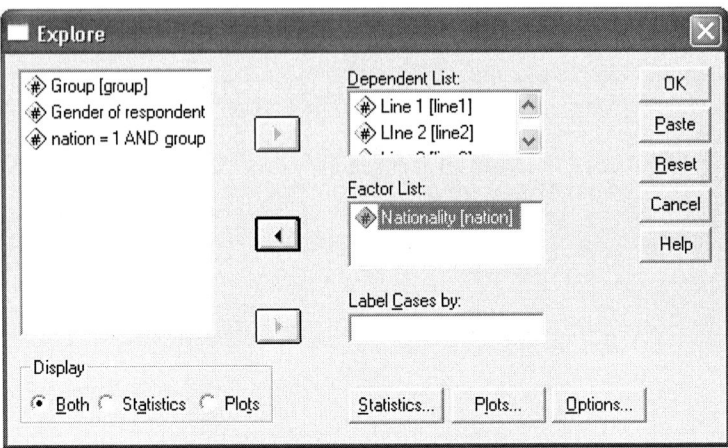

Figure 10.5: Dialog box to explore data

Now enter the DEPENDENT VARIABLE in DEPENDENT LIST, e.g. nine lines of poem. Click on STATISTICS (the default options are fine here), then on PLOTS.

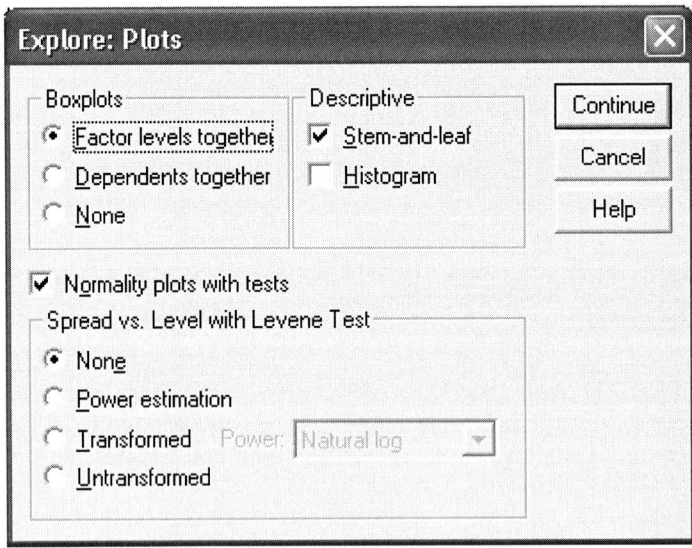

Figure 10.6: Dialog box to show normality plots

STEM AND LEAF has already been marked as default; click on NORMALITY PLOTS WITH TESTS, then on CONTINUE. In the SPSS output, look (below the descriptive statistics) at the following table:

Tests of Normality

	Kolmogorov–Smirnov*			Shapiro–Wilk		
	Statistic	df	Sig.	Statistic	df	Sig.
Line 1	0.169	250	0.000	0.929	250	0.000
Line 2	0.129	250	0.000	0.936	250	0.000
Line 3	0.134	250	0.000	0.926	250	0.000
Line 4	0.149	250	0.000	0.909	250	0.000
Line 5	0.158	250	0.000	0.896	250	0.000
Line 6	0.171	250	0.000	0.886	250	0.000
Line 7	0.179	250	0.000	0.871	250	0.000
Line 8	0.203	250	0.000	0.854	250	0.000
Line 9	0.103	250	0.000	0.915	250	0.000

*Lilliefors significance correction

Figure 10.7: SPSS output of Kolmogorov–Smirnov test

The table shows the statistics for each line in the rows. Ignore the right-hand side of the table, where it says 'Shapiro–Wilk', and concentrate on the left-hand side, under Kolmogorov–Smirnov. The information we are after is in the column titled 'Sig.', as usual. You see that the p-values listed here are highly significant in all cases: this indicates a deviation from normality. Hence the distributions of the responses to the individual lines are *not* normally distributed! Therefore, you cannot use parametric tests.

You can also inspect this in the plots you have requested.

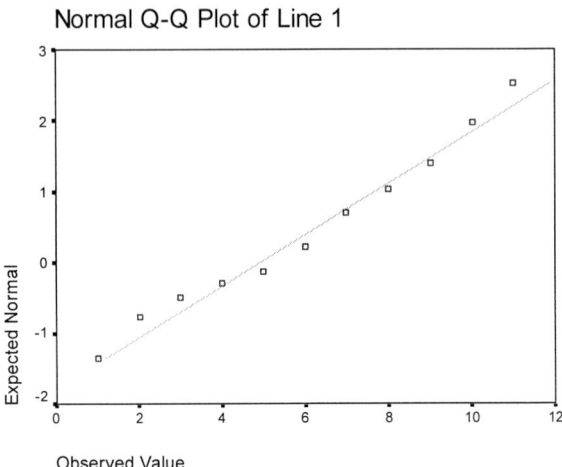

Figure 10.8: SPSS output of Q-Q plots

In this plot the straight diagonal line represents the normal distribution, the dots the actual observations (11, for the 11 points on the scale). If the data were normally distributed, all dots would fall exactly on that straight line. Any deviation from the straight line is a deviation from the normal distribution. You can inspect the plots for each line separately, but it is not, in fact, necessary, as you already know from the Kolmogorov–Smirnov test that these data are not normally distributed.

What do you do in such a situation? You choose *non-parametric* tests! These are also called assumption-free tests because they do not make the assumptions of the parametric tests, for instance that the data are normally distributed, or that the variances of the groups are roughly equal. In case these assumptions are broken, you can still perform inference statistics, by using so-called non-parametric tests. However, this comes at a price: non-parametric tests do not use the information in your data in an optimal way, unlike the parametric tests. Hence these tests have less *power*: this means that they are less able to detect a genuine effect that is there in the data. In other words, by using non-parametric tests, you run an increased risk of a *Type 2* error!

Now that we know how to find out whether our data are normally distributed, let us look at the decision matrix that allows you to determine which statistical test to use in which situation – see the flow-chart below.

Inference Statistics: Test Selection, *t*-test and Non-Parametric Equivalents 259

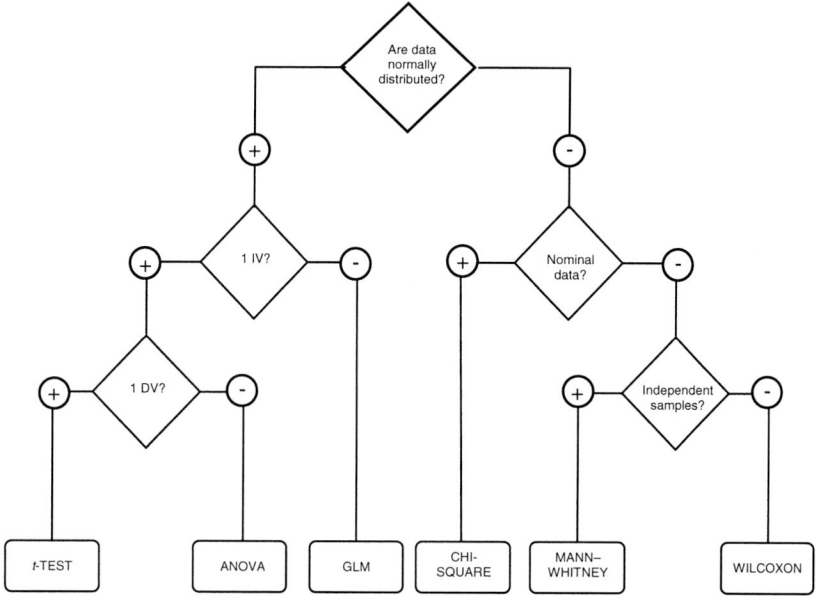

Figure 10.9: Decision flowchart for test selection

Let us go through the flow chart step by step, to see how it works. As you can see, the first question in the flow chart is whether the data are normally distributed. If they are, you follow the left hand side of the chart, which contains the tests that are called *parametric* tests, and ask the next question, which is whether you are dealing with one *independent variable*. When the answer is no (so you are dealing with more than one independent sample), follow the arrow straight down to where you see a box containing 'GLM' (General Linear Model): that is the test you will need in this case. If you are dealing with only one independent variable, the next question becomes whether you are dealing with one *dependent variable*. If yes, then follow the line straight to the bottom, where you find '*t*-test' in a box. That means simply: in this situation, choose the *t*-test! In applying this test, you will have one more choice to make, namely to choose between the situation where your samples were independent from each other or where they were dependent. SPSS uses a number of synonyms for such terms, which tends to be somewhat confusing to the novice, so it is good to know that dependent samples are also called 'paired' or 'related'. These are, of course, samples used in a *within-subjects* design; independent samples are the ones that go with a *between-subjects* design – if you have forgotten this distinction, refer back to Chapter 6.

If, however, the answer to the previous question was 'no' (so there was more than just one dependent variable, then follow this line down to where you find the box containing 'ANOVA': indeed the ANOVA is the (parametric) test you use when you are looking for the influence of one independent variable on several dependent variables.

If, however, the answer to the initial question was negative, i.e. your data were *not* normally distributed, you follow the lines to the right of the flow-chart, and ask whether the data are in the nominal scale of measurement. If they are, choose the Chi-square test. If they are not, ask whether the samples are dependent or independent. In the former case, choose the Wilcoxon test, in the latter use the Mann–Whitney test.

Now that we know which test to use in which situation, let us have a closer look at the tests themselves. We start out with the simplest ones in this chapter, the (parametric) t-test and its non-parametric counterparts.

10.2. *t*-test

Suppose we wish to examine how members of different cultures in the experiment on the nine poetry lines (introduced in Chapter 1) reacted. The informants belong to either one or another group; hence there is no overlap between the samples. They cannot be both Brazilian and Ukrainian. Here we are not discussing the possibility of double nationalities, but whether the participants in both groups belonged to the Ukrainian or Brazilian groups. They could not possibly have been at the two places simultaneously when the data were collected! Such samples are called independent (not to be confused, of course, with independent variables!) We will later give an example of samples that are not independent.

To obtain a t-test, click on **ANALYZE**, then on **COMPARE MEANS**, then on **INDEPENDENT SAMPLES *T* TEST**. The following window now opens:

Inference Statistics: Test Selection, *t*-test and Non-Parametric Equivalents 261

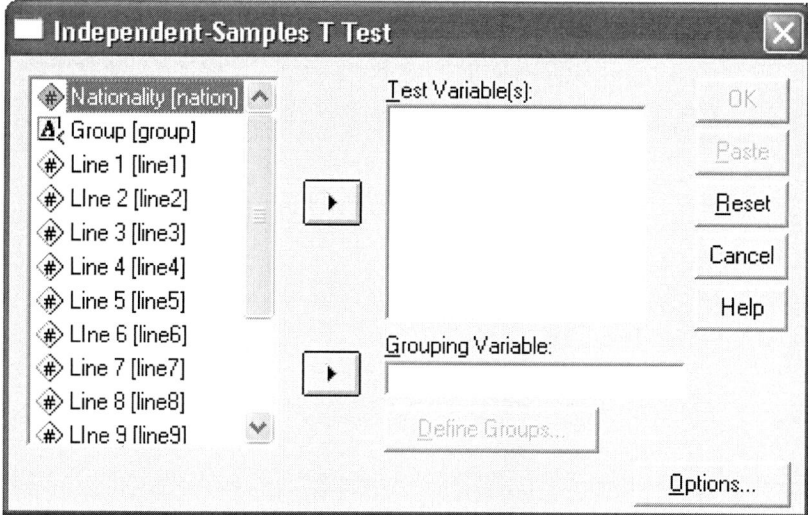

Figure 10.10: Dialog box to obtain an independent-samples *t*-test

On the left-hand side of the window, click on the variables **LINE 1**, **LINE 2**, etc, which will light up, then transport them into the box **DEPENDENT LIST** by clicking on the arrow. In the **GROUPING VARIABLE**, enter **NATION**, then click on **DEFINE GROUPS** – a new window now opens:

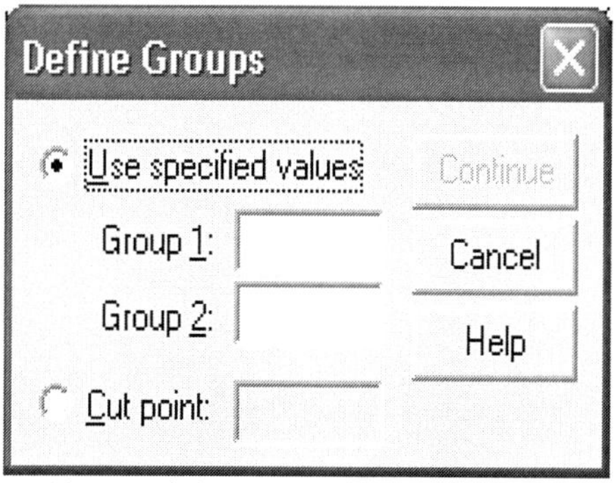

Figure 10.11: Dialog box to Define Groups in *t*-test

Enter the number of the nations you want to compare in each of the dialog boxes (e.g. 1 for Brazilians, 2 for Ukrainians – always go to **VARIABLE VIEW** if you have forgotten!) Then click on **CONTINUE**, then on **OK** in the previous window. The results shown look as follows:

Group Statistics

	Nationality	N	Mean	Std. Deviation	Std. Error Mean
Line 1	Brazilian	42	3,2143	2,69177	,41535
	Ukrainian	34	6,0882	2,84304	,48758
Line 2	Brazilian	42	3,2857	2,63453	,40652
	Ukrainian	34	5,6176	2,65164	,45475
Line 3	Brazilian	42	3,6429	3,03493	,46830
	Ukrainian	34	5,2647	2,57386	,44141
Line 4	Brazilian	42	3,1429	2,42519	,37421
	Ukrainian	34	5,5000	2,78796	,47813
Line 5	Brazilian	42	3,2143	2,37400	,36632
	Ukrainian	33	5,1515	2,76271	,48093
LIne 6	Brazilian	42	3,3095	2,30046	,35497
	Ukrainian	34	4,9118	2,81088	,48206
Line 7	Brazilian	42	3,5952	2,44011	,37652
	Ukrainian	34	4,5000	2,91548	,50000
Line 8	Brazilian	42	3,8333	2,60316	,40168
	Ukrainian	32	4,5313	3,22275	,56971
LIne 9	Brazilian	42	8,0000	3,21581	,49621
	Ukrainian	34	8,5588	2,63072	,45116

Figure 10.12: Descriptive statistics in independent-samples t-test

The first table on the output in SPSS is called **GROUP STATISTICS**. It contains the descriptive statistics for the nine lines, split according to nationality. You find the mean and standard deviation for each group response. You can inspect this table to see whether any differences occur between the groups. For instance, the average group response to line 1 shows a value of 3.21 for the Brazilian informants but of 6.08 for the Ukrainians – a considerable difference. Is that difference also significant? The answer to that question can be found in the next table in the SPSS output (scroll down!)

Independent Samples Test

		Levene's Test for Equality of Variances		t-test for Equality of Means						
									95% Confidence Interval of the Difference	
		F	Sig.	t	df	Sig. (2-tailed)	Mean Difference	Std. Error Difference	Lower	Upper
Line 1	Equal variances assumed	.086	.770	-4.513	74	.000	-2.8739	.63678	-4.14277	-1.60513
	Equal variances not assumed			-4.487	69.019	.000	-2.8739	.64051	-4.15172	-1.59618
Line 2	Equal variances assumed	.083	.774	-3.826	74	.000	-2.3319	.60954	-3.54647	-1.11739
	Equal variances not assumed			-3.823	70.552	.000	-2.3319	.60996	-3.54830	-1.11557
Line 3	Equal variances assumed	1.452	.232	-2.477	74	.016	-1.6218	.65485	-2.92667	-.31702
	Equal variances not assumed			-2.520	73.820	.014	-1.6218	.64355	-2.90419	-.33950
Line 4	Equal variances assumed	.070	.792	-3.940	74	.000	-2.3571	.59825	-3.54919	-1.16510
	Equal variances not assumed			-3.882	65.907	.000	-2.3571	.60716	-3.56941	-1.14487
Line 5	Equal variances assumed	.040	.843	-3.264	73	.002	-1.9372	.59358	-3.12023	-.75423
	Equal variances not assumed			-3.204	63.278	.002	-1.9372	.60455	-3.14522	-.72924
Line 6	Equal variances assumed	.492	.485	-2.733	74	.008	-1.6022	.58615	-2.77017	-.43431
	Equal variances not assumed			-2.676	63.469	.009	-1.6022	.59865	-2.79838	-.40610
Line 7	Equal variances assumed	.520	.473	-1.473	74	.145	-.9048	.61426	-2.12869	.31917
	Equal variances not assumed			-1.446	64.376	.153	-.9048	.62591	-2.15502	.34550
Line 8	Equal variances assumed	2.026	.159	-1.031	72	.306	-.6979	.67726	-2.04801	.65217
	Equal variances not assumed			-1.001	58.543	.321	-.6979	.69707	-2.09298	.69715
Line 9	Equal variances assumed	3.314	.073	-.816	74	.417	-.5588	.68498	-1.92368	.80603
	Equal variances not assumed			-.833	73.987	.407	-.5588	.67065	-1.89513	.77748

Figure 10.13: SPSS output of *t*-test for independent samples

Again we find the results for the nine lines in the nine rows. The first group of columns here is called LEVENE'S TEST FOR EQUALITY OF VARIANCES, the second is called *t*-TEST FOR EQUALITY OF MEANS. Each of these is subdivided into further columns. Thus in the latter case you see *t*, df, Sig. (two-tailed), mean, etc. It is the Sig. column that interests us most. The abbreviation stands for 'significance', of course, and contains the *p*-value. However, you also notice that for every line there are two different numbers in the Sig. column, one in the row EQUAL VARIANCES ASSUMED, the second one in the row EQUAL VARIANCES NOT ASSUMED. What does this mean?

One presupposition for the *t*-test is that the variances of the two groups under consideration are roughly equal. (For other presuppositions, see Section

10.6 of this chapter). The variance of a distribution is, you may remember, the square of the SD. If this assumption about equal variances is not met, however, adjustments can be made. This is what the two rows provide. The Levene's test checks the assumption that the two groups' variances are equal. *If the Levene test is significant* ($p < 0.05$), it means that the variances of the two groups are not equal, hence the assumption of homogeneous variances has been violated. In that case, *read the second line of the* t-*test*, which contains the correction for the unequal variances – that is why it reads "equal variances not assumed"! If the Levene test is not significant ($p > 0.05$), then accept the H_0, i.e., the assumption (that the variances are equal) is tenable, hence read the first row, labeled "equal variances assumed".

In Figure 10.13 above, for instance, you see that for Line 1 the significance of the Levene test is 0.77, i.e. non-significant. The appropriate *p*-value of the corresponding *t*-test is 0.000. Notice that if you had had to read the second row, there would have been no difference because it reads 0.000 there as well. As a matter of fact, none of the Levene tests is significant here, so you have to read the first row in all cases. But notice that for some lines the significance of the *t*-test differs in the first and second rows (e.g. in line 3)! In any case, none of the results of the Levene test here are significant.

So far we have been dealing with a *t*-test for independent samples – called a *between-subjects* design in Chapter 6. We have seen that the groups of participants in the different cultures form such independent samples. Now consider that we would like to know whether informants judged line 1 and line 9 of the poem differently. This could apply to all informants of the two groups together, or only the informants of one group, or the informants of both groups separately. In all such cases, the informants responding to lines 1 and 9 are the same. Hence they are not independent because there is a complete overlap between the subjects who rated line 1 and those who rated line 9. Such samples are called *dependent*, but there are also other terms in use (also in SPSS!), such as *paired*, *related*, or *repeated measures*. In Chapter 6 we called such a design a *within-subjects* design. Typical for such samples is that they are composed of the same persons. That is, the lines are different but the readers are the same. To obtain this test, click on **ANALYZE**, **COMPARE MEANS**, then on **PAIRED SAMPLE *T*-TEST**. The following window opens up:

Inference Statistics: Test Selection, *t*-test and Non-Parametric Equivalents 265

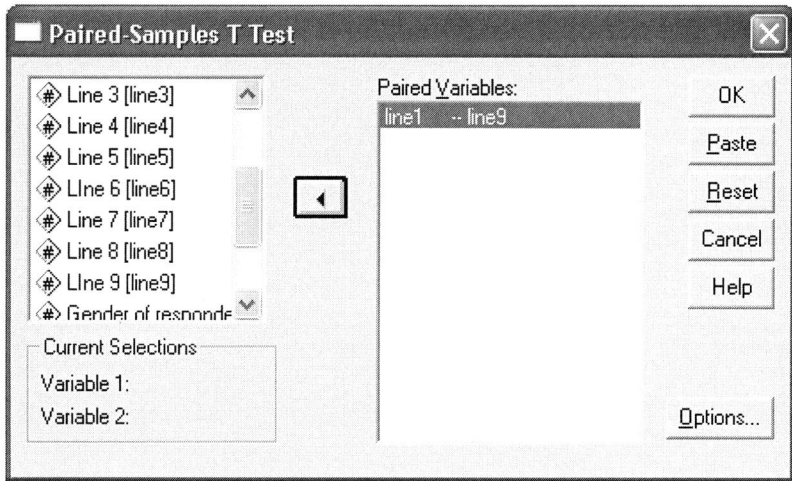

Figure 10.14: Dialog box to obtain a paired-samples *t*-test

In the box **PAIRED VARIABLES** you will then see the two variables selected. Click on **OK**; the result looks as follows:

Paired Samples Statistics

		Mean	N	Std. Deviation	Std. Error Mean
Pair 1	Line 1	4.9528	254	2.76013	0.17319
	Line 9	6.5157	254	3.39462	0.21300

Figure 10.15: Output of descriptive statistics in paired-samples *t*-test

First you get the descriptive statistics. You can check them and see whether the difference between line 1 (4.95) and line 9 (6.51) is in the predicted direction, that is, the larger the number, the higher they have rated the line. It is. Next, look at the results of the *t*-test down the page:

Paired Samples Test

	Paired Differences					t	Df	Sig. (two-tailed)
	Mean	Std. Deviation	Std. Error Mean	95% Confidence Interval of the Difference				
				Lower	Upper			
Pair 1 Line 1 - Line 9	1.5630	4.56161	0.28622	2.1267	0.9993	5.461	253	0.000

Figure 10.16: SPSS output of paired-samples *t*-test

There is no Levene's test to be applied here, so you can go directly to the *t*-value (−5.48), the degrees of freedom (253), and the significance (0.000). The conclusion is clear: the difference between the evaluations of lines 1 and 9 differs considerably, and in the direction predicted, and this difference is statistically highly significant ($p = 0.000$).

You again see the words 'two-tailed' between brackets in the significance column? As you saw in Chapter 9, this has to do with the design of your study, more particularly with the kind of hypothesis you are testing. Basically there are two types of (alternative) hypotheses: directional and non-directional ones. A non-directional hypothesis claims that there is a difference between the groups, but it does not specify which of the groups will score higher on a particular variable. This is precisely what a directional hypothesis does: it predicts not only that there is a difference, but also which of the groups will score higher on a variable. Hence non-directional hypotheses are of the form

$$A \neq B$$

while directional ones are of the form

$$A > B \text{ or } A < B$$

Thinking back about the distribution of the data in a graph, a non-directional hypothesis looks at both ends of the distribution, a directional one at only one of the ends. These ends are called 'tails' and this explains the term in the table. SPSS always calculates the *p*-values for a non-directional hypothesis, which is called two-tailed. If you have a directional hypothesis, you are dealing with one-tailed statistics, and this means you must divide the p-value by two. In the case of our example it does not make any difference because the p-value is already very low. But suppose p was 0.08, i.e. non-significant. If I divide this value by two, p becomes 0.04, which is now significant! In our case, however, the hypotheses were non-directional: we expected differences between the various cultures, but we did not have any idea which culture would score which lines higher.

So can you not just play around with this, so when the p-level is not significant then simply declare the hypothesis as directional and divide the p-level by two? Of course this is not allowed: you must specify the directionality/non-directionality of hypotheses in advance! Many students are also puzzled that the same data give rise to two totally different outcomes, but that is simply a result of the fact that a directional hypothesis runs a higher risk of being defeated than a non-directional one. To make up for this extra risk, the threshold for accepting the alternative hypothesis is halved.

10.3. Wilcoxon test for paired samples

There are situations in which you are not really allowed to use the t-test, but must use so-called non-parametric tests instead. (For the reasons why, see Section 10.6). Why do we say 'not really'? Because in practice, there is not a complete consensus among social scientists, and certainly common practice deviates somewhat from what you find in the theoretical literature. More about that later.

In cases where you should not use the t-test to compare the means of two dependent (or paired, or related) samples, click on **ANALYZE**, then on **NON-PARAMETRIC TESTS**, then on **RELATED SAMPLES**. Click first on the variable **LINE 1**, then on **LINE 9**. Only then can you enter the pair in the **TEST PAIR(S) LIST**. (If you click on one variable only, you cannot transport it!). In our case, we want now to compare whether respondents rated the first and ninth (foregrounded) lines differently, just as with the t-test.

268   Chapter Ten

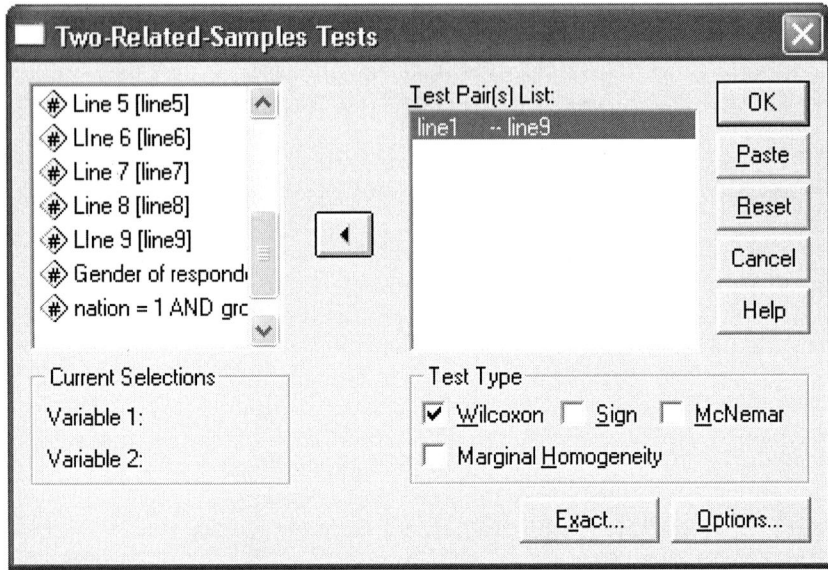

Figure 10.17: Dialog box to obtain a Two-Related-Samples Wilcoxon test

In the box **TEST TYPE**, the Wilcoxon has already been entered as the default. Next, click on **OPTIONS**. You now see the following window.

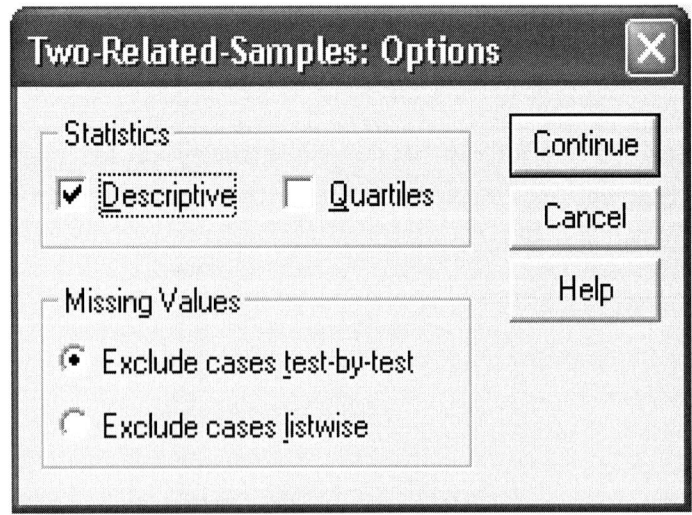

Figure 10.18: Options for descriptive statistics with the Wilcoxon test

Click on **DESCRIPTIVE** in this window, then on **CONTINUE**, then on **OK** in the previous window. The SPSS output now shows you (as usual) the descriptive statistics first:

	N	Mean	Std. Deviation	Minimum	Maximum
Line 1	254	4.9528	2.76013	1.00	11.00
Line 9	254	6.5157	3.39462	1.00	11.00

Figure 10.19: Output of descriptive statistics in the Wilcoxon test

As you can see, also the Wilcoxon test shows an average higher evaluation of line 9 over line 1, hence in the predicted direction. The table containing the test statistics reveals to what extent this difference can be generalized:

Test Statistics†

	Line 9 - Line 1
Z	−4.919*
Asymp. Sig. (2-tailed)	0.000

*Based on negative ranks.
†Wilcoxon Signed Ranks Test

Figure 10.20: Output of Wilcoxon test

As Figure 10.20 indicates, the difference is highly significant ($p = 0.000$), meaning that it is highly unlikely that this is the result of random errors. You notice that the error probability here is the same as with the previous t-test, but in some cases the p-value for the Wilcoxon test may turn out to be a bit lower. This is because non-parametric tests have somewhat less power, a notion to which we will return in the following chapter. But what if you cannot use a t-test when you wish to compare the mean responses of two independent groups? In such a situation you use the Mann–Whitney (U-)Test

10.4. Mann–Whitney ('*U*-Test') for independent samples

In order to obtain this test, click on **ANALYZE**, then on **NON-PARAMETRIC TESTS**, then on **TWO INDEPENDENT SAMPLES**. Then enter **LINE 9** under **TEST VARIABLE LIST** and **NATIONALITY** under **GROUPING VARIABLE**, and then define this variable with the numbers **1** (Brazil) and **2** (Ukraine), then click on **OK**. The output looks as follows:

NPar Tests

[DataSet2] C:\Dokumente und Einstellungen\Willie

⇒ Mann-Whitney Test

Ranks

	Nationality	N	Mean Rank	Sum of Ranks
Line 9	Brazilian	42	37,33	1568,00
	Ukranian	34	39,94	1358,00
	Total	76		

Test Statistics[a]

	Line 9
Mann-Whitney U	665,000
Wilcoxon W	1568,000
Z	-,523
Asymp. Sig. (2-tailed)	,601

a. Grouping Variable: Nationality

Figure 10.21: Output of Mann–Whitney U-Test

As the first table in the output shows, the difference is small: 37.33 is the average response of the Brazilian, 39.94 of the Ukrainian respondents. The table containing the Mann–Whitney test statistics shows that this difference is not significant: $p = 0.601$. Hence the conclusion is clear: we must, in this case, accept the H_0: there is no difference between the average response of the two groups. This is confirmation, of course, of our theory that novelty creates a sense of beauty, as outlined in Chapter 1. We find here further empirical evidence of the correctness of this view.

Now this could spur us on to ask: how about the other groups of respondents? Did they also react in similar ways to this foregrounded line? To answer this, we need a test that can compare more than two cultures at a time. This is the Kruskal–Wallis test.

10.5. The Kruskal–Wallis Test

You are now quite familiar with the following process: click on **ANALYZE**, then on **NON-PARAMETRIC TESTS**, then on **K INDEPENDENT SAMPLES TEST**. K is a symbol often employed in methodology for 'more than two'. Again enter **LINE 9** in the **TEST VARIABLE LIST** and **NATIONALITY** in the **GROUPING VARIABLE**. Now click on **NATION**, and then on **DEFINE RANGE**. If

you want to know the differences between all groups we studied, then enter **1** as
MINIMUM and **7** as MAXIMUM. SPSS produces three tables, the second and
third one of which are useful to us. First we get the descriptive statistics, i.e. the
average group responses to line 9:

Ranks

	Nationality	N	Mean Rank
Line 9	Brazilian	42	161.52
	Ukrainian	34	174.16
	German	50	136.58
	Egyptian	44	117.24
	German oral	18	156.44
	Dutch communication	42	75.61
	Dutch literature	25	78.22
	Total	255	

Figure 10.22: Descriptives output of Kruskal–Wallis Test

The column *N* lists the number of participants in each group, the column **MEAN RANK** lists the average rank allocated to line 9. We notice a relative coherence among the different cultures, with one exception: the two Dutch groups differ markedly from all other groups. Next we look at the test statistic:

Test Statistics*†

	Line 9
Chi-Square	59.627
df	6
Asymp. Sig.	.000

*Kruskal–Wallis Test
†Grouping Variable: Nationality

Figure 10.23: Output of Kruskal–Wallis test

As we can see, the test is highly significant, which means that for all cultural groups (in contrast to the previous comparison of Brazilian/Ukrainian groups only) we have to accept the H_a: there is a significant difference in the reaction to line 9 across all groups.

Now that we have seen how we can calculate non-parametric tests for multiple comparisons between independent groups, the question could be raised whether there are similar tests for comparisons between dependent groups. Yes, there are, for instance the Friedman test, or Kendall's W.

10.6. Friedman test

Suppose we wish to know whether reactions to the nine lines differ significantly from each other. Since every respondent has ranked all nine lines, the respondents are the same, and thus the groups of reactions (to line 1, line 2, etc.) are the same. In such a situation we are dealing with dependent (or paired, or related) samples. To obtain a test for this, click on **ANALYZE**, then on **NON-PARAMETRIC TESTS**, then on **K RELATED SAMPLES**, **K** again denoting any number larger than two. The dialog box that now opens is the following one:

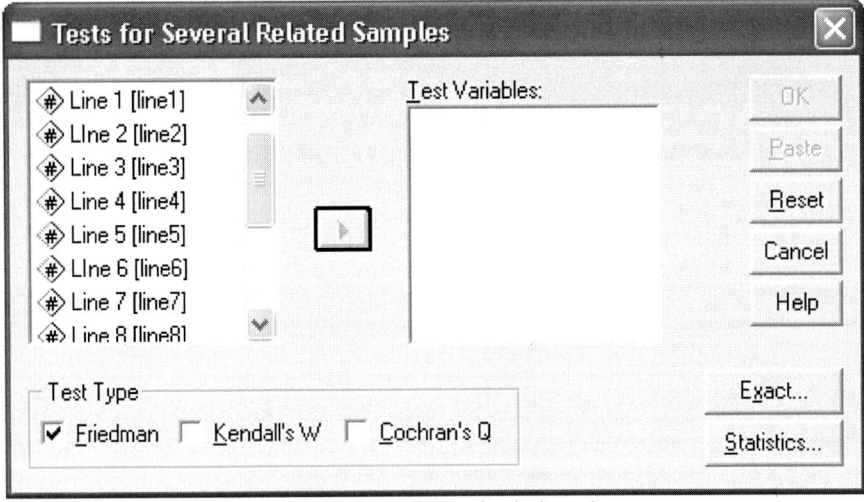

Figure 10.24: Dialog box of Friedman's test

You can enter all the lines in the right-hand window **TEST VARIABLES**, and you can request descriptive statistics if you wish. Below left you see the three tests that are available: Friedman, Kendall's W, and Cochran's Q. You can choose either of these, they will yield the same results – Friedman is the default value in SPSS. By clicking on **OK** you get the following results:

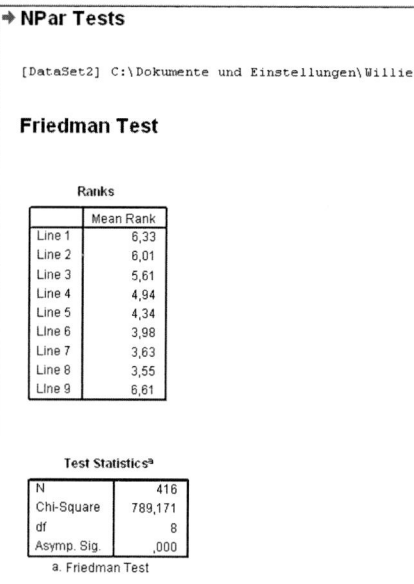

Figure 10.25: Output of Friedman test

The upper table lists the descriptive statistics, i.e. the average ranks allocated to each of the nine lines. The bottom table gives you the test statistics, confirming that the overall differences in reaction to the nine lines are highly significant.

10.7. Crosstabs

You may have noticed that several of the test statistics in the previous sections had a Chi-square as test. This is a test that you can also, and nearly always, use: it is the non-parametric test with the widest possible applications.[1] To obtain it, click on **ANALYZE**, then on **DESCRIPTIVE STATISTICS**, then on **CROSSTABS**. Enter **NATIONALITY** in the box **COLUMNS** and then **LINE 1** through **LINE 9** in **ROWS**, then click on **STATISTICS**, which will bring forward the following window:

---

[1] Chi-squared is the usual annotation nowadays. In older publications, you may also find it with the corresponding Greek letter, as χ^2, pronounced [kai].

274　　　　　　　　　　　　　　Chapter Ten

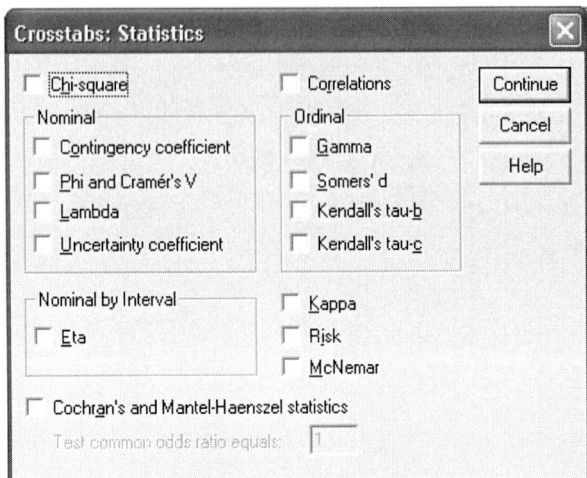

Figure 10.26: Requesting chi-square with Crosstabs

Click in the box next to **CHI-SQUARE**, then on **CONTINUE**, then on **OK**, which will produce the following output:

Crosstab

Count

		Nationality							
		Brazilian	Ukrainian	German	Egyptian	German oral	Dutch Communication	Dutch Literature	Tunisian
Line 1	1,00	18	2	17	4	1	0	2	4
	2,00	6	3	12	0	2	0	2	0
	3,00	4	5	6	2	4	2	0	1
	4,00	1	0	3	4	0	6	2	1
	5,00	2	2	1	3	1	5	2	1
	6,00	5	5	5	9	2	16	8	4
	7,00	2	4	3	5	3	12	4	1
	8,00	2	4	2	4	4	0	2	1
	9,00	1	6	1	9	0	1	2	1
	10,00	1	3	0	2	0	0	1	3
	11,00	0	0	0	2	0	0	0	3
Total		42	34	50	44	17	42	25	20

Figure 10.27: Output of chi-square with Crosstabs

The title above the table says **LINE 1 * NATIONALITY**: this means that the interaction between two variables is listed: on the one hand, the responses to line 1, on the other hand the various nationalities that took part in the investigation. So what you see here is a line-by-line distribution of the number of responses to the 11 points of the scale we used (the rows) across the various cultures that participated in the experiment (the columns). Below this there is the table containing the test statistics for this interaction between line 1 and nationality:

Chi-Square Tests

	Value	df	Asymp. Sig. (two-sided)
Pearson Chi-Square	155.951*	60	0.000
Likelihood Ratio	164.853	60	0.000
Linear-by-Linear Association	18.785	1	0.000
No. of Valid Cases	254		

*63 cells (81.8%) have expected count less than 5. The minimum expected count is .13.

Figure 10.28: Chi-square statistics in Crosstabs

Look at the first row only: the first column contains the value of Chi-square, the second one the degrees of freedom (df), and the third one the p-values. Since p is highly significant, you may assume a relationship between rows and columns – the chances that this relationship is due to chance are extremely low. The conclusion, therefore, is that members of the various cultures rated line 1 significantly differently. The SPSS output further lists the same tables and test statistics for the eight further lines. Here, for instance, are the ones concerning line 2 (with the bottom part of the descriptives on top, the Chi-square test in the middle, and the beginning of the descriptives for line 3 at the bottom):

Crosstab

Count		Nationality							
		Brazilian	Ukrainian	German	Egyptian	German oral	Dutch Communication	Dutch Literature	Tunisian
Line 2	1,00	14	2	20	3	2	1	2	1
	2,00	9	5	12	1	3	2	0	3
	3,00	6	2	6	2	3	5	3	0
	4,00	1	2	0	5	0	11	4	2
	5,00	1	4	3	2	2	10	6	1
	6,00	6	3	3	8	2	8	3	2
	7,00	1	7	2	7	3	5	4	2
	8,00	2	5	3	3	3	0	2	2
	9,00	0	2	1	9	0	0	0	1
	10,00	2	2	0	3	0	0	1	3
	11,00	0	0	0	1	0	0	0	3
Total		42	34	50	44	18	42	25	20

Chi-Square Tests

	Value	df	Asymp. Sig. (2-sided)
Pearson Chi-Square	309,525[a]	100	,000
Likelihood Ratio	316,571	100	,000
Linear-by-Linear Association	84,544	1	,000
N of Valid Cases	426		

a. 94 cells (77,7%) have expected count less than 5. The minimum expected count is ,46.

Figure 10.29: Further output of Chi-square test

Whenever you wish, you can always employ the cross-tabs function with Chi-square to cast your data in a table with multiple rows and columns. The Chi-square test then investigates how likely the relationship between rows and columns is. If the *p*-values turn out to be significant, you may conclude that there exists some kind of relationship between the variables involved. The test can be used with data at all levels of measurement, including nominal data. As a matter of fact, the Chi-square test is one of the very few tests that can be used with nominal data.

10.8. Overview

At various points in this chapter we have pointed out which tests to use in various situations. Table 10.1 summarizes the major divisions, whereby the distinction between parametric and non-parametric will be further elucidated in the following chapter. Note that in this chapter we have outlined parametric tests (the *t*-test) for comparing *two* groups only; the ANOVA test listed in the following table will likewise be explained in the next chapter.

		TWO INDEPENDENT SAMPLES	TWO DEPENDENT SAMPLES	MORE THAN TWO INDEPENDENT SAMPLES	MORE THAN TWO DEPENDENT SAMPLES
	ALL				
PARAMETRIC	T	T for independent samples	T for dependent samples	(ANOVA / GLM)	(ANOVA / GLM)
NON-PARAMETRIC	CHI-SQUARE	MANN–WHITNEY	WILCOXON	KRUSKAL–WALLIS	FRIEDMAN

Table 10.1: Overview of inference tests

As can be seen in the above table, so far we have dealt with only two situations in which a parametric test can be used: when comparing two dependent variables in independent and in dependent samples. What remains to be done in the next chapter, therefore, is, first of all, to outline when and how to use an ANOVA, which can (should) be used whenever you compare more than two dependent variables.

Note that the table above also presupposes that you are comparing the effect of only one *independent* variable on one or more dependent variables. In research, however, we often wish to investigate the influence of more independent variables at once. For instance, you may wish to see whether people who are prone to empathy identify differently with characters or situations when viewing a movie, but you would at the same time like to know the influence of gender on such identification processes. What to do in such situations will occupy us further in Chapter 11. Finally, we will come back to the difference between parametric and non-parametric tests, and provide you with rules when to choose which tests for which situations.

CHAPTER ELEVEN

INFERENCE STATISTICS: ANOVA

11.1. Analysis of Variance

Until now we have discussed tests that compare two groups at a time. In some situations you want to be able to compare more than two. In these cases you turn to Analysis of Variance tests (ANOVAs). Imagine you want to examine the influence of television ads on people's norms, attitudes, and knowledge. You hypothesize, for instance, that there is an effect on people's ideal of bodily beauty. Often it is claimed that television advertisements are responsible for many women wanting to be skinny, and that it could even lead to *anorexia nervosa*. Alternatively, you may be interested in the effects of ads on people's notion of happiness (e.g. what is the perfect composition of a family), or their knowledge of the world (e.g. hard water is bad for your washing machine). To examine these hypotheses you decide to compare three groups: (1) one group that hardly sees any television ads at all; (2) a middle group that watches television ads regularly; (3) and one group of 'heavy users', people who watch television ads as an integral part of their lifestyle. Such data need to be investigated with an analysis of variance.

Why not do a number of comparisons, you may ask? In our example we have three groups. So we could make three comparisons: using the *t*-test, we compare the means of group 1 with 2, that of 2 with 3, and that of 1 with 3. The problem is, however, that when you make more than one comparison, the probability that one will turn out to be statistically significant increases. The more comparisons you make, the likelier it is that you will find one or more pairs to be statistically different (a Type I error, as we explained in Chapter 8). How can this be? For each *t*-test you run there is a 5% probability of rejecting the null hypothesis while there is actually no difference between the groups. So, the probability of *not* making a Type I error is 95%. This is an acceptable level of certainty in the Social Sciences. What happens with this probability when you run three *t*-tests? Because each test is independent, the principles of statistics tell us that we must multiply the probabilities of each test: $(0.95)^3 = 0.95 \times 0.95 \times$

0.95 = 0.86, meaning that there is now an 86% chance of not making a Type 1 error. This is not acceptable anymore. In other words, the chance that we reject a null hypothesis while we should not is 14%! Compared to a situation where you run only one *t*-test, the chance of a Type I error is almost three times as large. This is what is called in statistics the *familywise error rate*; in formula: $1 - (0.95)^n$, where *n* stands for the number of tests that you run using the same data. (Note, of course, that what has been said above about the use of multiple *t*-tests applies equally well when you run several non-parametric tests!)

A way to avoid this problem is by using an ANOVA, short for Analysis of Variance. ANOVA extracts and uses more information from the data than the tests we dealt with in Chapter 10. Its main function is to analyze distributions *within* groups as well as *between* groups. To illustrate the importance of this, look at the graphs in Figure 11.1 presented below.

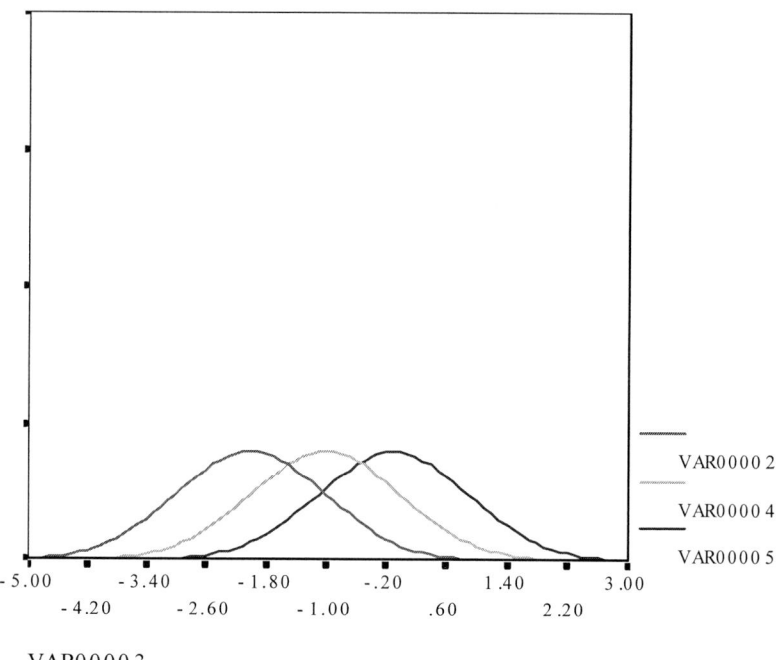

Figure 11.1a: Distribution within and between groups (ANOVA)

Imagine that these graphs represent the three groups of low, middle, and heavy users of television ads. The *y*-axis represents the number of

280 Chapter Eleven

respondents, while on the *x*-axis we find the scores on a 'world knowledge test' (e.g. responses to questions like "does hard water harm your washing machine" or "what chemical substance keeps your hair smooth", etc.). In the first graph you see a large spread. The average of Group 3 is -.20 (do not worry about the meaning of the numbers), but among respondents of Group 3 we also see that there are those who only score -.2.60. Looking at the overlap of the Group 3 distribution with that of Group 1, and even more so that for Group 2, we can already guess that the differences between the three groups are negligible: perhaps television advertisements do not enhance world knowledge after all.

Now imagine a different situation: the graph in Figure 11.1b.

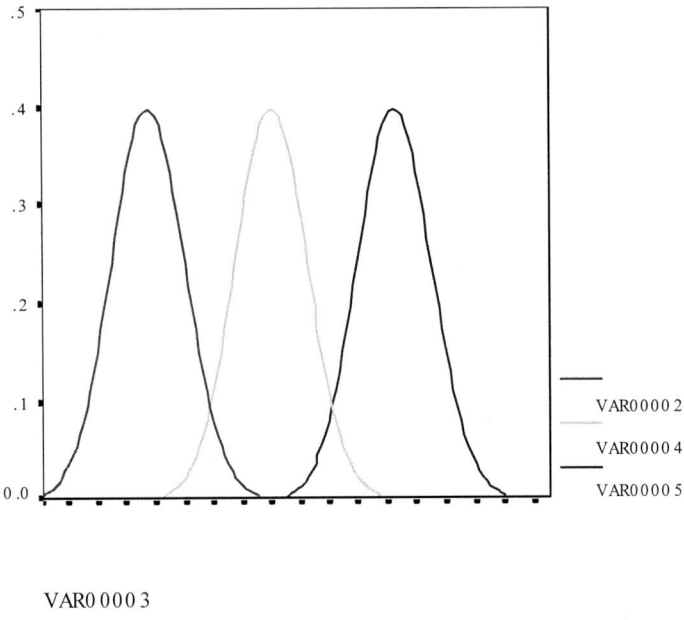

Fig. 11.1b: Distribution within and between groups (ANOVA)

You see that there is much less overlap here between the three groups. Obviously it is important to analyze not just the variance between groups but also of within group variance. ANOVA does exactly this, and is therefore more sensitive to actual differences between groups.

The *t*-tests produce a *t*-value (and a probability of that value). In a similar vein, ANOVAs produce an *F*-value, also accompanied by a significance level. The letter *F*, by the way, refers to the name of the statistician who invented the *F*-tests, Sir Ronald A. Fisher. Here is the formula:

$$F = \frac{\text{Between-groups Mean Square}}{\text{Within-groups Mean Square}}$$

The 'Mean Square' is a concept that we have already encountered: refer back to Section 8.5 in chapter 8. Perhaps you can have a look again at Figure 8.3, which represents the number of books read last month by six people we asked. As you can see, the average response is five (the line in the middle), but there is considerable deviation from this mean in the individual responses. If we add up all these deviations (and square them, to get rid of the pluses for deviations above and minuses for deviations below the average) we get some measure of how well the individual answers match the mean. (We called that the *sum of squared errors, SS*.) Because this measure becomes larger with each new participant added, we divide this number by the number of participants (minus 1). This is what we call the Mean Square, also called *variance*. What an ANOVA does is compare this variance *between* the groups with the variance *within* the groups. If the null hypothesis is true, the Mean Square values for between and within groups are the same, or almost the same. This means that when we divide one by the other, the *F*-value is close or equal to 1. Looking back at Figure 11.1, you can imagine that the graphs for low, middle and heavy users overlap completely: there are no differences between the groups, and we can or cannot conclude that our independent variable had an effect on world knowledge. However, the larger the value of *F*, the more the variance *between* the groups exceeds the variance *within* the groups, because the graphs for the separate groups will overlap less, and will look more like those presented on the graph in Figure 11.1b. In other words, the *F*-value tells us something about the strength of the independent variable's effect.

Before we look at how to carry out an ANOVA and how to interpret the results, there are a few things we need to discuss. First, an ANOVA requires that your data meet certain criteria: some of them should be taken into account even before you start collecting your data; others require the exploration of the data before the ANOVA.

1. One assumption is that you measured your dependent variable at an interval or ratio level. Hence our plea in Chapter 6 that when you make your questionnaire you aim at measuring your dependent variables at the highest possible level.
2. The groups that you compare must be distinguished from each other using a nominal (e.g. gender, because you compare men and women) or ordinal (e.g. in our example we had three levels of exposure to ads) level of measurement.
3. The samples that you use should be independent (that is, no participant can be a member of more than one group).
4. It is also important to realize that participants must be chosen randomly from the population.
5. In that population you need a normal distribution on your dependent variable. Analysis of variance is not too sensitive for this criterion. While you are exploring your data, you should hope for at least a symmetrical distribution. That is, in the distribution graph, what is left of the mean should be mirrored by the right side.
6. Finally, there is the assumption of homogeneity of variance. Like in the *t*-test procedure you use the Levene's test; however, here you specifically have to instruct SPSS to run this additional test. When all groups are the same size, you do not take this test too strictly.

In cases where these conditions are not met you need to refer to non-parametric tests. There is one more thing you need to know about ANOVA before we explain how to obtain this test. There are actually two types of analyses of variance: the one-way ANOVA and the General Linear Model. To compare more than two groups, with one independent variable defining the groups, we use a one-way ANOVA. In the case we discussed above, the effect of television ads, we dealt with one independent variable. We distinguish the groups in *one way*, namely using the amount of exposure to television ads as a criterion. However, sometimes we want to group our respondents using more than just one variable. Say we also want to take into account that level of education affects the possible impact of television ads on real world knowledge. Within each of the three groups defined by exposure to ads, we distinguish three more groups: those with a low, middle, and high educational level. Thus, we end up with nine groups. In situations like these, when groups are formed by more than one independent variable, we use the General Linear Model.

To explain the procedures of these tests, and how to interpret the results, we will work with a data set that you can find on the CD-Rom, called **MOVIEZONE.SAV**. This document contains the data of a research project conducted by two of our students. They were asked to evaluate a program that promotes art cinema among young people in the Netherlands. The program is called MOVIEZONE and is part of art education in Dutch High Schools, which we will refer to as Culture and Art Education (CAE).

To obtain a one-way ANOVA click on **ANALYZE**, and select **COMPARE MEANS**. This opens a new menu, from which you need to select the last option: **ONE-WAY ANOVA**. SPSS produces the following Dialog Box.

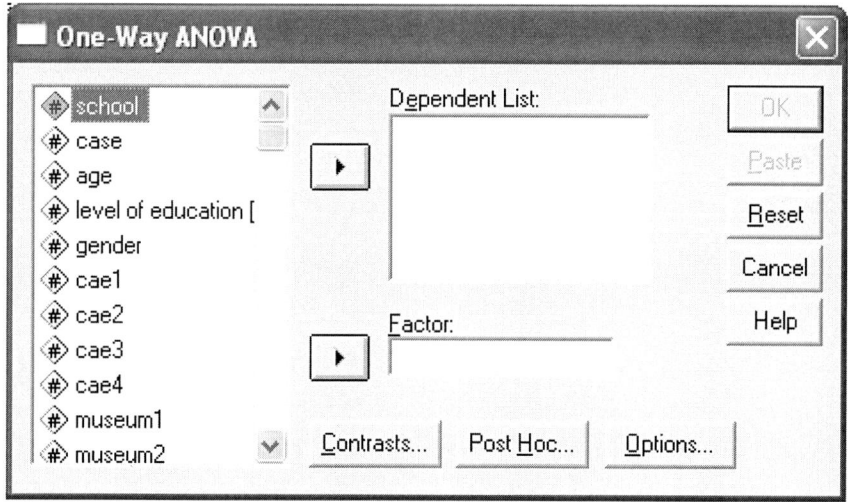

Figure 11.2: Dialog Box for one-way ANOVA

Now select your dependent variable from the variable list on the left and transport it to the field marked **DEPENDENT LIST**. In the example we will be using, choose **MUSEUM1**. This variable is participants' response to the statement "I find visiting a museum…" on a five-point scale ranging from "no fun" to "fun". So the higher the scores, the more participants enjoy going to a museum. Now select your independent variable, that is, the variable that you expect to affect the dependent variable. In the example we select **LEVEL (OF EDUCATION)** of participants.[1] The researchers wanted to know whether the level of education

---

[1] In this study, the researchers were interested in the opinions of students' at three **LEVELS OF EDUCATION**, arranged from low to high with 4 HAVO being the lowest, 5 VWO being the highest, and four VWO in the middle. HAVO stands for **HIGHER GENERAL EDUCATION**; it prepares students for higher education, but not for University. VWO is a higher level of education and does allow graduates to go to University. A 4 means the fourth grade and a 5, the fifth.

had an influence on the appreciation of museums. The independent variable **LEVEL (OF EDUCATION)** is entered under **FACTOR** in the dialog box presented in Figure 11.2.

By now you will be used to the multitude of options that SPSS offers. You will have noticed that not all of these options are relevant. In this case we do need to give SPSS a few more instructions to make the output intelligible. Click on the **OPTION** button. This opens the following dialog box.

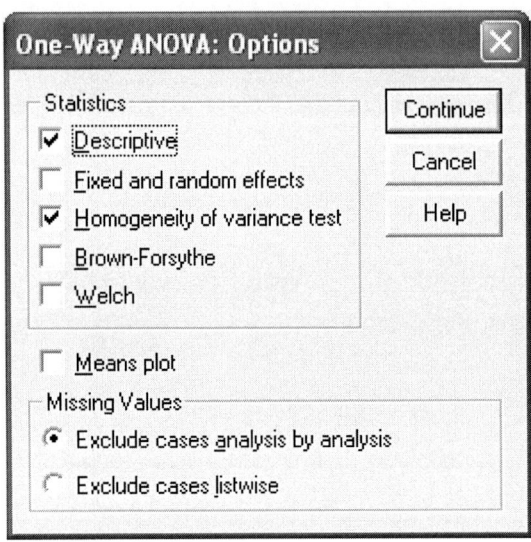

Figure 11.3: Dialog Box for One-Way ANOVA: Options

Here we need to do two things. First tick the box for **DESCRIPTIVE** here. Now SPSS will not only produce the statistics for the one-way ANOVA, but also the group means and other descriptive statistics. This will help you to interpret the results of the ANOVA. SPSS will now generate the means and standard deviations for each of your (sub)groups, so that you can see what the differences look like: which of the levels had the highest average score? Are these large or small differences? Second, you can run a Homogeneity-of-variance test. This is the Levene's test that you already encountered when we discussed the *t*-test. Tick this box as well, and click on the **CONTINUE** button. You return to the dialog box presented in Figure 11.2. Now you can click on **OK** and SPSS opens the Output window, which reveals the following results.

Descriptives

MUSEUM1

	N	Mean	Std. Deviation	Std. Error	95% Confidence Interval for Mean		Minimum	Maximum
					Lower Bound	Upper Bound		
4havo	242	2.3140	1.17394	0.07546	2.1654	2.4627	1.00	5.00
4vwo	240	2.6000	1.13447	0.07323	2.4557	2.7443	1.00	5.00
5vwo	183	2.7869	1.18759	0.08779	2.6137	2.9601	1.00	5.00
Total	665	2.5474	1.17758	0.04566	2.4577	2.6370	1.00	5.00

Test of Homogeneity of Variances

MUSEUM1

Levene Statistic	df1	df2	Sig.
0.154	2	662	0.857

ANOVA

MUSEUM1

	Sum of Squares	Df	Mean Square	F	Sig.
Between Groups	24.337	2	12.169	8.986	0.000
Within Groups	896.421	662	1.354		
Total	920.758	664			

Figure 11.4: SPSS output of descriptive statistics with ANOVA

Now let us see how we interpret this outcome. We will go through the process step by step. First, look at the descriptive statistics in the top table of Figure 11.4. You have seen data like these before, in Chapter 8. In the first column you see the three groups that were compared: **4 HAVO, 4 VWO, 5 VWO**. In the second, under *N*, we see how many participants the researchers had per group. In the third column you have important information, the mean scores per group on the five-point scale: the higher the score, the higher the participants' appreciation for museums. This information is important because it will help you to interpret the results of the test. For now, we can already see that the highest level of education (**5 VWO**) also has the highest score (rounding off upwards: 2.79), and the lowest level (**4 HAVO**) has the lowest score (2.31). So, enjoyment of museums differs per education level, but does it differ significantly?

Before we answer that question, we first look at the fourth column in the first table, were we find the standard deviations. As you may remember from Chapter 8, means are always accompanied by standard deviations. Here we see that they do not vary strongly, 1.17, 1.13, and 1.8 respectively. Imagine that in one group, **4 HAVO**, you had a SD of say 2.5, while the **VWO** groups have a much smaller SD (i.e. 0.82 and 0.97, respectively). In such cases it may be advisable to look at the distribution in the three groups. That would indicate a high consensus among the **VWO** students, but that responses among **HAVO** students may reveal a different pattern. In some cases you may want to consider dropping some outliers from your data set before you continue (see Chapter 8).

You ignore the next three columns, and look at the last two, where you see the minimum and maximum scores for each of the three groups: here you simply check whether the scores are between 1 and 5. If the maximum is, for instance, 55, then you know something went wrong during the data entry. Of course you would need to correct this first before moving on.

As mentioned before, one of the assumptions of analysis of variance is the homogeneity of variance. To see whether our data meet this criterion, we consult the second table in Figure 11.4. The Levene's test yields a probability indicating that the variances are equal: the p-value is 0.857, which means that the variances do not differ significantly. (Note the similarity with null hypotheses that all statistical tests try to reject.) That is good news, because now we know that the data allow us to use an ANOVA. But what if it wasn't? In cases were the p-value is 0.05 or lower, first look at the group sizes: if there are an equal number of participants in each group, then do not worry too much. Statisticians would simply recommend you to use an ANOVA anyway, because it can take moderate violations of the assumption of homogeneity of variance. If group sizes are far from equal, you need to consider using a non-parametric test.

Considering the present results of the Levene's test, we can go ahead and look at the third table. We will briefly go through the information, but focus on columns 5 and 6, the two last at your right-hand side. You need these to decide whether the null hypothesis should be accepted or rejected – the null hypothesis being that there are *no* differences between the three group averages on appreciation for museums. In this example, the F-ratio is calculated as follows:

$$F = \frac{\text{Between-groups means square}}{\text{Within-groups mean square}} = \frac{12.169}{1.354} = 8.9874446$$

Remember that the further the F-value is removed from 1, the less overlap there will be between the groups, the more the distributions will look like the one represented in the lower graph in Figure 11.1, the stronger the effect of the independent variable. Here we have a considerably larger F-value, which means that the groups seem different, and that we have here a powerful effect of education level. That is something, but we need more before we can draw our conclusions. As in every statistical test, the outcome should be accompanied by a probability estimate. In this case this is the chance that we would find the same, or even a larger, F-value if we were to run the test again using a sample from the same population. Look at the table. What you see here is that the p-value is well below the 0.05, namely 0.000. Does this mean that there is a zero chance? No. It means that the probability is less than 0.0005. SPSS prints probabilities to only three decimal places. Therefore, anything less than 0.0005 is printed as 0.000. In your research paper you report "$p < 0.000$". What percentage of chance is there that we would find an F-ratio of 8.99 or larger while the null hypothesis is actually true? To find out, you move the decimal point two positions to the right: this shows that there is a mere 0.05% chance that the independent variable exerted an influence by chance only. In other words, we can conclude that education level has a significant effect on appreciation. Of all these calculations, it is important that you at least remember two things: first that the value of F tells you something about the power of the effect; second, that you need to report the probability of the F-statistic.

Something that may come in handy for you is that SPSS offers you the opportunity to enter several dependent variables at once. In one go, you could examine the effect of, for instance, **LEVEL** on appreciation for museums, theater, film, etc. This produces, for each of the dependent variables that you have entered under Dependent List (see Figure 11.2), a separate F and p value that will tell you for each variable separately whether level of education had an effect on them.

In many designs you need to do more than a one-way ANOVA. How can you tell? Let us look at our example to illustrate this. What we know is that the null hypothesis that there are no differences in museum appreciation between the groups can be rejected. In other words, there are differences between the groups that are significant. But this does not necessarily hold for all the groups! Just by looking at the group means we can already see that the differences are small, especially between **4 VWO** and **5 VWO**. We could suspect that only the difference between **4 HAVO** and **5 VWO** is significant, and that there is no significant difference between **4 VWO** and **5 VWO**. To check this, we need to conduct an additional procedure, a *post hoc test* (called Bonferroni,[2] after its designer). Simply rerun the one-way ANOVA to find out how it works. Choose **COMPARE MEANS** from the **ANALYZE** menu and select **ONE-WAY ANOVA**. Click on the **POSTHOC ...** button, and SPSS will open the following dialog box (see Figure 11.5).

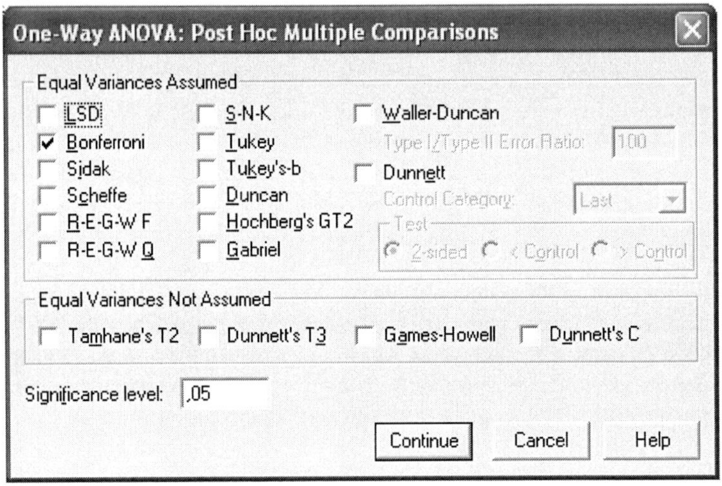

Figure 11.5: Dialog box One-Way ANOVA: Post Hoc Multiple Comparison

As you can see, SPSS offers you a great number of options, as usual. The only thing you need to do here is to tick the box for the **BONFERRONI** test. Now click **CONTINUE** and then the **OK** button. Below you see the results that SPSS produces.

Post Hoc Tests: Multiple Comparisons

Dependent Variable: MUSEUM1
Bonferroni

(I) level of education	(J) level of education	Mean Difference (I-J)	Std. Error	Sig.	95% Confidence Interval	
					Lower Bound	Upper Bound

---

[2] In case you cannot assume equal variances, use the Tamhane test.

4havo	4vwo	−0.2860(*)	0.10601	0.021	−0.5404	−0.0315
	5vwo	−0.4728(*)	0.11400	0.000	−0.7464	−0.1992
4vwo	4havo	0.2860(*)	0.10601	0.021	0.0315	0.5404
	5vwo	−0.1869	0.11420	0.307	−0.4610	0.0872
5vwo	4havo	0.4728(*)	0.11400	0.000	0.1992	0.7464
	4vwo	0.1869	0.11420	0.307	−0.0872	0.4610

* The mean difference is significant at the 0.05 level.

Figure 11.6: SPSS Output for Bonferroni test in a one-way ANOVA procedure

The table in Figure 11.6 makes multiple comparisons, which are all listed in the first two columns, for instance, **4 HAVO** is compared with **4 VWO** and **5 VWO**. The third column lists the results of these comparisons, the mean differences: the average of **4 HAVO** minus that of **4 VWO** (−0.2860, or −0.29), that of **4 HAVO** minus that of **5 VWO** (−0.47). As you can already see here, the asterisk indicates that both differences are significant at the 0.05 level. You can turn to the fifth column to see the exact level (0.021 and 0.000 respectively). Running down the table we find that the means for **4 VWO** and **5 VWO** differ significantly only from that of **4 HAVO**; the means of **4 VWO** and **5 VWO** do not. This is a crucial addition to the findings we discussed earlier: level of education does have an effect on appreciation for museums but this does not hold when we compare grades **4** and **5** of **VWO**.

So, to answer some essential questions, the one-way ANOVA procedure has to be complemented with post hoc analysis. What if you have more than one independent variable? How many does your design have? Look at your questionnaire and try to determine what factors potentially influence your dependent variable(s). In our example: would it not be possible that both education level *and* gender influence appreciation of cultural activities? What if the effect of education on the dependent variables is not the same for boys as it is for girls? We saw that education level seemed to have had an effect, but maybe this holds only for the female respondents. We do not know. In other words, gender may be a second independent variable that we want to take into account. When this is the case, you are dealing with what is called an interaction effect. In your analyses you need to make a distinction between main effects and interaction effects. *Main effects* are the effects of individual independent variables on dependent variables: like in every statistical test, what is examined is whether the groups are equal (e.g. boys versus girls, **4 HAVO**, versus **4 VWO** versus **5 VWO**). *Interaction effects* are the effects of combined factors. What is tested here is whether subgroups are equal (e.g. **4 HAVO** boys versus **4 HAVO** girls, **4 VWO** boys versus **4 VWO** girls, **5 VWO** boys versus **5 VWO** girls).

When interpreting the results of an analysis of variance, you always look at such interaction effects *first*. When these are significant you do not need to look at the main effects. This is because the differences between the subgroups already explain the differences between the groups. In case the interaction effects are not significant, it is useful to look at the main effects. For example, if education has the same effect on appreciation for museums among boys and girls, we still want to know whether it had an effect at all, and whether boys like museums just as much as girls.

These interaction effects are one of the reasons why researchers prefer working with parametric tests: these allow them to look for such effects (non-parametric tests do not), and enhances the complexity of their account of the phenomenon they are describing. It gives researchers the opportunity to move beyond mono-causal explanations. This requires tests that are more advanced than the one-way ANOVA. These will be discussed in the next section.

11.3. General Linear Model

In many research designs you will be dealing with more than one independent variable. In those cases you need to use a General Linear Model (often abbreviated as GLM). The procedure is much the same as for the one-way ANOVA, only SPSS offers you more options to analyze your data.

To obtain a GLM, click on **ANALYZE** and select **GENERAL LINEAR MODEL**. Now a new menu is presented with the following options: **UNIVARIATE**, **MULTIVARIATE**, **REPEATED MEASURES** and **VARIANCE COMPONENTS** (an option that will not be described here because too few of you will actually need it). When you examine the effects of more than one independent variable on only *one* dependent variable, you need to choose the *Uni*variate ANOVA; when you examine effects on *more than one* dependent variable, you select the *Multi*variate ANOVA. A *Repeated Measures* is required when you used a within-subject design in your study: participants responded to the same questions more than once, and you want to examine whether there are significant differences between the different measures. This test will be discussed later. For now we will focus on the second option, **MULTIVARIATE**. Univariate ANOVA works the same and is even simpler. To illustrate this, click on both these options just to compare the dialog boxes: you will see that **UNIVARIATE** allows only one dependent variable, and **MULTIVARIATE ANALYSIS OF VARIANCE** (which is also called MANOVA) has room for more. For the rest, things look just the same. Now continue with **MULTIVARIATE** for the example.

Above we discussed the familywise error rate. When doing a series of tests the chance of a Type 1 error increases considerably. The same holds for ANOVA. We may be interested in the effects of one independent variable on a number of dependent variables and be tempted to run a number of ANOVAs. This increases the chance of falsely rejecting the null hypothesis, just as running a number of t-tests would. We can avoid this problem by using a MANOVA, which is, as we just pointed out, one form of the GLM, namely a form of analysis of variance (like the ANOVA) in which we examine the influence of more than one independent variable on more than one dependent variable.

Again, before launching into the test, first be aware of the assumptions. When can you use this test, and when do you need to look for alternatives? First, let us look at the conditions. These will be illustrated later using an example.

1. The dependent variables should be measured at interval or ratio level. Refresh your memory by referring to Chapter 5, especially Section 5.2 concerning the levels of measurement. In our example, appreciation is measured using Likert scales. This results in data being at the interval level.
2. You need a conceptual reason to analyze the effects of your independent variable(s) on several dependent variables. This is extremely important. We strongly advise against entering a number of independent and dependent variables wildly. Keep to your plan of analysis. Remember the hypotheses with which you started. Statistics is designed to test clear-cut predictions that are generated by a sharply formulated theory. Put in any kind of data, potentially interesting or uninteresting combinations of dependent and independent variables, and you will surely find some spectacular significant results. The problem is they will not mean a thing and nobody will be interested in them. Again one important reason to refer back to Chapter 3, especially Section 3.3.
3. Use a scatterplot to examine the relation between the dependent variables: these should be linear (a straight line) (see Chapter 9, Section 9.4). The scatterplot sets scores for one variable on the y-axis, and the other on the x-axis. When the graph presents a curve of some kind as opposed to a straight line, the data violate one of the assumptions of the MANOVA and you should consider using a non-parametric alternative.
4. You need to explore your data to check whether they are normally distributed. See Chapter 8, Section 8.4, e.g. check for outliers.
5. Make sure that the number of cases in each cell is greater than the number of dependent variables. Most data sets meet this criterion.

When you examine five dependent variables, check whether subgroups are not smaller than six. This is something that you can easily check as you run through the MANOVA procedure.
6. Homogeneity of variance is required. As for the ANOVA procedure, you can check this along the way.
7. You need to make sure that the dependent variables do not correlate (for correlations, see Chapter 9, Section 9.4). This too is part of the SPSS procedure. The correlation coefficients for any pair of dependent variables should not exceed 0.90. If they do, it will be hard to say what contributed to the overall effect: was it the effect of your independent variable on the one or the other dependent variable? The SPSS output for MANOVA will not clarify this.

Do check these assumptions before running a MANOVA, but also realize that modest violations of these assumptions are acceptable.

To make these conditions more concrete let us look at an example again. To do this, run through the following steps to obtain a MANOVA. Open the following dialog box by selecting **MULTIVARIATE** from the **GENERAL LINEAR MODEL** options in the **ANALYZE** menu.

Inference Statistics: ANOVA

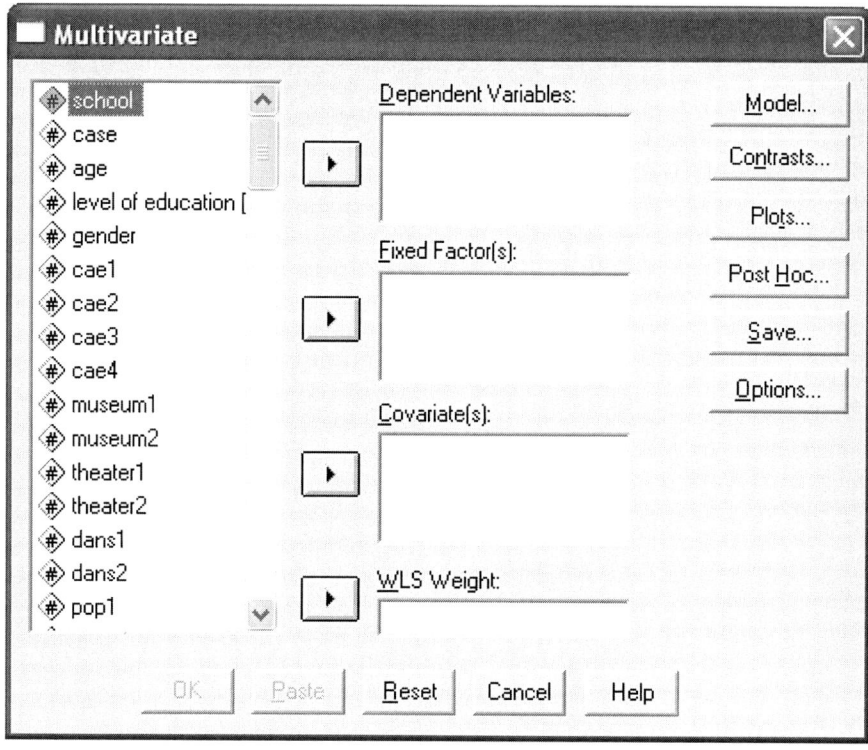

Figure 11.7: Dialog Box Multivariate GLM

Besides the possibility of entering several dependent and independent variables, you can include covariates in this procedure. *Covariates* are the control variables of your conceptual model (see Chapter 3). They are not part of your experimental manipulation, but you assume they may have an influence on your dependent variables. Suppose you want to examine the effect of gender on appreciation of museums, while keeping the possible effect of age constant. One of the possible outcomes could be that irrespective of age, gender has an effect on appreciation of museums. To examine this, you enter age in the present dialog box as a covariate. SPSS will look at each level of the variable age and examine the effect of the independent variable GENDER on the dependent variables MUSEUM1 and MUSEUM2. This is an extremely useful procedure. Covariates make your conclusions much more valuable. You show your (potential) critics that you have taken into account that other factors besides the independent variables could affect your dependent variables. Hence it is important to think of such possible intervening variables, and include them in your measure (see Chapter 5 on Questionnaires). However, do think carefully about the purpose of your study. Does it require you to examine the effects of age as an independent variable or merely as a control variable? In case you are involved in a developmental study, maybe you need to enter it in your analyses as a fixed factor rather than a covariate.

Let us assume that the students who collected these data constructed a conceptual model that predicts the effects of education on an individual's interest in new and unexpected experiences. In the context of their study they hypothesize that the higher the level of education the more participants will be curious about a type of movie that is different from the standard Hollywood movie that they can see every day on television. To examine this they put three statements in their questionnaire to which participants were asked to respond: (1) I'm interested in the kind of movies shown in art houses (**FILMINT**); (2) Knowing more about these movies would stimulate me to go and see them (**VISIT**); (3) Seems like fun to get to know more about these movies through educational materials (**CURIOUS**). These three variables appear to measure three different aspects of one construct, "openness for art cinema". What we want to do now is to see what effect level of education has on these three aspects of openness for art cinema, and how this effect interacts with the effect of gender. In addition, we want to find out whether these effects are irrespective of possible influences of age.

We just discussed the list of assumptions: the conditions for running a MANOVA. Let us assume that the data were explored, and that they meet criteria 1–4. The other assumptions will be tested during the MANOVA procedure. Run with us through the following steps. Open the dialogue box presented in Figure 11.7. Now enter **FILMINT**, **VISIT** and **CURIOUS** as dependent variables, **GENDER** and **LEVEL** as fixed factors, and **AGE** as a covariate. In Section 11.1 we learned that to interpret an ANOVA it is essential that we have the descriptive statistics at hand. Therefore click on **OPTIONS** (this opens a dialog box similar to Figure 11.3 but slightly more complicated). Tick the box for **DESCRIPTIVE STATISTICS**. Remember that homogeneity of variance is one of the assumptions of ANOVAs. Therefore, also tick the box for **HOMOGENEITY TESTS**. Moreover, to examine the magnitude of the effect of the fixed factors, tick the box for **ESTIMATES OF EFFECT SIZE**. This will give you a statistic called the *partial eta square*. How to interpret this statistic will be discussed later.

A click on **CONTINUE** brings you back to the dialog box as seen in Figure 11.7. Now click on **OK**, and SPSS starts working for you. If all went well, you now have the following output on your screen. (Note: we have left out

Inference Statistics: ANOVA

some of the output and focus on those parts we need for the interpretation of the results).

	LEVEL OF EDUCATION	GENDER	Mean	Std. Deviation	N
I'm interested in the kind of movies shown in art houses.	4havo	Male	2.1048	1.14290	105
		Female	2.3390	1.14892	118
		Total	2.2287	1.14949	223
	4vwo	Male	2.2813	1.01259	96
		Female	2.5851	1.07172	94
		Total	2.4316	1.05060	190
	5vwo	Male	2.7571	1.26761	70
		Female	2.8182	1.08856	88
		Total	2.7911	1.16779	158
	Total	Male	2.3358	1.15861	271
		Female	2.5567	1.12145	300
		Total	2.4518	1.14358	571
Knowing more about these movies would stimulate me to go and see them.	4havo	Male	2.6952	1.19393	105
		Female	3.1780	1.23088	118
		Total	2.9507	1.23474	223
	4vwo	Male	2.9479	1.10853	96
		Female	3.2340	1.22189	94
		Total	3.0895	1.17171	190
	5vwo	Male	3.4000	1.27859	70
		Female	3.6364	1.13646	88
		Total	3.5316	1.20334	158
	Total	Male	2.9668	1.21518	271
		Female	3.3300	1.21354	300
		Total	3.1576	1.22676	571
Seems like fun to get to know more about these movies through educational materials.	4havo	Male	2.5333	1.36626	105
		Female	3.1864	1.22613	118
		Total	2.8789	1.33175	223
	4vwo	Male	2.6979	1.17983	96
		Female	3.0426	1.30273	94
		Total	2.8684	1.25084	190
	5vwo	Male	2.8000	1.41011	70

		Female	3.0909	1.36151	88
		Total	2.9620	1.38640	158
	Total	Male	2.6605	1.31483	271
		Female	3.1133	1.28816	300
		Total	2.8984	1.31930	571

Figure 11.8(a): SPSS output of GLM: Multivariate

The first table for descriptive statistics looks a little more complicated than what we saw before in the output for a one-way ANOVA. The means are given for six subgroups: for the three levels of education and for male and female participants separately. In a moment you will be using these group means to interpret the test. Think also of the possibility of including the means (and, of course, the standard deviations) in your report, as well as in a separate table (using EXCEL, for instance – we advise against cutting this part of the SPSS output and pasting it into your report; see Chapter 12, Communicating results). For now, making out patterns in the results by just looking at the averages seems far too complicated: there are so many differences to look at, some small, some a little larger. Who is to say what is going on? Which of these differences are important? We need to look further down the SPSS output to make sense of all this.

Box's M Test of Equality of Covariance Matrices*

Box's M	28.760
F	0.945
df1	30
df2	599092.884
Sig.	0.551

Tests the null hypothesis that the observed covariance matrices of the dependent variables are equal across groups.
*Design: Intercept+AGE+LEVEL+GENDER+LEVEL * GENDER

Levene's Test of Equality of Error Variances*

	F	df1	df2	Sig.
I'm interested in the kind of movies shown in art houses.	1.265	5	565	0.277
Knowing more about these movies would stimulate me to go and see them.	0.865	5	565	0.504
Seems like fun to get to know more about these movies through educational materials.	1.817	5	565	0.108

Tests the null hypothesis that the error variance of the dependent variable is equal across groups.
*Design: Intercept+AGE+LEVEL+GENDER+LEVEL * GENDER

Figure 11.8(b): SPSS output of GLM: Multivariate

First, however, let us look at some of the assumptions. Instead of one test you will find the results of two tests here. For the one-way ANOVA we looked at the Levene's test to check for homogeneity of variance. Here we also have the Box's M Test. The thing you need to understand here is that we are looking for p values *above* 0.05. Again, as with every test, we examine whether we can reject the null hypothesis that says that there are no differences between the groups. Here we see that we cannot reject this hypothesis. In other words, we have to assume that variances are equal for the dependent variables. This means that we can move on. The Box's Test is very sensitive. It is possibly too strict when your sample sizes are large and equal. When your sample sizes are small and/or unequal, this is the place to look for homogeneity.

Let us take you further down the SPSS output, and look for the table that reports the multivariate tests results on openness to art cinema (Figure 11.8c). SPSS runs four different tests here. Which of the four you should use is a matter of discussion among statisticians, and it is far beyond the scope of this chapter to even start explaining the issues that are at stake here. Remember that the purpose of this book is to help you on the way using statistics; this cannot be a comprehensive introduction (see Field, 2005). For our purposes, in most cases, using the Wilks' Lambda will suffice. This is what most researchers do (Brace et al., 2003). However, use *Pillai's Trace test* when groups vary along more than one variable, and when your sample size is small.

Multivariate Tests‡

Effect		Value	F	Hypothesis df	Error df	Sig.	Partial Eta Squared
Intercept	Pillai's Trace	0.018	3.403*	3.000	562.000	0.018	0.018
	Wilks' Lambda	0.982	3.403*	3.000	562.000	0.018	0.018
	Hotelling's Trace	0.018	3.403*	3.000	562.000	0.018	0.018
	Roy's Largest Root	0.018	3.403*	3.000	562.000	0.018	0.018
AGE	Pillai's Trace	0.007	1.315*	3.000	562.000	0.269	0.007
	Wilks' Lambda	0.993	1.315*	3.000	562.000	0.269	0.007
	Hotelling's Trace	0.007	1.315*	3.000	562.000	0.269	0.007
	Roy's Largest Root	0.007	1.315*	3.000	562.000	0.269	0.007
LEVEL	Pillai's Trace	0.045	4.293	6.000	1126.000	0.000	0.022
	Wilks' Lambda	0.955	4.329*	6.000	1124.000	0.000	0.023
	Hotelling's Trace	0.047	4.366	6.000	1122.000	0.000	0.023
	Roy's Largest Root	0.045	8.511†	3.000	563.000	0.000	0.043
GENDER	Pillai's Trace	0.031	6.073*	3.000	562.000	0.000	0.031
	Wilks' Lambda	0.969	6.073*	3.000	562.000	0.000	0.031
	Hotelling's Trace	0.032	6.073*	3.000	562.000	0.000	0.031
	Roy's Largest Root	0.032	6.073*	3.000	562.000	0.000	0.031
LEVEL * GENDER	Pillai's Trace	0.007	0.647	6.000	1126.000	0.692	0.003
	Wilks' Lambda	0.993	0.646*	6.000	1124.000	0.693	0.003

Hotelling's Trace	0.007	0.646	6.000	1122.000	0.694	0.003
Roy's Largest Root	0.005	0.952†	3.000	563.000	0.415	0.005

*Exact statistic
†The statistic is an upper bound on F that yields a lower bound on the significance level.
‡Design: Intercept+AGE+LEVEL+GENDER+LEVEL * GENDER

Figure 11.8(c): SPSS Output. Multivariate tests

In the data set we use the sample sizes are not exactly small, so we refer to the Wilks' Lambda test results to see what the overall effects were. At this point the choice of test may seem irrelevant to you since the results of the tests do not seem to differ much. In practice you will find, however, that it is sometimes a matter of effect or no effect. When we interpret the results of this table, we first need to look at the interaction effects, which are indicated toward the bottom of the table, where you find LEVEL * GENDER: interactions between variables are indicated by * in SPSS outputs. We see that these are not significant. This means that we can look at the main effects separately. For both gender and level of education we see highly significant effects ($p < 0.000$ in both cases). This means that the average scores of subgroups on the new combined dependent variable "openness to art cinema" differ significantly: males and females differ, and among the three levels of education we find significant differences. The *partial eta square* values show the proportions of the variance in the new combined dependent variable that can be accounted for by the two independent variables. Take as a rule that values larger than 0.14 indicate large effects. Here, however, the effect sizes are small: 0.023 (or 2.3%) for level of education, and 0.031 (or 3.1%) for gender. Hence we will need to be modest in our conclusions! Apparently our model is not able to explain much of what is going on in our data. Still, the effects were significant, which means that there is a good chance that we would obtain an F value as large as or even larger than reported here if we repeat the study.

What happened with our control variable, the covariate AGE? As the table shows it does not seem to have had an effect ($p = 0.269$). Nevertheless, we know that the effects for gender and age are controlled for possible influences of age. In your report you need to pay attention to what happened to your covariates. For now, remember as you look at the rest of the results that any variance due to age is sifted away so that we can obtain a more reliable idea of the effects of the two main variables (level and gender).

Because the results of the MANOVA for the main variables are significant, you need to look further down the output, at the table for TEST OF

BETWEEN-SUBJECT EFFECTS. These test results are univariate ANOVAs. Here we can find out what exactly the contribution was of each relation between the independent variables on the one hand and the dependent variables on the other, to the significant overall result of the MANOVA. But wait! Did we not say a minute ago that we advised against running a number of ANOVAs, just like it was unadvisable to do a number of t-tests? True. What we need to do here is apply what is called a *Bonferroni correction*. What we usually do is take a p-value of 0.05 as a rejection criterion. When we run more than one ANOVA we need to divide this value by the number of dependent variables that we are looking at. So in the case of two dependent variables, the criterion for significance is $0.05/2 = 0.025$. We need to be even tougher when dealing with three dependent variables, as in the present example. Running three separate ANOVAs means that the criterion for significance is $0.05/3 = 0.017$.

Tests of Between-Subjects Effects

Source	Dependent Variable	Type III Sum of Squares	df	Mean Square	F	Sig.	Partial Eta Squared
LEVEL	I'm interested in the kind of movies shown in art houses.	20.299	2	10.150	8.100	0.000	0.028
	Knowing more about these movies would stimulate me to go and see them.	22.562	2	11.281	7.897	0.000	0.027
	Seems like fun to get to know more about these movies through educational materials.	1.762	2	0.881	0.519	0.595	0.002

GENDER						
	I'm interested in the kind of movies shown in art houses.	5.566	1	5.566	4.442	0.035	0.008
	Knowing more about these movies would stimulate me to go and see them.	15.635	1	15.635	10.945	0.001	0.019
	Seems like fun to get to know more about these movies through educational materials.	25.631	1	25.631	15.101	0.000	0.026

*R Squared = 0.052 (Adjusted R Squared = 0.042)
†R Squared = 0.061 (Adjusted R Squared = 0.051)
‡R Squared = 0.035 (Adjusted R Squared = 0.025)

Figure 11.8(d): SPSS Output: Multivariate test results

Again we print only part of the output simply to save space. As you can see, even with the adjusted significance level the effect of education level still stands for all three separate components of "openness to art cinema." Now look at the effects of gender. How many effects are significant here? On two of the dependent variables we cannot reject the alternative hypothesis because the probability that there are no differences between boys and girls exceeds the criterion of 0.017. Hence our conclusions need to be specified as far as the gender effect is concerned. What you do is report this in your research paper.

11.4. Repeated Measures

In the previous sections we have seen that ANOVA and MANOVA offer attractive alternatives to the *t*-test. When running an ANOVA we have more options, and provided we meet certain assumptions, our analysis will be sounder and richer, methodologically speaking. The *t*-tests are used when comparing two groups; in an ANOVA we can compare more than two groups in one go. We have learned that if we can, we should use omnibus tests like the ANOVA rather than relying on a number of *t*-tests.

One of the techniques we familiarized ourselves with was the paired samples *t*-test: here we compared within subjects two points of measurement: for instance you conducted a pretest and a post-test and you want to see whether a particular treatment affected the scores. For instance, you believe that laughter is good for you. You have the experience yourself. When you feel bad, you rent a comedy from the local video store and after a good laugh you feel much better.

Intuitively this sounds like a plausible idea. But does it work this way? That is exactly what four of our students wanted to find out. Right before and after showing an episode of *Friends* they asked their respondents how they felt: to what degree did they feel tense, happy, sad, etc. In addition they used standard heart rate equipment, available from any runners' or sports' shop, to also have a physiological indication of their inner state. To illustrate the use of the ANOVA we will look at the effects on heart rate. They had seven times at which they measured heart rate. One after giving participants their instructions, one just before they started the videotape, then four during the showing, and one afterwards. To analyze the effects of the tape on heart rate we need to run an omnibus test instead of a number of paired samples *t*-tests.

For the example: open the actual dataset that the students compiled: catharsis.sav. To obtain a Repeated Measures ANOVA, click on **ANALYZE**, **GENERAL LINEAR MODEL**, and then select **REPEATED MEASURES** from the menu. This opens the following dialogue box.

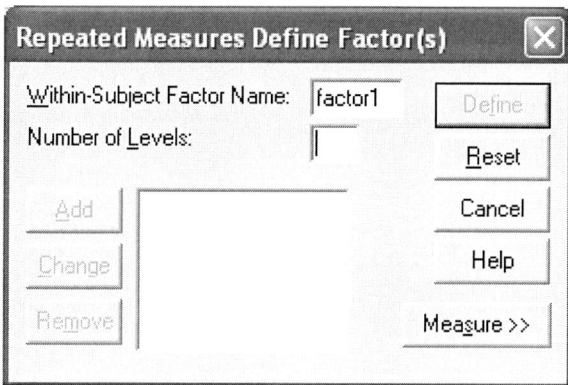

Figure 11.9: Repeated Measures ANOVA

The within-subject factor name is already entered for you. As you see SPSS suggests 'factor1'. This is of course not all that informative: in your output you want a name that is easier to interpret. The within-subject factor is the factor on which you compare scores of each individual subject. In the example it may be helpful to change the default setting to something that indicates that you are looking at heart rates; you could for instance type **HEART** in the first field. What is important is that it is a name that is easy for you to interpret. In the second field, you can enter the number of levels of the within-subjects factor. In our example there are seven. The students entered these data as separate variables in SPSS, but in fact they are the same test, over and over again. As you enter seven in the second field you will see SPSS activates the button **ADD**. Click on it to transport your factor to the third field. As soon as you are ready, the **DEFINE** button is activated. Click on it and if all went well the following dialogue box is opened.

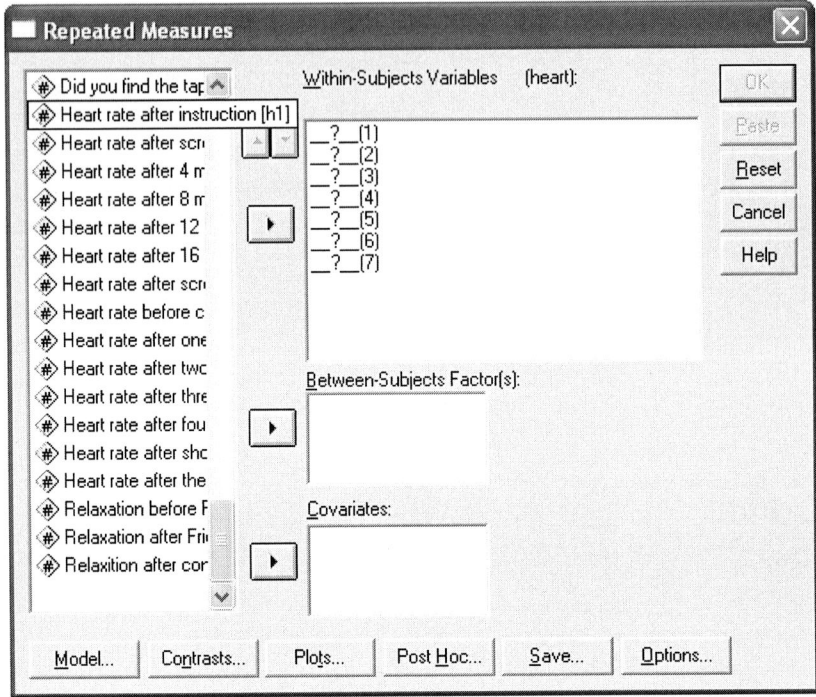

Figure 11.10: Dialog box for Repeated Measures

A part of the box will look familiar: a list of variables to the left, and on the right the various fields where you can enter dependent and independent variables, as well as a field for covariates. Also, again SPSS offers you several buttons, and behind these buttons you will find a variety of options. It is important that you realize that many of these are irrelevant to you now. Simply go through the following steps, and ignore all the rest for the time being. We already defined the within-subject variable, and we entered the number of levels of this variable, namely seven. This corresponds with the number of spaces you need to fill in the field to the right, labeled **WITHIN-SUBJECTS VARIABLES** (**HEART**). Run through the list of variables in the left field until you locate the heart measurements variables (h1 through h7, that is, **HEART RATE AFTER INSTRUCTION** through to **HEART RATE AFTER SCREENING OF FRIENDS**). Select these seven variables (you can select them all at once by holding the left mouse button while you scroll down). Transport all seven to the field on the right.

Now there is one important thing you need to understand about this step. The *order* in which you enter the variables here is crucial: if there is a possible meaningful order, then you should enter the variables in that order.

SPSS will look at possible trends in your data, and for this it will use the order. In our example it is the chronological order of the measure. Another example would be that you look at participants' responses to three poems; each participant evaluates three poems, and you expect that appreciation will increase with complexity. When poem 3 is the most complex and poem 1 the most simple, you need to enter the evaluation of the poems in this order: evaluations of poem 1, poem 2 and poem 3. SPSS will now test whether there is indeed a linear relation between complexity and appreciation, but the program can also show you whether the relation is curvilinear, best represented by a (reversed) U-curve, (or, of course, that there is no relation at all).

Returning now to our own example, when you have all the seven heart rate variables in the top right field, click on **OPTIONS**. As you are accustomed by now, you tick **DESCRIPTIVES**, and then on **CONTINUE** to go back to the dialog box presented in Figure 11.10. As you know, you want descriptives in your output so that you can interpret the results. What will also help is to visualize the results for each point in time. To do this, click on the **PLOTS** button in the dialog box. On your screen you will now see the following:

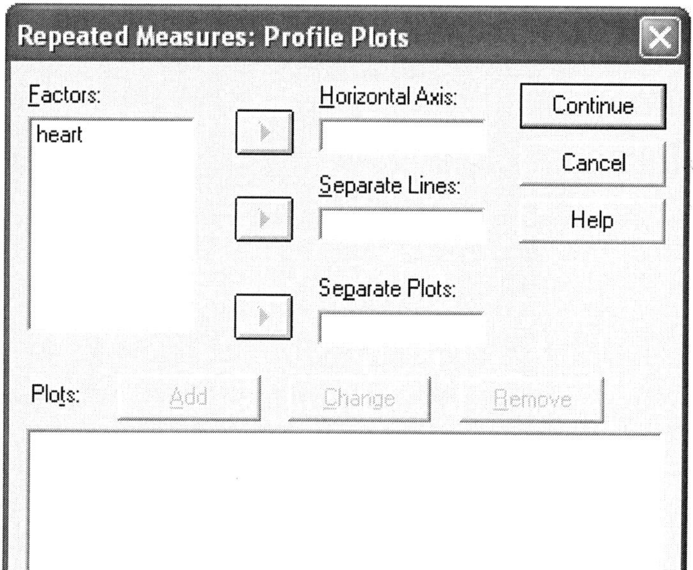

Figure 11.11: Dialog box for Repeated Measures: Profile Plots

To obtain a graph that represents the average heart rate for the separate moments, select **HEART** from the 'list' under **FACTORS**, and transport it to the field labeled **HORIZONTAL AXIS**. As you can see, there is only one variable that you can use. In some more complex designs, you will have more; in many of your designs you will also have between-subjects variables, as, for example, gender; if students had incorporated gender as an independent (subject) variable (see Chapter 6), they would obviously be interested in looking at the changes in heart rate for male and female respondents separately. Under **FACTORS** they would have needed gender, and would enter it under **SEPARATE LINES** to obtain the desired results. For now, click on **ADD**, and then on **CONTINUE**. This brings you back to the dialogue box represented in Figure 11.10.

There is one last thing we recommend. As with the other omnibus tests presented in this chapter, we can find out whether, in general, there are significant differences between the different points of measurement, but additional tests are needed to figure out where exactly those differences are significant. In our example, there are seven moments during the experiment when students measured heart rate. Imagine that they would find an overall effect. To interpret this finding they would need to know when the difference is significant, and when it is not. Is it after the entire episode of *Friends* that people feel more relaxed? Is it during the show itself right after some particular humorous scene? Does the effect disappear after the screening? To find out, click on **CONTRASTS**.

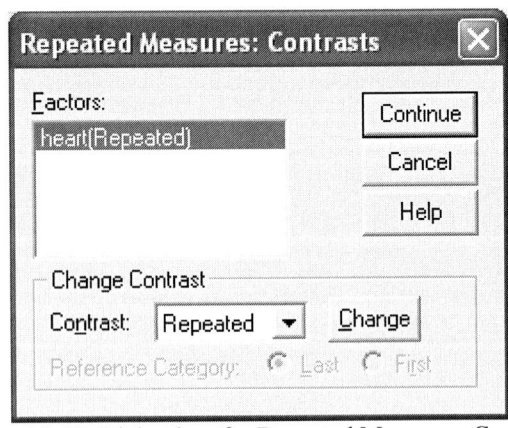

Figure 11.12: Dialog box for Repeated Measures: Contrasts

Click on the drop down menu for **CONTRAST** (the arrow pointing down, on the right of the field below). You now see that SPSS offers you (as usual) a great number of options here from which you can choose. For each research design there is a particular test. It is beyond the scope of this book to explore all the options offered by SPSS. However, there are two that are most relevant to the audience of this book: SIMPLE and REPEATED. You use SIMPLE when you have a control condition or situation. Every other measurement or variable is compared to scores on this variable. You could argue that in the present example we do have a control situation: the pretest. We could compare every heart rate measurement with the respondents' heart rate before the experiment started. When you choose SIMPLE contrast, it is important to pay attention to the order in which you enter the variables in the REPEATED MEASURES procedure (see the dialog box in Figure 11.10). When you do have a control variable (like a pretest) make this variable either the last or the first (this makes no difference), and indicate which of the two using the radio buttons below, and right of REFERENCE CATEGORY: the button for LAST when you entered your control measurement last, of course, and FIRST when you entered it first.

However, the REPEATED option seems more useful here: using this particular type of contrast, every subsequent measurement is compared to the previous one. This would allow us to find out whether there were significant changes from one moment to the next, and maybe we could find out when during the experiment, and thus also during which particular moment in the episode of *Friends*, we see an important effect of the treatment. For the purpose of our example, select REPEATED from the drop down menu, click on the CHANGE-button to affect your choice. As you will see, in the field marked FACTORS, it will now be indicated that you have chosen this particular contrast. Clicking on CONTINUE will bring you back to the dialogue box in Figure 11.10. Now click on OK.

We will only discuss parts of the output: some of the results will be very familiar to you; other parts are not relevant for your interpretation of the outcome. The first table you will see on your screen gives you the means (with, of course, the standard deviations) and number of respondents for each variable. You have seen such tables before, and we will not go further into the interpretation of such basic statistics. More important is the following information that you will find further down your SPSS output.

Mauchly's Test of Sphericity†

Measure: MEASURE_1

Within Subjects Effect	Mauchly's W	Approx. Chi-Square	df	Sig.	Epsilon*		
					Greenhouse–Geisser	Huynh–Feldt	Lower-bound
HEART	0.036	39.052	20	0.008	0.495	0.642	0.167

Tests the null hypothesis that the error covariance matrix of the orthonormalized transformed dependent variables is proportional to an identity matrix.
*May be used to adjust the degrees of freedom for the averaged tests of significance. Corrected tests are displayed in the Tests of Within-Subjects Effects table.
†Design: Intercept Within Subjects Design: HEART

Figure 11.12(a): SPSS Output: Mauchly's test of Sphericity

The test results you see here are probably new to you. You need Mauchly's test of Sphericity to see whether your data meet the criteria for certain tests. Sphericity is a complicated concept. For a more extensive discussion, see Field, 2005, p.324). For the purpose of this book, it is enough for you to know that sphericity is similar to homogeneity of variance, the assumption that the data need to meet in between-groups designs. Earlier we used the Levene's test (automatically included in the relevant SPSS procedures) to test assumptions of homogeneity of variance.

Sphericity is the equality of variances of the differences between the treatment levels, so here the different moments during the episode of *Friends*. If you were to take each pair of measurements (so the first moment and the second, the first and the third, the first and the fourth etc.) and calculate the differences between each pair of scores (heart rate in our example), then it is required that these differences have equal variances. Now, what do we see in Figure 11.12(a). We can interpret the results just like the results of a Levene's test. If $p > 0.05$ the data meet the criteria for conducting a Repeated Measures. However, as you can see for yourself, $p < 0.05$ (0.008), which tells you that the assumption of sphericity is violated. This information is important for the interpretation of the rest of the test results. Look further down the output until you see the following table.

Tests of Within-Subjects Effects

Measure: MEASURE_1

Source		Type III Sum of Squares	df	Mean Square	F	Sig.
HEART	Sphericity Assumed	404.629	6	67.438	3.427	0.004
	Greenhouse–Geisser	404.629	2.967	136.363	3.427	0.026
	Huynh–Feldt	404.629	3.853	105.016	3.427	0.015
	Lower-bound	404.629	1.000	404.629	3.427	0.085
Error(HEART)	Sphericity Assumed	1653.086	84	19.680		
	Greenhouse–Geisser	1653.086	41.542	39.793		
	Huynh–Feldt	1653.086	53.942	30.645		
	Lower-bound	1653.086	14.000	118.078		

Figure 11.12(b): SPSS Output: Test of Within-Subjects Effects

As you can see, SPSS executed four tests instead of one. Earlier we saw something similar for the Multivariate ANOVA. To make your choice you use the results of the Mauchly's test of Sphericity. As you may already have guessed, since the assumption of sphericity is violated, we cannot use the statistics mentioned in the row labeled "sphericity assumed". You look here only when, as in Table 11.12(a), $p > 0.05$. As you can see the F-value would have been highly significant ($p < 0.004$). But, what you need to understand here is that F-ratios are unreliable when sphericity cannot be assumed. In that case you need to refer to tests that correct for the lack of sphericity. The exact workings of these tests go beyond the scope of this book; we will simply tell you where you have to look for the correct test results (see for a brief discussion of the discussions among statisticians, Field, 2005, p.333–338).

The correction of the F-ratios resulting from Greenhouse–Geisser's test is the most conservative one. 'Conservative' here meaning careful: with this F-ratio the chance that you *reject* a null hypothesis that is actually *true* is relatively small. This is an advantage of course, but on other hand being careful in your interpretation of the data you might reject *too few* null hypotheses. We advise you to take as a rule of thumb that you use the Greenhouse–Geisser corrected F-ratio when the results of the test presented in the table of Figure 11.12(a) is smaller than 0.075. However, when this value is larger than 0.075 refer to the corrected F-ratio you find in the row labeled "Huynh–Feldt". In the present example this value is 3.427. So following the rule, you know that in the present case it is best to refer to the Greenhouse–Geisser correction. You can see the *F*-ratio there is the same as for the row "Sphericity Assumed", but we do have a different *p*-value. Nevertheless, the result is significant ($p < 0.026$). In conclusion, we can say that there is an effect of the episode of *Friends* on heart rate. Look up again in your output (not included here) you will find the mean heart rates per point of measurement. This shows you that heart rate drops after the first measurement (that is after the instruction is read to the participants). When during the procedure is the change in heart rate significant? For this we selected a (repeated) within-subjects contrast in the dialog box represented in Figure 11.12. This produces the following table in your output.

Tests of Within-Subjects Contrasts

Source	HEART	Type III Sum of Squares	Df	Mean Square	F	Sig.
HEART	Level 1 vs. Level 2	448.267	1	448.267	11.983	0.004
	Level 2 vs. Level 3	4.267	1	4.267	0.129	0.725
	Level 3 vs. Level 4	13.067	1	13.067	0.447	0.514
	Level 4 vs. Level 5	15.000	1	15.000	0.510	0.487
	Level 5 vs. Level 6	35.267	1	35.267	1.544	0.234
	Level 6 vs. Level 7	1.067	1	1.067	0.180	0.678
Error(HEART)	Level 1 vs. Level 2	523.733	14	37.410		
	Level 2 vs. Level 3	463.733	14	33.124		
	Level 3 vs. Level 4	408.933	14	29.210		
	Level 4 vs. Level 5	412.000	14	29.429		
	Level 5 vs. Level 6	319.733	14	22.838		
	Level 6 vs. Level 7	82.933	14	5.924		

Figure 11.12(c): SPSS Output: Test of Within-Subjects Contrasts

Each level (point in the procedure when participants' heart rate was measured) is compared with the next (see the first column). Each comparison results in an F-ratio and a significance level (see the last two columns). As you can see, only the drop in heart rate from the first to the second was significant ($p < 0.004$). Other fluctuations were not. Thus we can conclude that the effect had already set in from the very beginning.

11.5. Conclusion

In this chapter we discussed more complex statistical tests. Below we summarize their uses once more:

- you use an ANOVA when you want to examine the effects of one independent variable on one dependent variable;
- you use the GLM (General Linear Model) when you want to examine the effects of more than one independent variable. The GLM comes in three varieties:
    - UNIVARIATE, which is the version you use when you wish to examine the effects on one dependent variable;
    - MULTIVARIATE (also called MANOVA), which is the version you use to examine the effects on more than one dependent variable; and
    - REPEATED MEASURES, which you use for a within-subjects design, i.e. when you compare dependent samples.

Maybe you are somewhat confused by all this new terminology and by the sheer complexity of the tests themselves. That is perfectly normal because we have been going through concepts and methods that are already somewhat advanced. Do not despair. All you now need is a little practice. Sometimes you may run into a problem. Our advice, again, is: no, do not despair. Ask a student who knows more about statistics, or your supervisor. In our experience, which now stretches over a decade, all students can master the essential techniques of analyzing their data statistically.

In the Epilogue, we present some typical reactions of students who have read the materials contained in this book, or have gone through our classes. They are real utterances, giving vent to real concerns and anxieties, so we take them seriously. But we also believe, as we have witnessed so often in our professional lives, that they can be overcome.

CHAPTER TWELVE

COMMUNICATING RESULTS

After having gone through the work of developing your initial hypotheses or research questions, studying the literature on the subject, designing your research, carrying it out, analyzing the data collected and interpreting the results you obtained, this effort can vanish in thin air if you do not communicate your results. This chapter will help you to present your research in two ways: learning how to deliver your results orally to an audience (whether at a conference or even in the seminar) and writing them up as a paper for publication.

12.1. Oral presentations

The first place where your results are usually presented officially is at conferences. These can be local, regional, national, or international. What is presented at such conferences is generally, in your case, a short presentation of roughly half an hour (including discussion time), called a 'paper'. This may sound an odd name to you, as there is actually no real paper involved, but that is generally the designated name for such academic activity. Besides papers, there are other kinds of presentations at conferences, such as: opening address and keynote lectures, but these are usually given by invited speakers, who tend to be established or even well-known researchers in their field. Other types of activities are workshops, symposia, and poster sessions. Workshops are more informal discussion groups where one special topic is prepared by the workshops coordinators, usually by setting a number of questions that the participants are requested to discuss. Workshops can also be conducted by junior researchers, but as a high degree of expertise is needed in the area the workshop deals with, senior researchers may also take part in it. You can take part in workshops yourself if you wish to. They are usually a good hunting ground for new ideas, and – because the atmosphere is more relaxed – workshops allow you to develop appropriate listening and (improvised) discussion skills. Symposia are more formal, but also deal with a designated theme. They are usually set up by a small group of people (mostly senior, but this is neither necessary nor always the case) who give short presentations on the topic at hand, after which there is a general discussion. Because the time for discussion is more limited, symposia are less suited if you wish to develop your skills in presenting your arguments. In the case of poster sessions, a room is booked in which mainly junior researchers can put up posters on panels communicating their research, stand for an allotted period of time before these panels and briefly comment or answer the questions of passers-by. Although poster sessions are presented mostly by young researchers, we propose that you try to aim for the more challenging task of delivering a paper because you will get more out of the experience: on the one hand, you will learn more, by virtue of it being more challenging, especially regarding your presentation and discussion skills, and on the other hand there is more prestige attached to it.

One of the great advantages of delivering a paper is that if you are lucky, you can obtain highly interesting feedback. Remember that this is one of the main reasons why you are presenting your work. Of course you also wish to inform other researchers about your work, but you do not want to sell a product! On the contrary, you want to get as much criticism as possible, so that you are able to go over your study once again and make it better. So, make sure you leave enough time for questions after your presentation and that you present your paper in a clear and stimulating way.

In many situations you will be before an unknown audience of professionals, having to speak in a foreign language and within a very strict time limit. That puts high demands on your presentational skills. Therefore, you have to be well prepared. This chapter will guide you through the various demands that such a preparation puts upon you.

12.1.1. Submitting an abstract

The first action you take when you have decided to go to a conference is to look at the deadline for submitting your abstract. All the details are in the *Call for Papers* the organizers advertise and send out by mail, through posters or over the Internet. Make sure that you meet all the requirements (including number of words) and send your abstract **before** the deadline. There are many publications on how to write an abstract but a very good tip is for you to read published abstracts, so that you can familiarize yourself with the style. Try to write abstracts like the ones in refereed journals such as *Language and Literature*, *Poetics*, *SPIEL*, *Empirical Studies of the Arts*, *Discourse Processes*, *Style*, etc.

In your abstract you should describe the research problem, the methods used, including the participants and/or materials employed, the results and the discussion, preferably indicating further developments. Because it generally has to be written in 100 to 150 words, you have to be very concise and precise. To draw the reader's attention, you should start the abstract stating the problem. A good abstract should always contain the reason for your research, your hypothesis, your methodology, and the results at which you arrived. Here is an example of an abstract submitted to the 1998 IGEL Conference:

Children's understanding of hypermedia

Stefan Aufenanger (University of Mainz, Germany)
One of the main components of media literacy is certainly the understanding of texts. New media offer children new kinds of texts: verbal ones and pictorial ones. The integration of different media with different texts in one presentation is called multimedia, and the combination with a hypertext structure is called hypermedia.
In a pilot study it is investigated how children in the age from 4 to 14 years understand such new kind of texts. For that reason different hypermedia are presented to the children, and they were asked to solve given tasks. Further they were encouraged to think loud about what they are doing. Screen recording and video recording record the way of navigation in hypermedia or the children's commentaries, respectively. First results indicate that children need different pre-requirements to understand hypermedia. Children with media experiences, in particular experiences in computer games, do better than children without such experiences.
(in http://www.arts.ualberta.ca/igel/IGEL1998/abstract.htm)

As you can see, the author first situates the problem. Then, he describes the study, mentioning briefly the hypothesis, the participants, and the methodology, ending by pointing at the results and stating the conclusion.

Here is another abstract from the same conference. Although the presenter does not carry out an experiment, she provides an introduction, mentions the theoretical support, and describes very precisely how the argument will develop and end.

> **Reading socialization in an electronic environment**
> Laurel Brake (University of London, U.K.)
> The relationship between books or reading behavior and television has always been a complex and ambivalent issue and it is still discussed very emotionally by the public and the media: There are processes of competition and even displacement, but also of supplementation and support.
> The presentation will give an overview of what is known a) about the influences of television on the process of reading socialization and b) about the possibilities and limitations of the medium television for reading education. First, I will talk about the competition and partnership or even synergy between 'Books' and 'Television' in a more macroscopic or system perspective, while the topic of the next part will belong to the micro level: What kind of studies do we have and what can be said about the empirical evidence of the impact of television viewing on book reading behavior? Then, I will discuss both the chances and the limitations of information campaigns in general and book promotion programs in particular. The last part is dedicated to some considerations about strategies of reading promotion.
> (in http://www.arts.ualberta.ca/igel/IGEL1998/abstract.htm)

If you outline these basic elements of your research in a clear and transparent manner, you have good chances of having your abstract accepted.

12.1.2. Presenting yourself

Once you are accepted and attend the conference, dress and behave naturally. The scientific community is generally not interested in your clothes or your hairstyle and tolerates a wide variety of life styles. Just make sure you do not direct the attention of the audience from your paper to your appearance, although you may notice that some researchers may cultivate a taste for the eccentric. Especially at international conferences, you will notice national and cultural differences in clothing, behavior, and ways of interacting. Participants tend to be distanced and formal in countries like France or Germany, informal in Scandinavian countries, the Netherlands, and in North, Central and South America. At international conferences, the Anglo-Saxon style of interaction, which tends to be highly egalitarian and informal, is generally the norm. Also, make sure that you separate the social and the academic activities in conferences. If you went out dancing or drinking the previous evening, this will not be an excuse for you to be late for the morning activities or too intimate with colleagues.

12.1.3. Organizational aspects

Most paper presentations at international conferences are limited to 20 minutes, followed by a 10-minute discussion. Sessions are chaired by someone who has been appointed by the local organizers. Usually chairs are senior or at least experienced participants, so you may trust that they know how to handle the session. The task of the chair is fourfold:

- To introduce you to the audience;
- To make sure that your paper starts on time and to guarantee that you stick to the time schedule. Usually the chair will show you a card saying '5 minutes' after a quarter of an hour, and another card saying '1 minute' when your time is nearly up. Often the chair will interrupt you after 20 minutes, though sometimes he or she may let you speak on, but never over 30 minutes.
- To help you out with handouts, equipment, and any other things where you may need assistance.
- To thank you for the presentation, to invite questions and contributions from the audience, and to preside over the discussion. The chair may want to help you, for instance, by rephrasing a question for you. But there are considerable differences between people in this respect, so do not always take this assistance for granted.

Whenever possible, try to find out who the chair of your session is, and introduce yourself to him or her before your session, preferably during coffee breaks. If you are unable to do so, go to the chair immediately before the session and introduce yourself.

Sessions at international conferences are generally composed of three or four papers in a row. It is important that you stay in the room for the entire session, for three reasons:

- If your paper is not the first one in the session, you cannot guarantee when exactly your paper will begin. You should never rush into the room for your paper.
- It is rather impolite to present your paper and then walk out on the next person presenting a paper in your session.
- Organizers try to schedule papers with similar interests in the same session so as to generate discussion. In this way, you may also profit from listening to subsequent papers and their ensuing discussions.

12.1.4. Preparing a script

Especially if you are not an experienced speaker yourself, or if you are presenting in a foreign language, it can be highly useful to prepare a script prior to your presentation. You can print out the script and take it to the conference.

Do not, however, read the script. Rehearse it often enough before the conference so that you know it more or less by heart. Remember that your visual aids (see below) will help you. You can always resort to your script if you get stuck during the presentation. Preparing a script has yet another advantage: it can be the first step in writing up a text that you may wish to submit for publication. For the time being, however, we will concentrate on the use of the script in oral presentations. If you have 20 minutes, limit yourself to a maximum of six pages (with double line spacing).

- Write in a simple and clear way, reproducing everyday speech. The English-speaking academic tradition favors this, so do not be afraid to use simple sentences written in a direct and clear way. Avoid subordination and long sentences. You do not want your audience to get lost in winding prose.
- Several days before the conference, read your script aloud to yourself several times to check whether its structure is clear, whether the sentences are easy to understand, whether the ideas are flowing in an easy and logical way, and whether you are saying exactly what you want to say. Revise your script as many times as need be until it sounds perfectly natural to you.
- Read out your script to your supervisor or to friends to get feedback on your paper's content, structure, and wording.
- Make sure that you pronounce all words correctly. Mark the text to help you remember the correct pronunciation and intonation. Sometimes the audience's attention may be lost by the way you pronounce a certain word or by ticks such as 'ok' at the end of each sentence!
- Especially important in English is where the stress falls in a word. Many dictionaries list the pronunciation of words: check when you are uncertain, and mark the stress by underlining the syllable that is stressed in a different color.
- Some words that are bound to turn up regularly in your paper are inherently difficult to pronounce for speakers of English as a second or foreign language. One such word is *hypothesis*. As you will have to pronounce this word several times, exercise it until you can say it flawlessly and without effort.
- Print out the text at least in Font 14, double spaced so that you can read the script easily from a distance or in a darkened room (if you are using a PowerPoint presentation).

For many different reasons, some people find it hard to face an audience and speak without reading. This requires training. On the other hand, you can rely on the audio-visual resources. So, if you rehearse your presentation using the visual support many times, you will be able to put your script aside. In any case, if you find this very difficult, it is better to do a dramatic reading of your paper rather than to tremble or collapse before the audience. They will start worrying more about your health than about your paper! Here are some more tips that may help you succeed.

12.1.5. Speaking to an audience

- Control your nerves. Many other ordinary people have done this before and have survived.
- Especially important in controlling your nervous reactions is your breathing. Concentrate and try to breathe deeply and slowly. This will have a calming effect on you.
- Concentrate for a few minutes before you enter the room. Try to remain (or become) calm. If you are used to meditating, do a brief meditation. In any case, remember that there is no way out at this point, that you have prepared yourself well, and that everything will be fine.
- Never sit during your presentation! Stand before your audience and cheer up! If possible, try to get close to them. This may sound the most threatening thing to do, but, paradoxically, it often helps you feel more at ease.
- Establish eye contact with the audience. They are human beings just like you, and most of them have gone through the agonizing experience of delivering a first paper themselves. They know how it feels; therefore, many people in the audience will be sympathetic toward you. Avoid looking at your friends or colleagues, as this may disrupt your concentration or even set you giggling! Instead, establish eye contact especially with people in the audience you do not know personally.
- Also when you are doing a dramatic reading of your paper, keep eye contact with the audience. Read in such a way that the audience will not notice you are doing it ... like reporters in the TV news broadcast.
- Check the audience's reactions. Are they paying attention?
- Usually the chair will have introduced you. So, people are already paying attention. If they are not, and people are still talking or moving around, stand in front of the audience, look into their eyes and wait. Sooner than you think they will understand that you want to begin. You may also ask the chair to interfere and ask for silence. If this does not

work (which is highly unusual), simply ask them in a polite way: "Can I have your attention, please?"
- Speak loudly and clearly. Ask people in the back whether they can hear you. This creates an informal atmosphere and makes you look confident.
- Speak slowly. Remember you have timed your paper before, so you know how long it will take, and there is no need to rattle through it.
- Be careful not to be carried away and improvise. You may start elaborating on things you do not need to say, and which will take up valuable time. You may also lose track of the structure of your paper and get lost. Also remember the time you have allocated for each slide. Twenty minutes are very tight, and so now is *not* the time to improvise. Otherwise, there would not have been any need for all the preparatory work!
- If you feel comfortable about it, use some humor, but be careful not to overdo it. Also try not to use too much irony! Of course it will be easier if you insert the humor when you are preparing your script. If you use it in the right way, you will be able to create a relaxing atmosphere. Beware of jokes: if your audience does not find them funny, your attempt may backfire.
- Do not freeze. Relax and let your body follow its normal rhythm of speaking. Be natural, as if you were talking to friends. Vary the presentation (voice, body posture, position from where you are speaking, etc.)
- If you finish before your 20 minutes are up, do not panic. Audiences generally approve of this: it makes it less strenuous for them, gives them more time for interaction with you, and shows professionalism on your part. Especially if you place yourself in a position to answer questions and receive criticism. You can even prepare some questions beforehand to provoke some discussion, if nobody comes up with anything to say.

12.1.6. Discussion time

This part is, of course, what every beginner dreads most, since you are at the mercy of the audience, and cannot really prepare yourself for it. Here are some hints that can help you make the discussion time a very productive moment rather than an ordeal.

- Remain calm: people in the audience will only ask questions and make comments … they do not bite.

- If an irrational attack is launched against you, keep calm. Simply say you disagree, that you are of another opinion, and that you think you have good reasons to believe that your position is not completely wrong. This shows that you have a backbone and know how to handle disagreement. (But note the following point).
- Make sure you listen carefully to what the speaker is saying or asking. Check whether the person has understood your points clearly.
- Do not panic if you do not understand a question or a remark. Simply request that the person repeat it by saying: "I am sorry, but I am not sure I understand what you are aiming at. Can you please explain what you mean?"
- If you do not know the answer to a question or remark, do not beat about the bush. Simply admit that you do not know the answer and say that you will think about this point. Take notes. This will help you remember what you should look into later.
- If a sensible piece of criticism is offered, acknowledge it. This is why you are presenting a paper. So, say you will take that into account, or that you will consider it further. Write it down!
- Although this is not really necessary, it is always polite to thank the person who has taken the trouble to ask a question or offer a piece of criticism. Always thank a person who has provided a useful suggestion, a reference, or a piece of advice.
- Sometimes a question is asked about an aspect of your research that you had no time to present in those 20 minutes. If you have prepared sheets or slides on that aspect, you can show these now and talk about them.
- If you disagree with the speaker, do not be rude. Simply say so in a polite and non-personal way, like "Well, I am not so sure ...". Often this can be done courteously by putting your disagreement in the form of a question, like "But what if ...?", or "But wouldn't you think that ...?" You may also say that you will look into that point later.
- Do not be embarrassed about your English: everybody makes mistakes and the audience will appreciate your efforts to communicate in a foreign language. Do not draw attention to how a word should be pronounced. Just speak naturally and forget the mistakes. What is important is that you keep a discussion going and not how well you are communicating in English.
- Generally at international conferences, speakers of English as a first language tend to adapt their English so that communication is not disrupted. Most often they will avoid slang, regional variations, or idioms that other conference participants may not know. If a speaker of

English as a first language goes too fast (as they often tend to do when speaking in their own language), just ask him or her to please speak slower. There is nothing embarrassing about this, especially as many speakers of English are themselves in poor command of a foreign language (and usually too well aware of this).

Remember: the purpose of the discussion is to improve the quality of academic work. So consider it as a means to discover shortcomings your research may have. It generally does. Make notes during and immediately after the discussion so that you can use the criticism when you write up the final version of you paper for publication later.

12.1.7. Using media

Whatever the media you will be using, make sure you provide the title of your paper, your name, affiliation, and e-mail address. The reason for that is that you want people to remember what you presented and be able to get in touch with you if they are interested in your presentation. For your presentation, you can use audio-visual media that are adequate and balanced in number. In conferences on empirical studies, presenters tend to use three kinds of media: PowerPoint presentations, transparency sheets, and handouts. Of course, if you are dealing with theater, film or television, you may wish to use video or DVD equipment, but remember that most visual material can also be incorporated in a PowerPoint file.

PowerPoint presentations offer most in terms of possibilities: they look professional, can contain any kind of information you need, and allow you to create special effects to emphasize certain points. They can also be entertaining to watch. But beware of the dangers of too much variation. Too many showy illustrations may distract people in the audience, who will tend to enjoy the pictures and wonder what will be the next gadget you will use, rather than listen to the core of what you are saying.

PowerPoint presentations do not cost anything (if you already have the facilities). They are easy to create and can be edited at any time. They also pre-structure your talk to a high degree, making it easier for you to talk freely: the information is there on the screen and you will not run into the problem of getting the transparencies or pages mixed up, or placing them on the projector upside down.

The best way to use PowerPoint is to take your laptop with you to the conference. Always familiarize yourself with the beamer connections hours before your presentation. Some people even recommend you take a screwdriver with you to the conference to fasten the cable screws. One common problem is that you may produce your presentation on a disk at home and the file may not open on the computer in the conference room. So, if you do not have a laptop or do not wish to take yours with you, make sure that you can use your electronic document. You may send the organizers your document by e-mail and request them to save it on the hard disk of the desktop computer connected to the beamer in the room where you will be holding your presentation.

When using PowerPoint, you should:

- Ask the conference organizers whether you can use PowerPoint at all. If you can, request a room that is equipped with a beamer, and have its reservation confirmed.
- Make transparency sheets of your PowerPoint slides. You can print the .ppt document and then photocopy them onto transparency sheets. You should always think of different ways of presenting your paper for the situation when something goes wrong with the PowerPoint apparatus.
- **Transparency sheets** are also a good resource for illustrating your paper. As with PowerPoint presentations, check whether the organizers have booked an overhead projector for you ... and that it is working!
  - Prepare colored sheets. They are more fun to watch and you can use colors to emphasize certain aspects of your argument. Your graphs and tables here should be in contrasting colors.
  - Do not make too many sheets: for a 20-minute talk, 10 is enough. But again it will depend on how much time you spend with each transparency. Check your timing against the number of transparencies. This will also help you keep your pace.
  - Do not use fonts smaller than Font 20. You want your audience to be able to follow what you are pointing at and read what is on the sheet.
  - Do not put too much information on one sheet. For instance, do not write a long text if you want your readers to follow you. Transparencies should be used to support your talk, not as texts to be examined thoroughly, or, even worse, pages of your script! If you need the audience to have access to a long stretch of text, prepare handouts.
  - Make sure that your transparencies are in the right order. It is annoying when the audience has to wait while the presenter fumbles through the transparencies trying to find out what he or she was going to show next. If possible, ask a friend to help you with the transparencies. Make sure that your friend sits down quietly and does not stand in front of the projector.

- o Do not turn your back to the audience and look at the projected slide. Follow the slide by looking at the transparency on the projector's glass.
- **Handouts** are also a convenient way to help you present a paper. Remember that they should also contain the title of your paper, your name, affiliation, and e-mail address. It is also advisable to present an outline of what you are going to say. Just make sure that you:
  - o Have enough copies to go around. Generally 15 to 20 copies should be safe enough. In case they are not, ask the audience to share copies.
  - o Distribute the handouts before you begin your paper at both (or multiple) ends of the rows of seats to speed up distribution.

If you follow these guidelines, you will be on track for a successful presentation, one in which you learn by doing. Most importantly, be patient with yourself. Oral presentations require training and experience, which you will gain in time. The more conferences you go to, the better a presenter you will become.

12.2. Written presentations

Often after a conference (but sometimes also without having attended one), the question arises whether you want to communicate your findings to other colleagues in writing. It generally happens, for instance, that the conference organizers intend to bring out a volume with the papers presented. This is called the *Proceedings*, and can take the form of a collection of all or most papers that were held, or a selection of them. In the latter case, the selection is usually made by a small committee of two or three people. Organizers will send out a call for contributions to be submitted before a deadline. So you will have to decide whether you wish to send something in or not. If the organizers do not have such plans, you can still think of publishing your work, for instance, in a national or international journal. Also, a group of colleagues may get together and compose a book themselves. In this case, you may want to invite other colleagues to publish their work together with your own. This is not as impossible as it may sound to you at first.

In this section we will concentrate on the more basic production process by means of which you shape a written version of your research report and submit it for publication to someone else – in most cases an editor of a book or a journal. Here we will look at some of the steps you have to take in order to arrive at a publishable manuscript and will offer you some help in how to shape your report so that it meets the standards of academic publications. You will also find more details on where and how to publish, how to structure your paper, how to cite, and some important hints you should consider.

12.2.1. Where to publish

When you are ready to write up your results, you should decide where you are going to publish them (proceedings, collections, journals, etc.). We strongly recommend that you submit your paper to refereed journals. These are journals that publish any article only after it has been approved by two or three referees. Referees are senior researchers in the area who will be able to criticize your work and give recommendations. Publishing in refereed journals requires you to set higher standards and hence involves more work, but there are very good reasons to do so. One obvious reason is that articles in refereed journals have more prestige and therefore attract more attention of scholars in the area. Another reason is that experts will give you interesting and relevant feedback. Doing academic work should be a humbling experience, one in which you are constantly being criticized. So do not feel hurt if you get too many comments, or if your paper is rejected. Good referees spend a considerable amount of time substantiating their criticism so that you may improve the paper.

12.2.2. Structuring your paper

Although rules may vary, papers on empirical studies are generally divided into the following sections: Title page, Abstract, Keywords, Introduction, Method, Results, Discussion, References, Appendix, and Acknowledgements. We will discuss each of these sections below:

12.2.2.1. Title page

This is the sheet of paper that covers your work. It is good practice to suppress page numbers on the title page, but all the other pages must be numbered. Prepare a *header* which displays, in the upper-right hand corner of all pages and on the even-numbered pages, the author's name plus the number of the page. On the odd-numbered pages, it should display an abridged title plus that page number. Although this is not mainstream practice in papers on empirical studies of literature (but it is for psychology), it is highly recommended because it helps to identify the manuscript if the pages get out of control.

The title page also contains the full title of the paper, the author's name (or authors' names in case you did your research together with colleagues) and affiliation centered between the right and left margins. Under your names it is also advisable to write your e-mail address(es).

Here is an example:

Metaphors of violence in daily papers

Danielle Menezes
and
Olivia Fialho
Federal University of Rio de Janeiro

damenezes@aol.com
olivia@infolink.com.br

The title should be short (no more than 15 words), informative, and alluring. You want to catch your potential readers' attention, so that their curiosity is aroused and they wish to read on.

12.2.2.2. Keywords

These are the words that will be entered into databases like *PsycINFO*, so that other researchers who are doing a literature search may hit upon your article. So choose them very carefully. For instance, for the paper above, we could choose: **violence, metaphor, cognition, reader response, newspapers**. It is interesting to pick out words from your hypotheses, but if you are uncertain of how to make the selection, ask for advice from your supervisor or from more experienced researchers. It may also be helpful to read some keywords used in the journal to which you are intending to submit your paper.

2.2.3. Abstract

This usually appears as a single paragraph with no paragraph indentation in the centre of the page and comes on page 2. The abstract is a brief summary of your study. It is often printed later in collections or on the Internet so as to inform your readers of what the paper is about, and to allow them to decide whether its content is relevant to them. To write the abstract, you should follow the same instructions on how to write an abstract in response to calls for papers (see 12.1.1 above). In case you would like to refresh your memory, here is another abstract of a paper published online:

What is literariness? Three components of literary reading

David S. Miall and Don Kuiken

Departments of English and Psychology, University of Alberta
Discourse Processes, 28 (1999), 121-138.
© Copyright Lawrence Erlbaum Associates

Abstract

It is now widely maintained that the concept of "literariness" has been critically examined and found deficient. Prominent postmodern literary theorists have argued that there are no special characteristics that distinguish literature from other texts. Similarly, cognitive psychology has often subsumed literary understanding within a general theory of discourse processing. However, a review of empirical studies of literary readers reveals traces of literariness that appear irreducible to either of these explanatory frameworks. Our analysis of readers' responses to several literary texts (short stories and poems) indicates processes beyond the explanatory reach of current situation models. Such findings suggest a three-component model of literariness involving foregrounded textual or narrative features, readers' defamiliarizing responses to them, and the consequent modification of personal meanings.

As you can see, the abstract starts with a claim that is then supported from two perspectives. The claim is then called into doubt both by a literature search and an empirical study. Finally, an alternative approach with its components is proposed.

Now, here is an example of an abstract published in a journal. You will notice that the comments made for submitting a paper also hold when you write an abstract for a journal:

> *Cheating history: The rhetorics of art forgery*
>
> Abstract: Art forgery is a curious crime. If aesthetic appreciation is based only upon the beauty of the work itself, forgery should not be considered a crime. However, art appreciation may be defined to include more than the form and content of the work itself. Appreciation can be connected to historical, biographical, legal, and economic issues which create the context of the work of art. I examine how art forgery is viewed by various participants in the art world and by the general public. Typically, forgers emphasize the beauty of the symbol abstracted from its circumstance, claiming that the value of the art work is not a function of its history. The establishment art critic insists on seeing the art symbol in its social and historical context, and defines a forgery as a work which cheats history. In order to examine the sociological nature of art appreciation and deviant art question, I examine three case studies of forgers: 1) Han van Meegeren, the Dutch forger of Vermeer and De Hooch, 2) Elmyr de Hory, the Hungarian-born forger of modern French art, and 3) Tom Keating, the Cockney forger of Samuel Palmer and other artists. In these case studies I describe how the forger entered his trade, his attitude to the art world, the extent to which his works were accepted, his justifications for forgery, and the rhetorical strategies used by others to define his "crime". (Fine, Gary Alan in *Empirical Study of the Arts*, *1*:1, 1983, 75-93).

In this example, the author starts with a general statement. He then puts forward his hypothesis, details his material and methodology, and arrives at a conclusion.

12.2.2.4. Introduction

On page 3 of your paper, you start by stating the problem you will investigate. Open with two or three sentences referring to a wider context or perspective. The advantage of this is that readers who are unfamiliar with the problem at hand will be able to contextualize the problem you are focusing on and see the importance of your research. These opening sentences are followed by problematizing the issue, after which a review of the literature is presented, showing what previous researchers have done and what they have not. Especially go into questions like:

- What definitions and/or theories about your topic exist?
- What is already known about the subject and what is not?
- How does your study relate to this earlier work?
- How is your research embedded in the general theoretical approaches to the issue?

When dealing with work from other researchers, it is important to introduce their contributions as a kind of discussion and not as a listing. That means you should avoid giving an account of the various things that have been written on the subject. Instead, you should structure the overview according to particular problems or areas that will later relate to (or be taken up by) your own study. Also make sure that you review the evidence at hand critically. That is, do not just paraphrase, but also show where the shortcomings of these previous studies lay (from a philosophical, theoretical, methodological, statistical, etc.) point of view. Show where your study avoids the problems that previous studies encountered, and point out contradictions in theories or/and research. It is important that you remember that this section does not have to (and cannot) be exhaustive. However, your study may sometimes take on an entirely new problem and you may find yourself in a situation where there is hardly any research available (though do not be satisfied too soon, and make sure that your literature study is thorough enough to be certain on this point). In any case, try to avoid the possibility that readers will be able to point out important publications that you have not considered. The guideline should be that you describe studies that are clearly related to the research problem at hand: make this relation explicit for your readers! This should clarify why you conducted the study. Your readers will want to know how each study you mention contributed to the development of your hypotheses. This is why the hypotheses come at the end of the introduction, as the outcome of a natural development. They indicate the predictions you make about your study. Therefore, formulate exactly what the hypotheses you are testing are, and what results are to be on the basis of the existing literature or your own expansion of it. Your hypotheses, then, come in the last paragraph of your introduction. You can write your hypothesis in full, like the following authors did:

> In narratology and discourse processing, it is common to describe the structure of events in the story world independently of the manner of narration and the perspective of the narrator. In contrast, we argue that readers generally process the narrative as if they were communicating with the narrator. As a consequence, they represent only those aspects of the story world that are relevant to the point or message the narrator seems to intend. For example, it is usually assumed that readers track the goal structure of characters so that they can interpret characters' plans and understand motivations for their actions. However, *we hypothesize that characters' goals are represented only to the extent that the narrator appears to signal that such goals are relevant to his or her communicative purpose*[our italics]. In order to test this hypothesis, we developed passages in which two characters share a superordinate goal (e.g. taking a fishing trip) that can be accomplished if both characters succeed in their respective sub-goals (e.g. getting a fishing license and renting a boat). Sentence reading time was measured as a function of the relationship between the sub-goals and the manner in which the passage was introduced by the narrator. When the narrator emphasized the relevance of the superordinate goal, readers took additional time to coordinate information from the two sub-goals when they both succeeded. However, when the narrator emphasized only the relevance of one of the sub-goals, no such effect was found. This result suggests that readers' representation of goal structures is mediated by their representation of the narrator and his or her apparent communicative intent. In general, this study supports the view that readers represent goals, make inferences, and generate expectations primarily in service of understanding the narrator as a conversational participant.
> (Dixon, P. & Bortolussi, M. *"Narratorial Relevance and Character Goals"* in Abstracts for the IGEL Conference, Toronto, 2000)
> http://www.arts.ualberta.ca/igel/Conf%202000%20abstracts.htm;

Here, the hypothesis has been clearly spelled out in the sentence – we have italicized it. When several hypotheses are involved, you can number them, as in the following example:

> In their study, Wiseman & van Peer (2000) observed that grief is associated with the sounds of the vowels "a", "o" and "u" and the sounds of the nasals "m" and "n". Differently, the sounds of the vowels "i" and "e" and the plosives "b", "p" and "d" are better suited to express joy. The hypotheses to be tested here are the following:
> H1: The sounds of the vowels "a", "o" and "u" are suited to express negative feelings.
> H2: The sounds of the vowels "i" and "e" are suited to express positive feelings.
> H3: The sounds of the consonants "m" and "n" are suited to express negative feelings.
> H4: The sounds of the consonants "p", "b" and "d" are suited to express positive feelings.
> (Fialho, O. & Zyngier, S. *"Revisiting phonetic iconicity: an empirical study"*, paper presented at the 4th ECEL conference in Rio de Janeiro, 2003)

There are also other ways of formulating hypotheses. For instance:

> The main question of this study was whether the low degree of updating is caused by superficial reading (skipping) or by a refusal to change the model in rejecting the transformative information of the second text (rejecting). If superficial processing (skipping) is the cause of a poor updating, then we might expect that the following think-aloud activities are of great importance in relation to processing of the transformative information and – negatively – related to the judgment performance: "incomplete repetition," "incorrect repetition," and "careless metacomment." If skipping is plausible, we might expect that a high frequency on these categories is related with low test performance. In other words, the more often subjects make incomplete or incorrect repetitions or utter careless metacomments while processing the new (transformative) information, the lower their judgment test performance should be.
> (Oostendorp, H. van *"Holding onto Established Viewpoints"*, in van Peer, W. & Chatman, S. *New Perspectives on Narrative Perspective*, NY: State University of New York Press, 2001: 182-183)

In this example, the author preferred to present the hypotheses by describing what to expect in the cases where each of them turned out to be the case. Once you have formulated your hypothesis, you then set out to describe the way you have conducted your research, which is the object of the next section.

12.2.2.5. Method

This section follows the Introduction (without having to start a new page). Here you describe step-by-step the procedures you carried out, justifying your actions. You will have to decide how detailed you must be, bearing in mind that your reader may want to replicate your study. You are reporting to fellow researchers. Therefore, you can count on their understanding of terms like "random sample", "control condition", or "matching". Precisely how you did the study is unknown to them, however; so you should describe the steps you took clearly and explicitly. This section is divided into subsections in which you discuss:

- **Your Research paradigm:** an overview of the perspective you opted for, that is, what theoretical notions or background the research is embedded in or makes use of, whether your research is quantitative, qualitative, mixed, etc.
- **Participants:** if your study does not involve people, as in the case of a text analysis, you may skip this item. Here is where you describe the people involved in the study, that is, who they were, how many were assigned to each of the conditions, and how this was done (randomly, along existing groups, etc). There may be several things that are relevant in describing your sample, depending on the purpose of your

study, but at least mention how many male and female subjects participated, what the mean age was (when reporting means, always mention the standard deviation as well), what the general characteristics of your subjects is in terms of socio-economic status, education, where they live (in large towns, in the countryside, etc.), whether they have special characteristics (for instance, whether they are bilingual, or learners of English as a foreign language, what level of proficiency they have, etc.). If you are conducting qualitative research, you should describe each of the participants and the context in which the research took place in much more detail. For instance, if your participants are students, what the school conditions are, or what kind of family they live in; in short, describe everything that you think is relevant for your reader to have a comprehensive picture of the conditions under which you have worked and which may have influenced the results at which you have arrived.

- **Materials** (when relevant): which materials were used (e.g. the text(s) participants read, or the movie they saw, etc.). You should also explain how and why they were selected.
- **Apparatus or instrument** (when relevant): In case you used special instruments to conduct your research, like WORDSMITH Tools, you should report the brand name, model number of the equipment used, etc. If you use SPSS, there is no need to report it. Your analysis will make it evident. If you used a questionnaire, this is the place where you detail it and, if necessary, describe the instructions that preceded their distribution, how the questionnaire was developed, which categories were used, etc. Questionnaires are generally appended to your study. Here you may also detail whether you conducted interviews, and how you made transcriptions. In short, in this section you should give as accurate a description as possible of the way in which your instruments were prepared.
- **Procedure:** a description of how the study was conducted. In the case of quantitative research, you must detail how independent variables were identified and/or manipulated and how dependent variables were measured, the design of the study and all the control features (e.g. randomization), and step by step, what happened to participants during the study. As to dependent measures, you should include a description of the tests that were administered or which questions were answered, how these questions were structured in relation to the hypotheses, and so forth. Often it is instructive when you quote one or two questions to illustrate the types of questions that were asked. Also include how the participants were debriefed. This is also the place for you to describe

the pilot test you conducted to test your instruments. In quantitative studies, in this section, you should also mention the statistical tests carried out (and why they and not others were chosen), together with your choice of an alpha level (conventionally set at 0.05).

12.2.2.6 Results

This section comes immediately after the methods and reports the results of the descriptive and inferential statistics (in quantitative research) or the data you obtained from your qualitative method. These results are commented on with respect to the predictions that were derived from the hypotheses. Do not, however, try to explain here why some predictions were borne out while others were not, since that is the subject of the *Discussion* section. The structure of your report, here, is best based on your hypotheses and predictions. You could, for instance, dedicate one paragraph to each of your predictions; and preferably deal with the predictions in the same order as they were presented in the Introduction. The same applies to qualitative research. Describe the data you obtained, the categories you found (while you have described *how* these were developed in the previous sections). In the case of quantitative research, do not describe that you "entered the data in the computer program SPSS." Simply start by listing the descriptive statistics first (see Chapter 8), and link them to the predictions. Always report descriptive statistics (see Chapter 8) before inferential statistics, but sometimes you can enter the results of inference statistics (see Chapters 9–11) together with the descriptives, for instance, by making use of the system of asterisks, as was explained in the Chapter 9, Section 9.4 where correlation matrices were explained. However, especially when you are doing somewhat complicated statistics, as with an ANOVA, you need to report the test statistics separately. As you have already mentioned which tests you carried out in the procedures section, here you follow the 'standard' rules and abbreviations (such as M for sample mean; SD for standard deviation) with which you must become familiar. Beware of technical meanings of words. It is very common for beginners to say that something is significant. In empirical studies, *significant* means *statistically significant*!

Conducting statistical tests requires that you are specific about how you conducted them and what results they yielded. Reporting on an ANOVA, for instance, report which covariates you used, and what the design was.

For reporting on the results of *t*-tests, ANOVAs, General Linear Models, Chi-square tests, or correlations, there are rules for reporting:

- ***t*-test:** Report the means for each group, as well as the standard deviations. Furthermore, report the *t*-value, the degrees of freedom and the value of *p*. Example: for group 1 the average [$M = 4.5$; $SD = 1.3$]

was significantly higher than that of group 2 [$M = 2.6$; $SD = 1.1$; $t = 4.2$, $df = 3$, $p < 0.05$]. Here M is the average; SD is the standard deviation; t is the t-test and p the probability.

- **Mann–Whitney U-test:** Report the z-score and the p-value.
- **Wilcoxon test:** Report the values of U, z, and p.
- **Kruskal-Wallis and Friedman tests:** Report the values of chi-squared, df, and p.
- **ANOVA and General Linear Model:** Report the means and standard deviations as above, and also the F-value, the degrees of freedom, and the value of p. Example: [$F = 6.3$, df = 1, $p < 0.01$].
- **Chi-square:** Report the value of Chi-squared, the degrees of freedom and the value of p. Example: [$Chi^2 = 8.3$, df = 20, $p < 0.001$].
- **Correlations:** Report correlation and the p-value. Example: [$r = -0.78$, $p < 0.01$].

In addition, always consider the difference between significance and effect size. Especially if your groups of participants were rather large, it may happen that differences between groups turn out as highly significant, even if the difference itself is small, or even marginal. That means that the difference will be reproduced if you repeat the investigation. But you should also consider whether so small a difference is worth considering, even if it occurs in the population! So what you do in the Results section is to revisit your research questions and show how the data you obtained cast light on these. Since you developed the hypotheses in a systematic way, there is no need to deviate from the order in which they have been presented before. As a matter of fact, keeping the same order will make it easier for your reader to follow the presentation. Make sure you summarize each of the findings after you have described them. There is always the danger that you resort to merely listing the results. You avoid that by giving the reader a clear picture of how the results answer your research questions. So, remind the reader at each turn what is at stake and how the details obtained and analyzed provide some answer to the questions you set out to investigate. Use advance markers here to guide the reader through the maze of data and details that you present. Do not forget that perhaps for you, who have been working on the study for weeks on end, things may be crystal clear, but for your readers, who have little time to look at your study, they may not be so obvious. Hence you need to make it as clear as possible.

One reminder: when reporting your results, do not put SPSS outputs straight into your text. That involves a lot of information that you will not need and makes your tables difficult to understand. The labels you use in your data set may be clear to you, but remember that they can be incomprehensible to your reader. If necessary, you can present SPSS outputs in Appendices.

- **Illustrations**

Sometimes it is too complicated to describe all your descriptive statistics in a paragraph and often a single graph can summarize pages of text. When it is clearly an advantage, present your data in a table or figure. Never use both ways to present the same data. Use a table when it is important to communicate the exact mean scores (in a figure it is often hard to determine what the exact scores were). Alternatively, use a graph when the exact scores do not matter too much, but you wish to display the general pattern of the different responses. You will also find that at some point there is too much information to present in a graph to make the results clear to your readers (too many bars for instance to still be able to make a clear distinction between the groups). Graphs can be handy to demonstrate a dramatic difference between groups, or to show an interaction effect in a factorial design. Use a bar chart, for instance, to present the mean scores on one variable in several conditions, or the differences between male and female subjects. Use a line graph when you want to show the relation between two continuous variables.

Each illustration should bear a number and a title (e.g. Graph 1: Difference between groups) either above or under it, depending on the style of the journal. You should always refer to the numbers of Figures, Tables, Diagrams, or Graphs in your text. Example:

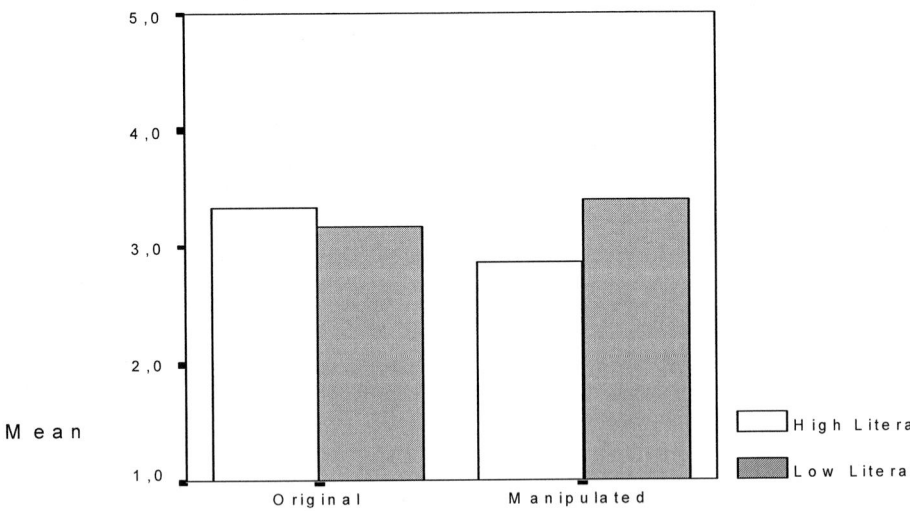

Figure 12.1: Level of appreciation (from Mendes & Menezes, 2003) showing differences between groups

In the example above, the authors wanted to show that appreciation was the same between two texts in the original group. However, in the manipulated version, a difference was noted: the non-canonical extract received a higher evaluation.

Be careful not to let yourself be carried away by the numerous fancy possibilities for making graphs that most computing programs offer. Too much can be very bad. Avoid colors in your written text, but do use them for oral presentations, and make sure that contrasts are clear.

It is important to realize that graphs and tables with means alone are not enough. You need to show that differences were large enough for your hypothesis(es) to be accepted (or rejected), given statistical significance, of course.

All in all, remember that illustrations mean exactly what they are: they help the reader to understand better what is being presented. Make sure that your tables, graphs, or diagrams are clear and present precise information – not more, not less.

12.2.2.7. Discussion

This section comes after the Results. Here you interpret your findings by teasing out their implications, discussing alternative explanations, outlining limitations, and embedding these results in the theoretical framework from which you started. A solid way of initiating the discussion is by referring to the original aims of your study and your initial expectations or hypotheses, and comparing them to the results you obtained. Here is where you also build bridges with the theoretical background you detailed, so as to establish a link between your findings and those of previous studies. Connections are also made between your results and the relevance of your study that you provided in the Introduction.

In addition, it is suggested that you also reflect self-critically on your own work: outline the limits of your statistical analysis, and provide *caveats* (that is, things one should be aware of) to your findings. Discuss the validity (see Chapter 6) of your conclusions. Try to imagine what objections readers may have to your method. Indicate here how any problem can be solved in further studies when pointing out what questions remain unanswered, what extra questions the study has generated, how to proceed from this point. Example:

> Regarding the items all together, there is, however, more conformity than disagreement between both sexes. In view of these results it must be said that the sex of the writer has no influence on the evaluation of the text. But further research is necessary to verify these results, because the chosen text had a feminine connotation, which may have influenced the results. Therefore, a study with masculine connotated material should be made. Also, other factors that could be relevant, like age or education of the readers should be examined.
> (Preuss, A. & Mentjes, A. "Gender and Reading. Do women read differently? In *Textual Secrets, The Message of the Medium, Proceedings of the 21st PALA Conference*, ed. Csábi, S. & Zerkowitz, J. Eötvos Loránd University: Budapest, 2002, 285)

As this section is the place where you interpret your results, do not torture your numbers or other data[1] until they confess. To avoid this, you must specify in the procedure section which statistical tests you intend to carry out. Not doing so means capitalizing upon chance. Since statistics is the realm of the probable, doing endless rows of calculations means you will 'probably' end up with some significance here or there. You will be criticized or frowned upon if you do, because that is not the logic by means of which statistics works. The purpose of statistical analysis is to show whether the pattern you predicted is there or not. Moreover, remember this maxim: No results are also interesting results ... and may even turn out to be more interesting than positive ones! When your results turn out to be contrary to your expectations, this is then a clear indication that your intuitions were fatally wrong! So, do not despair when your predictions are not borne out. On the contrary, point out the counterintuitive nature of your results, but stress their objective and reliable character, emphasizing the careful methodology you have used. Again, this is one important reason for publishing your results. You want other people to carry on from where you arrived.

End this section by showing directions you envisage for further study, as in the example above. If you think you need a longer conclusion, you can add **A Final Note** section. Conclude with some potent thought for further reflection formulated in your last sentence. Here is an example:

---

[1] A small note: *data* is Latin. It is the plural of *datum*. However, many authors have been using *data* in the singular. To be on the safe side, use *data* as a plural noun. Some other plurals you will need regularly are analysis/analyses; criterion/criteria, hypothesis/hypotheses, phenomenon/phenomena.

> It is disappointing that discourse psychologists lost interest in investigating theme representation and processing in the late 1980s. Informative progress was beginning to be made, but the paradigm ended rather abruptly as researchers pursued other directions. Some questions were never explored. For example, Seifert, Dyer and Black (1986) was one of the few studies that began to explore how themes are activated on-line during comprehension. No study has investigated how themes are both constructed and modified during on-line comprehension. We know that the theme of a story is not firmly established at its beginning. Instead, there is uncertainty over the appropriate theme as a plot unfolds in an unpredictable fashion (Graesser et al., 1994). What is the process of dynamically modifying the theme of a story? An answer to this question will hopefully emerge in the future, particularly if the attentions of discourse psychologists do turn to matters of theme.
> [Graesser, A. et al. "Psychological and computational research on theme comprehension" in *Thematics. Interdisciplinary Studies*, Louwerse, M & van Peer, W. (Eds.), Amsterdam: John Benjamins, 2002, 19–32]

12.2.3. Where to begin

Should you start writing from the Introduction? In no way! There is no rule here, but it would be advisable to start from the section you are most familiar with: a description of the methods and your results. Then, you could go on to the discussion of the literature on the subject so that you see your results in this light. It is very important that you make a connection between the theoretical part and the discussion of your results. Abstract, Introduction and Conclusion may be left to the end, when you already have an overall view of the whole paper. Remember that you will have to write and re-write the paper several times if you want it to be neat and clear, short and simple.

Research on writing developed by Flower & Hayes (1981) shows that there are two types of writers: those whose ideas are so well developed that the writer can formulate a general plan, and subsequently 'fill up' each part and subpart of the plan; the second type works 'chaotically'. Ideas are thought fragments with little organization. They collect bits here, write pieces there, paste them together without any plan at all, but gradually make their way toward a final whole. One type is not better than the other. They are just two ways of dealing with writing. Many professional researchers, including at least one of the authors of this book, belong to the 'chaotic' type.

So, try to find out to which type of writer you belong and what are the advantages and disadvantage of your type. In any case, experience has shown us that beginners should attempt to start from a general plan. It is less time-consuming and keeps you on track. Beyond that, follow your personal inclinations, but learn from your mistakes! Your supervisors should be of great help here, but also invite comments from colleagues and friends.

12.2.4. Some stylistic reminders

12.2.4.1. Pronouns

Authors vary in terms of using *I*, *we*, or the more impersonal academic style in which the passive voice predominates, as in the fourth quotation below.
I have argued that LA must focus its efforts primarily on teacher education.
— van Lier, L. "Not the nine o'clock linguistics class: investigating contingency grammar" in *Language Awareness, 1,* 2: 104

While there might have been some slim justification for this in the dim past, such a charge does not seem to me to stick to any current or recent stylistic practice.
—Stockwell, P. "(Sur)real stylistics: from text to contextualizing" in *Contextualized Stylistics, In Honour of Peter Verdonk*, ed. Bex, T. et al., Amsterdam, Rodopi, 2000,p. 16

The reason why we need a concept such as interpretability is of course that it involves a dimension different from that of other success concepts.
—Enkvist, N.E. "Context" in Sell, R. & Verdonk, P. *Literature and the New Interdisciplinarity*. Amsterdam: Rodopi, 1994, p. 49

As can be observed from this brief analysis, the study of texts translated into a minoritized language and culture, such as the Galician, could be considered as an examination of the problems inherent in the life and existence of the Galician language itself.
—Millán-Varela, C. "Hearing Voices" *Language and Literature 13* (1), 2004: 52–53

A good policy is for you to check whether the journal to which you are submitting your paper is particular about this issue. Look at some of the papers that have already been published there. If there is no tendency to use one of the pronouns, just choose the one that makes you feel more comfortable and the style flow easily. Be careful when you switch pronouns, however. Sometimes this can be a highly functional strategy. For instance, you may switch from the impersonal academic style to the use of a first person pronoun when personal perspective is introduced. The same applies to verb tenses. The rule you should follow here is to be consistent. Any shift will produce some effect. It depends on whether you want this effect to take place.

12.2.4.2. Markers

Mark any transitions. If a new topic is to be broached, introduce it, and also relate it to what has been mentioned:

- "*In contrast*, there are only two rhymes of obstruents which differ in place…"
- "*Moreover*, the practice of allowing differences in voice in rhymes seems to have a longer history in English than is commonly acknowledged…"
- "*More recently*, Sylvia Plath routinely rhymes…"
- "*Admittedly*, the statistical difference between two rhymes with place differences …"
(Hanson, K. "Formal variation in the rhymes of Pinky's *Dante*" *Language and Literature 12* (4), 2003, 322 *passim*; our italics).

Check the structure of your text very carefully so that every transition from paragraph to paragraph and section to section runs smoothly and there are no abrupt changes or lack of coherent links.

12.2.4.3. Gender

When you write, use neutral formulations and gender-neutral language: do not use *he, his, man, man's*, etc. when you are referring to both men and women. One easy way out is to resort to plural forms. For instance, "The reader's absorption in the text depends on his personal history," could be replaced by "Readers' absorption in the text depends on their personal history." Or "The biographer needs to bear in mind the fact that he recreates characters," can be replaced by "Biographers need to bear in mind that they recreate characters." Only use "s/he" when you really need to. This form does not enhance the attraction of your writing style and can sometimes become awkward. Some writers have opted for the use of a general "she" instead of a "he". For instance: "When the researcher chooses her sample. She must make sure, etc.". But this does not do away with the implications that the use of either "he" or "she" suggests. It is up to you to decide and take the responsibility upon yourself. Again, be consistent.

12.2.4.4. Politeness

When you formulate criticism of other people, be polite and avoid offensive language. For instance, "They were very stupid to think of such a hypothesis," or "They were totally wrong in their conclusions." Instead, you may say "They missed the point," or "Although their contribution was valid to a certain degree, they did not address the crucial point, namely ...".

12.2.4.5. Tone

Bear in mind that very few researchers manage to produce a breakthrough in scientific terms. Most papers are just a tiny light that kindles for a short period of time but they are not really so small – together, these brief lights make us explore and experience the world. So, keep the tone of your paper down and describe in as business-like manner as possible what you have done, step by step, avoiding any expressions that may exaggerate your results. Do not try to be overly funny, ironic, poetic, nor to create suspense or rely on any style that may produce more ambiguity than necessary. You want to be optimally understood. So, think of each and every word you use. Clarity and simplicity are keywords, and modesty is the tone.

12.2.5. Sources and citing

Do not forget to mention all the sources you used in the text and in the reference section. Avoid plagiarism, which means copying stretches of text from other authors without using quotation marks and/or acknowledging the original source. Plagiarism is more than an ethical issue. It is a crime. It is also unethical to paraphrase an idea or change the wording in order to snatch the idea. You must always report where you encountered that idea, if you did not conceive of it yourself. So, whenever you use other people's words or ideas, make a clear reference to the sources you used, whether they are manuscripts of fellow students, texts in internet sites, or published works. Always make clear "who says what," that is: make sure that readers understand which statements, claims, or arguments in your text are your opinion or your findings, and which ones are someone else's.

When you quote, you should avoid long quotations. In general, it is best to formulate things in your own words, unless it is the specific wording that you want to draw the reader's attention to. When quoting make clear why you are doing so, by writing an 'announcement' of the quotation and a justification for it in the sentences directly preceding or following the quotation.

Check whether all the sources listed in your bibliography are actually referred to in the text of your article. Likewise, make sure that every reference in your text makes its way into the reference section. There is nothing more annoying to the reader of a paper than to look for a reference and not find it.

Remember that journals always print "Instructions for Authors" with each issue, which you must read carefully so as to get important information as to the kind of style they will accept, the length of the paper, spacing, margins, the style for referencing, how they expect sections to be presented, etc. Rules vary from one journal to another. They may also vary from one discipline to another. Authors in our area tend to rely on *the MLA (Modern Language Association) Handbook* and the *Publication Manual of the American Psychological Association* (APA-style). If you do not want to purchase these manuals, you can check the homepages of these associations. In any case, here are some major guidelines:

12.2.5.1. Citing sources APA style

- **Citation in your text**
  Examples:
  o Similar effects were found by Peterson (1998).
  o Similar effects were found in other studies (e.g. Peterson, 1998).
  o Peterson (1998) states that "significant differences were found between the two groups" (p. 40).
  o In general we may expect "significant differences between the two groups" (Peterson, 1998, p. 40).
- **Journal article, one author**
  Cupchik, G. (1994). Emotion in aesthetics: Reactive and reflective models. *Poetics, 23,* 177–188.
- **Article, two authors**
  Levy, S.G. & Fenley, W.F. (1979). Audience size and likelihood and intensity of response during a humorous movie. *Bulletin of the Psychonomic Society, 13* (6), 409–412.
- **Book, one author**
  Tan, E. (1970). *Emotion and the Structure of Narrative Film: Film as an Emotion Machine.* Mahwah: Lawrence Erlbaum.
- **Book, two authors**
  Bortolussi, M. & Dixon, P. (2003). *Psychonarratology: Foundations for the empirical study of literary response.* New York: Cambridge University Press.
- **Book, edited**
  Schram, D.H. & Steen, G. (Eds) (2001). *The psychology and sociology of literature.* Amsterdam, Philadelphia: John Benjamins.
- **Article in edited book**
  Gerrig, R.J. (1988). Text comprehension. In R.J. Sternberg & E.E. Smith, (Eds). *The Psychology of Human Thought* (pp. 242–266). Cambridge: Cambridge University Press.
- **Web document on university program or department Web site**

Chandler, D. (1995) *Text and the Construction of Meaning*. Retrieved April 14, 2004, from University of Wales, Aberysthwyth, Web site: http://www.aber.ac.uk/media/Documents/short/texts.html
- **Stand-alone Web document (no date)**
  Nielsen, M. E. (n.d.). *Reading Hypertext. Theoretical ambitions empirical studies*. Retrieved April 13, 2004, from http://www.daf.uni-muenchen.de/DAF/PERSONEN/PEERDE/REDES/MIALL_Vortrag_Hypertext.pdf
- **Stand-alone Web document (no author, no date)**
  How has new technology changed your life? (n.d.). Retrieved April 4, 2004, from http://newsvote.bbc.co.uk/mpapps/pagetools/print/news.bbc.co.uk/2/hi/talking_point/33...

12.2.5.2. Citing sources MLA style

- **Journal article, one author**
  Cupchik, Gerald. "Emotion in Aesthetics: Reactive and Reflective Models." Poetics 23 (1994): 177–188.
- **Article, two authors**
  Benjafield, John and Keith McFarlane. "Preference for proportions as a function of context." Empirical Studies of the Arts 15:2 (1997): 143–151.
- **Article or Chapter in Anthology**
  Sinclair, John McH. "Lines about 'Lines'". *Language and Literature*. Ed. Ronald Carter. London: George Allen & Unwin, 1982, 163–176.
- **Book, one author**
  Simpson, Paul. *Language, Ideology and Point of View*, London: Routledge, 1993.
- **Book, two authors**
  Van Dijk, Teun A. and Walter Kintsch. *Strategies of Discourse Comprehension*. New York: Academic Press, 1983.
- **Book, edited**
  Cameron, Deborah, ed. *The Feminist Critique of Language. A Reader*. London and New York: Routledge, 1990.

2.6. Some words of caution

- **Length:** a question that is often asked is how long the manuscript should be. A general norm has emerged of something like 20 to 25 pages with spacing 1.5 or double, including references and illustrations. Many journals today refer to length in terms of word count (6,000 words, etc.) Although in some cases it may be useful to submit manuscripts (often abbreviated as MSS.) that are shorter or longer, if you follow this norm, you may assume you are on the safe side, at least where length is concerned. We would like to note in passing that for this reason, there is good ground to make students write seminar papers of about 20 to 25 pages too, so that they get used to dealing with this length of writing.

- **Spelling:** do run a spelling check often but do not rely on it totally. Sometimes the spelling check may accept a word that is not the one you really intended. So, if you check your writing often enough, you may pick up problems like the use of *rely* instead of *reply*, which no computer will notice. Always ask someone else to read the paper for you before you submit it. This is not just because you wish someone else to check your spelling, your grammar, and your style, but also to receive feedback on the content of your article: whether its content is clearly presented, whether the arguments hold, whether your conclusions follow from your observation, etc. You should realize that even senior professionals in the field do this as a standard practice: you can witness that in the many thanks that are included in published books and articles, where often the first acknowledgement is to the people who have read earlier versions of the manuscript. If you are in doubt, read the preface to some academic books and see for yourself what we mean. You will realize that even highly famous people often rely heavily on many such earlier readers of their manuscripts.
- **Distancing yourself from your work:** if you have the time, let your article sit for a couple of days – perhaps even a week or more. You yourself will read the paper with different eyes and be able to produce a better revision.

12.2.7. Final checklist before submitting

Here are some points you should check at this stage. Have you:

- Double spaced throughout the entire manuscript?
- Used margins at least one inch (2.5 cm) throughout?
- Checked whether all the works that you refer to are included in the Reference section? Have you also checked the other way round?
- Verified whether all the works that you mention in the Reference section are actually referred to in your text?

- Done a final check of your spelling?
- Asked a colleague to read the final draft for you before sending it out?
- Reread your final version one last time before sending it out?

12.2.8. Submitting your paper

When sending out your article, you should accompany it by a covering letter, a (fictive) example of which could run along the following lines.

Date
Dr Johnson, Editor, *Journal of Empirical Cultural Studies*
Address

Dear Dr Johnson,

Please find, hereby enclosed, five copies of my manuscript "Do ethnic jokes contribute to the formation and maintenance of stereotypes? A qualitative-quantitative study" for publication in your *Journal of Empirical Cultural Studies*.
The article, which is not under review by any other journal, contains original material which I believe is of relevance to the readers of your journal.
I look forward to hearing from you.
Yours truly,
Signature.

As you derive from the above example, many journals request that you send multiple copies. Why this is so is explained in the next paragraph.

- In a refereed journal, your manuscript will be sent to two or three colleagues (hence the multiple copies, which avoid the editor having to do all the copying himself) – which is why the practice is called 'peer review'. They will receive it together with a covering letter from the editor requesting that they indicate both the quality of the work and a recommendation whether to publish or not. Reviewers are often asked to indicate the quality of your work on the kind of scales you are now familiar with, such as, for instance, the following:
    o   Is the manuscript innovative in some way?
        (1)   (2)   (3)   (4)   (5)
    o   Is the conceptual part of the manuscript clear?
        (1)   (2)   (3)   (4)   (5)
    o   Has the existing literature been reviewed adequately?
        (1)   (2)   (3)   (4)   (5)

- Is the design of the study adequate for its purposes?
  (1)   (2)   (3)   (4)   (5)
- Has the research been carried out properly?
  (1)   (2)   (3)   (4)   (5)
- Is the statistical treatment of the data appropriate?
  (1)   (2)   (3)   (4)   (5)
- Are the results interpreted correctly?
  (1)   (2)   (3)   (4)   (5)

Journals will differ in their approach and style in this respect, but all refereed journals give instructions of some kind or other to judge the quality of the work under consideration, and as you can see from the example, the process works as a kind of vetting procedure.

- As to the recommendations, these usually come in four variants. (1) Publish as it stands – something better not to expect! (2) Publish with minor alterations (usually typos, small bibliographical errors, correcting a sentence here and there. (3) Publish after serious revision (along the lines indicated by the referees). (4) Do not publish. You should realize that most submissions are returned with recommendation (3) or (4), so do not despair if you do not get (1) or (2) on your first round!
- When the reviewers are ready with their evaluation, they will send in their reports. On the basis of these, the editor will send you his summary and decision. How long this process will take, is difficult to say in general. Most journals try to let you have a decision as soon as possible, but this will at least take months, as editors have often to deal with dozens of submissions on a monthly basis. Do not become dissatisfied if you do not have an answer after a fortnight, as publishing in journals and learned books is often an exercise in patience. One of the authors of this book may hold a record in this respect: between the moment of submission and the actual publication of one of his articles lay nine years!
- Note that as author you are the one who is responsible for copyright permission. Hence if your article contains longer quotes from texts, or whole (literary) texts, you should seek copyright permission. Make sure that you learn about the rules of copyright in case you are citing long stretches of text, adverts, poems, etc. It would be interesting for you to check details in http://promo.net/pg/vol/pd.html and http://www.utsystem.edu/ogc/intellectualproperty/copypol2.htm
- If your results were presented earlier in a paper at a conference, you may mention this in a note. It is courteous to thank any discussants who provided you with interesting remarks – or indeed to thank the audience in general.

12.3. Poster sessions

The last section in this Chapter includes a very typical event at an international conference: a poster session. Being invited to present a poster means that in a room filled with rows of bulletin boards you will find one that is reserved for you. This is where you can put up your poster, briefly describing, or rather *showing* your research project. Here and there you will see other researchers too, busy with pushpins or Sellotape, trying to get their poster hanging straight. After a while, people will be pouring in. Researchers will be standing next to their bulletin boards, awaiting the audience, ready to explain their research project and become engaged in discussions.

The reason behind such an event is, first of all, one of efficiency. While you will often have just two paper presentations in one hour, you can have many more poster presentations in the same amount of time. As a visitor, you have much more flexibility to quickly browse around, check out projects, select those that are of particular importance to your own work, and interact with the researchers. As a presenter, you will have the unique opportunity to meet people who share your research interests, discuss alternative explanations of your findings, get the feedback that you need to improve your future work, or maybe even make contacts for joint research. Poster sessions are an excellent environment for networking, which is essential for good research. Young researchers generally find their way into the international academic world first through poster sessions. However, senior researchers understand the advantages of poster presentations just as well, and sometimes prefer them to paper presentations. Because you will, in general, have a greater chance of being invited to present a poster rather than a conference paper, we will give you some suggestions on how to make one (see Hess & Lieger, 2004, and many other websites for more tips, examples, and software).

What *is* a poster? It is simply a large piece of paper (or a number of A4 sheets), stuck on a board, that presents (a) the title of your project, (b) your name, and that of your university, (c) an abstract, (d) a brief introduction, (e) your hypotheses, (f) the method of your study, (g) possibly a description of your apparatus, (h) the results, preferably in a few tables or figures, (i) your conclusions, and (j) a brief list of references.

We can give you some general guidelines for preparing your poster. Keep in mind though, that the conference organizers may have their own requirements. Also, as to planning, when you are new to all this, it will probably cost you a lot of time to prepare a poster: count on at least a week for planning and producing the presentation.

12.3.1. Preparations

The first step is to find out whether there are indeed rules for poster presentations issued by the conference organizers. This may sounds too obvious to you, but do not underestimate the number of times people ignore the obvious. For example, it may save some time (and embarrassment) to find out what the required size of your poster is. Second, before you get to work, reread the abstract that you submitted. Often it is months after you sent it in. Check whether the information is still valid.

One rule of thumb is that your audience should be able to understand the purpose and the results of your study in two minutes, or preferably even less. To be able to do this, you first need to reflect on the central message that you want to bring across.

Here is another important hint: first make a sketch of your poster. One way to go about this is to first draw a number of columns (four, five at most). People will walk past your poster: organizing your information in columns instead of horizontally, allows for more people to be reading your poster simultaneously, and facilitates traffic in the (sometimes crowded) room. Considering the way people are used to read texts, it makes sense to have the introduction to your study at the top left, and the conclusion at the bottom right (see Figure 12.2)

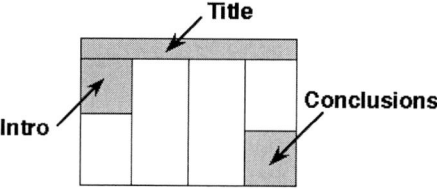

Figure 12.2: Example of a poster layout

What lies between the introduction and conclusion can be filled with a description of your methods and results. Plan how to arrange this information. For this you need to keep two things in mind. First, posters are very much a visual medium. If you can summarize your information in a smart looking graph, or make a statement with a cartoon or photo, do so! Remember, though, that it cannot replace the content of your poster. Second, try to make a clear distinction between the essence of what you want to communicate and the details. Distinguish these in your presentation too, and make use of layout to do so. Even better, leave out the details; you can discuss them when someone starts asking questions.

Your sketch should also include a plan for sizes and fonts. As to the title: make sure it is visible from 4 to 6 meters (15–20 feet) away. Therefore, make your title 4 centimeters high (1.5 inch), and your name and that of your university a bit smaller. Use a font that is easy to read, like Arial, Geneva or Helvetica. If space allows, include your first name; this will facilitate interaction with your audience. Choose the shortest possible name of your institute or university. Sometimes the conference organizers assign a poster number to your presentation; do not forget to include it in your title.

The font of the section headings (e.g. Method, Results, etc.) should be at least 36 pt. Use a font of 24 pt for the (brief but crystal-clear) figure captions, and 18 pt for the text itself. You want to attract people's attention, so using colors may help but keep in mind that your central aim is transparency, and too many different colors can be confusing.

12.3.2. Graphs, tables, illustrations

Make sure that people can clearly see your visual material from a distance of around 2 meters (6 feet). The title, as explained above, should be visible from a greater distance. The graphs and figures should be self-explanatory, so that in your text you need few words to explain what can be seen. Do not include data that are not discussed in the text. Do not use unnecessary grid lines in tables and figures. You may want to use arrows to direct viewers' attention from one section to another. Use substantial borders around the visual material to distinguish things from other information.

12.3.3. The text

As for the other aspects of your poster, restrict the text to what is absolutely necessary. Use double spacing, and align to the left side. Consider using a larger font for the Conclusion section. Try to fit each section on one page. Use short sentences, simple words, and bullets. Avoid jargon and unusual abbreviations. Most importantly, make sure that the take-home message is included (see below).

12.3.4. Making the poster

Before you start actually making the poster, put all the different pieces out on the floor or on a table to get an overview. Is everything clear? Does your poster focus on the central question or are there still superfluous parts that could be omitted? Is everything spelled correctly?

When you are satisfied with your work, the simplest thing to do is to take the model of your poster and go to a copy shop and ask whether they can make it for you. However, this can be quite expensive, and there are cheaper alternatives. Here is what you could do for a title banner: Under the **FILE** menu in Word select **LANDSCAPE** as page set up. Distribute the title, your name, and that of your university over four A4. Let it run over to the next page rather than to the next line. Doing this is quite a puzzle. Take your time to figure it all out. What you want is the text to overlap a little, so you have the second sheet overlapping the first, the third overlapping the second, etc. Make the right hand margin of the first sheet as small as possible, both the left and right margins of the second and third sheet too, and for the last sheet only have a small margin for left side. Restore the normal margin for the last sheet to default. Print the four sheets, and put them on the table to do your final editing. Then use double-sided Sellotape to put the pieces together. You can use a single mat board, or several pieces to have a solid background for your poster. Generally, we would advise you to use soft colors in the background, so as to let your poster stand out well.

Some final suggestion: since poster presentations are places where you make useful contacts, bring your business cards, and an ample supply of copies of a brief version of your paper (also including your contact information, of course). Do not stand or walk too far away from your bulletin board, but make yourself available for discussion or answering questions. Keep a copy of your poster on disk or memory USB pen and preferably also one somewhere on the Internet. Also, bring your own pushpins or Sellotape. The organizers are supposed to take care of sufficient supply, but you never know. If possible, prepare a small envelope or box and glue it on the bottom of your poster. Leave all the information you would like people to take home there, including an outline of your presentation and how to contact you.

12.4. Final words

By now you should be quite ready to carry out your own research and present it to an audience[2]. We hope you have enjoyed the challenges this book has posed and that in return, you feel you want to proceed in empirical work and contribute to studies in the area. In case you still have some doubts, please read the epilogue we prepared for you.

---

[2] We suggest you visit the IGEL website at http://www.igelweb.org

EPILOGUE

As our book comes to a close, we would like to go back to some questions that might have come to your mind as you were working through the concepts and methods. Using empirical methods to study Literature, Arts and other media is still a challenge because of the way we have traditionally been made to think of things in the Humanities. Here we offer some statements by our own students and colleagues that we would like to share with you, in the hope that our discussion of them will help you gain a clearer picture yet of the power of empirical research:

1. *What I have read so far makes me uncertain: there is so much one has to be aware of that such research is not something you can expect from a novice like me.*

That you feel uncertain is definitely not surprising, as doing research is indeed a challenge. But that is true for every new thing you start in life. Is that a reason not to embark on new projects? We view uncertainty as something that can be highly productive.

2. *How can I do this if my professors / university do not foster such a type of investigation?*

This is exactly why this book is needed. Very few scholars have been doing empirical research in the Humanities, and so one will be bound to meet with resistance, as all things new are initially suspect. We hope to have convinced you of the need for empirical research and we hope that, in turn, you will effect changes in your own academic context. If you do not have support for this kind of investigation and you are convinced it is necessary, it is time you started working towards the goals you set for yourself and for the future of research. Here we offer arguments that you can count on. Remember you can find support with other students and scholars from associations like IGEL and REDES, who may share your ideas.

3. Empirical work is too slow: I can cover much more ground by theoretical reflection. Why would I bother to invest so much time and energy in doing this kind of research?

Well, of course we also need people who do theoretical work. But would you not want to know whether your theories are correct? If so, you will need to test them independently, and empirical methods offer you the best way to do so.
There is also another reason why empirical work is a vital complement to theory: the latter is always constrained by our intuitions about the world, and we know that these intuitions are only partially reliable. Empirical data nearly always bring out aspects of reality that we had not thought of, that we might not even have conceived of. These data then lead to new directions in theoretical thinking. The enrichment goes both ways.

4. Empirical research is unpredictable and sometimes the results are upsetting. When doing empirical research, the results may not turn out the way I had predicted. I don't like that. Suppose you work hard to carry out a piece of empirical research, and then the results come out all different from what you had expected. Then I have done all that work for nothing!

What you say is correct, but that is exactly where the great value of empirical work lies: that our ideas about the world can be totally misconceived. If your results show that your expectations were not met, do not despair. You are not alone. Your results may show that nearly everyone else also had misconceptions. One of the healthy aspects of research is that it sometimes proves us to be wrong! So your work is not for nothing, but has actually revealed an important fault in our thinking about the world.

5. But it is so frustrating that the type of studies that students are involved in often leads to the conclusion that there are no differences where you expected there would be.

Of course you may be right. Often there is something seriously wrong in student research projects, sometimes because of mistakes on the part of the students or supervisors, or simply because of practical reasons. But do not disregard your findings too fast. It is always important to note the limitations of your research. If you find that you have to reject a hypothesis that you considered almost too obvious to put to the test, you have made an important contribution to our knowledge. Now we know that, given the circumstances of your study, the attempt to falsify the hypothesis succeeded. Anyone who would have asked you why you waste time proving the obvious, was now shown to be wrong.

6. *Students have to study so many disciplines they get mixed up… I do not know how to make connections with all that I have been learning.*

If students get mixed up, it is often the fault of their teachers… Teaching certainly is not an easy task, and demands a lot of creativity and dedication. But we should do our best to make sure that the points are clear and that our students learn how to make connections. As Richard Feynman, a famous physicist and physics teacher, said the aim of teaching should be to explain even the most complex things in such a way that anyone can understand them. As to be getting a bit mixed up, do not forget that often that can be fruitful too. Sometimes it is also unavoidable, because you are learning things that are contrary to your entrenched ideas. And entrenched ideas are not very productive in the realm of research.

7. *I simply can't believe that students are able to do research.*

What can we say? Ours certainly are. On the website of one of us (van Peer), there is a list with the names of students who have presented their research results at international conferences, with their e-mail addresses: you can contact them if you want, and ask about their experiences. You can also see the papers that have been published by other students of ours, both by graduate and undergraduate students. The website of REDES (www.redes.de) gives further evidence of the research that students were (and are!) involved in.

8. *OK, perhaps some students can, those who are especially gifted or highly motivated.*

Although some of them may be, and although we are very proud of our students, we are convinced that they are not particularly different from you. And do not forget that one of us works in a developing country, where there are very few resources for students in terms of infrastructure and online access to periodicals. Nevertheless, these students go to international conferences, give papers and publish their work. Students learn how to work in research teams where they support each other.

9. *The kind of research dealt with in this book is a kind of psychology, and has little to do with literature or culture.*

Why draw such strict boundaries? Isn't it interesting to venture out in different directions and in different fields? Literature, arts, and media certainly have a lot to do with psychology. It used even to be said that psychology students can learn more about the human soul through reading literary works or watching plays. For instance, emotions are an important issue in culture, both in the sense that a lot of literature or art is 'about' different kinds of emotions, but also in the sense that most people read literature or go to museums because they want to experience particular forms of emotions. Why not use the tools of emotion psychology to understand such issues at a more than superficial level?

10. *I know that if I have to present something in front of an international audience, I will be so nervous that I will not be able to bring out a single word.*

That may be what you think but in reality things are often different. If you have prepared yourself in the way we have described in Chapter 12, and if you have tried out your paper a couple of times before a group of peers, as we strongly recommend, you will not be as nervous as you initially believe, because you know nothing can go wrong. Here your teachers should coach you, of course, and make sure you receive the right kind of support that will see you through the ordeal.

11. *Research may be all well and good, but I see little use for it – it is all too far away from the real world. I am more something of a practical person, I prefer to get on with a job!*

Research is eminently practical. It is about questions we have in daily life, real questions, to which we need real answers. Getting into research is trying to find practical solutions to such real problems, solutions that help us improve our world. We would say: yes, get on with the practical work of research immediately: we need such practical people in research! It is high time Humanities researchers leave the armchair and go out into the world, where their insights and skills are needed!

12. *In what way can empirical studies help me to interpret literary texts, plays, films, etc?*

There are many ways in which empirical investigations can help us to interpret cultural artifacts. For instance, by showing which devices are the most important ones in people's reactions, or by showing in what way a particular device guides readers' attention, or how certain features bring forward unexpected emotional reactions. But it is important to ask why interpretations should be that important in the first place. It certainly does not play a predominant role in cultural life outside the university. Empirical research of culture is its own justification, in that it investigates questions of culture in its own right.

13. *How can I be certain that what I found in my research is the case generally speaking?*

If you still have this question in mind, you should go back to Chapters 9–11. There we showed that this is possible with the help of statistics. As a matter of fact, this is one of the great advantages of empirical research: it allows you to reach reliable conclusions on how strongly your generalizations can be made (or not). Much non-empirical work is just guessing.

14. *OK, you do an empirical investigation, but there are dozens of factors that you cannot control which may influence the results.*

That is right, and in principle you never know which factors are at play. The only thing you can do is to try to control as much as possible, to approach the problem from different angles and with different methods, and in the end compare all the information and try to draw conclusions from it.

15. *I cannot think of an exciting and original topic to research by myself. I have to ask my supervisor if he or she knows one.*

This is not just a problem for you: finding a good question or formulating a problem in the right way is even a difficult task for experienced researchers. But that is exactly why you must start training yourself in this respect immediately. Also, there is no way out: you simply have to go on trying. In our practice with our students, we tend to avoid providing topics at all cost, because developing hypotheses is an integral part of the research process. (A different situation is the one in which several researchers work together on a common project – there it will be necessary to divide various aspects of the problem, and hence it may happen that one gets a particular topic assigned.)

16. *All individuals are different, so my results will not apply to individuals other than the ones who took part in my research.*

In some respects this is correct, in that no two people are identical. However, empirical results usually allow you to detect general patterns and tendencies. Even when these do not apply to every single individual, maybe not even to *any* individual at all, such conclusions are nevertheless insightful, as they reveal underlying structures and regularities in the real world. Moreover, your statistical analyses will also allow you to accurately describe how strongly (or weakly) individual respondents agree to these general patterns and tendencies.

So even if we cannot say much about individuals, the information gained in this way is nevertheless important if we wish to understand how culture functions.

17. *Most research described here has been done with students as participants. So one cannot say anything about the way other people respond to art, music, film, or literature.*

The first sentence is absolutely correct. The question is, however, whether the 'so' in the second sentence is valid. In many cases, where we are investigating cognitive reactions to art works, we may not have good reasons why students would differ in their reactions from other groups. In other studies, however, there may well be reasons to expect such differences to show up. In general, however, you are right and we wish to encourage you to use other groups of people as respondents. Interesting locations to find participants are places where people have to, or are inclined to, kill time, such as airports, railway and bus stations, schools, the entrance of a zoo, theatres, concert halls, etc.

18. *Instead of empirical studies it is much more important to bring forward new interpretations of texts, plays, or movies.*

What is so special about interpretation that it deserves a prominent place? We do not wish to downplay the importance of interpreting cultural products, but we have serious hesitations about the overworked emphasis on interpretation that has been the current fashion in cultural studies. There are many aspects to culture and its functioning that need to be studied if we wish to understand human culture at a deeper level, and interpretation is certainly not the only, not even the best, method for getting there. We are also a bit critical of the armchair approach that most interpretations involve.

19. *If you want me to do research, you put me on the level of my lecturers and professors, so there is no difference between students and staff any more!*

That is right! When it comes to research, we are all equal – or near-equal, because some people have more talent, and staff has more experience. But research is basically an anti-authoritarian business, which fares best without strong hierarchies. Instead, we recommend reliance on flat organizational structures, easy and open access to resources, and efficient and egalitarian communication between all involved.

20. *I am simply afraid of getting involved in research.*

That is an honest reaction, and one that a lot of students have initially. After all, it is something that involves new and complex skills that you have not practiced before. Here lies an important task for your supervisor(s): the best way is to bring these emotions into the open, not to suppress them, and look for ways to deal with them. Bertrand Russell always emphasized that the ultimate goal of education should be to get rid of fear!

21. *Making students do research is a way to let students do the work that staff should do. In that way life becomes rather easy for staff members.*

If you have never done research yourself, you have not been at a university, but instead at some kind of extended school, since producing new knowledge is what distinguishes a university from a school. But what we have advocated in this book is not that students do research to replace the research done by staff. Instead, it complements it. And it is certainly *not* the case that making students carry out research makes the life of staff members easier. Our experience is that the opposite is the case: it demands much more involvement on the part of the staff – but is also much more rewarding.

22. *In order to achieve real insight, one has to do dozens or more empirical investigations.*

That is why we have no time to lose, but should start right away. And that is why we should work together, also in teams, to study particular problems in a coherent and efficient way. And that is why we need to network and create efficient communication channels, so that we can disseminate new insights and developments rapidly.

23. *My time is simply too valuable to be lost on such small-scale investigations as the ones outlined here.*

Then you must be a really important person! Because even Nobel Prize winners do this kind of research. In many cases, they are even given that prestigious prize *because* of such small-scale investigations that they have carried out. It is a misconception that research is only (or mainly) about 'big' questions.

24. *If we all do empirical research, we will be isolated from each other and there will be no interaction in the classroom any more.*

Quite the contrary. Good research is done in teams, where information is exchanged regularly, even internationally, where methods and results are critically discussed, where people cast ever wider nets of communication by going to conferences, workshops, summer schools, and the like. On another note: do you really need classroom interaction? Is it not much more profitable to learning if we abolish the classroom and start doing research actively? The idea that one has to sit in a seminar room each week for a number of hours, and that this is the best way to learn is in sharp contrast to almost everything we know about knowledge acquisition and dissemination. We invite you to critically gauge the value of traditional teaching methods in the Humanities …

25. *I cannot see research as part of my life as a whole … where does it fit? And what do I get from all this investment in research?*

That is a very important question, and one that needs your personal answer, not ours. The only thing we can give as a testimony is that having done research, even in a limited way, is enrichment to life, to critical thinking, and to one's satisfaction with one's position in the world.

BIBLIOGRAPHY

Aaftink, C. (2004, August). *Reading related to pivotal life experiences.* Paper presented at the Ninth Conference of the International Society for the Empirical Study of Literature and Media, Edmonton, Canada.
American Psychological Association (1994). *Publication manual of the American Psychological Association,* 4th ed. Washington, DC: American Psychological Association.
Andringa, E. (1986). Perspektivierung und Perspektivenübernahme: Zur Wahrnehmung literarischer Figuren. *Spiel, 5,* 135–146.
Bailey, K.M. (1990). The use of diary studies in teacher education programs. In J.C. Richards & D. Nunan, (Eds). *Second language teacher education* (pp. 215–226). Cambridge: Cambridge University Press.
Baker, R. & Wright, H. (1955). *Midwest and its children.* Evanston, IL: Row, Peterson.
Bales, R. & Cohen, S. (1979). *SYMLOG: A system for multiple level observation of groups.* New York: Free Press.
Bandura, A., Ross, D. & Ross, S.A. (1963). Imitation of film-mediated aggressive models. *Journal of Abnormal and Social Psychology, 66,* 3–11.
Barros, H. S.(2003). Desfamiliarização ou Preferência? O Estranhamento na Cidade de Deus. *Caderno de Letras 20,* 121-127.
Bauer, M.W. (2000) Classical content analysis. In M. W. Bauer & Gaskell, G.. (Eds). *Qualitative Researching with Text, Image and Sound: A Practical Handbook* (pp. 131–151). London: Sage.
Bechtel, R. (1967). Hodometer research in museums. *Museum News,* March, 23--5.
Bechtel, R.B. & Zeisel, J. (1987) Observation: The world under a glass. In R.B. Bechtel, R.W. Marans & W.M. Michelson, (Eds.). *Methods in environmental and behavioral research* (pp. 11–40). New York: Van Nostrand Reinhold.
Berlyne D.E. (1971). *Aesthetics and Psychobiology.* New York: Appleton-Century-Crofts.
Birdwhistell, R. (1970). *Kinesics in context: Essays on body motion communication.* Philadelphia: University of Pennsylvania Press.
Bourg, T., Risden, K., Thompson, S. & Davis, E.C. (1993). The effects of an empathy-building strategy on 6th graders' causal inferencing in narrative text comprehension. *Poetics, 22,* 117–133.

Bower, G.H. (1978). Experiments on story comprehension and recall. *Discourse Processes*, *1*, 211–231.
Brace, N., Kemp, R. & Snelgar, R. (2003). *SPSS for Psychologists; A guide to data analysis using SPSS for Windows*. New York: Palgrave.
Bronowski, J. (1976). *The Ascent of Man*. London: BBC.
Cantor, J. (1984). Effect of forewarning on emotional responses to a horror film. *Journal of Broadcasting*, *28* (1), 21–31.
Cantor, J., Ziemke, D. & Sparks, G. (1984). The effect of forewarning on emotional responses to a horror film. *Journal of Broadcasting*, *28*, 21–31.
Carp, F.M. & Carp, A. (1981). The validity, reliability and generalizability of diary data. *Experimental Aging Research*, *7*, 281–296.
Conrad, F.G. & Schrober, M.F. (2000). Clarifying question meaning in a household telephone survey. *Public Opinion Quarterly*, *64* (1), 1–28.
Cook, Th. and D.T. Campbell. (1979). Quasi-experimentation : design and analysis issues for field settings. Boston: Houghton Mifflin
Davis, S. & Andringa, E. (1995). "Narrrative Structure and emotional response". In G. Rusch, (Ed.). *Empirical Approaches to Literature* (pp. 50–60). Siegen: Lumis-Publications.
Descartes, R. (1637/2006). A Discourse on the Method. New York: Oxford University Press, 2006.
Dilthey, W. (1985). *Poetry and experience. Selected Works*, vol. V. New Jersey: Princeton University Press.
Dilthey, W. (1994). The hermeneutics of the human sciences. In K. Mueller-Vollmer (Ed.), *The hermeneutics reader: texts of the German tradition from the enlightenment to the present*. New York, NY: Continuum.
Earthman, E.A. (1992). Creating the virtual work: Readers' processes in understanding literary texts. *Research in the Teaching of English*, *26*, 351–384.
Field, A. (2005). Discovering statistics using SPSS : (and sex, drugs and rock 'n' roll). London: Sage.
Flerx, V.C., Filder, D.S. & Rogers, R.W. (1976). Sex role stereotypes: Developmental aspects and early intervention. *Child Development*, *47*, 998–1007.
Flower, L.S. & Hayes, J.R. (1981). A cognitive process theory of writing. *College Composition and Communication*, *32* (4), 365–387.
Freud, S. (1975). *The psychopathology of everyday life*. In J. Strachey (Ed. & Transl.) *The Pelican Freud Library*, vol. 5, Harmondsworth and New York: Penguin.
—. (1979). *On psychopathology*. In J. Strachey (Ed. & Transl.) *The Pelican Freud Library*, vol. 10, Harmondsworth and New York: Penguin.

—. (1984). *On metapsychology: The theory of psychoanalysis*. In J. Strachey (Ed. & Transl.) *The Pelican Freud Library*, vol. 11, Harmondsworth and New York: Penguin.

Frost, W. (1969). The development of a technique for TV programme assessment. *Journal of the Market Research Society, 11,* 25–44.

Gadamer, H.G. (1975). *Truth and method.* New York, NY: Continuum.

Gerrig, R.J. & Prentice, D.A. (1991). The representation of fictional information. *Psychological Science, 2,* 336–340.

Gibbs, A. (n.d.). *Focus Groups.* Retrieved December 28, 2004, from http://www.soc.surrey.ac.uk/sru/SRU19.html.

Gibson, R., Aust, C.F. & Zillmann, D. (2000). Loneliness of adolescents and their choice and enjoyment of love-celebrating versus love-lamenting popular music. *Empirical Studies of the Arts, 18* (1), 43–48.

Goodwin, C.J. (2002). *Research in psychology: Methods and design.* New York: Wiley.

Goss J.D. & Leinbach T.R. (1996). Focus groups as alternative research practice. *Area, 28* (2), 115–23.

Hakemulder, J. (2000) *The Moral Laboratory.* Amsterdam: John Benjamins.

Hawkes, D.L. (1990). *Communicating your results*: *A guide for postgraduates.* Wales: The Polytechnic of Wales.

Hess, R.G. and Lieger, L.H. (2004) *Creating effective poster presentations.* Retrieved June 6, 2005 from http://www.ncsu.edu/project/posters/

Holland, N. (1975). *Five readers reading.* New Haven: Yale University Press.

Homan, R. (1991). *Ethics in Social Research.* Harlow: Longman.

Hunt, M. (1993). *History of Psychology.* Philadelphia: Temple University Press.

Iser, W. (1975). Die Appellstruktur der Texte. In R. Warning, (Ed.). Rezeptionsisthetik Theorie und Praxis (pp. 228–52). München: Fink.

—. (1978). *The Act of Reading: A Theory of Aesthetic Response.* Baltimore: Johns Hopkins University Press.

Kelle, U. (Ed.). (1995). *Computer-aided qualitative data analysis: Theory, methods and practice.* London: Sage Publications Ltd.

Kinkade, R.G. (1974). *Thesaurus of psychological index terms.* Washington: APA.

Kitzinger, J. (1995). Introducing focus groups. *British Medical Journal, 311,* 299–302.

Kreuger, R.A. (1988). *Focus groups: a practical guide for applied research.* London: Sage.

Lachenmann, J. (1999). *Interviews mit Lesenden. Wirkungen von Literatur auf Musiker und Mediziner. [Interviews with readers. Effects of literature on musicians and physicians].* Unpublished MA-thesis, University of Munich.

Limbert, W.M. & Polzella, D.J. (1998). Influence of music style on observers' perception of representational and abstract paintings. *Empirical Studies of the Arts*, 16.1, 33–39.

Martindale, C. (1990) *The Clockwork Muse*. New York: Basic Books, Harper Collins Publishers.

McInerney, D.M. (2001). *Publishing your Psychology research: A guide to writing for journals in psychology and related fields*. London: Sage.

McNamara, C. (n.d.). *Basics of Conducting Focus Groups*. Retrieved December 28, 2004, from http://www.mapnp.org/library/evaluatn/focusgrp.htm.

Mattos, M.J. & Mendes, M. (2002) Grupo de Enfoque na Ciência Empírica da Literatura: atitude dos alunos em relação à literatura. Paper presented at the III ECEL (Encontro de Ciência Empírica da Literatura) in Rio de Janeiro.

Mendes, M. & Menezes, D. (2003) The influence of authorial prestige on Brazilian students. Paper Presented at the IV ECEL (Encontro de Ciência Empírica da Literatura) in Rio de Janeiro.

Merton, R.K. & Kendall, P.L. (1946). The Focused Interview. *American Journal of Sociology*, *51*, 541–557.

Miall, D.S. (1990). Readers' response to narrative: Evaluating, relating, anticipating. *Poetics*, *19*, 323–339.

Morgan, D.L. (1988). *Focus groups as qualitative research*. London: Sage.

Morgan, D.L., Krueger, R.A. & King, J.A. (1998). *The focus group kit*. Thousand Oaks, California: Sage.

Morris, D. (1977). *Manwatching: A field guide to human behavior*. London: Cape.

Patton, M.Q. (1990). *Qualitative evaluation and research methods*. Newsbury Park: Sage.

Piaget, J. (1948). *The moral judgment of the child*. M. Gabain, (Transl.). Glencoe, IL: Free Press.

Plato (1906). *The Trial and Death of Socrates*. F. J. Church (Transl.), New York: Macmillan and Company, Ltd.

Powell, R.A. & Single H.M. (1996). Focus groups. *International Journal of Quality in Health Care*, *8* (5), 499–504.

Powell, R.A., Single, H.M. & Lloyd, K.R. (1996). Focus groups in mental health research: enhancing the validity of user and provider questionnaires. *International Journal of Social Psychology*, *42* (3), 193–206.

Radway, J.A. (1984). *Reading the romance; women, patriarchy, and popular literature*. Chapel Hill: University of North Carolina Press.

Riessman, C.K. (1993). *Narrative analysis*. London: Sage.

Rogers, E.M. & Shoemaker, F.F. (1971). *Communication of innovations: A cross-cultural approach*. New York: Free Press.

Rose, J. (2001) *The Intellectual Life of the British Working Classes*. Cambridge MA: Yale University Press.
Russell, B. (1999). *The Problems of Philosophy*. NY: Dover Publications
—. (2006). *The Conquest of Happiness*. NY & London: Routledge.
Saris, W. & Stronkhorst, H. (1984). *Causal modelling in nonexperimental research*. Amsterdam: Sociometric Research Foundation.
Schreier, M. (2001). Qualitative methods in studying text reception. In D. Schram & G. Steen (Eds.). *The Psychology and Sociology of Literature* (pp. 35-56). Amsterdam & Philadelphia: John Benjamins.
Shklovsky, V. (1917/1965) Art as Technique. In L.T. Lemon and M. Reis (Eds.). *Russian Formalist Criticism* (pp. 3–24). Nebraska: University of Nebraska Press.
Sinclair, J.McH. (1991). *Corpus, concordance, collocation*. Oxford: Oxford University Press.
—. (Ed.). (1987). *Looking up*. London & Glasgow: Collins ELT.
Skaife, A.M. (1967) The role of deviation and complexity in changing musical taste. *Proceedings of the American Psychological Association*, Vol. 2, pp. 25–26.
Slater, A., Quinn, P.C., Hayes, R. & Brown, E. (2000). The role of facial orientation in newborn infants' preference for attractive faces. *Developmental Science, 3* (2), 181–185.
Snow, C.P. (1959/1993). *The two cultures*. Cambridge: Cambridge University Press.
Sternberg, R.J. (1988). *The Psychologist's Companion: A guide to scientific writing for students and researchers*. Cambridge: Cambridge University Press.
Stolnitz, Jerome (1991). On the Historical Triviality of Art. *The British Journal of Aesthetics, 31*, 195–202.
Van Peer, W. (2001). Justice in Perspective. *New Perspectives on Narrative Perspective*. In W. Van Peer & S. Chatman (Eds) (pp. 325–38) .Albany, NY: SUNY Press.
Van Peer, W. & Stöger, I. (2001). Psycho-Analysts and Day-Dreaming. In G. Steen & D. Schram (Eds) *The Psychology and Sociology of Literature* (pp. 185–200). Amsterdam / Philadelphia: John Benjamins.
Van Peer, W., Zyngier, S. & Hakemulder, F. (2007) "Foregrounding: Past, Present, Future". In D. Hoover (Ed.). *Prospect and Retrospect. Papers from the Poetics and Linguistics Association International Conference, New York, 2004*. Amsterdam / Atlanta: Rodopi (in press).
West, R.F., Stanovich, K.E. & Mitchell, H.R. (1993). Reading in the real world and its correlates. *Reading Research Quarterly, 28* (1), 34–50.

Windelband, W. (1894). *Geschichte und Naturwissenschaft*. Straßburg: Straßburger Rektoratsrede.
Zill, N. & Winglee, M. (1990). *Who reads literature?* Cabin John, MD: Seven Locks Press.
Zillmann, D. & Bryant, J. (1975). Viewer's moral sanction of retribution in the appreciation of dramatic representations. *Journal of Experimental Social Psychology*, *13*, 155–165.
Zwaan, R. A. (1991). Some parameters of literary and news comprehension: Effects of discourse-type perspective on reading rate and surface structure representation. *Poetics*, *20*, 139–156.

Some Relevant URLs

APA Style: http://www.uwsp.edu/psych/apa4b.htm or
http://www.vanguard.edu/faculty/ddegelman/index.cfm?doc_id=796 or
http://webster.commnet.edu/apa/apa_index.htm.
Bulletin of Psychology and the Arts:
http://www.apa.org/divisions/div10/bulletin.html.
Creativity Research Journal: http://www.leaonline.com/loi/crj?cookieSet=1 and
http://gort.ucsd.edu/newjour/c/msg03406.html.
Culture and Psychology: http://www.sagepub.com/journal.aspx?pid=23.
Discourse Processes: http://www.psyc.memphis.edu/dp/dp.htm.
Empirical Studies of the Arts: http://ume.maine.edu/~iaea/esaabstr.html and
http://www.baywood.com/journals/previewjournals.asp?id=0276-2374.
IAEA (International Association of Empirical Aesthetics):
http://www.ume.maine.edu/~iaea/.
IGEL (Internationale Gesellschaft für Empirische Literaturwissenschaft):
http://www.arts.ualberta.ca/igel/ or
http://www.lumis.uni-siegen.de/igel/en/frames.htm.
Imagination, Cognition and Personality:
http://www.baywood.com/journals/previewjournals.asp?id=0276-2366.
Journal of Creative Behavior:
http://www.creativeeducationfoundation.org/jcb.shtml.
Journal of Cross-Cultural Psychology:
http://www.sagepub.com/journal.aspx?pid=197.
Language and Literature: http://www.sagepub.com/Journalhome.aspx.
MLA Style: http://webster.commnet.edu/mla/index.shtml or
http://www.wisc.edu/writing/Handbook/DocMLA.html.
PALA (Poetics and Linguistics Association): http://www.pala.lancs.ac.uk/.
Poetics: http://www.elsevier.com/wps/find/.
Poetics Today: http://www.jstor.org/journals/03335372.html.

Society for the Psychology of Aesthetics, Creativity, and the Arts: http://www.apa.org/about/division/div10.html.
STD (Society for Text and Discourse): http://www.psyc.memphis.edu/st&d/st&d.htm.

INDEX OF NAMES

Aaflink, C. 93
Andringa, E. 85, 118
Aristotle 34, 35, 36, 37, 38, 39, 48, 55
Aufenanger, S. 314
Aust, C.F. 124, 125
Bailey, K.M. 86
Baker, R. 85
Bales, R. 106
Bandura, A. 83
Barlow, M. 107
Barros, H.S. 136
Bechtel, R. 81, 82, 106
Benjafield, J. 342
Berlyne, D.E. 11, 12, 14, 162
Bex, A. 338
Birdwhistell, R. 106
Bortolussi, M. 329, 341
Bourg, T. 140, 151
Bower, G. 99, 100, 101, 149
Brace, N. 297
Brake, L. 315
Brody, M. 73
Bronowski, J. 44
Brown, D. 164
Brown, E. 14
Bryant, J. 79, 80
Cameron, D. 342
Campbell, D.T. 81
Cantor, J. 142
Carp, A. 116
Carp, F.M. 116
Carter, R. 342
Chandler, D. 342
Chatman, S. 330
Cohen, S. 106
Conrad, F.G. 130, 131
Cook, T. 81
Csabi, S. 336
Cupchik, G. 341, 342
Davis, S. 85

Descartes, R. 3
Dilthey, W. 2, 3, 4, 5, 6, 7
Dixon, P. 329, 341
Earthman, E.A. 62, 85, 86
Enkvist, N.E. 338
Faulkner, W. 85
Fechner, T. 14
Fenley, W.F. 341
Fialho, O. 325, 329
Field, A. 195, 297, 308, 309
Filder, D.S. 150
Fine, G. A. 327
Flerx, V.C. 150
Freud, S. 20, 21, 47, 73
Frost, W. 87
Gadamer, H.G. 4, 5
Galilei, G. 37, 38, 39, 40, 48
Galton, F. 6
Gauss, C.F. 196
Gerrig, R. 76, 341
Gibbs, A. 95
Gibson, R. 124, 125
Goodwin, C.J. 148
Graesser, A. 337
Habermas, J. 4
Hakemulder, J. 13, 170, 38
Hanson, K. 339
Hayes, R. 14
Holland, N. 93
Hunt, M. 8
Iser, W. 62, 86
Johns, T. 107
Kelle, U. 102
King, C.M. 73
Kintsch, W. 342
Kohl, S. 136
Kuiken, D. 326
Lachenmann, J. 90, 91
Lehmann, L. 11
Levy, S.G. 341

Limbert, W.M. 108, 109, 110
Louwerse, M. 337
MacNamara, C. 96
Martindale, C. 14, 15, 42
Mattos, M.J. 95
McFarlane, K. 342
McGinn, C. 42
Mendes, M. 95, 334
Menezes, D. 325, 334
Mentjes, A. 336
Miall, D. 93, 326
Millán-Varela, C. 338
Mitchell, H.R. 87, 116, 117, 136
Morgan, D.L. 94
Morris, D. 77
Newton, I. 39
Nielsen, M.E. 342
Nuhoff, E. 137
Oostendorp, H. 330
Patton, M.Q. 93
Piaget, J. 79
Plato 2
Polzella, D.J. 108, 109, 110
Popper, K.R. 42, 43, 45, 48, 50, 228, 235
Powell, R.A. 94
Prentice, D.A. 76
Preuss, A. 336
Quinn, P.C. 14
Radway, J.A. 93
Riessman, C.K. 93
Rogers, R.W. 150
Rose, J. 82
Saris, W. 105
Schram, D.H. 341
Schreier, M. 101
Schrober, M.F. 130, 131
Scott, M. 107
Sell, R. 338

Shaughnessy, J.J. 106
Shklovsky, V. 15
Simpson, P. 342
Sinclair, J. 102, 342
Single, H.M. 94
Skaife, A.M. 18
Slater, A. 14
Smith, E.E. 341
Snow, C.P. 5, 6
Socrates 49
Sparks, G. 142
Stanovich, K.E. 87, 116, 117, 136
Steen, G. 341
Sternberg, R.J. 341
Stockwell, P. 338
Stöger, I. 20, 21
Stolnitz, J. 38
Stronkhorst, H. 105
Tan, E. 341
van der Velde, V. v.d. 142
van Dijk, T.A. 342
van Lier, L. 338
van Peer, W. 13, 21, 170, 329, 330, 337
Verdonk, P. 338
West, R.F. 87, 116, 117, 136
Windelband, W. 4
Winglee, M. 131
Wiseman, M. 329
Wright, H. 85
Wundt, W. 1, 8, 9
Zechmeister, E.B. 106
Zeisel, J. 82, 106
Zerkowitz, J. 336
Ziemke, D. 142
Zill, N. 131
Zillmann, D. 79, 80, 124, 125
Zwaan, R. 139, 140, 141
Zyngier, S. 13, 170, 329

INDEX OF SUBJECTS

Abstract 73, 313ff., 325ff.
Activation 12
Advertising 94
Aesthetics 11ff., 109ff.
ALL CASES 188
Alternative explanation 27, 155ff.
Alternative hypothesis 235
ANALYZE 208
ANOVA 194, 278ff., 333
anti-naturalism 3
anxiety 154
APA 82, 341ff.
approximation 38, 49, 55
arithmetic mean 191ff.
arousal potential 12
arousal 12
art history 41
Astronomy 57ff.
Audio tour 108
AURA 87
Authenticity 87, 88
Author Recognition Test 116
authoritarianism 40, 44, 46, 56, 355
automatism 15
bar charts 215ff.
BASIC TABLES 208
behavior checklist 83
bell curve 196ff.
between subjects effects 300
between-subjects design 141ff., 264
Biology 57ff.
birdwatching 77
BIVARIATE 246
block randomization 148
bold hypotheses 48, 56
BONFERRONI 288, 300
Book of Q 54ff.
Box's M test 296
Boxplots 223ff.

CAQD 101
Card-sorting techniques 94
Carry-over effects 146
Case study 157
Category system 84, 94, 95, 101, 102
Causality 2, 60, 97ff., 103, 138ff.
Ceiling effect 123, 160
CELL STATISTICS 210
Central limit theorem 198
Central tendency 191ff.
Ceteris paribus 17, 30, 46
CHART EDITOR 220
CHARTS 254
Checklist 115, 117
Chi-squared test 273, 333
Choice of statistical tests 253ff.
Citations 340
Classical experimental design 148
Clockwork Muse 15
Closed questions 108ff.
Coding 106
Coherence 7, 36, 40, 56
Cohort studies 105
Collative properties 12
Communicating results 312ff.
COMPARE MEANS 260
Comparison of theories 38
Complexity 12, 17ff.
COMPUTE 179ff.
Conceptual model 62ff.
Concordance 102
Conditions 99, 139ff.
Conferences 312ff.
Confounding variables 99, 100, 158, 162, 229ff.
Constant errors 229ff.
Constant-sum rating scale 115, 127
Construct validity 164
Constructs 110

Consumer preferences 94
Content analysis 101ff.
Context of discovery 44ff.
Context of justification 44ff.
Contradiction 7, 35ff.
CONTRASTS 306
Control group 31, 148ff., 152ff.
Control of variables 78, 98
CORRELATE 246
Correlation coefficient 239ff.
Correlation 239ff., 333
Counterbalancing 147ff.
Covariates 293ff.
Creativity 45ff.
Critical tradtion 41, 42, 48
Critique 40ff., 49, 50
Cronbach's alpha 211ff.
Cross-section study 104
CROSSTABS 273ff
culture 3, 5, 6
data collection 75ff.
DATA VIEW 169ff.
Decision flowchart for test selection 259ff.
delayed post-test 150
demarcation criterion 48
dependent variables 99, 110, 138, 171ff.
descriptive research 60
descriptive statistics 190ff.
design matrix 163
developmental psychology 79
direct unobtrusive measures 81
directional hypothesis 238, 266
dispersion 193ff.
dogmatism 46, 56
double blind research 79, 83
dropouts 106, 161
Dualism 3
Effect size 201
Emotional reactions 25, 85, 88, 89, 92, 353
Empirical 7, 20, 37, 40, 55ff
Entering data 177ff.
Entering graphs into Word 210, 217
ERIC 69
Error elimination 44, 46

Errors 28
ESTIMATES OF EFFECT 294
Ethics of research 81
Ethology 57
Evolutionary epistemology 46
Experiment 97ff., 138ff.
Experimental design 141, 148ff.
Experimental factors 157
Experimental group 148ff., 153, 155
Explaining 1ff., 38, 39, 76
Explanatory research 60, 94
Exploratory research 60, 109
EXPLORE 256
EXPORT 222
Exposure to print 116
External validity 161
Extra-experimental factors 148
Extreme values 225
Factorial design 151
FACTORS 306
Fairy tale 20, 21
Fallibilism 46, 48, 228
Falsification 42ff., 55
Family-wise error rate 279
Feasibility 61
Field studies 78, 98, 152
FILTER ON 188
Filter questions 133
Floor effect 123, 160
Foils (in checklist) 117
Folk theory 37
Formulating questions 130
Foundations 35, 39, 50
Fractionation scale 127
F-ratio 281ff.
 Gaps 86
Gauss curve 196ff.
General Linear Model 290ff., 333
Generalization 29, 30, 93, 162, 164
Geology 5, 30
GLM 290ff.
Graphic rating scale 122, 123
Graphs 215ff.
Greenhouse-Geisser's test 309ff.
Group dynamics 97
GROUPING VARIABLE 261

Hawthorne effect 81
Hedonic value 12ff., 17, 18
HISTOGRAMS 254
HOMOGENEITY TESTS 294
Homogeneous sample 101
Horror movies 142ff.
Humor 69ff.
Huynh-Feldt test 309
Hypothesis generation 76, 94
Hypothesis 36, 39, 47, 48, 52, 54, 55, 56, 62
Identification 98, 99, 130
Idiographic 4, 5
IGEL Society 350
Immunization of theories 46ff.
Impartiality 28, 44, 46
Independent evidence 7, 15, 88
INDEPENDENT SAMPLE T-TEST 260
Independent variable 99, 110, 138ff., 171ff.
Indirect unobtrusive measures 82
Individual differences 31, 194ff.
Inference statistics 227ff.
Inference tests (overview) 277
Informed consent 82
Instruction for questionnaire 133
Instruction variable 139ff.
Interaction effect 152, 289
Interaction 19, 162, 275
Interfering variables 99, 100, 158
Internal focalisation 21, 22
Internal validity 156ff.
Interpretation 27, 76, 109, 355
Inter-rater reliability 83
Interval measurement 113, 123
Intervening variables 99, 100, 158, 162, 229ff.
Interview 61, 76, 88ff.
Introspection 7
Itemized rating scale 123ff.
Jpeg files 222
K INDEPENDENT SAMPLES 270ff.
K RELATED SAMPLES 272
Kendall's Tau 251
Kendall's W test 272ff.

Kinkade's Thesaurus 66
Kolmogorov-Smirnov test 255
Kruskal-Wallis test 270ff., 333
KWALITAN 107
KWIC 102
KWOC 102
Laboratory research 98, 152, 162
Latent effects 146
Laughing 69ff.
Layout of questionnaire 134
Learning effects 146
Level of measurement 110, 141
Levene's test 263ff., 286
Likert scale 127
Line graph 222ff.
Lisrel-analysis 105
Literature search 62, 65ff., 131
Logic 36, 39
Long-term effects 151
Magazine Recognition Test 116
Main effect 152, 289ff.
Manipulated factor 27, 139
Manipulating data 179
Manipulation 98, 99
Mann-Whitney test 269ff., 333
MANOVA 291ff.
Marketing research 94
Matching 144
Maturation effect 160
Mauchly's test 308ff.
Mean square 281
Mean 191ff.
Measurement 26, 39, 56, 94, 98
Measures of central tendency 191ff.
Measures of dispersion 193ff.
Media use in presentation 321
Median 192ff.
Metaphor 15, 190
MICROCONCORD 107
Misconception about empirical studies 25ff.
missing values 178
MLA style 342
mode 193
Moderator 95
modesty 29, 49

370 Index of Subjects

Monism 3
MONOCONC 107
Monomethodology 57ff.
Moral beliefs 79
Motion 34ff.
Multiple choice questions 118
Multiple perspectives 96
MULTIVARIATE 290
Naïve participants 141
Narratology 22, 23
naturalism 3
naturalistic observations 81
negative correlation 239ff.
nominal measurement 111, 118
nomological 4, 5
nomothetic 4, 5
non-directional hypothesis 238, 266
non-equivalent control group design 152
non-parametric tests 249; 267
NORMAL CURVE 254
normal distribution 196ff., 234, 253ff.
normality plots 256; 257
note taking 92
novelty 12ff., 42
Null-hypothesis 235ff.
objectivity 27, 28, 44, 46, 83
observation 8, 38, 39, 77ff.
observer bias 82ff.
OLD AND NEW VALUES 184
ONE-WAY ANOVA 283
open-ended questions 109
order effects 146
ordinal measurement 112, 113, 123
orientation in research 84
outliers 192, 225
PAIRED SAMPLE T-TEST 264
panel study 104
parametric tests 251
partial eta square values 299
participatory research 80
Pearson correlation 246
piecemeal engineering 7
Pillai's trace test 298
pilot study 123, 128, 135, 161
placebo control group 153

planning research 61, 65, 84ff., 96ff.
PLOTS 256, 305
pluralism 58
positive correlation 239ff.
Positivism 29, 42, 43
Post hoc tests 288ff.
Poster sessions 313, 346ff.
Post-post test 150
Post-test 142ff., 148
Power 114, 251, 258, 269
prediction 36, 48, 52
preparing a script 315ff.
pretest 142ff., 148
probability 233ff.
problem solving 34, 50
procedure for data collection 135
ProQuest 68
Protocols 85, 86, 92, 93, 95, 101
psychoanalysis 20ff., 31, 47
PsycINFO 65ff.
p-value 233ff.
qualitative methods 58ff., 75ff., 101, 107
quantitative methods 58ff., 75ff., 101
quasi-experiments 98, 163
questionnaire design 131
questionnaires 60, 91, 93, 94, 108ff.
quotations 340
random errors 229ff.
randomization 100, 143, 152, 156
range 193ff.
rank order rating scale 126
ratio measurement 113, 114, 115
reading habits 87
RECODE 183ff.
REDES project xx, 350, 352
REFERENCE CATEGORY 307
Region of rejection 234ff.
Regression line 245
REGRESSION 244
RELATED SAMPLES 267
reliability 23, 87, 97, 110
repeated-measures 142, 145ff., 302ff.
res cogitans 3
Res extensa 3
research design 57ff.

research methodology 57ff.
researcher involvement 80ff.
reverse randomization 148
R-square measure 245ff.
Russian Formalism 42
Sample size 163
SCALE IF ITEM DELETED 213
SCATTER 242
Scatterplot 195, 242ff.
Science fiction 93
Science 2, 4, 6, 7, 20, 33, 50, 55, 56
Semantic dictionaries 102
Semantic differential 109, 128ff.
Semantic precision 39, 41, 63
Semi-structured interview 89
SEPARATE LINES 306
Sequence effects 146
Shapiro-Wilk test 257
Significance level 236ff.
Significance 164, 201, 235ff.
Situation variable 139
Skepsis 49
Social Science Citation Index 69
Solomon design 159ff.
SORT 178
Spearman correlation 246
Speculative methods 7, 20
Sphericity 308ff.
SPSS 165, 166ff.
Standard deviation 194ff., 286
Statistical validity 161
STEM AND LEAF 257
Straight control group 153
Structured interview 89ff.
Structured research 78ff.
Subject reactivity 81ff.
Subject variable 140ff.
Sum of squared errors 196, 281
Survey 103ff.
SYMLOG 106
TABLES 208
TACT 107
Tails 198, 238
Target behavior 78, 83
TARGET VARIABLE 181
Task variable 139

Tautology 7
Taxonomy of measurement 111
Team work 356, 357
Telephone interview 93
Television violence 103
Tendency toward significance 238
Test effects 158
TEST PAIRS 267
Testing 45, 55
Theatre-going habits 104
Theory 25, 34, 36, 39, 43, 54
Think-aloud method 85ff., 136
Third Culture 5, 6, 33
Threats to external validity 162ff.
Three-way design 151
Time intervals 84, 88
TRANSFORM 180
Trend studies 105
Trial and error 44
t-test 260ff., 332, 333
Two Cultures 5ff.
Two-tailed test 238, 248, 266
Two-way design 151
Type 1 error 236ff., 278
Type 2 error 236ff., 258
Types of questions 115ff.
Uncertainty 235ff., 350
Understanding 1ff., 94
Unstructured interview 89
Unstructured research 78ff.
U-test 269ff.
Validity 40, 110, 155ff.
VALUE LABEL 174
Values 6
VARIABLE VIEW 169ff., 261
Variance 194ff., 281
Verification 43
Vienna Positivists 42
Waiting-list control group 154
Wilcoxon test 267ff., 333
Wilks' Lambda 297
Within-subjects design 141ff.
WORDSMITH 107
Written presentations 323
Wundt curve 1, 9ff., 17, 19, 30, 31
Yoked control group 155